THE THEOPOLITICAL DISCOURSES OF MOSES:

THE BOOK OF DEUTERONOMY IN POLITICAL PERSPECTIVE

PART ONE

BY

MARTIN SICKER

iUniverse, Inc.
New York   Bloomington

The Theopolitical Discourses of Moses

The Book of Deuteronomy in Political Perspective, Part One

iUniverse books may be ordered through booksellers or by contacting:

iUniverse
1663 Liberty Drive
Bloomington, IN 47403
www.iuniverse.com
1-800-Authors (1-800-288-4677)

ISBN: 978-1-4401-4513-1 (pbk)
ISBN: 978-1-4401-4514-8 (ebk)

Printed in the United States of America

iUniverse rev. date: 6/2/009

CONTENTS

INTRODUCTION

The Book of Deuteronomy, the last of the Five Books of Moses or Pentateuch, consists in the main of Moses' final discourses or sermons delivered to the children of Israel as they stood poised on the banks of the Jordan awaiting the signal to cross the river and begin the conquest and settlement of the land originally promised to the Patriarchs, Abraham, Isaac, and Jacob. In the course of presenting these discourses Moses reprises a good deal of the biblical legislation recorded earlier in other books of the Pentateuch in addition to introducing a large number of new provisions. It is quite common to find commentators asserting that the book is actually made up of primarily three discourses. This however is by no means certain and numerous equally plausible alternate schemes have been proposed. In any case, establishing the number of discourses, while perhaps of some literary interest, is of no consequence for understanding the text and its implications, and will not be discussed further in this study.

The central concern of Moses, as reflected in these discourses, is with the challenge of nation building, creating an Israelite nation out of a mélange of ethnically related tribes and clans that were just liberated from centuries of subjugation and servitude in a relatively sophisticated pagan environment. That which is to bind them together is not a compact between them but rather a common covenant with God to which all are equal parties. The covenant, first made with Abraham, and renewed with Isaac and Jacob, was again renewed with the children of Israel during the convocation at Mount Sinai following the exodus from Egypt, its terms being revealed incrementally in the earlier books of the Pentateuch. However, it is only here in Deuteronomy that Moses begins to give it the clearly discernible shape of a constitution for the covenantal society to be established as a nation-state in its divinely assigned territory. Within the constitutional framework set forth in the work is a range of precepts, rules, and regulations governing both those matters that are between man and God and those between man and man, understood as the two sides of a common coin, the covenant.

The covenant, however, "signifies a form of social relation in which the integrity of each party, in this case God and Israel, remains intact. The human partner, both as individual and as group, does not lose his humanness. Thus we can say that a certain sphere of unalloyed humanness or legitimated secularity remains foundational to the covenantal social and political order."[1] The covenant stresses the divine desiderata in terms of outcomes and reflects these goals within the broad parameters set forth in the Torah, but leaves it to man to figure out how best to achieve the indicated ends, especially where it deals with those things that are between man and man, matters that are by their nature more secular than sacral. By not providing a detailed recipe on how to deal with such issues, the Torah relies on man's divinely granted capacity for rational decision-making and thereby creates a certain tension between acting on one's inclinations and satisfying the demands of the covenant.

The critical problem that Moses seeks to confront and deal with in these discourses is the difficulty in reorienting the perceptions of the people from the pervasive polytheistic paradigm that shaped their attitudes and beliefs regarding the world in which they lived for centuries to the monotheistic paradigm demanded by the covenant. This fundamental change in mindset proved to be very difficult for many and resulted in numerous incidents of recidivism during the course of the forty years between the exodus and the delivery of these final discourses. Moses' perhaps greatest fear was that if this pattern of polytheistic recidivism, even in its milder form of syncretism, continued after the people crossed the Jordan and undertook the conquest and settlement of the promised land, their potential viability as an independent nation there would be in grave doubt, because it would have violated the essential terms of the covenant that unequivocally demanded belief and faith in the one and only God. Accordingly, Moses devotes a substantial amount of space in his discourses to dealing with this problem, beginning with pointed reminders of the people's past rebelliousness against God, followed by specific commandments regarding how they are to deal with the residual vestiges of polytheism in the lands that come under their control. In addition, in an effort to prevent assimilation to such beliefs and practices, Moses proclaims a series of laws designed to impede social intimacy with members of the pagan societies they would encounter in the land.

Another major concern that Moses sought to address was the creation of a sense of national cohesion among the tribes and clans that made up the children of Israel, and towards this end insisted on the creation of a central national sanctuary that would serve as the exclusive portal for communal as well as personal interaction with God through a formal and highly structured sacrificial rite. By precluding the offering of sacrifices at any other site, Moses evidently hoped to create a sense of national cohesion; all the children of Israel, regardless of tribal or clan affiliation, would be obligated individually to make pilgrimages to, and make votive and other sacrificial offerings at, the central sanctuary, a requirement that would have the effect of blurring tribal distinctions and emphasizing the commonality of the children of Israel.

In the course of his presentations, Moses also recalled the incident that led to the divine decision to cause the children of Israel to wander as nomads through the wilderness for four decades until the lives of the entire generation of men of military age (twenty and older) at the time that divine decision was made had come to an end, as well as other historical events such as the conquests of territory in Transjordan just prior to the time that he was making these final addresses to the people. In regard to these references to earlier events recorded in Scripture, the question relentlessly pursued by historians for generations is whether the accounts presented in the biblical texts are in fact historical or merely mythological, much ado being made of archaeological or other ostensibly corroborating evidence, and in some cases the lack thereof, as a basis for drawing often highly contentious conclusions. It should be noted at the outset that the historicity of the biblical account of the story of Moses and the children of Israel in the period between the exodus and their entry into the promised land some four decades later is not the concern of the present study, which is focused entirely on attempting to understand the meaning and implications of the text as it is recorded in the Masoretic version of the Hebrew Scriptures.

Moreover, I would argue that, from the standpoint of the history of the children of Israel and their descendants through more than three millennia, the question of the historicity of the events described in Deuteronomy and elsewhere in Scripture is far less significant than the fact of the existence of the biblical narrative itself. That narrative has played a critical role in Jewish history, its theological, ethical, social, and political teachings serving as points of convergence for adherents of Judaism throughout the world, without which the children of Israel would long ago have disappeared. In other words, the existence of the narrative is itself an indisputable fact that has shaped Israel's history over the millennia. In the words of one noted scholar:

> What is important is not the rediscovery of the origins of the promise to Abraham, but the recognition that that promise was so interpreted from age to age that it became a living power in the life of the people of Israel. Not the mode of its origin matters, but its operation as a formative, dynamic, seminal force in the history of Israel. The legend of the promise entered so deeply into the experience of the Jews that it acquired its own reality. What Jews believe to have happened in the Middle East has been no less formative in world history than that which is known to have occurred.[2]

Although, with the exception of a few sentences at the end of Deuteronomy, the work purports to be the verbatim addresses delivered by Moses to the people shortly before his death, the numerous parenthetical explanatory passages clearly indicate the intervention of an editorial hand, and arguably parts of the text attributed to Moses may also betray the work of that same hand. In any case, the question of whether or not Moses actually said these things or any part of them is not a matter of concern in this book. What is of concern here is the meaning of the text that has been transmitted to us for the last two and a half millennia, regardless of how and by whom it was originally composed and edited, or from what earlier sources it may have derived some of its material. It goes without question that the ancient Israelites did not live in a cocoon and like everyone else were influenced by surrounding cultures. However, it is a fact of Jewish history that when external influences were absorbed they tended to be transformed into something other than what they were originally, and it is only the final product that is of interest for purposes of this study. The fact that covenantal language corresponds to ancient Hittite treaty language or that some aspects of the story of Abraham reflect elements of Hurrian law docs not constrain the use or importance assigned to these data by the biblical writer or editor. The only relevant question is what does the final statement mean? Accordingly, a proper reading of the text must be concerned not only with what it relates but also what Moses or his literary alter ego intended to convey through his choice of words and selection of what he chose to convey to us.

Comprehending and explaining the biblical text, which is written in the terse mode of expression typical of the Torah, presents a number of problems for the modern commentator, especially one writing in English. First of all, there is the problem of language. While there is an abundance of English translations currently available, every translation of necessity is also an interpretation, and for this reason I have resisted the temptation to add yet another translation of the texts. Ideally, the biblical text should be presented in its Hebrew version and the interpretation presented in English or any other language. However, because this is impractical for a work intended for readers who may not have adequate knowledge of the original language, I have chosen what I consider to be the least problematic of English translations currently available, principally because it is the most literal, notwithstanding that it may not be the easiest to read. Accordingly, passages cited from the Torah in this book are based on the King James Version as modified by the old Jewish Publication Society version, as further modified by me when deemed appropriate, especially with regard to the names of God, which I give in their Hebrew transliterations rather than the arbitrary translations used in the earlier works. Moreover, although some of the language used is now archaic it has the advantage of making distinctions that tend to be blurred in modern English, especially with regard to the use of second person pronouns, which in modern English employ "you" and "your" for both singular and plural, whereas using "thou" and "thy" for the singular and "you" and "your" for the plural better capture the meaning of the Hebrew which does distinguish between the singular and the plural, and there are instances where the distinction is important to comprehension of the text. However, because this translation also is an interpretation, it is often problematic. Accordingly, wherever necessary, I will point out the difficulties that need to be resolved to capture what most likely is the intent of a particular verse or expression.

A second problem results from the fact that one can hardly construct a sensible analysis of a biblical text that has been studied almost to exhaustion over a period of more than two millennia without referring to the work of those who preceded him. The difficulty one encounters in doing this lies in the fact that there is little if any consensus among the commentators, ancient, medieval, or modern, as to the meaning or significance of the texts. To deal with this problem, on occasion I will propose alternate interpretations that reflect different but plausible approaches to the text, indicating as appropriate my own preferences.

A third problem concerns the wide number of differing interpretations of any given text that are available. Since it is not my purpose to compile a compendium of interpretations, it was necessary to set some parameters for inclusion, by mere mention or actual citation, irrespective of whether or not I agree with them. Accordingly, in this study I have elected to consider only those interpretations that expound or contribute to the understanding of the plain meaning of the given text. In other words, with rare exceptions, no consideration is given here to mystical, esoteric, or homiletic interpretations that tend to take a particular text out of its context for rhetorical purposes. I have also avoided any reference to source criticism, which, although of interest from both a literary and historical point of view, contributes little if anything to understanding the straightforward meaning of the texts as they have been transmitted through the ages to us. However, because of the importance of these texts to the unfolding of Jewish law as formulated by the talmudic sages and their rabbinic successors, in a number of instances I have taken the liberty of illustrating how the laws given in the text were elaborated upon in the rabbinic halakhic literature. Regrettably, there also are a few biblical texts that seem to defy rational explanation, and I must leave attempts at their explication to others.

This problem in itself should not be too surprising when considering writings dating back centuries let alone millennia. Although it may be asserted that the biblical texts have eternal meaning and significance, it seems self-evident that those writings, to have survived the generation in which they first appeared, would of necessity had to be comprehensible to their readers. It seems reasonable to suggest that if this had not been the case, those writings would have been ignored, and failing to be copied they would have soon disappeared. The problem for any subsequent reader is that language is dynamic and the meaning of words in one era may have very different connotations in another. The implication of this is that if one reads a passage of the Hebrew Bible, it may not mean the same thing in Modern Hebrew as it did in Biblical Hebrew, even though the words literally may be the same.

Moreover, it is not only a question of the meaning attached to the individual words but also their connotation, that is, the idea that the words are being used to convey to the reader. How does one determine the meaning of a biblical word or phrase that does not appear self-evident in the context in which it is found? The usual method of doing so is by analogy to its use in other texts where its meaning is unambiguous, or by its similarity to words in cognate languages. Although this approach is by no means certain or flawless, it does represent an attempt to understand the text objectively, that is, what it conveyed to the reader of the period in which it was written. An alternative approach to the biblical texts is more subjective in nature, namely, that of asserting what the text is attempting to convey to its reader by its choice of language, not only by what it actually states but also what it may be understood as implying. These two alternate approaches, the objective or straightforward reading of the text, called the *peshat* and the subjective interpretive reading called *derash* in Hebrew respectively, can lead to very different understandings of the biblical word.

The ancient rabbis and their successors were well aware of the intellectual dangers inherent in the subjective approach to the texts, which might not only involve *exegesis*, drawing out the author's ideas from the text, but also *eisegesis*, reading one's own ideas into the text. To prevent distorting the biblical text by failing to be appropriately circumspect in applying the subjective approach, they adopted the interpretive principle that although one may infer subtexts from a particular word or passage, the text itself never loses its objective meaning. In other words, they accepted the notion that a biblical text might contain layers of meaning that might be extruded from it in addition to its objective meaning, but not in place of it.

In a sense, the objective approach is historical in that it conveyed a particular meaning to the audience to which it was originally addressed. By contrast, the subjective approach is ahistorical, divorced from time and place, but perhaps containing a message for future generations. The interplay of these alternate approaches can also produce incompatible results that may prove to be troublesome, especially when the biblical texts being interpreted are legal in nature or have normative implications.

Finally, a word about sources used in the study. In approaching the biblical narrative, I initially drafted my impressions of what the texts were relating, without reference to any commentary, a process that left me with great gaps in my understanding and a host of questions. I then turned more or less systematically to the classic rabbinic commentaries imbedded in the talmudic and midrashic literature, as well as to the major and a number of minor primarily but not exclusively rabbinic commentaries on the biblical texts composed in both the medieval and modern periods, to fill the gaps. Unfortunately, there are very few contemporary commentators that do not seem to be obsessed with source criticism, which in my opinion, as indicated above, has little if anything to contribute to an actual understanding of the written text as we have it. As a result, I make scant reference to their very considerable body of work. As for philological deconstruction of the biblical texts, there is hardly a verse or word in the biblical texts that has not already been subjected to microscopic scrutiny in the vast rabbinic literature, and as has pointedly been remarked: "The vessel of Scripture, afloat in the immense ocean of rabbinical dialectic, can hardly be endangered by the squalls of a few philologists who do not even know the vessel's draught."[3]

The references listed at the end of the book reflect those works either cited in the book or those which led me to the interpretations considered in the following pages. As a matter of practice, whenever I found that an earlier commentator had already noted my own initial impression of a text, I have referenced that work. However, the reader should be aware that when I actually cite a commentator or a work, I do so because of the felicity of expression it reflects and not necessarily because I agree with the context in which the original statement was made. In other words, the context in which I use a citation may not conform to the actual view of the author or work cited, much as the biblical writer's use of extraneous source material may have little or no correspondence to its original meaning or intent.

Finally, because of the volume and variety of material contained in Deuteronomy, it is difficult to find a way of sensibly dividing the book into discrete coherent sections for the benefit of the modern reader. Because I find some problems in this regard with the placement of breaks in the text in the commonly accepted chapter subdivisions of Scripture adopted in the medieval period, I have elected to follow traditional rabbinic practice and subdivide the work according to the named standard *parshiot* or sections of the text of the Torah as read in the synagogue throughout the annual cycle of weekly recitals of the texts that comprise the Pentateuch.

1

DEVARIM

(1:1-3:22)

Deut. 1.1 *These are the words which Moses spoke unto all Israel beyond the Jordan; in the wilderness, in the Arabah, over against Suph, between Paran and Tophel, and Laban, and Hazeroth, and Di-zahab.* *1.2* *It is eleven days' journey from Horeb unto Kadesh-barnea by way of mount Seir.*

This seemingly awkwardly stated passage appears to be saying that the essence of the discourses or sermons that follow was delivered to the Israelites repeatedly, at various locations, throughout their long sojourn in the wilderness. Now, and for the last time, Moses speaks *unto all Israel beyond the Jordan,* on the plains of Moab, shortly before their entry into Cisjordan from the east. The bulk of the initial discourse that follows this brief introduction would perhaps better be described as a chastising sermon that contains a reprise of the significant and problematic events that took place during the four decade-long period from the exodus to the point where the children of Israel now found themselves, finally poised to enter the land promised to them as part of their covenant with God.

The focus of Moses' remarks is the repeated displays of lack of faith in God on the part of the people and their consequent rebelliousness that caused them to be condemned to wander as nomads in the wilderness for such a long period, even though their ultimate destination was within easy reach, at least geographically. The approach taken by Moses in his presentations differs markedly from how he addressed the children of Israel during their wilderness sojourn. The reason for this, it has

1

been suggested, is that in the past Moses was highly circumspect in the manner in which he delivered his message of reproof to the people, perhaps because he was concerned that repeated open confrontation and reprimand might have the negative effect of driving the people even farther from the desired path than was already the case. Now, however, sensing that he personally was coming to the end of his road in life, the time had come no longer to deal with mere allusions to past improprieties but to be straightforward about them, raking up the coals of the past, so to speak, and to warn the people in as explicit terms as appropriate of the consequences any continued waywardness with respect to what was required of them under their covenant with God would incur once they entered the land promised to them.[4]

The timing of these final discourses was critical because, as has often been observed, it seems to be a natural tendency for people to ignore predictions of impending disaster at a time when no such event is on the generally foreseeable horizon. It takes an event of some major significance to cause people to pause and take stock of their lives, opening their minds to the critical self-examination that may be engendered by carefully crafted words of reproof and admonition. For an individual, such a moment may arrive through witnessing some unexpected calamity, such as the illness or death of a loved one. For a nation as a collectivity, the impending death of the only leader it has known for most if not all of their collective lives, would likely serve as just such an event that might shake them to the core.[5] Moses, sensing that his remaining time was short, seized the opportunity to present a series of farewell addresses to the nation that he hoped would serve to awaken them to the need to begin to take their relationship to God more seriously than had been the case, not only in the distant past but even quite recently. This was essential because they were about to enter the final phase of the venture that began with the exodus from Egypt, one in which Moses would no longer be available to intercede with God in their behalf. Thus, out of deep concern for their welfare, he undertook the distasteful but necessary task of prodding them to face the reality of their existential situation.

The statement *These are the words which Moses spoke unto all Israel* appears to be an odd way of introducing his discourses; it could simply have stated "and Moses said to the children of Israel," or some something similar. The expression, *These are the words*, raises the question not only about the content of *the words* but also whose words they are, Moses' or God's. One opinion understands *the words* as alluding to the various laws and precepts that Moses will present later in these discourses to supplement those previously revealed to the people, which in the aggregate will constitute the whole of the covenant legislation revealed by and through him. However, against this view it has been argued that the wording of the text does not support the notion that *the words which Moses spoke* at the time refer to the laws and precepts of the Torah, given that the latter are the words of God, and not of Moses.[6] Thus, although they would be revealed through Moses later, they are not what the opening verse of the passage is referring to. Moreover, it has been argued that God evidently did not specifically instruct Moses to prepare and deliver his tirade against the people, but that he did so on his own initiative, as the wording of the text suggests.[7] Indeed, according to some, Moses delivered all of the denunciations and curses voiced later in the book of Deuteronomy at his own discretion.[8] One of the implications of this is that the text is drawing a distinction between the harsh words in the present text and those that are found in the earlier books of Scripture, effective asserting that *these are the words which Moses spoke*, that is, these alone were originated by Moses, whereas the others were the direct word of God that were merely repeated by Moses.[9]

The text emphasizes that Moses' words were directed to *all Israel* even though the brunt of the remarks applied only to a small part of the people. A number of possible reasons for this have been proposed. One suggestion in this regard argues that because the remarks contained a message of reproach and Moses did not want to humiliate those individuals of the generation of the exodus that were still alive, or embarrass the descendents of those who had died in the wilderness during the decades of wandering, for whom the reproach was both deserved and intended.[10] By generalizing his comments to the entire people, he avoided obviously aiming them at specific individuals. Another opinion suggests that the children of Israel as a collective body indeed merited rebuke, and that Moses addressed his remarks to *all Israel* may be taken as a sign that "they were deserving of rebuke and able to stand up under rebuke."[11] Moreover, the assertion that Moses *spoke unto all Israel beyond the Jordan; in the wilderness* has been understood as suggesting that his words of rebuke dealt with events that had taken place most recently, during the brief period when the Israelites were *beyond the Jordan*, that is, in Transjordan, in addition to those events that took place earlier *in the wilderness*, thus making his words of reproach to the people as a whole quite appropriate.[12]

As a practical matter, the notion that Moses was able to speak directly to *all Israel* is quite unrealistic, given that the text earlier spoke of Israel as having some 600,000 men of military age alone, which together with the women and children, as well as older people may have amounted to as many as two million. Even assuming, as most scholars do, that these are conventionally inflated figures, the means by which Moses might have communicated directly to the people remains an unresolved issue. Generally speaking, it would appear that whenever Moses has something to say to the people as a whole, the text has him addressing the *children of Israel*, which evidently does not refer a general assembly of the entire population, but more probably to whatever crowd assembled to hear him, in the expectation that his words would be repeated by them to others, unmediated by the leaders of the community. Here, however, because of the nature of what he wishes to convey to the people, he wants to address them all simultaneously and therefore directs his remarks to *all Israel*, by which term the text must necessarily be understood as referring to the tribal leaders and elders, who bore the responsibility for informing, educating, and remonstrating with the people at large, and who were to be held accountable for the public's misconduct should they fail to do so.[13] Presumably, they were charged with the task of repeating his words verbatim to their constituencies.

The identification of some of the places mentioned in the text is uncertain, but it seems reasonable to assume that the ancient reader was quite familiar with them; if not, there would be little purpose in mentioning them. Although the *Arabah* generally denotes the long narrow depression that is geologically part of the East African Rift Valley system, which extends south from Lebanon to the Gulf of Eilat, in the present context it would seem to refer more specifically to that section of the depression located between the Dead Sea and the Gulf that separates the hills of Edom to the east from the hills of the Negev to the west. With regard to Shittim, in the Plains of Moab and the final stop for the Israelites before they crossed the Jordan into Cisjordan, an earlier text informed us that it was there that *the people began to commit harlotry with the daughters of Moab* (Num. 25:1). Some assume that *Suph* may be a shorter form of *yam suph* or the Sea of Reeds, where the psalmist asserts that *they were rebellious at the sea, even at the Sea of Reeds. Nevertheless, He saved them* (Ps. 106:7-8). In this regard it was suggested that they exhibited little faith even as they were being saved, saying: "Just as we go up from this side, so will the Egyptians go up from the other side."[14] However, others speculate that it may refer to a site in Moab, mentioned elsewhere in the biblical texts as *Suphah* (Num. 21:14).

It seems likely that *Paran* refers to the wilderness of Paran, which is in the area between the wilderness of Zin and the wilderness of Sinai, an area west of the *Arabah* and identified by some as the wilderness of al-Tih. The oasis of Kadesh-barnea (so named to distinguish it from other sites named Kadesh) is located there, and it was from there that spies were sent to scout out the defenses that the Israelites would have to overcome to penetrate the land of Canaan from the south, the overwhelming acceptance of the validity of their negative report being instrumental in causing the Israelites to be forced to remain in the wilderness for almost four decades. With regard to the remaining four sites listed, none are explicitly mentioned in connection with any especially contentious or grievous public event. Some have identified *Tophel* as the site of the village of al-Tafile, about fifteen miles southeast of the Dead Sea. *Laban* and *Hazeroth* appear to be sites mentioned as *Libnah* and *Hazeroth* (Num. 33:17-20), where the Israelites stopped during their long sojourn in the wilderness. It does appear, however, that God's punishment of Miriam for challenging Moses' authority took place at *Hazeroth* (Num. 11:35-12:16). The location of *Di-zahab* remains a mystery. It also remains quite unclear why the rest of these named locations are singled out, although it is quite possible that Moses did have issues with the people that arose at these locations but which for some reason have not been recorded in the text. It has been suggested in this regard, that instead of rebuking the people for other specific instances of past rebellion, Moses chose merely to allude to them by mentioning where their misconduct took place, perhaps in order not to embarrass them or make them feel any more uncomfortable about past behavior than he considered necessary.[15]

The significance of the mention in the preface to Moses' discourse of the distance between Horeb (lit. 'desolation'), the name given to the desolate district in which Mount Sinai was located, and Kadesh-barnea, is that it serves as a subtle reminder to the reader that after receiving the covenant at Mount Sinai, it took only eleven days of travel from there by *way of mount Seir*, the easternmost trail from the Sinai, to reach Kadesh-barnea, the southern entry point to the Negev, from which it was but a metaphorical 'stones throw' to their ultimate goal. Nonetheless, because of their errant behavior as a people, what should have taken but a few days to enter the promised land took them some four decades of wandering in the wilderness and untold hardships. In other words, what these opening verses are stating is that at all of the various sites where they stayed during their wanderings, Moses repeatedly reminded the people that *it is eleven days' journey from Horeb unto Kadesh-barnea by way of mount Seir*. That is, had they acted properly, they need not have spent an additional thirty-eight years to reach the point of entry into the land promised to them from Transjordan; they already had been at the point of entry at *Kadesh-barnea* a mere eleven days after concluding the covenant at Sinai, but squandered the opportunity presented to them to proceed into the promised land.[16]

Their failure to proceed directly from Horeb to their ultimate destination, in effect, was a direct consequence of their lack of faith in divine providence, which resulted in their remaining stuck in the wilderness until the errant generation, or at least most of it, passed away from natural causes. It was not because God arbitrarily compelled them to remain in the wilderness, but rather because they were virtually immobilized by their timidity. It was a generation whose mature members clearly reflected "the inability of humans to outgrow a trauma of mammoth proportions to an entire nation."[17] The challenges that they would face in the conquest and settlement of the land clearly indicated the need for a new generation whose attitudes had not been shaped by the experience of slavery but rather by the experience of freedom.

The point that Moses is making is that the men of that generation were given the freedom to choose their course of action and they chose badly, something that would not have happened had they maintained their faith in the God who had liberated them. It may be argued that man is given moral autonomy but is confronted internally by his competing impulses, for good or bad, between which he must choose. It is at that point that faith in God can alter the balance in favor of the inclination toward good. Thus, although the biblical doctrine of reward and punishment is predicated on man's moral autonomy, and God does not compel him to choose one course in preference to the other, He is nonetheless dispositive of the consequences of that choice.[18]

> *1.3 And it came to pass in the fortieth year, in the eleventh month, on the first day of the month, that Moses spoke unto the children of Israel, according unto all that YHVH had given in commandment unto them; 1.4 after he had smitten Sihon the king of the Amorites, who dwelt in Heshbon, and Og the king of Bashan, who dwelt in Ashtaroth, at Edrei; 1.5 beyond the Jordan, in the land of Moab, took Moses upon him to expound this Torah, saying:*

It is assumed by some that Moses, perhaps following the precedent set by the patriarch Jacob (Gen. 49), sensing that his end was near, chose to present the people with the equivalent of an ethical will delivered in the form of a discourse in which he recapitulated the basis for and the stipulations of the covenant between God and the children of Israel. However, this alone does not explain why the text specifies the exact date on which the discourse was delivered, which remains something of a mystery. Moreover, it seems likely that the text is merely indicating the date on which Moses commenced his final discourses, and not that they were concluded that same day. Indeed, one midrashic source calculates that it took thirty-six days for Moses to *expound this Torah* from the first day of the eleventh month, later known as Shevat to the sixth day of Adar, when he concluded it just prior to his demise the following day, assumed by tradition to be exactly one hundred and twenty years after his birth.[19]

The text notes that the discourse was delivered not long after Moses' successful leadership in the military conflicts with the Amorite king Sihon, who had recently extended his sway from his base in Cisjordan and taken control of the area of Moab north of the Arnon River as far as the Jabbok (Num. 21: 21-26), and Og, the Amorite king who extended his control to the region north of the Jabbok as far as southern Syria. Og's northern capital at Ashtaroth has been identified as Tell Ashterah, a site in Syria along the ancient King's Highway. In the southern part of his realm, Og also had a capital at Edrei, identified as modern Deraa, situated along an eastern tributary of the Yarmuk.[20] The struggles mentioned, discussed below, would still have been fresh in the minds of Moses' Israelite audience, as they stood poised to face new struggles for control of the land once they crossed the Jordan.

The assertion that Moses took this occasion *to expound this Torah* suggests, as one commentator put it, "Deuteronomy is thus 'preached law'—that is, law explained with prophetic urgency, divine authority, and a preacher's clarity."[21] This seems to imply that what follows will be such an exposition. However, this is not the case, at least not immediately. What does follow is a recapitulation of the events that brought them to the place where they finally now found themselves in Transjordan, some four decades after they left Egypt, ready to enter the land promised to them. An exposition of the terms of the covenant will come later. As a result, some have understood these introductory verses primarily as an introduction to the opening discourse, rather than to the entire book, as others maintain, an issue that is merely of peripheral interest for the purpose of this study. What is clear is that this preface calls upon the people to reflect on what caused them to wander in the desert for forty years, all the while being within physically easy reach of their final destination.

It is noteworthy that *torah*, as the term is employed in the other books of the Pentateuch, generally refers to instruction in specific cultic-religious regulations and practices. In Deuteronomy, however, the concept of *torah* is broadened to comprehend the entire range of Mosaic legislation and teaching and the introductions and comments accompanying its revelation.[22] In this particular instance, the *torah* that Moses is about to expound is what Israel should have learned from their long and difficult sojourn in the wilderness, and does not seem to apply to law at all. Recounting the experience of the past forty years, characterized by complaints, backbiting, and outright rebellion by a stubborn and often ungrateful people, must have been very difficult for Moses. Nonetheless, as painful as these recollections were, he thought it important to expound them and their implications to the younger generation before they crossed into the land promised to them in accordance with their covenant with God.[23] Following this brief preface, the text begins the presentation of Moses' final discourses to the people of Israel as they stood on the threshold of crossing the Jordan.

It has been suggested that the reason why Moses chose this point in time to deliver these discourses was precisely because the children of Israel were about to enter the promised land and he was concerned that they should be spiritually prepared for what was expected of them, especially since he would not be with them to instruct them with regard to carrying out the divine commandments in practice, or to resolve any issues in this regard that were likely to emerge.[24] The content of the opening discourse is a brief survey of Israel's history since the exodus, clearly illustrating its malfeasance with respect to God, which began but did not end at Horeb with the golden calf affair, an idolatrous rebellion that infuriated God and caused Moses to smash the original tablets containing the Decalogue. The point of departure for this initial discourse is the aftermath of that event and Moses' successful intercession with God on behalf of the people, and the renewal of the covenant between God and Israel.

1.6 YHVH our Elohim spoke unto us in Horeb, saying: 'Ye have dwelt long enough in this mountain; 1.7 turn you, and take your journey, and go to the hill-country of the Amorites and unto all the places nigh thereunto, in the

> *Arabah, in the hill-country, and in the Lowland, and in*
> *the South, and by the seashore; the land of the Canaanites,*
> *and Lebanon, as far as the great river, the river Euphrates.*
> *1.8 Behold, I have set the land before you: go in and*
> *possess the land which YHVH swore unto your fathers, to*
> *Abraham, to Isaac, and to Jacob, to give unto them and to*
> *their seed after them.'*

Moses recalls God's instruction to him, after the golden calf incident and his successful intercession on behalf of the children of Israel to assuage divine anger, *Depart, go up hence, thou and the people thou hast brought up out of the land of Egypt, unto the land of which I swore unto Abraham, to Isaac, and to Jacob, saying: Unto thy seed will I give it* (Ex. 33:1). In his recounting of the divine instruction, Moses now reveals a bit more of what was said at the time. Because of God's anger at the people for their perfidious behavior, He said *I will send an angel before thee . . . for I will not go up in the midst of thee* (Ex. 33:2-3). However, without assurance that God personally would be directly engaged with the people, rather than indirectly through a divine messenger or agent, Moses hesitated to move, perhaps sensing that it might be futile to do so without His direct involvement. For Moses' sake, and to alleviate his concern, God relented somewhat and said, *My presence shall go with thee* (Ex. 33:14). However, the meaning and significance of this revised commitment was not self-evident and Moses continued to hesitate and again pleaded, *let Adonai, I pray Thee, go in the midst of us* (Ex. 34:8). Presumably, he was unclear about what was meant by *My presence* and whether that *presence* would be actively engaged with events or merely passively cognizant of them. Moses desperately wanted further assurance that it would be God himself that would accompany the children of Israel. He evidently believed this to be necessary because he was concerned that the people might not accept any intermediary, even of a divine character, between them and the God they experienced during the theophany that took place earlier. Nonetheless, a more precise divine commitment of direct personal involvement was not to be forthcoming, and Moses indicates that God had had enough of his procrastination, telling him bluntly, *Ye have dwelt long enough in this mountain,* that is, it was time to move on the basis of the assurance that His *presence* would accompany them. With the instruction, *turn you, and take your journey,* in effect, God insisted that Moses carry out the leadership role for which he was chosen, without further hesitation.

How long did they remain in the vicinity of Mount Sinai? It was related in the earlier account, *In the third month after the children of Israel were gone forth out of the land of Egypt, the same day they came into the wilderness of Sinai* (Ex. 19:1). Then we are informed, *And it came to pass in the second year, in the second month, on the twelfth day of the month, that . . . the children of Israel set forward by stages out of the wilderness of Sinai* (Num. 10:11-12). Accordingly, the duration of the Israelites' stay in Horeb was eleven months and nineteen days.[25] Presumably, the organizational issues about to be discussed arose and were dealt with during this protracted period.

It is noteworthy that the early scribes may have sought to reflect God's simmering anger at the Israelites at the time by spelling the Hebrew *Horeb* defectively, allowing the unvocalized word to be read as *herev* or sword. That is, the opening words of the passage, *spoke unto us in Horeb,* could also be read as "spoke to us with a sword," intimating that if the people failed to comply with the covenant, the sword awaited them.[26] As the rabbis of the talmudic period put it, at Horeb, "a scroll and a sword tied together descended from heaven. God said to them, 'If you observe the Torah written in the one, you will be saved from the other; if not, you will be smitten with it.'"[27]

Moses was instructed to direct the people to *go in and possess the land which YHVH swore unto your fathers.* It has been suggested that this text "expresses Israel's theology of land in a nutshell." That is, Israel's ability to take possession of the land against the wishes of its multinational inhabitants would in itself represent tangible proof of divine faithfulness to His commitment in accordance with the obligations God undertook in the covenant. The idea that Israel received title to the land as a divine gift was critical to Israel's self-understanding of itself as a nation. Because of it, "they could never consider themselves an autochthonous people ("sons of the soil"), for they would have been no people and would have had no land apart from the divine gift."[28] Throughout history nations have emerged out of the people living in a land. In the unique case of Israel the process was radically different. Israel became a nation in the wilderness, in a land in which the children of Israel had no roots, and only subsequently planted its national roots in the land that God bequeathed to them. However, the divine gift of the land did not of itself mean that the peoples residing in the land would voluntarily acknowledge Israel's right to claim that gift. Israel would have to *go in and possess the land* by force if they wanted to exercise their right to it. However, Moses also is told, *I have set the land before you,* which has been interpreted as saying that God had already instilled fear into the hearts of the peoples of the land, causing many to flee and generally weakening the will to resist on the part of many others, so that the children of Israel should not be concerned about their ability to succeed in achieving their goals.[29]

As a matter of priority, Moses begins the substance of his discourses by drawing a verbal map of the territories that are to comprise the heritage of the Israelites by the grace of God. The Israelites are to cross the Jordan to invade and conquer Cisjordan, beginning with the hill-country dominated by the Amorites, a term often used generally to describe the mélange of peoples in ancient Cisjordan, remnants of the invasions and wars that took place along the landbridge between Africa and Asia since time immemorial. The sway of the peoples grouped under the rubric of Amorites had already extended across the Jordan to Moab and Bashan, where it was recently undone by force of Israelite arms. However, in the present text, the reference to *the hill-country of the Amorites* may actually be referring to the Amorites as a distinct people.

The Amorite presence in the hill-country of Cisjordan had been established centuries earlier, the biblical text itself recalling that Abraham, while residing at Hebron in the Judean hills, had formed an alliance with certain Amorite chiefs (Gen. 14:13). Now the time had come, in the divine scheme, for them to relinquish control of the hill-country to the Israelites. The same applied to the other regions of Cisjordan, the Negev in the south, the Canaanite coastal region and the Lowland or Shephelah, the foothills between the central mountain range and the maritime plain in the west, the Arabah, which in this instance refers to the region of the Jordan rift north of the Dead Sea in the east, and the mountain range of Lebanon in the north as far as the Euphrates, as indicated in the covenant with Abraham, *Unto thy seed have I given this land, from the river of Egypt unto the great river, the river Euphrates* (Gen. 15:18). It is noteworthy that the divine instruction to Moses is essentially reiterated in the revelation to Joshua that appears at the beginning of the biblical book bearing his name. *Every place that the sole of your foot shall tread upon, to you have I given it, as I spoke unto Moses. From the wilderness, and this Lebanon, even unto the great river, the river Euphrates, all the land of the Hittites, and unto the Great Sea toward the going down of the sun, shall be your border* (Josh. 1:4). All this was intended to be Israel's patrimony, presumably if Israel adhered to their covenantal obligation to heed God's commands.

Viewing these texts in retrospect, notwithstanding the prevailing realities and history of the Middle East, they may be seen as reflecting a remarkable degree of geopolitical and geostrategic prescience. The creation of a viable and secure model covenantal society in Cisjordan, the relatively short landbridge between Africa and Asia, required full control of its frontiers in all directions. In the north, this meant control of the historical invasion routes from Mesopotamia to Egypt which transited the western region of what is today Syria and Lebanon, passing through the Bekaa valley between the Lebanese mountain chains into northern Israel and from there southward along the coastal military and trade route, known in Roman times as the Via Maris, to Egypt. It was for this reason that, in the days of David and Solomon, a chain of Israelite fortresses were established in the north, from Hazor in the Galilee to Iyun (modern Marjayoun) at the bend of the Litani river in Lebanon, to protect the country from invasion along this classic military route. One can only idly speculate, from a biblical perspective, on what the history of Israel might have been had the Israelites as a nation remained sufficiently and consistently faithful to the covenant to earn the divine beneficence they so sorely needed. The narrative before us is a testament to that failure.

> *1.9 And I spoke unto you at that time, saying: 'I am not able to bear you myself alone; 1.10 YHVH your Elohim hath multiplied you, and, behold, ye are this day as the stars of heaven for multitude. 1.11 YHVH, the Elohim of your fathers, make you a thousand times so many more as ye are, and bless you, as He hath promised you! 1.12 How can I myself alone bear your cumbrance, and your burden, and your strife? 1.13 Get you, from each of your tribes, wise men, and understanding, and full of knowledge, and I will make them heads over you.' 1.14 And ye answered me, and said: 'The thing which thou hast spoken is good for us to do.'*

It would appear that the original context of this passage was the period during which the Israelites were still at Horeb, looking forward to their imminent entry into the promised land. At that point it became essential for Moses to introduce a hierarchical structure in the organization of the people to facilitate the conquest of the land. The tasks ahead would require internal harmony and a unified vision of purpose and goals, if they were to succeed.[30]

One may ask why Moses begins by stating *I spoke unto you at that time* when it is clear that the great majority of the people he was addressing were either still unborn at the time or very young. However, Moses appears to be engaging the people in a vicarious recollection of the collective past, conveying to them, regardless of age, that they are part of a common history, and that they have received and must bear the burden and legacy of their parents and ancestors.[31] One also may note another nuance in the phrase *at that time*, namely that it is directly connected to the immediately preceding texts, *turn you, and take your journey, and go to the hill-country of the Amorites . . . go in and possess the land which YHVH swore unto your fathers.* That is, Moses is indicating that the people of a nation that is about to go to war against a powerful enemy must be united and organized in a manner that will maximize the potential for success. Thus, given the prevailing contentiousness among the tribes and clans and quarreling among the people, he declares, *I am not able to bear you myself alone*;

that is, he feels that it is beyond his ability to singlehandedly resolve the great number of issues that impede achievement of the degree of social solidarity needed to meet effectively the challenges facing the nation.[32] In effect, Moses told them that the current arrangement wherein he personally was expected to govern the people personally and directly was impracticable as well as counterproductive, and that he was fully prepared to devolve some of his authority to others in an ordered hierarchical national management structure that could cope with the needs of the people in a more efficient and effective manner.

Moses recalls that at the time of the exodus from Egypt, the children of Israel were a motley collection of more or less cohesive tribes and clans, with whom he dealt through their respective elders. Moses' task was to transform these extended family associations into a coherent nation governed not by tribal and clan traditions but in accordance with the laws divinely set forth for them. Moreover, for this nation to enter and settle the land promised in the covenant against the opposition of the peoples still in the land, it would require a greater degree of organization and structure than that which now existed, in which the only acknowledged national authority was Moses himself. This placed an overwhelming burden on him personally, which he bore to the best of his ability. However, he was becoming exhausted and was forced to acknowledge that continuing in this manner was impracticable in consideration of the growing internal as well as the newly emerging external challenges the nation would have to confront.

Accordingly, he had already told them at Horeb, *I am not able to bear you myself alone; YHVH your Elohim hath multiplied you, and, behold, ye are this day as the stars of heaven for multitude*, a clear allusion to the promise given to Abraham, *I will multiply thy seed as the stars of the heaven* (Gen. 22:17). Moses was not complaining that there were too many of them, on the contrary, he prayed that *YHVH, the Elohim of your fathers, make you a thousand times so many more as ye are, and bless you, as He hath promised you!* It is noteworthy that the expression for God commonly found in Deuteronomy is *YHVH your Elohim*, the phrase employed earlier in the passage. Now, he employs the phrase *the Elohim of your fathers*, which seems to be employed only when the context in which God is invoked concerns the covenant or the divine promises made to the Patriarchs.[33]

It may be observed that Moses' allusion to the promise made to Abraham only deals with the first part of the actual statement, *I will multiply thy seed as the stars of the heaven*, which continues, *and as the sand which is upon the sea-shore* (Gen. 22:17). As one commentator observed, a careful parsing of Moses' words will reveal not only praise and blessing for Israel, but also some subtle implicit criticism. "The stars look at us from high above, they glimmer in the distance, proud and individualistic, each star to itself. The sand is under our feet, lowly and humble, but the grains are grouped together, compactly. Moses hints that now they are only like the stars, worlds apart . . . God's full promise combines the imagery of the stars with the imagery of the sand, individualism and togetherness."[34] What Moses wanted was to see was a balance of both characteristics in his people; so far, all he only saw was the individualism. Fostering the sense of togetherness was critical to the national enterprise they were about to undertake.

The immediate issue that troubled Moses was not the growth in the number of the children of Israel for whom he had become responsible. Indeed, as far as he was concerned, the more they grew in number the better it would bode for their future. What deeply concerned him was the essential weakness of the existing central authority structure and the increasing difficulty of his personally attending to the myriad matters that government entailed. He was particularly disconcerted about the disposition of internal conflicts of interests that, if not dealt with judiciously and fairly, might impair the social harmony necessary to achieve their common goals. Ironically, it has been suggested, instead of relishing the idea that they were about to be brought to what would become their own land, after centuries of servitude, an idea that should have given them a new spirit of brotherhood, they used their freedom to engage in seemingly limitless quarrels among themselves that demanded resolution if the society were to be held together.[35] This produced a number of conflicts to be resolved through adjudication or arbitration that simply was overwhelming for one man, even a Moses. As he put it, *How can I myself alone bear your cumbrance, and your burden, and your strife?* By *cumbrance* or "troublesomeness," it has been suggested that he was referring to the lack of cooperation and assistance by some elements in the community that were essentially troublemakers.[36] It has also been assumed that the *burden* of which he spoke concerned his responsibility for assuring adequate supplies of food and water, shortages of which produced hostile demonstrations against his leadership.[37] Finally, he felt overburdened by their *strife*, which has been understood as referring to their excessive litigiousness.[38] In short, Moses, who had no difficulty in confronting Pharaoh and leading the people out of Egypt, defeating the Amalekites, and overcoming innumerable obstacles on the long journey to Sinai and then to Kadesh-barnea, was at a loss when confronted by the these negative traits in his people. Moses was not prepared to turn his back on people whom he had come to love truly. He simply felt unable to continue to deal personally and effectively with their seemingly constant bickering, while at the same time dealing with the larger issues facing the people and nation.

Confessing his inability, notwithstanding his unique background and leadership training, to continue to meet the public's demands on him for authoritative leadership as well as the resolution of disputes, he sought to involve more people directly in the governmental process. It was evident that he needed assistance. However, he did not want to impose his own choices of officials to assist him; he preferred that the Israelite public make those choices and thereby give them a direct stake in the proper governance of the nation. Accordingly, he undertook to set forth the required qualifications for public office, namely that the chosen candidates for such office be *wise men, and understanding, and full of knowledge*, but left it up to the people to select the actual candidates. Once they were chosen, he would *make them heads over you*, that is, formally designate them to be their leaders, to whom he would delegate some of the authority that he bore entirely at the moment. In other words, the candidate officials would be selected from among those proposed by the tribes, but would derive their operating authority from Moses, who would oversee them.

What Moses proposed was extraordinary for the world in which he lived. It was unheard of for a ruler to voluntarily relinquish authority, and if one needed assistance as even autocrats always did, he alone would choose with whom to share any of his authority. Moses was willing not only to cede some of his authority but also to accept the choice of the people as to whom it should be granted. As a practical matter, given the very large number of officials to be appointed, he could not possibly have selected them personally since he surely had limited direct contact with those outside the traditional tribal and clan leadership. In any case, it was a proposal that must have seemed miraculous in itself, and one that the people evidently savored. Their reply to it was, *The thing which thou hast spoken is good for us to do.* Not only would it relieve the overwhelming pressure on Moses, they acknowledged that it was *good for us to do.* It was not only that they were being given the opportunity to have a direct voice in their own governance; their response also implied that it was good for them to assume at least that degree of responsibility for the proper functioning of their society, a responsibility that had previously and universally been restricted to the ruling class.

What should not be glossed over in Moses' proposal is his instruction *Get you, from each of your tribes.* Moses clearly wants to retain the tribal structure, presumably because it is based on family allegiances and he considers their retention critical to passing on the traditions associated with the covenant from generation to generation. There were no public educational institutions in which the covenant and its provisions could be taught to successive generations of children; whatever education there was for the people took place at the family hearth and this would continue to be the case for the foreseeable future. Accordingly, supporting the tribal structure also supported the cohesion of the family and enhanced the probability of inculcation of the covenant and its values from the generation of the exodus to succeeding generations. It has also been suggested that, as a practical matter, Moses realized that the children of Israel had not yet learned to think of themselves as members of a nation instead of as members of different albeit ethically related tribes. To appoint leaders, no matter how competent, from one tribe to serve over a different tribe would have been found unacceptable and resisted by the tribes.[39]

It is also noteworthy that Moses chose not to rely on the existing tribal elders to provide the candidates for this process, notwithstanding that he relied heavily on them in the past. One might reasonably assume that his reason for this was that the qualities he wanted in the leadership of the tribes that he hoped to transform into a federation under his central leadership were not necessarily to be found among the elders, who often achieved their status for reasons unrelated to their specific qualifications for the role. In other words, it would appear that Moses wanted to retain the tribal structure but alter significantly the way its leaders were chosen. In effect, he wanted to introduce the idea of a meritocracy to replace the inter-clan politics that often determined the composition of tribal leadership. However, it is by no means clear that he succeeded in this and there is good reason to believe that he did not.

Although the text does not address the issue, it may be concluded from events in the forty-year stay in the wilderness as well as subsequent events that were recorded, that the traditional tribal leadership remained essentially intact. Indeed, the text records that at one point, not long after the covenant at Sinai, Moses was virtually distraught over the burden under which he was laboring and pleaded with God for relief. *And YHVH said unto Moses: 'Gather unto Me seventy men of the elders of Israel, whom thou knowest to be elders of the people, and officers over them; and bring them unto the tent of meeting, that they may stand there with thee. And I will come down and speak with thee there; and I will take of the spirit which is upon thee, and will put it upon them; and they shall bear the burden of the people with thee, that thou bear it not alone* (Num. 11:16-17). That is, by endowing the existing leadership cadre with a portion of Moses' prophetic power, their enhanced influence in the camp would enable them to silence the persistent murmurings of discontent and help put an end to the repeated instances of moral recidivism and faithlessness.[40] This clearly suggests that Moses' proposed reorganization of the people did not take place, and that he had to rely upon the existing tribal elders to share his authority and burden. However, it is possible to assert that what this last text is talking about is the establishment of an advisory council and not a group with executive functions. In any case, the text does not portray his attempt to introduce a meritocracy into the tribal system as having a divine imprimatur, and the tribal leadership may have been reluctant to divest itself of power simply because Moses thought it best.

> *1.15 So I took the heads of your tribes, wise men, and full of knowledge, and made them heads over you, captains of thousands, and captains of hundreds, and captains of fifties, and captains of tens, and officers, tribe by tribe.*

Moses records that following the popular acceptance of his proposal and their selection of candidates, he installed them as leaders of their respective tribes in the indicated hierarchical structure. It is noteworthy that the candidates Moses appointed were *wise men, and full of knowledge,* whereas the qualifications he earlier stipulated were that they be *wise men, and understanding, and full of knowledge.* It would appear that of the three qualifications set forth by Moses, whether one was wise and knowledgeable was easily ascertainable. However, whether the candidate could be characterized as *understanding* was evidently far more difficult to determine, and it would seem that since Moses personally was making the appointment he had no choice but to accept this reality and therefore dropped the requirement of *understanding* as a necessary albeit desirable attribute for a leader.[41]

What remains to be reconciled is the earlier statement, *Get you, from each of your tribes, wise men, and understanding, and full of knowledge, and I will make them heads over you,* and the present assertion, *So I took the heads of your tribes, wise men, and full of knowledge, and made them heads over you,* which clearly seem to be incompatible. It has been suggested that Moses initially ignored the tribal leadership structure and appointed new judges as indicated. Speaking now, from the vantage point of thirty-eight years later, the stature of these popular appointees "grew within the nation, and they naturally evolved into the leaders who represent the different tribes." Moses is thus able to point to the *heads of your tribes* as reflecting those men of ability that "were not chosen because they were 'tribal heads' but rather, as a result of having been chosen as judges, they were given the status of 'tribal heads.'"[42]

The governing structure that Moses instituted was initially proposed to him by his father-in-law Jethro, but with significant differences. Jethro proposed that Moses *provide out of all the people able men, such as fear Elohim, men of truth, hating unjust gain; and place such over them, to be rulers of thousands, rulers of hundreds, rulers of fifties, and rulers of tens* (Ex. 18:21). The text then states: *So Moses hearkened to the voice of his father-in-law, and did all that he had said. And Moses chose able men out of all Israel, and made them heads over the people, rulers of thousands, rulers of hundreds, rulers of fifties, and rulers of tens. And they judged the people at all seasons: the hard causes they brought unto Moses, but every small matter they judged themselves* (Ex. 18:24-26).

But did Moses really do everything that Jethro recommended? A careful reading of the text suggests that this was not the case. For one thing, we are told that Moses *chose able men out of all Israel*, but no mention is made of the other qualifications that Jethro proposed, that is, men that *fear Elohim, men of truth, hating unjust gain*. As a practical matter, the only demonstrable qualification among those proposed that Moses could be sure of was *ability*, whether in leadership, management, or business acumen. He could not see into the human psyche to assess a person's morality or true religiosity, and therefore had to ignore these desirable qualifications, which he replaced with wisdom, understanding, and knowledge, which as it turned out was also a bit overly ambitious, at least with regard to the attribute of understanding. As one paraphrase of the text put it, "So I took the chiefs of your tribes, and moved them kindly with words; wise men, masters of knowledge, but prudent in their thoughts, I found not."[43] It has been suggested that there is another fundamental distinction between what Jethro proposed and what Moses stipulated that accounts for several of the other distinctions between their organizational ideas. Jethro, according to this argument, was primarily interested in establishing a judicial system that would significantly reduce the burden on Moses, whereas Moses was primarily concerned about establishing a system of governance that would include an expanded judiciary as but one albeit very important element in a hierarchical political structure. This would help account for some of the differences in qualifications for office holders in the two proposals.[44]

Moreover, although the text assures us that Moses agreed and *did all that he [Jethro] had said* (Ex. 18:24) it is clear that he did so only within a much narrower context than Jethro proposed. For one thing, he did not choose candidates from *out of all the people*, including the "mixed multitude," but only *out of all Israel* (Ex. 18:25). Moses applied the proposed hierarchical structure to the tribes of Israel, but not to *all the people* as a collective non-tribal constituency. In effect, while he accepted Jethro's advice regarding delegation of leadership and authority, he rejected his father in-law's broader political advice about reconstituting the people, presumably including the "mixed multitude," as a single constituency under a centralized government. He rejected the latter idea, presumably because it would have undermined the communal cohesiveness of the Israelites provided by the tribal structure, and with it the family structure that was critical to the transmission of the covenant from generation to generation. His mission was to preserve the children of Israel so that they could serve God's purpose, and not to create an artificial nation out of a mixed population united only by a common disaffection for Egyptian rule.

Some have expressed surprise that Moses never mentions that he had discussed this issue with his father-in-law Jethro, as recorded in the book of Exodus, who gave him some specific advice on how to deal with then problem, advice that Moses followed to some extent. It has been suggested that Moses might have refrained from so doing because it might represent a slight to the Israelites that he had to receive advice from a Midianite, a member of a people with whom the children of Israel recently had some troubled relations.[45] Alternatively, it has been suggested that Moses neglected to mention his father-in-law out of personal embarrassment because he had married a non-Israelite, Cushite woman, which his own brother and sister thought improper for a leader of Israel (Num. 12:1).[46] That is, if the Cushite woman were none other than Jethro's daughter Zipporah, mentioning Jethro would only have highlighted and exacerbated the problem by appearing to boast of the wisdom of the Midianite leader. On the other hand, if as many suggest, Moses divorced Zipporah after he undertook his mission, the fact that he then married another woman made it inappropriate to recall the scandal by mentioning Jethro, who had become his ex-father-in-law. The essential point raised by these and other commentators is that Moses, despite his exalted status as interlocutor with God, was nonetheless flawed to some extent, with a proverbial skeleton in his closet, as is the case with every other human being.

What Moses attempted to institute within each of the tribes was a magistracy whose *sarim*, translated as *captains* but more likely referred to magistrates that served both as judicial and executive officials, as needed. Presumably, these same captains would serve as unit commanders in the wars of conquest that would have to be fought for possession of the land. He also appointed *shotrim* or *officers*, whose most likely responsibility was to enforce the decisions of the magistrates when such became necessary. In this regard it has been suggested that the enormous cadre that Moses imposed on the tribes not only involved quantitative considerations but also qualitative ones. Thus it is proposed that the *captains of thousands* were to serve as the key tribal leaders and generals, the *captains of hundreds* were the actual magistrates, the *captains of tens* were the *officers* whose responsibility it was to enforce compliance with the law, and the *captains of fifty* were the tribal elders who were responsible for the moral and religious education of the people, as suggested by the prophetic statement, *YHVH will enter into judgment with the elders of His people* (Isa. 3:14), who presumably would be held accountable for their failure to inculcate the proper principles of conduct in them and their leaders.[47] The basis for the assumption that *captains of fifty* referred to teachers appears to derive from a midrashic play on word, suggesting that the biblical phrase *sarei hamishim* or *captains of fifty* be read as *sarei humashim* or *captains of the Humash*, that is, masters of the Five Books of Moses or Pentateuch.[48] It has been suggested that even if one declines to accept all of this explanation, it seems reasonable to assume that there were discrete functions assigned to the various leadership levels, bearing in mind the Hebrew term *shoftim* connotes more than "judge," and that *shotrim* or *officers* are considered in other biblical writings to be Levites (2 Chron. 19:11; Neh. 8:11).[49]

It seems clear that the precipitating factor that caused Moses to take these steps was not only the need to be ready to respond effectively to the military challenges that would face the people, but also his abiding interest in and concern about preserving harmony within the Israelite communities, or at least preventing interpersonal disputes from disturbing the public order. This surely was necessary because prudence alone was a calming factor while they were in servitude in Egypt, subject to the arbitrary decisions of Egyptian overlords and taskmasters. Fear of doing anything to arouse the concerns of their masters effectively forced the people to make accommodations that would have been rejected under other circumstances. Their sudden liberation from Egyptian rule changed all this, allowing people to vent their grievances and to seek justice for their complaints. Without an effective judicial system in place, the burden of resolving or adjudicating disputes automatically fell upon the sole accepted authority, which was Moses. It was this burden that had to be redistributed if Moses was to be left free to deal with the broader issues involved in transforming the children of Israel and their tribes and clans into a coherent and cohesive nation. And it was to assuring justice and social harmony that Moses directed his attention as a matter of highest priority.

Moses recalls that upon inducting the new cadre of magistrates he stressed the importance of their conducting themselves in a manner that would give credibility and respect to the judicial system he was putting in place.

> *1.16 And I charged your judges at that time, saying: 'Hear the causes between your brethren, and judge righteously between a man and his brother, and the stranger that is with him. 1.17 Ye shall not respect persons in judgment; ye shall hear the small and the great alike; ye shall not be afraid of the face of any man; for the judgment is Elohim's; and the cause that is too hard for you ye shall bring unto me, and I will hear it.' 1.18 And I commanded you at that time all the things which ye should do.*

He admonished them to *hear the causes between your brethren*, an instruction that seems quite superfluous. After all, it was to hear and adjudicate cases that they were made judges in the first place. It has been argued, in this regard, that prior to this command, the judges were able to choose what cases they were willing to hear. Now this freedom was taken from them; they were obligated to *hear the causes between your brethren*, meaning any case that came before them, even though they may have preferred not to become involved in certain litigation.[50]

Considering the text from a jurisprudential perspective, it has been suggested that the intent of the admonition is that the judges are to give equal attention to each of the litigants.[51] Another suggestion is that *hear . . . between your brethren* means, "not to listen to *ex parte* statements, but to all that is said on both sides."[52] According to one reading, the admonition "is a warning to the court not to listen to the claims of a litigant in the absence of his opponent; and to the litigant not to explain his case to the judge before his adversary appears."[53] Approaching the matter from yet another perspective, the text has been understood to mean, "So hear your brethren that one may not (be permitted to) speak all his words, while another is compelled to cut his words short; and so hearken to their words, as that it may be impossible for you not to judge them, and deliver a judgment in truth."[54] Another approach takes the text as addressing the psychology of the judge. That is, the text should be understood as though it read, "I said to them, Be deliberate in judgment. If a case comes before you two or three times, do not say, 'Such a case has already come before me repeatedly,' but be deliberate in judgment," treat it as though you are hearing it for the first time.[55] However, it is also possible that the imperative *hear* means more than merely to give ear to, but adjures the judge to grasp the motives and intentions of the litigants and not to overly rely on the superficial merit of their respective claims, in the absence of compelling evidence.

The magistrates were also charged to *judge righteously between a man and his brother, and the stranger that is with him.* The idea of "righteous judgment" is a value concept that can be defined in a variety of ways. Considering the concept from a legal perspective, it was asserted, to *judge righteously* means to "consider rightly all aspects of the case before giving the decision."[56] Others maintained that righteous judgment meant basing the decision on the preponderance of credible evidence.

"The righteous litigant brings a just claim and offers just evidence."[57]
Moreover, given the reality of the non-Israelites living among them,
the judges are admonished to make no distinctions between Israelite
and non-Israelite in cases that come before them. The reference to *the
stranger that is with him* is understood to mean the stranger that lives
in Israelite society and whose very life or livelihood may depend on his
receiving righteous judgment, that is, fair treatment at the hands of the
court.[58]

In addition, Moses also set forth some principles of ethical
judgment, the first of which is *Ye shall not respect persons in judgment.*
The judge must demonstrate complete impartiality with regard to how
he treats the litigants before him. This was understood to prohibit
acknowledging the presence of one of the litigants, even if he is a friend,
and ignoring another because he is perceived as an enemy.[59] Moreover,
as one rabbinic sage put it, "when the litigants stand before you regard
them as guilty; and when they leave you, regard them as acquitted,
(when they have accepted your judgment.)"[60] It is noteworthy that
this admonition has also been understood as applicable to a person
who has the authority to appoint judges. He is not to allow personal
considerations of any kind to influence his choice in such regard,
which should be based solely on the person's judicial qualifications.
Otherwise, "the result might be that such a judge might free the guilty
and convict the innocent, not because he is wicked but because he is
simply not knowledgeable; yet he will be regarded as having respected
persons in judgment."[61] His ignorance may be interpreted as favoritism
and thus bring the judicial system into disrepute.

Another stipulation is *ye shall hear the small and the great alike.*
This requirement has been interpreted in alternate but not inconsistent
ways. Thus, it has been understood as saying that the same judicial
diligence must apply to a minor suit involving a small amount of money
as to a major one involving large amounts. However, this explanation
was objected to as being unnecessary because the point is self-evident.
Instead, it was argued that what the text means is "to give the due
priority, if it should be first in order.[62] That is, the judicial schedule
should not be adjusted to give priority attention to major litigation
over less dramatic suits if the latter were presented first. Alternatively

the text has been understood as cautioning the judge not to insert his own predilections into the judicial decision. That is, on the one hand, he is not to reason that because one litigant is poor and the other wealthy, and since the Torah requires that the poor be sustained, that he should be inclined to rule in favor of the poor litigant. On the other hand, it also cautions him against being reluctant to find in favor of the poor litigant because of a sense that to do so might cause the wealthy litigant unnecessary embarrassment for what might be a trivial amount for him. In such a case, he is cautioned not to rule in favor of the wealthy litigant, while making an extra-judicial arrangement for him to actually give the amount in question to the poor litigant, and thus satisfy the needs of both, the latter for his sustenance and the former for his honor.[63] Instead, the judge is admonished to *hear the small and the great alike,* and to render his judgment without taking into account any such considerations, which, although well intentioned, tend corrupt the judicial process.

Moreover, the judge is admonished, *ye shall not be afraid of the face of any man.* A judge in a contentious proceeding is always open to possible intimidation by threats to his or his family's well being as a means to secure a favorable decision. He must not succumb to such intimidation, but must remember always that he is acting in the name of the judge of all men, *for the judgment is Elohim's.*[64] This assertion was later amplified by a king of Judah in his charge to the judges he appointed: *Consider what ye do; for ye judge not for man, but for YHVH; and [He is] with you in giving judgment. Now therefore let the fear of YHVH be upon you; take heed and do it; for there is no iniquity with YHVH our Elohim, nor respect of persons, nor taking of bribes* (2 Chron. 19:6-7). A slightly different interpretation suggests that the phrase *for the judgment is Elohim's* is intended to convey the notion that the judge should consider the litigant before him not as a weak mortal but rather as though it were God that was a party to the judgment, and therefore in rendering judgment the judge *shall not be afraid of the face of any man.*[65] In what sense would God be a party to a lawsuit? As one rabbi put it, God has said with regard to those judges who fail to act appropriately: "It is not enough for the wicked [judges] that they take away money from one and give it to another unjustly, but they put Me to the trouble of returning it to its owner."[66] That is, as one commentator remarked, "the final verdict is always given to *Elohim* for completion."[67]

Nonetheless, the categorical rabbinic position taken by a straight reading of the text was deemed impracticable by some and was subsequently modified to suggest that in anticipation of a personal threat, the judge might legitimately recuse himself from hearing the case, either before the case has been heard, or even after, as long as he is in doubt about how he would rule in the absence of such threats. However, if he had already decided in his mind how he would rule, all agree that it would be morally impermissible for him to withdraw from the case because of the threat.[68] The presumption here appears to have been that once the judge had decided on a verdict, even though it had not been announced, it was considered by heaven as a *fait accompli*, and the idea of opening that settled judgment in favor of one litigant to possible reversal by another judge was deemed morally unacceptable.

Moses also advised the cadre of magistrates that they need not fear having to render judgments in cases where they felt unable to reach a solidly grounded conclusion. If they encounter such a problem, *the cause that is too hard for you ye shall bring unto me, and I will hear it*. In effect, Moses would personally adjudicate those cases that the appointed magistrates felt exceeded their competence. However, this probably should not be interpreted as an indication that Moses intended to establish an appeals system, with him serving as chief appellate judge to whom such appeals would be referred.[69] According to the traditional rabbinic reading of biblical law, there is no provision for an appellate judicial system.

It is of interest to note that the rabbis saw in this statement a degree of arrogance unbecoming to Moses. He had just told the judges *the judgment is Elohim's*. Accordingly, they maintained that he should have said that if they were presented with a case too difficult for them to decide, they should bring it to God for resolution, perhaps consulting God through Moses, but not leaving it for him to decide on the basis of his presumably superior wisdom.[70] They therefore taught: "Said the Holy One, blessed is He, to Moses: 'You think that you can decide difficult cases—by your life, I shall make you know that you cannot decide difficult cases. I shall bring you a case that your pupil's pupil will be able to judge, but you will not.'"[71] And, indeed, a number of such cases did arise, perhaps the most famous being one regarding the inheritance rights of daughters that Moses was forced to bring before God, because he could not decide it by himself (Num. 27:5).

It has been suggested that Moses' final statement in this passage, *and I commanded you at that time all the things which ye should do*, was not directed only to the magistrates but also to the people at large, as originally proposed by Jethro, when he advised Moses, *thou shalt teach them the statutes and the laws, and shalt show them the way wherein they must walk, and the work that they must do* (Ex. 18:20). Moses was taking the virtually unparalleled step in antiquity of establishing the practice of public education, of teaching *the statutes and the laws* promulgated by God to the entire citizenry, so that they should know and understand what was required of them as citizens.[72]

Having instituted the restructuring of the tribes in the manner described earlier and having set in place a theoretically responsible judicial system, Moses ordered the movement of the people from Horeb, the environs of Mount Sinai, to Kadesh-barnea, the staging point for entry into the promised land.

> *1.19 And we journeyed from Horeb, and went through all that great and dreadful wilderness which ye saw, by the way to the hill-country of the Amorites, as YHVH our Elohim commanded us; and we came to Kadesh-barnea. 1.20 And I said unto you: 'Ye are come unto the hill-country of the Amorites, which YHVH our Elohim giveth unto us. 1.21 Behold, YHVH thy Elohim hath set the land before thee; go up, take possession, as YHVH, the Elohim of thy fathers, hath spoken unto thee; fear not, neither be dismayed.'*

The meaning of *that great and dreadful wilderness* is clarified later in the text where it is described as a place *wherein were serpents, fiery serpents, and scorpions, and thirsty ground where was no water* (Deut 8:

15). The point is that God had them take this difficult route because it was the shortest one to Kadesh-barnea, which would be the staging point for their entry into the promised land while they were still enthused by the events they witnessed at Mount Sinai.[73] The ordeal of the trek to Kadesh-barnea took eleven difficult days, and the children of Israel were poised to enter the land at a point that would lead them directly into the hill country under control of the Amorites. Until they reached that point, notwithstanding the hardship of the trek, they had followed God's instructions faithfully, and Moses reminded them once again that God wanted them to invade the country and *take possession* of it without concern about the forces that would attempt to prevent them from so doing. The Hebrew term translated as *take possession* is *resh*, better rendered as "inherit," the implication being that they should go in and take possession of the land with the same ease as one might take possession of the inheritance left to one by his father.[74] God was on their side, and there was no reason to fear the Amorites, who were far less formidable than the Egyptians, and they had witnessed firsthand what happened to the latter at the hand of God.

> [1.22] *And ye came near unto me every one of you, and said: 'Let us send men before us, that they may search the land for us, and bring us back word of the way by which we must go up, and the cities unto which we shall come.'* [1.23] *And the thing pleased me well; and I took twelve men of you, one man for every tribe;* [1.24] *and they turned and went up into the mountains, and came unto the valley of Eshcol, and spied it out.* [1.25] *And they took the fruit of the land in their hands, and brought it down unto us, and brought us back word, and said: 'Good is the land which YHVH our Elohim giveth unto us.'*

It seems self-evident that the assertion *ye came near unto me every one of you* cannot mean that the entire people approached Moses, but must be understood as referring to a popular sentiment that was reflected in the demand that was made by the leaders of the tribes.[75] In this regard, it is noteworthy that in the earlier description of what took place it stated, *And YHVH spoke unto Moses, saying: 'send thou men, that they may spy out the land of Canaan, which I give unto the children of Israel; of every tribe of their fathers shall ye send a man, every one a prince among them* (Num. 13:1-2). Now we are told that the idea originated with the people, who evidently were unwilling to march into Canaan until they had a better idea of exactly where they were going and what they would encounter. In other words, they were no longer willing to rely on Moses' assurances that they were proceeding under divine guidance. It has been suggested that there is no real contradiction between the two passages, the earlier text focusing on the behavior of the scouts and the latter on the response of the people to their reports.[76]

However, a close reading of the Hebrew text indicates some subtle differences between the two accounts that may help explain the seeming incompatibilities. Thus, it has been suggested that the texts use alternate terms to describe the function of the people being sent to scout out the land. In the earlier text God instructs Moses, *send thou men, that they may spy out the land,* the Hebrew term translated as *spy out* being *veyaturu,* whereas in the later text the people demand of Moses *send men before us, that they may search the land for us,* the Hebrew term for *that they may search* being *veyahperu.* Both terms are understood to refer to "spying," but each in a different sense. In the first case, the term *veyaturu,* which may be understood as meaning sightsee, presumably refers to assessing the qualities of the various sections of the land for purposes of settlement, agriculture, and the raising of flocks and herds. Accordingly, God instructed Moses *of every tribe of their fathers shall ye send a man, every one a prince among them* (Num. 13:2). These representative tribal leaders were to assess and report to their respective constituencies about what they could expect to find in the territories allotted to them. In the second case, the term *veyahperu,* which means to search beneath, would seem to refer to revealing the military situation in the country, the character of its defenses and the forces that might be arrayed against their attempt to conquer it.[77] Thus, in the first instance, God is instructing Moses to send tribal leaders to see the goodness of the land and thereby quell any concerns about what they were inheriting; the matter of doing a military assessment is not even contemplated. In the second instance, the people demand of Moses that he send a reconnaissance team into the country precisely for the purpose of making a military assessment of the prospects for success and the potential losses to be incurred, to *bring us back word of the way by which we must go up, and the cities unto which we shall come.*[78] In this case, the role of God was completely ignored, even though Moses saw the military logic of what was being demanded. In effect, it has been suggested, it was not so much that the people had no faith that God would clear the way for them than it was that they were becoming increasingly uncomfortable with the idea of blindly walking into potentially dangerous situations without any idea of what awaited them.[79]

In a sense, if this latter interpretation is valid, what they were demanding from Moses was a more direct role in comprehending and shaping their collective destiny. It would appear that Moses was sensitive to the popular concern and also perhaps concerned about how the Israelites would acquit themselves in battle if their morale were low because of their implicit concerns.[80] Accordingly, he dispatched the twelve tribal chieftains, as God instructed him, but also, on his own initiative, gave them the additional mission of making the military assessment demanded by the people, a deviation from the divine instructions for which he was going to be punished by being denied the privilege of entering the country himself.

It is noteworthy, however, that the use of the term *veyahperu* in the people's demand has also been understood in a rather different manner than as referring to ferreting out military information. There is a view that it relates more directly to the later text, where Moses mentions the promise that when they enter the land God will give the people *houses full of all good things, which thou didst not fill* (Deut. 6:11). According to one interpretation of the text, what the people ostensibly were questioning was not whether they would be able to overcome the enemy, but whether the enemy would contrive to keep this divine promise from being kept. They assumed that when the peoples of the land became aware of the invasion by the Israelites they would bury their wealth in order to prevent its seizure. Accordingly, what they requested of Moses was to send spies to learn where these buried treasures might be so that they might readily be led to them once they entered the country, and for this reason they used the term *veyahperu*, which also means to explore or to excavate, instead of *vayeragelu*, which clearly means to spy out in a military sense.[81]

As discussed below, it would appear that their demand was acceptable to Moses, and it was he who was misled into broadening the mission to include a military assessment, which is what the people really wanted. Thus, when Moses sent the scouts on their mission, *they turned and went up into the mountains, and came unto the valley of Eshcol, and spied it out.* In this instance the text uses the term *vayeragelu*, meaning they did a military assessment that subsequently triggered the distrust in God that resulted in the protracted stay of the entire nation in the wilderness.[82] It is noteworthy that in this instance, just as was the case with the appointment of leaders and judges, Moses had to overcome tribal distrust by sending a scout from each tribe, even though a dozen such scouts were not really needed to carry out the assigned mission. This led to squabbling about commitment to the overall project, as it related to tribal self-interests, and resulted in the divided opinions about the feasibility of the invasion that led to its decades-long delay.[83]

It would seem that this spirit of rebellion against both him and God must have taken Moses aback. After all, this took place after he had established a hierarchical leadership structure, one purpose of which was to relieve him of the need to make virtually every decision. It would not have surprised Moses had it been representatives of the leadership cadre that proposed sending out scouting parties before they undertook an invasion that surely would be resisted strongly. However, it seems rather clear that it was not the leaders who approached him but the people as such, who were behaving as though the hierarchical structure he had established simply was of no significance. This surely troubled Moses.[84] Although the request they were making was not unreasonable in itself, it would appear that he was not sure quite how to respond to the popular demand when God informed him that he should accede to it.

Turning to the people, he announced that he agreed that it was prudent to scout out the land before entering it en masse, saying that the idea *pleased me well.* That is, it was acceptable to him since, presumably, he expected that such a reconnaissance mission would assuage any concerns they had and instill more trust in the divine word and confidence in his leadership.[85] The mission statement for the scouts set forth by Moses clearly indicates that he was a man with significant experience in military affairs. *'Get you up here into the south, and go up into the mountains; and see the land, what it is; and the people that dwelleth therein, whether they are strong or weak, whether they are few or many; and what the land is that they dwell in, whether it is good or bad; and what cities they are that they dwell in, whether in camps, or in strongholds'* (Num. 13:17-19). However, he omitted mentioning that although it pleased him it may not have pleased God, who nonetheless told Moses to comply with their wishes, surely knowing what would be the result of their demonstrated lack of faith in Him. Divine displeasure was clearly indicated as He told Moses, *shlah-lekha anashim*, which literally says, "Send *for yourself* men," hinting that God was disassociating from what was about to take place, implicitly leaving the matter to Moses' own judgment. By contrast, God earlier instructed Moses, *assaf-li shivim ish* or *Gather unto Me seventy men* (Num. 11:9), the choice of words indicating that God fully approved that assembly, but not this one.[86]

Caught between seeming divine indifference and the popular demand, Moses yielded to the latter, his only realistic choice under the circumstances, and selected a dozen men comprising one from each of the tribes to carry out the intelligence-gathering mission. The men chosen, presumably, were each a prominent representative of his respective tribe, something that was essential to ensure the credibility of their collective and individual reports. The scouts reconnoitered deep into the land and returned, laden with examples of the produce of the land and declared, *Good is the land which YHVH our Elohim giveth unto us.* Specific mention is made of *the valley of Eshcol* because it was there that, as related earlier, they cut down *a branch with one cluster of grapes, and they bore it upon a pole between two,* as evidence of the abundance of produce in the land. The locale where this took place was subsequently referred to as the *valley of Eshcol,* the latter meaning "cluster," presumably because of the prodigious cluster of grapes they brought from there (Num. 13:23-24). Although the scouts traveled throughout the land, the reason *the valley of Eshcol* is mentioned specifically, according to an alternate view, is not because of the fruits that were gathered there but because their visit there, where the remnants of the subsequently reported ancient race of giants were to be found, marked the turning point in the thinking of the majority of the scouts about their ability to conquer the land. This resulted in the tragedy of their betrayal of trust in God, which caused all of the people to be compelled to remain in the wilderness until that entire generation of those twenty years of age and older at the time passed away.[87]

With regard to their assessment of the military situation, it appears that the scouting parties were unable to arrive at a unanimous assessment of the situation, which resulted in the presentation of both a majority and minority report. The majority report asserted that, although the land itself was clearly desirable as a place of settlement, occupying it at that point in time was likely to be very costly because *the people that dwell in the land are fierce, and the cities are fortified, and very great* (Num. 13:28), and therefore capable of repulsing any Israelite attempt at a penetration from the south. The majority report also went farther and asserted that even an indirect approach was clearly impracticable because of the disposition of the various peoples that lived in the land. *Amalek dwelleth in the land of the South; and the Hittite, and the Jebusite, and the Amorite dwell in the mountains; and the Canaanite dwelleth by the sea, and along by the side of the Jordan* (Num. 13:29). In other words, there was no way of entering the land en masse without a major armed struggle, in which they saw little prospect of Israelite success. The assessment of the situation reflected in the majority report cast doubt on the viability of the proposed enterprise of establishing a permanent Israelite presence in the country. It asserted, in effect, that the ragtag, ill equipped, and untrained forces of the Israelite tribes were no match for the fortified towns and experienced armies of the Canaanite and other peoples in control of the country from the Mediterranean Sea to the Jordan River and the Dead Sea. The report clearly albeit implicitly suggested that no reliance could be placed either on Moses' leadership or on the divine promises that he purported to convey to them.

As indicated, there was also a minority report that offered a rather different assessment of the situation and the prospects for a successful penetration of the country. The spokesman for the minority view was Caleb, a leader of the tribe of Judah, who recommended, *We should go up at once, and possess it; for we are well able to overcome it* (Num. 13:30). What was the reasoning behind Caleb's optimism, which was later seconded by Joshua of the tribe of Ephraim, the leader of the expedition? In effect, Caleb did not dispute the objective information contained in the majority report. He did, however, dispute the conclusions drawn from it and the recommendation for inaction based on those conclusions. But on what basis did the minority reach an opposite conclusion from that of the majority? It would seem that, at least from the perspective of the biblical historiographer, Caleb was asserting that the majority report's assessment failed to take into account the divine role in history and the divine promise to Israel's patriarchs. With God on Israel's side, the balance of power on the battlefield would shift in Israel's favor. Does this mean that Caleb was anticipating a miracle that would enable Israel to prevail against the perceived odds? There is no indication in Caleb's words that he believed this to be the case. He argued quite explicitly that with regard to the opposition that would be mounted by the Canaanites and others, *we are well able to overcome it.* In other words, the conviction that God stood behind them would give the Israelites a superiority of morale that would compensate for the inferiority of their arms and battle experience.

Despite the protestations of Caleb and Joshua, the other ten scouts collectively took the position, *We are not able to go up against the people; for they are stronger than we* (Num. 13:28, 31), and their opinion prevailed and the Israelites of the time, because of their lack of faith in God, were immobilized by fear. Now, in his discourse, decades after the event, Moses refuses to allow the people to rationalize their elders' earlier behavior simply by blaming the scouts for misleading them; he insists that they acknowledge that, irrespective of the lack of unanimity among the scouts with regard to the feasibility of direct entry into the land, it was the people as a whole at the time that chose to heed the report of those who had little faith in God, a lack of faith that resulted in the prolonged sojourn in the wilderness. As one writer put it, "it was the spies who persuaded the people that they were no match for the Canaanites, but the people consented, accepting the spies' words, and therefore they shared the responsibility." Moses' message to their descendents, as well as to their elders who were minor children at the time, was that they could not salve the collective conscience by merely claiming that the spies were to blame for all the people's subsequent woes, which explains why Moses does not relate the story of the spies now, except for only the indisputably true part of their report, *Good is the land which YHVH our Elohim giveth unto us*, an assertion with which all the scouts or spies were in agreement. "The rest of the spies' report, such as the calumnies they spread about the land, is not relevant here insofar as they do nothing to mitigate the sin committed by the people,"[88] a sin which Moses now recounts in specific terms.

> [1.26] *Yet ye would not go up, but rebelled against the commandment of YHVH your Elohim;* [1.27] *and ye murmured in your tents, and said: 'Because YHVH hated us, He hath brought us out of the land of Egypt, to deliver us into the hand of the Amorites, to destroy us.* [1.28] *Whither are we going up? Our brethren have made our heart to melt, saying: The people is greater and taller than we; the cities are great and fortified up to heaven; and moreover we have seen the sons of the Anakim there.'*

Notwithstanding the divine commandment to do so, Moses reminded his listeners, *yet ye would not go up, but rebelled against the commandment of YHVH your Elohim.* It has been suggested that the reproach of rebellion goes beyond the issue at hand and that even if the scouts "had not demoralized them, the nation would have sought some other pretext for their disobedience."[89] The implication of this is that once they tasted freedom, many were disinclined to feel bound to another ruler even if that ruler were the God who liberated them in the first place. This would help explain why they were more influenced by the secondhand report of the scouts than by their firsthand witnessing of the miracles that liberated them from Egypt and allowed them to cross the Sea of Reeds unharmed and fed them in the wilderness.

They willingly and all too easily accepted the assertion, contested by two of their leaders who had participated in the mission, Caleb and

Joshua, that *the people is greater and taller than we; the cities are great and fortified up to heaven*, and the purely imaginative claim, *and moreover we have seen the sons of the Anakim there.* The latter clearly referred to *Ahiman, Sheshei, and Talmai, the children of Anak* (Num. 13:22), who lived in the area of Hebron. These, presumably, were tall men, a fact that the scouts embellished grossly when their report was challenged by claiming that they saw *the Nephilim, the sons of Anak, who came of the Nephilim; and we were in our own sight as grasshoppers, and so were we in their sight* (Num. 13:33). Mention of the *Nephilim* clearly refers to the mythical antediluvian giants mentioned in Gen. 6:4, suggesting that they survived the great deluge along with Noah and were now to be found living in Hebron. Although Abraham, who lived there for many years, never mentioned them, there is a thirteenth-century B.C.E. document that describes certain Bedouin as being between four and five cubits in height,[90] or between six and nine feet tall depending on the assumed length of a cubit. This suggests that the scouts might have seen some such men in the area, but surely not in the numbers to justify the mass hysteria that resulted from their report of the sighting. Their claim may well have been dismissed as nonsense if the people were not ready to grasp at straws to justify their fears born of their inability to place their trust in God and his servant Moses.

Caleb, supported by Joshua, attempted to reason with the people, assuring them that *the land, which we passed through to spy it out, is an exceedingly good land. If the Lord delight in us, then He will bring us into this land, and give it to us . . . Only rebel not against the Lord, neither fear ye the people of the land . . . their defense is removed from over them, and the Lord is with us; fear them not* (Num. 14:7-9). It was to no avail. In effect, the people dismissed out of hand the argument that superior morale would tip the military balance in favor of Israel, implicitly arguing that their high morale would quickly dissipate once the Israelites were faced by the reality of contending with an invincible foe. The wave of fear that spread throughout the camp soon turned to mass hysteria with people crying, *Would that we had died in the land of Egypt or would have died in the wilderness! And wherefore doth YHVH bring us unto this land, to fall by the sword? Our wives and our little ones will be a prey; were it not better for us to return into Egypt?* This infuriated God, who was prepared to wreak vengeance on them, and it was only because of Moses' intercession in their behalf that God did not destroy them (Num. 14:1-20).

Thus, Moses reminded them, *ye murmured in your tents, and said: 'Because YHVH hated us, He hath brought us out of the land of Egypt, to deliver us into the hand of the Amorites, to destroy us.'* The perverse logic of this assertion was surely the result of an irrational fear. If God wanted to annihilate the children of Israel, He surely could have contrived to make it happen in Egypt. However, the argument of this assertion is that God wanted the people suffer more by bringing them to the threshold of a new life as a nation in their own land, only to abandon them to their fate in the hands of the Amorites. Alternatively, it has been suggested that the logic of their complaint is not as irrational as may appear at first glance. Assuming that they believed that God would give the land to their descendants as promised both to the Patriarchs and to them, they nonetheless feared that God would deliver them *to fall by the sword*, with their wives and children becoming captives. With regard to the reason why God did not take retribution on the generation while still in Egypt, if He had done so there would have been no one to lead the children out of Egypt and to bring them into the land. By having the Canaanites or Amorites kill them, the children would remain in the land under divine protection to inherit it later when God decided to eliminate the Canaanites from the land. In other words, they feared that as members of the generation that was faithless before and after the exodus, they now were to pay for their faithlessness, while only their wives and children would survive.[91]

> [1.29] *Then I said unto you: 'dread not, neither be afraid of them.* [1.30] *YHVH your Elohim who goeth before you, He shall fight for you, according to all that He did for you in Egypt before your eyes;* [1.31] *and in the wilderness, where thou hast seen that YHVH thy Elohim bore thee, as a man doth bear his son, in all the way that ye went, until ye came unto this place.* [1.32] *Yet in this thing ye do not believe YHVH your Elohim,* [1.33] *who went before you in the way, to seek out a place to pitch your tents in: in the fire by*

> *night, to show you by what way ye should go, and in the cloud by day.'*

Moses relates that, at the time, he did all he could to reassure them that their fears were groundless; the Amorites, as well as the others they would encounter in the land, were no different than the Israelites with regard to stature and natural abilities. However, they, the children of Israel, were significantly different from the Amorites because God was on their side in the struggles that would of necessity take place, struggles that they would have to win if their future were to be assured. He thus assured them, *YHVH your Elohim who goeth before you, He shall fight for you, according to all that He did for you in Egypt before your eyes; and in the wilderness, where thou hast seen that YHVH thy Elohim bore thee, as a man doth bear his son, in all the way that ye went, until ye came unto this place.* Surely this statement should have made it clear to them that God did not intend to have them die in a vain attempt to invade the land promised to them. Yet, and despite everything that God did to help them survive and to lead them safely through the wilderness to the very doorstep of the land of Canaan, they nonetheless paid more heed to the words of a handful of rebellious men than to Him, working themselves into a paranoid state, unwilling to accept that God had forgiven them for their past lapses in faith.

The critical questions that the text does not address is why the open rebellion against Moses' leadership broke out at this particular point in time and what it was intended to accomplish. What was the underlying agenda of the ten scouts that led them to exaggerate the threat out of all proportion to reality, and to denigrate the potential divine role in their successful struggle against the peoples of the land? It surely was not to work the people up into a frenzy to want to return to Egypt. A clue to what they might have had in mind may be found in the earlier account where it states, *all the children of Israel murmured against Moses and against Aaron* (Num. 14:2). It may be that when the princes of the tribes went to scout out the land, they concluded that it would be more beneficial for the tribes to enter into a loose confederation with a weak national leadership rather than the much tighter federation headed by a strong centralized national government, as conceived and promoted by Moses and Aaron. If this were their goal, it seems reasonable to conclude that it would be best to accomplish this political restructuring before entering the land, before the exigencies of war and population movement would likely make it far more difficult to achieve in the foreseeable future. Accordingly, it would facilitate the implementation of such an arrangement to delay immediate entry into the land, as called for by Moses. However, because the popular expectations of doing the latter were so high, a highly plausible reason for delaying the invasion had to be conjured, and so the evocation of the images of giant warriors, impenetrable fortified cities, and powerful armies was employed to disenchant the people about the realism of their high expectations, and to discredit the central leadership of Moses. Of course by according greater credibility to the majority of the spies than to the lonely voices of Moses, Joshua, and Caleb, the people also, perhaps for the most part not intentionally, discredited God and His commitments under the covenant.

The simple reality, notwithstanding the self-serving predilections of the tribal leaders for retaining their autonomy, was that the newborn nation composed of those same tribes sorely needed the collective discipline and nurture that could only be provided by a strong central political and religious leadership. The latter was critical, as finally became evident to the people centuries later following the chaotic and volatile period of the Judges, if it were to be able to confront successfully the numerous military challenges that lay ahead, in addition to remaining simultaneously viable as a unique monotheistic religious community in the context of the seductive pagan world into which it was inserting itself.

This virtual collapse of faith in God reflected in the episode of the spies clearly was unacceptable to Him and constituted a grievous failure for which the children of Israel collectively would have to pay dearly, as made clear in the following passage, in which Moses recalls the divine reaction.

> *1.34 And YHVH heard the voice of your words, and was wroth, and swore, saying: 1.35 'Surely there shall not one of these men, even this evil generation, see the good land,*

which I swore to give unto your fathers, [1.36] *save Caleb the son of Jephunneh, he shall see it; and to him will I give the land that he hath trodden upon, and to his children; because he hath wholly followed YHVH.'* [1.37] *Also YHVH was angry with me for your sakes, saying: 'Thou also shalt not go in thither;* [1.38] *Joshua, the son of Nun, who standeth before thee, he shall go in thither; encourage thou him, for he shall cause Israel to inherit it.* [1.39] *Moreover, your little ones, that ye said should be a prey, and your children, that this day have no knowledge of good or evil, they shall go in thither, and unto them will I give it, and they shall possess it.* [1.40] *But as for you, turn you, and take your journey into the wilderness by the way to the Red Sea.'* [92]

It is noteworthy that Moses, in his recapitulation of these events, failed to mention that God told him that He was completely fed up with the children of Israel, saying: *How long will this people despise Me, and how long will they not believe in Me, for all the signs which I have wrote among them? I will smite them with pestilence, and destroy them, and will make of thee a nation greater and mightier than they* (Num. 14:9). It was only because of Moses' intercession that God relented in part. Thus Moses pleaded: *Pardon, I pray Thee, the iniquity of this people according unto the greatness of Thy lovingkindness, and according as Thou hast forgiven this people, from Egypt even until now* (Num. 14:19). However, Moses only succeeded in assuaging divine anger with regard to the younger generation, *that this day have no knowledge of good or evil,* and therefore cannot be held individually liable for what their elders had done. Nonetheless, Moses again emphasizes to his audience, all of which were either very young or unborn at the time of the episode of the spies, that, in so far as they are members of the nation, they had to bear the burden of their collective past and suffer for the sins of their fathers.

As made clear below, the implication of these texts is that it is only at the age of twenty that one is considered fully responsible and publicly accountable for his actions as a citizen; prior to that one is considered as still, at least partially, under the authority and influence of their parents. As for those who were already twenty years of age and older at the time of the incident, men of military age, who complained, *Would we had died in the land of Egypt or would we have died in the wilderness* (Num. 14:2), the divine response was, *As I live, saith YHVH, surely as ye have spoken in Mine ears, so will I do to you: your carcasses shall fall in this wilderness, and all that were numbered of you, according to your whole number, from twenty years old and upward, ye that have murmured against Me* (Num. 14:28-29).

It was the divine judgment that the mood of rebellion inspired by the tribal princes and fostered by the tribal elders was counterproductive and contrary to the vision of a people committed to the covenant. Accordingly, without effective central leadership a rapid conquest of the country would not be possible, making it necessary for the conquest to be delayed until a new generation nurtured under the leadership of Moses and Aaron matured and assumed leadership roles among the tribes. Thus God decreed, *Surely there shall not one of these men, even this evil generation, see the good land, which I swore to give unto your fathers*, the only exceptions were to be Caleb, who spoke out strongly against the majority report, and Joshua, whose loyalty was so well established that it did not require mention.

It is noteworthy that with regard to Caleb, God promised, *to him will I give the land that he hath trodden upon, and to his children.* The land spoken of in this text is Hebron and its environs, where Caleb confronted his colleagues over their unwarranted concern and fear of the descendents of the giants (Num. 13:33). As recorded, Caleb subsequently requested of Joshua: '*Now therefore give me this mountain, whereof YHVH spoke in that day; for thou heardest in that day how the Anakim were there, and cities great and fortified; it may be that YHVH will be with me, and I shall drive them out, as YHVH spoke.*' *And Joshua blessed him; and he gave Hebron unto Caleb the son of Jephunneh for an inheritance . . . because that he wholly followed YHVH the Elohim of Israel* (Josh. 14:12-14).

As for Moses, because of his failures as political and moral leader of the nation, in acceding to the timidity of the national leadership he himself had placed in office in the matter of the scouts, he too would not be permitted to enter the land. It has been suggested that it was because Moses' transgression was unintentional, an error in judgment, whereas that of the people was intentional, a conscious rejection of trust in God, he was not lumped together with them in the enunciation of the fateful divine edict that resulted in the demise of the entire generation of men twenty and older during the thirty-eight years of wandering in the wilderness. In effect, Moses would be the last of the older generation to succumb to death outside the promised land.[93]

Henceforth, Joshua would take his place as supreme leader of *your children, that this day have no knowledge of good or evil, they shall go in thither, and unto them will I give it, and they shall possess it*; Joshua would carry out the task that Moses had initiated but would not be permitted to see it through to completion. By juxtaposing God's rejection of his plea to cross the Jordan with the people and his replacement by Joshua, Moses' "intention was to impress also upon the minds of the people the fact, that even in wrath the Lord had been mindful of His covenant, and when pronouncing the sentence upon His servant Moses, had given the people a leader in the person of Joshua, who was to bring them into the promised inheritance."[94] As for the current generation, they were to return to the wilderness and live out their days, while the new generation that would be born there would be hardened by the experience and at the proper time follow God's instruction and take possession of the land promised to their ancestors.

Moses recalls that immediately following his delivery of the divine sentence levied against the entire generation, the popular reaction was one of shock and dismay, suggesting that it suddenly dawned on the people that they had overstepped the bounds of acceptable dissent, and that they needed to assuage the divine wrath as a matter of extreme urgency.

> [1.41] *Then ye answered and said unto me: 'We have sinned against YHVH, we will go up and fight, according to all that YHVH our Elohim commanded us.' And ye girded on every man his weapons of war, and deemed it a light thing to go up into the hill-country.* [1.42] *And YHVH said unto me: 'Say unto them: Go not up, neither fight; for I am not among you; lest ye be smitten before your enemies.'*

> *1.43* *So I spoke unto you, and ye hearkened not; but ye rebelled against the commandment of YHVH, and were presumptuous, and went up into the hill-country. 1.44 And the Amorites, that dwell in that hill-country, came out against you, and chased you, as bees do, and beat you down in Seir, even unto Hormah. 1.45 And ye returned and wept before YHVH; but YHVH hearkened not to your voice, nor gave ear unto you. 1.46 So ye abode in Kadesh many days, according to the days that ye abode there. 2.1 Then we turned, and took our journey into the wilderness by the way to the Sea of Reeds, as YHVH spoke unto me; and we compassed mount Seir many days.*

Terrified by the divine response conveyed to them by Moses, the people seemed to come to the realization that they feared the awesomeness of divine wrath far more than the enemies that awaited them across the frontier. In the context of what took place earlier, it seems reasonable to assume that it was a sudden reversal of public support of their position that caused the tribal leaders to publicly acknowledge that they had sinned against God by casting doubt on His trustworthiness and assert that they now sought to make amends, declaring: *We have sinned against YHVH, we will go up and fight, according to all that YHVH our Elohim commanded us.* Suddenly discounting all their expressed concerns about their inferiority to those who awaited them in the promised land, which had sewn such dissension among the people, the tribal leaders now proposed to invade the country as originally commanded. They then *girded on every man his weapons of war, and deemed it a light thing to go up into the hill-country.* The mythical giants of old suddenly vanished from their minds as quickly as they had been evoked earlier. Presumably, they expected that now that they had decided to do what they were told to do earlier, all would be forgiven and God would be with them.

It proved, however, to be too little too late. The divine edict would not be recanted, and Moses was told to inform them that they should desist because they will fail. He was to convey to them the divine command, *Go not up, neither fight; for I am not among you; lest ye be smitten before your enemies.* However, it was evident that they had learned nothing from their previous experience; they decided that they would attack even without divine approval and Moses' leadership or direction. Thus their decision to go ahead and invade the country clearly was not an act of contrition for their earlier rebelliousness but was rather yet another act of rebellion against God. That is, after God declared that it would only be the younger generation that *shall go in thither, and unto them will I give it, and they shall possess it,* they insisted *we will go up and fight,* as though their previous rebellion never took place.[95] As one commentator put it, they "went from criminal cowardice to criminal conceit." That which they doubted could be accomplished with God, they now believed they could achieve without Him.[96]

In an attempt to make sense of this somewhat bizarre episode, it has been suggested that the initial refusal to invade the country and the subsequent decision to do so were both manifestations of a desire to rebel against their vassalage to a divine sovereign. In the first instance, they refused to go into the country precisely because God was going to hand it to them in return for their obedience. In the second case, they wanted to go in precisely because God told them not to do so. In other words, the expressed concern of the tribal leaders about the overwhelming odds that would face them was nothing more than a subterfuge for rebellion against divine leadership. Thus, once it was withdrawn, all their fears of an awesome and overwhelmingly powerful enemy quickly dissipated. Now they were ready to invade the country without divine assistance, which they did not want, so that they could be free to live there as they chose and not according to the occasionally onerous requirements of the covenant.[97] Well aware of the obligations they undertook in exchange for their freedom from slavery, the sense of freedom proved so heady for some that they were prepared to renege on the covenant if necessary to resist any new encumbrance on that freedom, and to impose their views on the children of Israel through deception and demagoguery.

Moses recalled that *ye rebelled against the commandment of YHVH, and were presumptuous, and went up into the hill-country,* on your own initiative and without divine sanction, which proved to be a prescription for disaster. As anticipated by Moses, the incursion into the southern hill country dominated by the relatively powerful state of Arad was repulsed with heavy Israelite casualties (Num. 14:45, 21:1), as they were beaten back as far as Hormah. The name *Hormah* appears to be related to the Hebrew word *herem*, meaning either 'ban' or 'destruction,' and as one commentator noted, "There was a touch of irony in the fact that a defeated Israel fled to a place whose name suggested annihilation."[98] Perhaps also ironic, the intelligence report submitted by the majority of the scouting party, which argued strongly against such an attack, proved to be prescient once Israel's earlier qualitative edge was no longer a factor. It is noteworthy that according to the original account of the fighting, *then the Amalekite and the Canaanite, who dwelt in that hill-country, came down, and smote them and beat them down, even unto Hormah* (Num. 14:45). Accordingly, in the present description of their defeat at the hands of the Amorites, the term probably should be understood as a general designation for the various peoples found in the land, which included the Amorites as one component of the population. More significant is the earlier report that the Israelites underwent a major defeat at the hands of the Amalekites, whom they routed in battle at Rephidim under the leadership of Joshua, *And Joshua discomfited Amalek and his people with the edge of the sword* (Ex. 17:13), who had declined to lead them again in a battle that did not have divine sanction, as evidenced by the notice that *the ark of the covenant of YHVH, and Moses, departed not out of the camp* (Num. 14:44).

Moses then recalled, *And ye returned and wept before YHVH; but YHVH hearkened not to your voice, nor gave ear unto you.* It has been suggested that the divine lack of response was not the result of indifference to their grief over what happened, but rather because what they were crying over was not their offense against God, only the consequences of that offense, something that did not merit divine consideration.[99] They were left in the wilderness on their own—well, not quite on their own because the text indicates that divine beneficence in the form of the manna never ceased until they entered the land promised to them.

So, after remaining at the oasis of Kadesh-barnea for an unspecified period of time, Moses led the children of Israel back into the wilderness in the direction of the Sea of Reeds, avoiding the area of Mount Seir so as not to come in conflict with the Edomites. In all, the Israelites would remain in the wilderness at various locations for a total of another thirty-eight years. According to one tradition, they stayed at Kadesh-barnea for nineteen years, and spent the remaining nineteen at various other locations in the wildernesses of the Sinai region.[100] However, it is not known whether Moses and the Israelites remained at Kadesh-barnea only once for an extended period or whether, as they moved from site to site in the wilderness, they may have returned to Kadesh-barnea one or more times over the long period of their wandering. In any case, at the end of this long hiatus God instructed Moses that the time had arrived to begin maneuvering the people into position to cross into the land of Canaan from the east. In the course of doing so, they would have to pass through territories occupied or claimed by others as protectorates. However, Israel was not given the discretion to fight and conquer its way through the shortest route to its goal, but was instructed to by-pass certain territories and to conquer others. "In this way the precise extent of the land to be occupied was defined by God and selfish human ambitions were restrained."[101]

> *2.2 And YHVH spoke unto me, saying: 2.3 'Ye have compassed this mountain long enough; turn you northward. 2.4 And command thou the people, saying: Ye are to pass through the border of your brethren the children of Esau, that dwell in Seir; and they will be afraid of you; take ye good heed unto yourselves therefore; 2.5 contend not with them; for I will not give you of their land, no, not so much as for the sole of the foot to tread on; because I have given mount Seir unto Esau for a possession. 2.6 Ye shall purchase food of them for money, that ye may eat; and ye shall also buy water of them for money, that ye may drink. 2.7 For YHVH thy Elohim hath blessed thee in all the work of thy hand; He hath known thy walking through this great wilderness; these forty years YHVH the Elohim hath been with thee; thou hast lacked nothing.' 2.8a So we passed by from our brethren the children of Esau, that dwell in Seir, from the way of the Arabah, from Elath and from Ezion-geber.*

It has been suggested that the import of *Ye have compassed this mountain long enough* is that even though the anniversary of the divine decision that entry into the promised land would be delayed for another thirty-eight years had not yet been reached, the entire generation of those twenty and older at that time, with the exception of Moses, Joshua, and Caleb, had already passed away, and there was no other reason for waiting any longer. Accordingly, God told Moses to begin the process of entering the country from the east.[102]

It seems that it may have been while the Israelites were still at Kadesh-barnea that Moses received the word to bring his people into position to cross into Cisjordan from the east, and for this purpose he appealed to the king of Edom for permission to cut through his country and cross into Transjordan just south of Moab. The message he sent to the king stated, *Let us pass, I pray thee, through thy land; we will not pass through field or through vineyard, neither will we drink of the water of the wells; we will go along the king's highway, we will not turn aside to the right hand nor to the left, until we have passed thy border* (Num. 20:17). The request was refused, and to ensure that the Israelites would not attempt to cross Edomite territory anyway, the Edomites turned out in force to block their way, a challenge that Moses did not accept.

For years the Israelites had been camping some distance from Seir, and Moses was now told to lead the people on an easterly route that would bypass the Edomite heartland of Seir, which included the Arabah from the Salt Sea to Elath and Ezion-geber at the entrance to the Red Sea. It would appear that it was in the vicinity of the latter, although there is little agreement among scholars in this regard, that the Israelites crossed into Transjordan before heading north along the eastern face of the hills of Seir. The movement of the body of Israel along their eastern frontier was expected to raise alarm among the Edomites of the area, but Moses was cautioned not to threaten them in any manner. The Edomites were the descendents of Esau, and their territorial integrity was to be fully respected by the Israelites; there was to be no trespass because their territory was a divine grant and was not intended to be part of Israel's patrimony. It was permissible, however, to purchase provisions from the Edomites, if they would consider selling them to the Israelites, which as will be seen below, is what they did.

What was it that made the Edomites more accommodating now than they had been shortly before? It has been suggested that the topography of the region had a great deal to do with it. On the west, the hill-country of Edom has relatively high steep slopes that were easy to defend against encroachment and the Edomites took advantage of this to block passage of the Israelites through the transverse passes. However, once the Israelites crossed into Transjordan farther south and then proceeded north ward along the Edomite eastern frontier, where their hills only rose slightly from the tableland, making them highly vulnerable and difficult to defend, the Edomites elected to be more accommodating, especially since it was clear that the Israelites displayed no interest in seizing any of their land, even though they did not ask for rights of transit as they did the first time. Moreover, the text states specifically, *Ye are to pass through the border* [*bigevul*] and not [*al gevul*] *along the border*, indicating that the Israelites had no choice but to violate their territory if they were not to make a wide detour through the desert to go entirely around Edomite territory.[103]

Alternatively, it has been suggested that the Edomites essentially were split into two political entities, one of which occupied the western part of the hill-country under a king who categorically refused to allow the Israelites freedom of passage through his territory. The second consisted of unaffiliated Edomite tribes, ruled by their independent tribal leaders, that were to be found on the eastern side of the Edomite hill-country, and it was the latter that proved accommodating because of their vulnerability. Presumably, it was to the latter Edomites that the text refers in the assertion, *they will be afraid of you; take ye good heed unto yourselves therefore; contend not with them.* That is, the Israelites are not to take advantage of them, even though they could easily do so. Moreover, it is argued that the text itself draws the distinction between the two entities. Thus, the first time, *Moses sent messengers from Kadesh to the king of Edom* (Num. 20:14), who rejected his overture, *and Edom came out against him with much people, and with a strong hand* (Num. 20:20). Now, there is no mention of Edom, or its king, but only *the children of Esau*, even though the Edomites and the children of Esau are ethnically identical.[104]

The divine restriction on violating the territorial integrity of the land of the Edomites reflects an important geopolitical principle. As clearly indicated later in the biblical text, one facet of divine sovereignty over the universe is the determination of the borders of the nations of the world. In the present text and in those below that deal with Moab (2:9) and Ammon (2:19), it is made clear that, as Israel is about to gain its own territory, God demonstrates particular concern about assuring that Israel be respectful of the boundaries of the peoples tracing their descent not only from Abraham but also from Esau and Lot, whose lands also are a divine gift to them. "It compels the Jewish people to realize that beyond the sphere of Hashem's special care for them, they must respect the property of other nations and not feel as invincible conquerors."[105]

(It is noteworthy that in the Masoretic text verse 2:8 is interrupted at this point, and I have reflected this by designating the first part of the verse as 2:8a and its continuation below as 2:8b.)

> [2.8b]*And we turned and passed by the way of the wilderness of Moab.* [2.9]*And YHVH said unto me: 'Be not at enmity with Moab, neither contend with them in battle; for I will not give thee of his land for a possession; because I have given Ar unto the children of Lot for a possession.* ([2.10] *The Emim dwelt therein aforetime, a people great, and many, and tall, as the Anakim;* [2.11] *there also are accounted Rephaim, as the Anakim; but the Moabites call them Emim.* [2.12] *And in Seir dwelt the Horites aforetime, but the children of Esau succeeded them; and they destroyed them from before them, and dwelt in their stead; as Israel did unto the land of his possession, which YHVH gave unto them.)* [2.13] *Now rise up, and get you over the brook Zered.' And we went over the brook Zered.*

Moses, however, was also instructed to consider the territory of Moab, which at the time included the land between the Jordan rift valley in the west and the sparsely populated wilderness in the east, and from the brook or wadi of Zered in the south to the Arnon valley in the north, as inviolate. He therefore led the Israelites on a route that took them deep into Transjordan in order to bypass Moab, whose capital city of Ar was located in the valley of the Arnon, which was given as a heritage to the descendents of Abraham's nephew Lot. By moving east of the settled areas of both Edom and Moab, Moses also avoided the necessity of crossing the steep canyon separating Moab from Edom in addition to the fertile and settled districts before again moving north, crossing *the brook Zered*, a wadi which connects with the Arnon. It is noteworthy that in Israel's subsequent history the restriction on trespassing the territory of both Moab and Ammon was violated by David (2 Sam. 8:2, 11:1). Some have sought to vindicate David's actions by pointing to the wording of our text, *And YHVH said unto me: Be not at enmity with Moab*, and emphasizing that the phrase *unto me* merely imposed the restriction on Moses, but did not make it obligatory on subsequent generations that were permitted to violate it as circumstances dictated.[106]

The text also inserts a long parenthetic statement explaining the earlier history of the area, which included a people known variously as *Emim* or *Rephaim* that were uncharacteristically tall and therefore referred to as *Anakim* or giants. In the context of the earlier narrative, some remnants of this people may have remained in the region and it is possible that the Israelite scouts may have seen a few such remnants and exaggerated their observation into the claim that they could not enter Canaan because of the *Anakim* to be found there. The note makes clear that the *Anakim* as a group had long disappeared and had been supplanted first by the *Horites* or Hurrians, *but the children of Esau succeeded them; and they destroyed them from before them, and dwelt in their stead; as Israel did unto the land of his possession, which YHVH gave unto them.* It is assumed that the latter assertion relates to the Israelite settlement of the region north of Moab discussed below. It also has been argued that there is an important implication in the clause, *which YHVH gave unto them*, a statement that does not appear with regard to land occupied by the Edomites, Moabites, and Ammonites. Thus, it has been suggested that the fundamental difference between the inheritance of the land by Israel and the other territories by their respective peoples is the nature of the divine providence involved. That experienced by the other nations is "general providence," whereas Israel is the beneficiary of "individual [special] providence."[107]

It also has been suggested that this parenthetical statement was intended to raise the morale of the people in preparation for the impending struggle against the remnants of the fabled giants, "by reminding the people that under God's direction, equally gigantic nations had to give way before the sons of Lot and Esau, and these were now in undisturbed possession of their lands."[108]

> *2.14 And the days in which we came from Kadesh-barnea, until we were come over the brook Zered, were thirty and eight years; until all the generation, even the men of war, were consumed from the midst of the camp, as YHVH swore unto them. 2.15 Moreover the hand of YHVH was against them, to discomfit them from the midst of the camp, until they were consumed.*

The crossing of the Zered constituted a milestone, marking the beginning of the end of the thirty-eight year detention of the children of Israel in the wilderness. By this time, the entire generation of those who had already reached maturity at the time of the exodus, including the tribal leaders who had fomented the rebellion that resulted in the detention, had died as God had promised would be the case. The time had come for the new generation to be permitted to achieve what their forbears had failed to do because of their lack of faith. The text also makes clear that the demise of the older generation was not entirely natural, but the divine hand disposed of those that would have naturally lingered on, presumably through acceleration and intensification of natural processes such as diseases or exposure that hastened their demise. This intervention was necessary in order to fulfill the divine commitment that all the older generation would succumb by the fortieth year and thereby relieve the younger generation of any further unnecessary suffering on account of the rebellion of their fathers.[109]

> *2.16 So it came to pass, when all the men of war were consumed and dead from among the people, 2.17 that YHVH spoke unto me, saying: 2.18 'Thou art this day to pass over the border of Moab, even Ar; 2.19 and when thou comest nigh over against the children of Ammon, harass them not, nor contend with them; for I will not give thee of the land of the children of Ammon for a possession; because I have given it unto the children of Lot for a possession. (2.20 That also is accounted a land of Rephaim: Rephaim dwelt therein aforetime; but the Ammonites call them Zamzummim, 2.21 a people great, and many, and tall, as the Anakim; but YHVH destroyed them before them: and they succeeded them, and dwelt in their stead; 2.22 as He did for the children of Esau, that dwell in Seir, when He destroyed the Horites from before them; and they succeeded them, and dwelt in their stead even unto this day; 2.23 and the Avvim, that dwelt in villages as far as Gaza, the Caphtorim, that came out of Caphtor, destroyed them, and dwelt in their stead.) 2.24 Rise ye up, take your journey, and pass over the valley of the Arnon; behold, I have given into thy hand Sihon the Amorite, king of Heshbon, and his land; begin to possess it, and contend with him in battle. 2.25 This day will I begin to put the dread of thee and the fear of thee upon the peoples that are under the whole heaven, who, when they hear the report of thee, shall tremble, and be in anguish because of thee.'*

Moses continued his narrative by pointing out that it was only *when all the men of war were consumed and dead from among the people,* that God told him to cross the Zered, which was the southern border of Moab, and proceed north skirting Moab as far as the frontier of Ammon.[110] The possible implication of this assertion may be that there was no direct communication between God and Moses throughout the thirty-eight year period of Israel's detention in the wilderness.[111] In this regard, it is noteworthy that in previous references by Moses to communications from God, he phrases it as *YHVH said unto me* (Deut.

1:42, 2:2, 9), whereas here he states, *YHVH spoke unto me*. *Amirah* (saying) is understood only as referring to the communication itself, but not specifically to its mode of delivery, whereas *dibbur* (speaking) "designates the articulated words of the mouth, the spoken word."[112] The implication of this is that because of the lack of faith of the older generation, God did not communicate with Moses in the manner that distinguished him from all other prophets for as long as those denied the privilege of entry into the promised land were still alive. Now that they were gone, God once again spoke to Moses *mouth to mouth* (Num. 12:8).[113]

In any case, Moses was then warned that the territory of Ammon was to be considered inviolate because, like Moab, it too was granted to the descendents of Lot. Instead, he was to lead the people in a northwesterly direction to avoid Ammon, but would encounter *Sihon the Amorite, king of Heshbon,* with whom he was to contend and destroy and seize his land, which abutted the Jordan. As the text puts it, *behold, I have given into thy hand Sihon the Amorite, king of Heshbon, and his land,* the diametric opposite of the fear expressed by the earlier generation that *Because YHVH hated us, He hath brought us out of the land of Egypt, to deliver us into the hand of the Amorites, to destroy us* (Deut. 1:27). The battle was to be so decisive as to spread fear throughout the region at the approach of the Israelites, giving them a psychological advantage in the forthcoming invasion of Cisjordan.

The text also introduces here a long parenthetical note again emphasizing that the lands to be taken and settled by the Israelites were not populated by indigenous peoples but by foreigners who conquered the territories and displaced or absorbed the indigenous population. Just as the Amorites displaced those who came before them, the Israelites would now displace them in accordance with the divine prerogative in assigning those lands to Israel. Thus, the lands currently occupied by the Ammonites, with divine concurrence, were once *accounted a land of Rephaim,* whom the Ammonites referred to as the *Zamzummim, a people great, and many, and tall, as the Anakim; but YHVH destroyed them before them: and they succeeded them, and dwelt in their stead,* just as God did for the Edomites, *that dwell in Seir, when*

He destroyed the Horites from before them; and they succeeded them, and dwelt in their stead even unto this day.

Moreover, the same applied to the *Avvim that dwelt in villages as far as Gaza,* on the opposite side of Cisjordan. According to some, it is likely that the *Avvim* were either early Philistines or Canaanites that were closely associated with them. In this regard, it is noteworthy that at the time of the Israelite conquest, the Philistine confederation consisted of *the five lords of the Philistines: the Gazite, and the Asdodite, the Ashkelonite, the Gittite, and the Ekronite; also the Avvim* (Josh. 13:4). It has been suggested, "they alone of all the Canaanite tribes remained there when these were expelled by the Philistines."[114] It has also been suggested that the reason they are mentioned here is because the *Avvim* were actually a group of Philistines that were already present in the southern coastal district of Cisjordan in the days of Abraham, well in advance of the arrival of the main body of the Philistines that came with the Sea Peoples that invaded the region about the time of the exodus. According to this opinion, the capital of the *Avvim* was Gerar, and it was with Abimelech the king of Gerar that Abraham concluded a non-aggression treaty that was to continue in effect throughout the generations (Gen. 21: 22-24), a treaty that would have closed their territory to Israelite conquest and settlement. Therefore, "the Holy One, blessed be He, said, let the Caphtorim come and take away the land from the Avvim, who are Philistines, and then Israel may come and take it away from the Caphtorim."[115] Accordingly, it was *the Caphtorim, that came out of Caphtor* or Crete, who *destroyed them, and dwelt in their stead,* and that would subsequently be displaced by the Israelites. It is likely that the biblical reference to *the Caphtorim* refers to the later Philistines who were part of the Sea Peoples, and who therefore were not parties to Abraham's treaty with the *Avvim.*

2.26 And I sent messengers out of the wilderness of Kedemoth unto Sihon king of Heshbon with words of peace, saying: 2.27 'Let me pass through thy land; I will go along by the highway, I will neither turn unto the right hand nor to the left. 2.28 Thou shalt sell me food for money, that I may eat; and give me water for money, that I may drink; only let me pass through on my feet; ^{2.29} *as the children of Esau that dwell in Seir, and the Moabites that dwell in Ar, did unto me; until I shall pass over the Jordan into the land which YHVH our Elohim giveth us.'* ^{2.30} *But Sihon king of Heshbon would not let us pass by him; for YHVH thy Elohim hardened his spirit, and made his heart obstinate, that He might deliver him into thy hand, as appeareth this day.*

Having bypassed Moab, the Israelites were assembled in the wilderness of Kedemoth, assumed to be the region of the upper Arnon, and it was from there, ready for battle, that Moses dispatched agents to the Amorite king in an attempt to avoid the necessity for war. It is noteworthy that whereas Moses was instructed to *contend with him in battle*, he nonetheless first sought to negotiate an agreement that would allow the Israelites freedom of passage to the Jordan through the Amorite territory, a procedure later stipulated as a law of war (Deut. 20:10-14), which is discussed below. There is little consensus among commentators as how to reconcile the apparent contradiction between what Moses was instructed to do and what he actually did.[116]

In his request for safe passage, Moses promised to *go along by the highway*, referring to the King's Highway (Num. 21:22), the main trade route through the region, from which *I will neither turn unto the right hand nor to the left*. Moreover, rather than forage for supplies as was common for armies on the march to do, Moses offered to pay for whatever food and water his people might need. In effect, he pointed out that he had successfully made such an arrangement with both the Edomites and the Moabites, and the transit of the Israelites through or adjacent to their territories took place without incident. The difference, of course, was that Moses had no alternative way of reaching the Jordan other than crossing Sihon's territory. Despite his effort to reach an amicable agreement concerning transit rights, Moses asserts, God *hardened his spirit, and made his heart obstinate*, something that probably contributed to Sihon's misconstruing the reason for Israel diverting its route around Edom, Moab, and Ammon as indicating its reluctance to engage in warfare, which as he was to learn to his regret was not the case.[117]

It clearly was the divine wish that that Sihon should reject Moses' request for innocent passage through his territory, *that He might deliver him into thy hand, as appeareth this day.* Indeed, it clearly was the divine intention that Moses was to engage in battle with and disgorge the Amorites. It would seem that Moses, on his own initiative, sought to avoid what might have proved to be an unnecessary war, since his goal was to lead the people into Cisjordan, and he evidently saw no rationale for seizing territory in Transjordan. However, it is also clear that it would have been a strategic mistake to cross the Jordan without first securing the river's east bank, a well-intentioned blunder that God would not permit Moses to make, and this could not be done without seizing it from the Amorites, whose interests extended to Cisjordan as well.

> *2.31 And YHVH said unto me: 'Behold, I have begun to deliver up Sihon and his land before thee; begin to possess his land.' 2.32 Then Sihon came out against us, he and all his people, unto battle at Jahaz. 2.33 And YHVH our Elohim delivered him up before us; and we smote him, and his sons, and all his people. 2.34 And we took all his cities at that time, and utterly destroyed every city, the men, and the women, and the little ones; we left none remaining; 2.35 only the cattle we took for a prey unto ourselves, with the spoil of the cities which we had taken. 2.36 From Aroer, which is on the edge of the valley of Arnon, and from the city that is in the valley, even into Gilead, there was not a city too high for us: YHVH our Elohim delivered up all before us. 2.37 Only to the land of the children of Ammon thou camest not near; all the side of the river Jabbok, and the cities of the hill-country, and wheresoever YHVH our Elohim forbade us.*

The negotiations having collapsed, there was no alternative but war, which was in fact what God wanted. As He told Moses, *Behold, I have begun to deliver up Sihon and his land before thee; begin to possess his land.* That is, by strengthening Sihon's resolve to block the Israelites from entering his territory, God set the stage for the Israelite conquest of his land. Thus, He had *begun to deliver up Sihon and his land*; it would be up to the Israelites to complete the process by force of arms.

Sihon attacked the Israelites with all the force he could muster for a decisive battle at Jahaz, a site still unidentified, only to experience total defeat at the hands of Israel. For Israel, this was an existential war; defeat effectively would have meant their end as a nation, for they had no haven to which they could retreat. Following the norms of ancient warfare, the people would have been slaughtered and the few survivors made into slaves. As it turned out, the tide of battle went against the Amorites, *and we smote him, and his sons, and all his people. And we took all his cities at that time, and utterly destroyed every city, the men, and the women, and the little ones; we left none remaining; only the cattle we took for a prey unto ourselves, with the spoil of the cities which we had taken.* It is noteworthy that Moses attributed the victory to divine intercession. It served as a poignant reminder to the Israelites that with God on their side they could appear invincible.

The area conquered from Sihon was the entire region from the Arnon in the south to the Jabbok in the north and from the Jordan in the west to the then impenetrable defenses of Ammon in the East. The Israelites studiously avoided any intrusion into Ammonite territory in accordance with the divine constraints placed on them regarding any such trespass. The victory over the Amorites, as pointed out by one historian, "was of incalculable importance to the Israelites; it strengthened their position and inspired them with self-reliance. They at one took possession of the conquered district, and henceforth abandoned their nomadic life . . . The Israelites could now move about freely, being no longer incommoded by the narrow belt of the desert, nor the suspicions of unfriendly tribes."[118]

3.1 Then we turned, and went up the way to Bashan; and Og the king of Bashan came out against us, he and all his people, unto battle at Edrei. 3.2 And YHVH said unto me: 'Fear him not; for I have delivered him, and all his people,

> *and his land, into thy hand; and thou shalt do unto him as thou didst unto Sihon king of the Amorites, who dwelt at Heshbon.' [3.3] So YHVH our Elohim delivered into our hand Og also, the king of Bashan, and all his people; and we smote him until none was left to him remaining. [3.4] And we took all his cities at that time; there was not a city which we took not from them; threescore cities, all the region of Argob, the kingdom of Og in Bashan. [3.5] All these were fortified cities, with high walls, gates, and bars; beside the unwalled towns a great many. [3.6] And we utterly destroyed them, as we did unto Sihon king of Heshbon, utterly destroying every city, the men, and the women, and the little ones. [3.7] But all the cattle, and the spoil of the cities, we took for a prey unto ourselves.*

Having defeated Sihon and taken his kingdom, a further war with Og, the Amorite king of Bashan, the area bordering the Jordan north of the Jabbok, was virtually inevitable. It was a war which Moses made no effort to avoid, as was the case with Sihon. He marched north and engaged Og in battle at Edrei, the modern Edra'ah, about thirty miles southeast of the Sea of Galilee. It is noteworthy that Moses reported that God told him: *Fear him not; for I have delivered him, and all his people, and his land, into thy hand*, whereas with regard to Sihon, He did not say *Fear him not*, thus suggesting that, although there was reason to fear Og, Moses need not do so because of God's engagement in the forthcoming struggle. Why fear Og more than Sihon? Part of the reason may be that, as explained below, Og was a remnant of the ancient race of giants and as such generated fear among many people. Another reason may be that many of his cities were well fortified and the Israelites may not have had the equipment necessary for the siege and conquest of walled cities.[119]

Nonetheless, as was the case with Sihon, it was a total victory for Israel and an existential defeat for the Amorites of Bashan. It may well be that it was Og's arrogance that led to his defeat. Instead of having his army remain in their fortified positions and going out to attack the passing Israelite columns in a running war of attrition, as Moses noted, he *came out against us, he and all his people, unto battle at Edrei.* Having opted for a pitched battle, employing his entire army, that Og must have believed would have lead to the utter destruction of the Israelite forces, he left his cities virtually undefended, making it feasible for Israelites to break into them by scaling inadequately defended walls even without the equipment normally required for attacking defended walled cities. Moreover, absent any appreciation of the superior morale of the Israelites, he could not reasonably have anticipated that it would be his army that would meet with virtual annihilation on the battlefield, which it did surely to his astonishment.

Moses stated *we utterly destroyed them, as we did unto Sihon king of Heshbon, utterly destroying every city, the men, and the women, and the little ones*, an extreme action that evidently deviated from the norms of warfare in antiquity that did not demand the total obliteration of an enemy. It is noteworthy in this regard that in Moses' later codification of the laws of war for Israel, it was stipulated that if the enemy surrendered it was to be made a tributary. If the enemy chose to resist, all the men were to be killed, *but the women, and the little ones . . . shalt thou take as a prey unto thyself* (Deut. 20:13-14). This rule applied to foreign peoples and territories. However, with regard to *the cities of these peoples, that YHVH thy Elohim giveth thee for an inheritance, thou shalt save alive nothing that breatheth . . . that they teach you not to do after all their abominations, which they have done unto their gods, and so ye sin against YHVH your Elohim* (Deut. 20:16-18). By applying the provisions of the latter rule to the Amorite kingdoms in Transjordan, it seems clear that in the biblical view, the kingdoms of Sihon and Og were considered as part of Israel's covenantal heritage and were therefore treated according to the special rules of war that applied with regard to the territories covered by the covenant.[120]

> *3.8 And we took the land at that time out of the hand of the two kings of the Amorites that were beyond the Jordan, from the valley of Arnon unto mount Hermon (3.9 which Hermon the Sidonians call Sirion, and the Amorites call it Senir) 3.10 all the cities of the plain, and all Gilead, and all Bashan, unto Salcah and Edrei, cities of the kingdom of*

Og in Bashan. *(³·¹¹ For only Og king of Bashan remained of the remnant of the Rephaim; behold, his bedstead was a bedstead of iron; is it not in Rabbah of the children of Ammon? Nine cubits was the length thereof, and four cubits the breadth of it, after the cubit of a man.) ³·¹² And this land we took in possession at that time; from Aroer, which is by the valley of Arnon, and half the hill-country of Gilead, and the cities thereof, gave I unto the Reubenites and to the Gadites; ³·¹³ and the rest of Gilead, and all Bashan, the kingdom of Og, gave I unto the half-tribe of Manasseh; all the region of Argob (all that Bashan is called the land of Rephaim. ³·¹⁴ Jair the son of Manasseh took all the region of Argob, unto the border of the Geshurites and the Maacathites, and called them, even Bashan, after his own name, Havvoth-jair, unto this day.) ³·¹⁵ And I gave Gilead unto Machir. ³·¹⁶ And unto the Reubenites and unto the Gadites I gave from Gilead even unto the valley of Arnon, the middle of the valley for a border; even unto the river Jabbok, which is the border of the children of Ammon; ³·¹⁷ the Arabah also, the Jordan being the border thereof, from Kinneret even unto the sea of the Arabah, the Salt Sea, under the slopes of Pisgah eastward.*

The passage begins with a parenthetic note that describes Og himself as being a lone descendent of the Rephaim, the extinct race of giants referred to earlier as *Anakim*. The only evident purpose of this may be to point out once again the extent of exaggeration about giants populating the land that helped engender the rebellion that resulted in a thirty-eight year sojourn in the inhospitable wilderness, as well as to explain in part why people might fear him.

Moses summarized the extent of the conquests achieved as the result of the two wars, which included all the territory from the border of Moab at the Arnon as far north as Mount Hermon, presumably referring here to the southernmost part of the Anti-Lebanon range, and in some instances referring to the entire range in southern Lebanon. More significantly, this stretch of territory was assigned as their patrimony to the tribes of Reuben, Gad, and half of the tribe of Manasseh, namely to two of its large clans, those of Jair and Machir. Jair is later identified as *the Gileadite*, who *judged Israel twenty and two years* (Judg. 10:3). The territory between the Arnon and the Jabbok, the midpoint of Gilead, was allocated to the tribes of Reuben and Gad, the former taking the southern section and the latter the northern section of the territory. The remainder of the conquered territory was given to half of the tribe of Manasseh, from the Jabbok to the Yarmuk being assigned to the clan of Machir, and the rest of Bashan as far north as the frontiers of the Golan and the two small Aramaic tribes *of the Geshurites and the Maacathites*, to the clan of Jair. The significance of the mention of Geshur as beyond the bounds of Israelite conquest becomes evident later because King David marries a Geshurite princess, who bears him his favorite son Absalom (2 Sam. 3:3).

It should be noted that the distribution of the conquered territories in Transjordan raises a curious point. We were told earlier that the *children of Reuben and the children of Gad came and spoke unto Moses, and to Eleazar the priest, and unto the princes of the congregation,* pleading *If we have found favor in thy sight, let this land be given unto thy servants for a possession* (Num. 32:2-5). Reuben and Gad asked for the land, and their request was granted, but there is no mention in the text of a similar request from the clans of Manasseh. And if the latter did not request such an allocation of territory, why were they given it anyway? Although the text itself provides no information to support the idea, it has been suggested that when the Transjordan territories were initially assigned to Reuben and Gad, it was determined that the territories were too large for their populations and a request was made for volunteers from other tribes to help populate the large territory. Presumably, the two clans of Manasseh had large numbers of cattle for which the land was especially suitable, and they volunteered to split off from contiguity with their tribe to take advantage of the opportunity.[121]

An alternative approach suggests that Moses probably invited the Manasseh clans to settle in Transjordan because he was not pleased with the settlement there of any of the children of Israel. The scenario postulated by this notion is that at some point the clans would wish to reunite with the rest of their tribe and would relocate to Cisjordan, and that once this happened the solidarity between the Manasseh clans and the tribes of Reuben and Gad would be shattered and the entire settlement enterprise might be undermined. The evacuation by the Manasseh clans would create a political vacuum along their northern frontier of Israelite settlement that outside forces would seek to fill, making the territory of Gad, and secondly that of Reuben, vulnerable from a security standpoint. Presumably, this would encourage those tribes to relocate to Cisjordan as well.[122]

> [3.18] *And I commanded you at that time, saying: 'YHVH your Elohim hath given you this land to possess it; ye shall pass over armed before your brethren the children of Israel, all the men of valor.* [3.19] *But your wives, and your little ones, and your cattle—I know that ye have much cattle—shall abide in your cities which I have given you;* [3.20] *until YHVH give rest unto your brethren, as unto you, and they also possess the land which YHVH your Elohim giveth them beyond the Jordan; then shall ye return every man unto his possession, which I have given you.'*

This passage seems to gloss over the reality that some of the Israelite tribes, most notably Reuben, Gad, and some elements of Manasseh, were quite prepared to abandon the idea of settling in the land of Canaan. They were land-hungry and were content to remain in the lands they now occupied in Transjordan as a result of the defeat of the Amorite kings. It is not at all certain that this was part of the original settlement plan, even though the character of the war waged against the Amorite kingdoms suggests that it may have been such. In any case, the Israelite leaders understood that any such tribal defections before the crossing into Cisjordan would seriously weaken the tribal alliance and jeopardize the success of the ongoing penetration and conquest of Canaan. The biblical writer suggests that Moses had to use all of his considerable influence to retain the loyalty of the tribes of Reuben and Gad and some clans of the tribe of Manasseh to the Israelite alliance. He did this by making the legitimacy of their holdings in Transjordan contingent upon their continued participation in the conquest of Canaan, a ploy that apparently succeeded in holding the alliance together at a critical point in time. Accordingly, Moses recalls that at the time he demanded, *ye shall pass over armed before your brethren the children of Israel, all the men of valor. But your wives, and your little ones, and your cattle* were to remain behind. That is, only those men fit and ready for offensive operations were required to cross the Jordan, the others remained behind to provide security for their families and property. Thus, it was later recorded that, of the tribes of Reuben, Gad, and half of Manasseh, *about forty thousand ready armed for war passed on in the presence of YHVH unto battle, to the plains of Jericho* (Joshua 4:13). That is, they had to participate in the conquest of Cisjordan before they could return to their holdings in Transjordan. The need for Moses to take such a step made it clear that the Israelite tribal alliance was inherently unstable. In the absence of a more deeply ingrained sense of common purpose, it could only be held together by the charismatic personality of a Moses or a Joshua, who assumed the mantle of leadership after the death of the prophet-legislator. This portended serious future problems for the budding nation.

> *3.21 And I commanded Joshua at that time, saying: 'Thine eyes have seen all that YHVH your Elohim hath done unto these two kings; so shall YHVH do unto all the kingdoms whither thou goest over. 3.22 Ye shall not fear them; for YHVH your Elohim, He it is that fighteth for you.'*

Having obtained a secure fallback position in Transjordan, Moses then commanded Joshua to assume command of the Israelites and carry out the invasion and conquest of Cisjordan, with the knowledge that God would be with him and would do to the various kings of the area what He already had done to the Amorites. He adjured Joshua to approach the task assigned to him without fear; secure in the knowledge that he was acting as the instrument of God.

2

VAETHANAN

(3:23-7:11)

Moses continues his presentation to the people, taking pains to explain why he will be unable to accompany them across the Jordan, in an effort to calm any concerns they may have about his seeming to abandon them precisely at the point toward which he had led them for the past four decades.

> [3.23] *And I besought YHVH at that time, saying:* [3.24] *'O Adonai YHVH, Thou hast begun to show Thy servant Thy greatness, and Thy strong hand; for what god is there in heaven or on earth, that can do according to Thy mighty acts?* [3.25] *Let me go over, I pray Thee, and see the good land that is beyond the Jordan, that goodly hill-country, and Lebanon.'* [3.26] *But YHVH was wroth with me for your sakes, and hearkened not unto me; and YHVH said unto me: 'Let it suffice thee; speak no more unto Me of this matter.* [3.27] *Get thee up into the top of Pisgah, and lift up thine eyes westward, and northward, and southward, and eastward, and behold with thine eyes; for thou shalt not go over this Jordan.* [3.28] *But charge Joshua, and encourage him, and strengthen him; for he shall go over before this people, and he shall cause them to inherit the land which thou shalt see.'* [3.29] *So we abode in the valley over against Beth-peor.*

Moses *besought* or better, *implored* God *at that time*. It has been suggested that this depiction of Moses pleading on his own behalf illustrates the principle of the equality of all men before God, since even Moses, the greatest of the prophets, was forced to plead for divine forbearance like everyone else.[123] That is, he hoped that the recent victory over the Amorite kings in Transjordan, which clearly and tangibly reflected renewed divine engagement with the children of Israel, might also be the harbinger of a divine change of heart with respect to His decision that Moses would not be permitted to cross the Jordan with his people.[124] What was the basis for this expectation? Presumably, Moses concluded that the territories east of the Jordan, where he now stood, the conquest of which was undertaken at divine instruction, and which subsequently were allocated for settlement by the tribes of Reuben and Gad and part of Manasseh, were intended to be considered part of Israel's national patrimony, and that since he was permitted to enter them he might also be allowed to cross the Jordan to enter the rest of Israel's assigned territory.[125]

In framing his plea, Moses addresses God in an unusual manner, as *Adonai YHVH*, which begs for some explication. *Adonai* literally means *my Lord*, and is the way, in Judaic tradition, the Tetragrammaton is normally vocalized in actual speech, in which case the present text would normally be read aloud as *Adonai Adonai*. However, in this instance, the Masoretes applied the same diacritical marks to the Tetragrammaton as found in the name *Elohim*, so that the formulation is vocalized aloud as *Adonai Elohim*. Why Moses or the ancient scribes decided to use this formulation is unclear and awaits a compelling explanation. However, in Judaic tradition, both *Adonai* and *Elohim* are understood generally to refer to that aspect of God that is concerned with judgment and the Tetragrammaton, when used in conjunction with either, is understood to refer to that aspect of God that is concerned with mercy. Hence, the present formulation, *Adonai YHVH*, should be understood as God "merciful in judgment."[126] Or as another commentator put it, Moses is pleading that the justice of *Adonai*, who is sitting in judgment of him, be tempered with the mercy of *YHVH*,[127] as he pleads for a suspension of the divine decree regarding the prohibition of his accompanying the children of Israel across the Jordan. Alternatively, it has been suggested that *Adonai* "expresses the complete readiness for obedience, to do everything that God wishes." In this regard, it has been argued that both names relate to divine management of the universe; the Tetragrammaton refers to governance of the natural order, and *Adonai* refers to God in His aspect of sovereign of the world who can do with the natural order whatever He wills.[128] By using this name together with the Tetragrammaton, "Moses declares beforehand how without discontent he will not complain if God's decision finds it right to deny him his last and warmest wish."[129] It is noteworthy that the same formulation appears earlier in the story of Abraham where the Patriarch pleads with God over the absence of an heir to carry on the work he had undertaken (Gen. 15:2).[130]

Moses carefully avoids any suggestion that he has earned the right to cross the Jordan because of his long and difficult service to God that caused him to spend the last four decades of his life totally engrossed in his mission. In the course of his so doing, he had eschewed all personal interests, neglected his wife and children and any other human relationships that might have distracted him from the single-minded pursuit of preparing the children of Israel for their historic role in the land promised to their forefathers. God, of course, knew all this before He rendered His decision, so making this argument would be rather pointless. Instead, Moses takes a different approach, now that his own life was rapidly coming to an end. He pleads for divine accommodation of his most fervent desire to see the fruition of his efforts that began in Egypt come to a conclusion in the land of the Israelites. Thus, he argues, *Thou hast begun to show Thy servant Thy greatness, and Thy strong hand*, implicitly suggesting that in view of their long and extraordinary relationship it seems only fair that he might also see the consummation of the divine intervention in history that began with the exodus.

Somewhat surprisingly, Moses also added a note of adulation, *for what god is there in heaven or on earth, that can do according to Thy mighty acts*, that may strike one as out of place, a statement that more appropriately would be made to his fellow Israelites in praise of God rather than as a direct compliment to Him. The rabbis, however, understood Moses as arguing that precisely because God is omnipotent He need not act as humans; "Among the latter, a prefect who rules over his province fears that his co-prefect may not agree to revoking the judgment. But, Thou, who hast no co-prefect, why dost Thou not pardon me?"[131] That is, God is free to do as He pleases, and that includes rescinding His own decree, should He so choose. Moses then comes to the point of his plea, that he be permitted to *go over* the Jordan, not necessarily as the leader of the Israelites, since he had already invested his leadership authority in Joshua, but even as a private citizen to see at close quarters the goal toward which he worked for so long, the land he had never seen.

It is noteworthy that Moses specifically indicates his great desire to see the *goodly hill-country, and Lebanon.* Presumably, from the spot where Moses stood, in the plains of Moab, the whole of Cisjordan that he could see in the distance appeared as a single mountain chain reaching as far as Lebanon, something he longed to see close up. As one commentator noted: "The three great landmarks in his life were all connected with mountains. Horeb, where he was called to be the Leader of his people; Sinai, whence issued forth the Divine Proclamation for all time of the Law of conduct; and Nebo, the peak from which he was to behold the Promised Land from afar."[132]

However, Moses' plea, perhaps for the first time, went unheeded because, as he told his listeners, God *was wroth with me.* It has been pointed out that the Hebrew term *vayitaber,* translated as *was wroth,* is unique in the Torah and appears to be employed here as a pun. In the preceding verse, Moses pleaded *ebra-na* or "let me cross," and the divine response, employing the same word root, was that God "was cross" with him and told him he would not be permitted to cross.[133] Indeed, the response he received seems rather harsh, reflecting a degree of divine impatience with him. *Let it suffice thee; speak no more unto Me of this matter.* As far as God was concerned the matter was closed and there was no point to Moses raising the issue once again; he would not be allowed to cross the Jordan in any capacity and would have to be satisfied with viewing his heart's desire from a distance. Thus, he was told to go to *the top of Pisgah,* a promontory on the western slope of the range that includes Mount Nebo. Moses had pleaded that he needed to see the promised land, and God told him he could see it without crossing the Jordan. From the mountain height he could observe in all directions that which he was being denied the privilege of visiting.

Moses then explained in his discourse that the reason for God's intransigence on this point was because He *was wroth with me for your sakes*. The Hebrew term *lemaankhem*, translated as *for your sakes*, which is normally used in a positive sense, is understood here in a negative sense as meaning *because of you*, an interpretation that is questionable, because the latter phrase would normally be rendered in Hebrew as *biglalkhem*. However, because no substantively satisfactory explanation has yet to be offered as to why Moses' punishment served the interests of the people, it has been understood here in a negative manner.[134] This argument implicitly rejects the view of some commentators that "in some sense Moses died outside the promised land as a substitute for the people, i.e. he suffered vicariously for them."[135] In this regard, it is noteworthy that many traditional commentaries assume that Moses was alluding to the incident in the wilderness when the people again were suffering from the lack of sufficient water, and God instructed him: *Take the rod, and assemble the congregation . . . and speak ye unto the rock before their eyes, that it give forth its water; and thou shalt bring forth to them water out of the rock*. However, instead of speaking to the rock, as he was instructed to do, in his anger at the people for demonstrating so little faith in their divine benefactor, *Moses lifted up his hand, and smote the rock with his rod twice; and water came forth abundantly, and the congregation drank*. The divine reaction to Moses' actions, which was also directed at Aaron, was, *Because ye believed not in Me, to sanctify Me in the eyes of the children of Israel, therefore ye shall not bring this assembly into the land which I have given them* (Num. 20:8-12).

Presumably, Moses' offense in the incident was that by not following God's instructions to the letter, which would have made the gushing forth of water to be perceived clearly as a miracle, he struck the rock, making it appear that it was he and not God that caused the water to flow.[136] But God does not actually make this charge against him. He merely asserts that Moses' punishment was decreed *because ye believed not in Me*, a charge that seems quite improbable in the case of either Moses or Aaron. Indeed, the psalmist wrote with regard to this incident: *They angered Him also at the waters of Meribah, and it went ill with Moses because of them; for they embittered his spirit, and he spoke rashly with his lips* (Ps. 106:32-32). Was Moses being punished for what he did, or what he said? But what could Moses have said that would justify the charge, *ye believed not in Me?* The only plausible explanation of this seems to be that Moses and Aaron were being accused of a failure of leadership, and that because of that failure neither of them would be privileged to lead the people into the land.

However, with regard to Moses' revelation that God had told him *thou shalt not go over this Jordan,* which completely denies him entry into the land, the biblical text itself suggests that Moses' punishment was essentially unrelated to the incident of striking the rock but rather to his role in the incident concerning the scouts, regarding which he confessed that God *was angry with me for your sakes, saying: 'Thou also shalt not go in thither* (Deut. 1:37), a statement that does not appear in the original account of the matter of the scouts. It appears that texts describing each of these events are in conflict. Thus, with regard to the matter of striking the rock, Moses was told, *therefore ye shall not bring this assembly into the land.* That is, Moses is informed that neither he nor Aaron but Joshua would lead the people. But this does not say explicitly that Moses would be precluded from going along with the people as a member of the community. By contrast, as a result of Moses' agreeing to send the scouts, he set in motion a rebellion against God that was unforgivable, and for his unwitting role in this he subsequently was denied the right to enter the land, even as a private citizen. The problem, of course, is that the incident of the scouts took place prior to that of striking the rock. Accordingly, Moses was first told *Thou also shalt not go in thither,* and only later was told *therefore ye shall not bring this assembly into the land,* which clearly is a non sequitur; if he cannot enter the land he surely cannot lead the people into it. The only way to reconcile these conflicting statements is to assume that Moses may have wished to believe that, after thirty-eight years of contending with the people in the wilderness, he might have been forgiven for his failure in the matter of the scouts, and that although he would not be permitted to lead the people into the land because of the matter of striking the rock he might be permitted to accompany them as a private citizen, which evidently was not to be the case.

In any case, God's rejection of his plea did not bring an end to his mission; there were still matters to be dealt with by him. Perhaps first and foremost, he was to *charge Joshua, and encourage him, and strengthen him.* He had led the people for forty years and it was his responsibility to assure a smooth transition to a new leadership under Joshua, who was God's choice to carry out the task that Moses was not going to be permitted to complete. To charge Joshua with the task meant formally and publicly transferring Moses' authority to his most loyal and competent disciple, and to do so with enthusiasm and thereby facilitate full acceptance by the tribal leaders. This was essential because *he shall go over before the people.* It would appear that this statement is superfluous because it has already been established that Joshua was going to take Moses' place. However, some have seen in this assertion another nuance, namely, that Joshua's success was contingent on his direct and personal leadership of the invasion into Cisjordan; he would not succeed if he commanded it from afar.[137]

The implication of all this is that Moses would retire entirely from public office; it would not do for him to serve as a co-regent with Joshua. He had to show publicly his complete and unequivocal trust in Joshua by surrendering complete control to him. As one commentary put it, God said to Moses, "Long enough hast thou enjoyed the light of the sun that was with thee; thou canst not do so any more, for the time of the moon has come, and the moon cannot shine till the sun is gathered in."[138] For the task ahead, it was essential that the people see Joshua as the successor to Moses, and this would not happen completely if Moses were still with them. At the same time, Moses had to prepare Joshua for his role by thoroughly informing him of the military challenges ahead, and reassuring him that he was fully capable of dealing with them without Moses' oversight.[139] He also had to encourage him with regard to the internal politics of and between the tribes and the headaches and heartaches these would give him, while encouraging and instilling confidence in him that he would be able to deal with them successfully.

Moses concludes his recapitulation of past events with the notation that *we abode in the valley over against Beth-peor*, also referred to as *Baal-peor*, the significance of which is discussed below. Suffice it to note at this point that *Beth-peor* was a site in nearby Moab that was dedicated to the worship of the god Baal, where elements of the children of Israel allowed themselves to be seduced into gross sacrilege with horrendous consequences, an error that Moses wanted to caution them against ever repeating and thereby provoking divine retribution.

> *4.1 And now, O Israel, hearken unto the statutes and unto the ordinances, which I teach you, to do them; that ye may live, and go in and possess the land which YHVH, the Elohim of your fathers, giveth you. 4.2 Ye shall not add unto the word which I command you, neither shall ye diminish from it, that ye may keep the commandments of YHVH your Elohim which I command you. 4.3 Your eyes have seen what YHVH did in Baal-peor; for all the men that followed the Baal of Peor, YHVH thy Elohim hath destroyed them from the midst of thee. 4.4 But ye that did cleave unto YHVH your Elohim are alive every one of you this day.*

Having reprised some of the significant aspects of their history from the exodus to the present day, as they stood on the threshold of entering into the promised land, and recalling their flirtations with utter disaster as a result of their proclivity toward rebelliousness against God, Moses implicitly forewarns them not to squander the opportunity before them by reverting to past practices. If they want to survive as a nation in their own land, they will have to pay heed to the covenant into which they entered, which provides the guidance by which they are to govern their society, much of which is reflected in the divine commandments already conveyed to them through Moses in the form of statutes and ordinances.

It is noteworthy that Moses speaks of the laws *which I teach you*, marking him as the "teacher" of Israel. Thus, although Moses is both prophet and de facto ruler of the people, he traditionally has been known among Jews throughout the ages as *Moshe Rabbenu* or "Moses Our Teacher." It has been observed that this is the only occasion on which

Moses employs this particular expression; in all others it is primarily *which I command you*, and on occasion *which I speak in your ears* (Deut. 5:1), or *which I set before you* (Deut. 11:32). The reference of the latter three formulations is to the commandments, rules, statutes, ordinances or related specific adjurations or admonishments that he is presenting. However, it has been suggested, when he says in reference to the latter, *which I teach you*, Moses is speaking of going beyond the letter of the text to grasp the underlying significance and purpose of the stipulated directions; that is, Moses is teaching them that which is not written or codified but which provides context and practical meaning to that which is written, what would later be referred to as the Oral Torah.[140]

Moses' teaching is purposive; the people are to learn the statutes and ordinances not simply for the sake of knowledge but how to apply them in practice, *to do them, that ye may live.* That is, Moses is asserting that Israel's very existence as a nation, its national identity, is grounded in the observance of the statutes and ordinances that he is conveying to the people. Indeed, it has been argued that the children of Israel are being given the land solely in order to establish a society wherein observance of the statutes and ordinances becomes the societal norm.[141] The adjuration *to do them* has been understood as the source of the rabbinic teaching that that performance is the essence of study.[142] As one rabbi put it, "not the expounding [of the Torah] is the chief thing but the doing [of it]."[143]

The legal categories of statutes and ordinances are mentioned repeatedly in the texts, and are discussed further below. In general, statutes originally referred to authoritative enactments that were engraved in stone and therefore intended to be permanent and not amenable to subsequent modification. In biblical usage, statutes usually refer to laws governing the relations between man and God. Ordinances, by contrast, are generally concerned with societal matters and interpersonal relations, and also reflect adjudicated decisions that serve as precedents for future guidance, which suggests that they may be subject to modification in response to changing circumstances. In this regard, it has been suggested that *ordinances* most likely represent case law whereas *statutes* refers to apodictic law, that is, law intended to be permanent.[144] As a rule, when these categories of law are mentioned in the biblical texts, statutes always precede ordinances "in order to indicate the basic importance of unquestioning obedience to the Divine Will."[145] It also has been suggested that the reason why the seemingly arbitrary statutes are named before the more intelligible ordinances is to stress the idea that "it is not possible to understand the Torah solely on the basis of rational thought."[146] Alternatively, it has been proposed that the *hukim* or statutes are given primacy because they help incline people towards "spiritual matters and morality from whom a national life can be based on the equity of the *mishpatim*" or ordinances.[147]

It is noteworthy that the meanings of *hukim* and *mishpatim* in the biblical texts, depending on the context in which they are stated, have also been interpreted rather differently in rabbinic tradition. Thus, with specific regard to Moses' later statement, *These are the statutes and the ordinances, which ye shall observe to do* (Deut. 12:1), in one place it states, "*the statutes*—these are the interpretations—*and the ordinances*—these are the regulations."[148] Another later source asserts, "For our Rabbis taught: *These are the statutes*—this refers to the interpretations [that is, laws not explicitly stated in Scripture but derived by exegesis]; *and the ordinances*—to civil law . . . *to do*—to actual practice."[149] In another place it asserts, with regard to the statement, *that ye may teach the children of Israel all the statutes which YHVH hath spoken unto them by the hand of Moses* (Lev. 10:11), that "*all the statutes* refers to the expositions of the Law."[150] Taking into consideration these diverse interpretations, it has been argued that, in the present instance among others, *hearken unto the statutes and unto the ordinances, which I teach you* cannot reasonably be understood to refer to divinely ordained stipulations because, if that were the case Moses would have said "which I command you" rather than *which I teach you*. What we must assume Moses is teaching them are the basic methods of exegesis that may be applied to the written texts to derive and infer new rules and regulations in accordance with the needs of time and place, which is the essence of the talmudic enterprise.[151]

Returning to a non-exegetical reading of the text, Moses appears well aware of the human capacity for rationalization and the consequences it may have on the integrity of a revealed commandment or precept, and he insists that Israel must not attempt to substitute human for divine wisdom in establishing the ethos of the society they shortly will establish in the lands of which they are about to begin to take possession. In other words, they are not to tinker with or deviate in any way from these commandments, but are to follow them to the letter as given, neither to embellish nor diminish them in any way. It has been suggested that this caveat is a reflection of the consideration that because of a relatively minor infraction in this regard, Moses was forced to die outside the land along with the entire generation that perished because of their rebelliousness.[152]

The importance of the command *neither shall ye diminish from it* is self-evident, something that is not the case with the demand *ye shall not add unto the word.* "One may think that, by doing *more* than the law requires, one is doing better, being more religious, more observant, when one is in fact thus *violating* the law. And when one imposes such additions to the law on others, one puts them at risk of violation as well."[153] In this regard, it has been suggested that the caveat, *Ye shall not add unto the word which I command you*, calls to mind that the first sin, that took place in the Garden of Eden, may have been the consequence of the violation of this precept.[154] God told Adam, *of the tree of the knowledge of good and evil, thou shalt not eat of it* (Gen. 2:17), but Eve embellished the restriction by saying, *God hath said: ye shall not eat of it, neither shall ye touch it* (Gen. 3:3), and it was her addition of the restriction concerning touching it that presumably led her astray when she saw the serpent touching the tree without any ill effects.

However, Moses was surely aware that changing circumstances might require new rules governing contingencies not covered by the commandments. Accordingly, the biblical injunction has been understood as admonishing "not to add to the precepts of the Torah, nor to take any precept away from it; that is, not to impart to any regulation (evolved in the course of time) the character of an old, established law, as though it were a command embodied in the Written or Oral Law."[155] At least one commentator[156] links the interpretation of this injunction with the opinion of the rabbis that because it states, *These are the commandments, which YHVH commanded Moses for the children of Israel in mount Sinai* (Lev. 27:34), "eighty-five elders, including a number of prophets" regrettably concluded that the text means *these are the commandments*, and no others, therefore precluding any future prophet from adding anything new to them.[157] In effect, as one commentator put it, the revealed Torah, like the human body, is an organic whole, complete in itself, and to remove anything from it would be equivalent to amputating part of the human body, and adding anything to it would create an organic anomaly.[158]

However, another commentator points out that this specific injunction appears only in one other place in the Torah (Deut. 13:1), where, like here, the text is primarily concerned with warning against the worship of other gods. It is therefore suggested that the injunction here relates to matters concerning God; there is to be no deviation, by addition or subtraction, from acceptance of the unique oneness of God and its implications.[159] In this same vein, it has been suggested that the concern Moses is attempting to deal with in this passage is the difficulty many of the children of Israel were having in accepting fully the idea of an incorporeal God. Their struggle with this led to a tendency toward syncretism, adding familiar pagan practices to the adoration and worship of God, practices that that would corrupt the integrity of the monotheistic idea. Hence it was essential for Moses to emphasize that, particularly with regard to religious ritual, nothing was to be added from the practices of the peoples they would encounter.[160] Viewed from this perspective, the injunction does not preclude legislative innovations that do not touch on the latter concern. Indeed, some have inferred from this passage that any additional legislation that serves to preserve the integrity of the divine legislation is permitted, and any that does not meet that criterion is prohibited.[161] Seen from this perspective, the restriction on eating of the *tree of the knowledge of good and evil,* discussed above, was quite clear and was not at all enhanced by the addition of a broader restriction that clearly was being violated by a creature to which the original injunction was not directed.

Moses' positive message also includes a clear caveat: *Your eyes have seen what YHVH did in Baal-peor; for all the men that followed the Baal of Peor, YHVH thy Elohim hath destroyed them from the midst of thee.* Moses invokes their memory of the apostasy that had recently taken place at Shittim, their last stop prior to their crossing the Jordan, where many Israelites accepted the invitations of both Moabite and Midianite women to attend a sacrificial festival in honor of the god Baal of Peor, which involved licentious rites accompanied by worship in which the Israelites participated. The point, it has been suggested, is that the people involved did not attend the rites because they consciously chose apostasy, but rather because they were seduced by the licentiousness of the rites, as it states, *and the people began to commit harlotry with the daughters of Moab* (Num. 25:1), even though they were already forewarned against intimate fraternization with pagans, *and their daughters go astray after their gods, and make thy sons go astray after their gods* (Ex. 34:16). Nonetheless, each person involved was convinced that he could enjoy the sexuality of the rite without being spiritually corrupted, but events proved him wrong.[162]

God was enraged by what had occurred and He instructed Moses, *Take all the chiefs of the people*, that is, call for an assembly of the tribal and clan leaders of those who were to be called to account for their capital offense,[163] and order them to inflict the appropriate punishment, namely, to *hang them up unto YHVH in face of the sun, that the fierce anger of YHVH may turn away from Israel.' And Moses said unto the judges* [the assembled leaders] *of Israel: 'Slay ye every one his men that have joined themselves unto the Baal of Peor'* (Num. 25:4-5). At the same time, a plague broke out that threatened to decimate the population. The plague, which the text indicates brought about some twenty-four thousand deaths (Num. 25:9), struck primarily the tribe of Simeon,[164] which was located at the southern end of the Israelite encampment and in closest proximity to Moab. It would appear that the tribe of Simeon never quite recovered from this tremendous loss of manpower, which necessarily included a number of its leaders, and it ultimately was absorbed into the tribe of Judah. But, Moses reminded them, *ye that did cleave unto YHVH your Elohim are alive every one of you this day,*[165] that is, they did not suffer the losses that afflicted those who succumbed to the carnal temptations of the pagan rites. This in itself is extraordinary in that a plague is inherently indiscriminate, but, Moses tells them, you saw for yourselves that the plague discriminated between those *that did cleave unto YHVH your Elohim*, who remained unaffected, and those who were afflicted because of their perfidy.[166]

This reading of the text interprets it in an essentially physical sense. However, the assertion, *ye that did cleave unto YHVH your Elohim are alive every one of you this day,* has also been interpreted in a notably spiritual sense. Thus, with regard to the meaning of "life" in this text, it has been argued: "The uniqueness of the House of Israel lies in the fact that it views existence from the vantage point of holiness. It senses, with all the strength of its being, that life possesses value to the extent that it is godly, and that life which is not godly is worth nothing. It perceives that . . . a life which is not godly is not to be termed life at all."[167] Accordingly, the significance of the assertion about those who *did cleave* unto God goes beyond mere non-participation in the worship of Baal-peor; the affirmation reflects the notion that clinging to God gave them "life" in far more than the simple physical sense of the term.

The lesson of this calamitous episode was self-evident: God was not to be trifled with; the children of Israel had become parties to the covenant and could be held accountable for any non-compliance with it at divine discretion. Moses proclaims that "even regarding one single commandment, setting Man's opinion as being equal to the statutes of God is equivalent to a general defection to polytheism."[168]

Having reminded the people of the negative consequences of deviating from the norms set forth by the covenant, Moses turns to drawing their attention to the uniqueness of the covenant and the benefits of conformance with its statutes and ordinances.

> [4.5] *Behold, I have taught you statutes and ordinances, even as YHVH my Elohim commanded me; that ye should do so in the midst of the land whither ye go in to possess it.* [4.6] *Observe therefore and do them; for this is your wisdom and your understanding in the sight of the peoples, that, when they hear all these statutes, shall say: 'Surely this great nation is a wise and understanding people.'* [4.7] *For what great nation is there, that hath Elohim so nigh unto them, as YHVH our Elohim is whensoever we call upon Him?* [4.8] *And what great nation is there, that hath statutes*

> *and ordinances so righteous as all this Torah, which I set before you this day?*

Moses points out that he has already provided the people with the divinely promulgated code of conduct that they are to follow in their new homeland, in addition to the rules such as those concerning the Sabbath and the prohibition of idolatry that were to be observed regardless of location.[169] In rabbinic tradition, the adjuration, *Observe therefore and do them*, is not a redundancy, but an instruction to *observe* the negative commandments, that is, to withhold from violating them, and to *do* the positive commandments, that is, to actively carry out their provisions.[170] Should they do so, they will constitute a model civilization that will earn the admiration of all who be come aware of them, inspiring others to say, *Surely this great nation is a wise and understanding people*, to live by such standards, *great* in this context clearly meaning spiritually great. Indeed, Moses assures his listeners, this is as it should be because, after all, what other nation is privileged to be on such intimate terms with *Elohim*, the creator and sovereign of the universe, who assisted and assists them whenever necessary in their hour of need. There are, of course many nations that are more numerous and more powerful than Israel, but the civilization that they reflect pales in comparison with that established by the righteous statutes and ordinances of the Torah, which he has *set before you this day*. The righteousness of the statutes and ordinances, it has been presumed, relates to their being perceived as fair and acceptable.[171] Alternatively, it has been suggested, the righteousness spoken of reflects the idea that the laws are not designed to further the interests of any particular group, including the societal elite.[172]

This passage raises an obvious problem in that it suggests that when the peoples of the land observe Israel's performance of the statutes they will be deeply impressed by it, whereas in reality they are more likely to scorn them for some of these seemingly bizarre practices. Accordingly it has been suggested that what the passage means to say is that what will most impress outsiders is the body of ordinances, which portray a disciplined, moral, and just society, one that urges replication. When this perception takes hold, they will also accept the unknown wisdom behind the statutes for which no reasons have been given other than it is the divine wish that they be observed.[173] It has also been observed in this regard that the passage is in effect an assertion that the wisdom of the Torah is unique and not derived from the cultures of the surrounding nations, including Egypt and Mesopotamia, for if the latter were so there would be no basis for others being impressed by it.[174]

It should be noted, however, that the statement *for this is your wisdom and your understanding in the sight of the peoples* is unique in one respect. It is the only text in the entire Torah that is concerned with what others think about it. But why is Moses concerned about what the peoples the Israelites are about to conquer will think of them? One cultural response is, "This verse makes the claim that inherent in the Torah is its capacity to be understood by non-adherents. The claim here is that the Torah is universal, that everyone can understand its teachings ('statutes and ordinances'). The Torah is not self-referential, not self-enclosed . . . In a word, this verse maintains the religious legitimacy of reason, of that tool by which any person can objectively convey ideas to another."[175] Alternatively, it is suggested that Moses is not really concerned about what outsiders think about Israel's body of laws, but that the statement is actually intended for the benefit of the Israelites themselves, making them aware that the only essential difference between them and the peoples they are about to conquer and dispossess is their possession of the code of laws that will shape a unique society, the only purpose of their having been divinely granted the land they are taking away from others.[176]

The implications of Moses' opening statement in this passage are far reaching. For one thing, his assertion *that ye should do so in the midst of the land whither ye go in to possess it* puts people on notice that many of the laws that have been and are about to be revealed do not and were not intended to apply to children of Israel living outside the land.[177] For another, the normal process of nation building is for the people of a land to form themselves into a nation and then develop or adopt laws by which it is to be governed. In the case of Israel, however, the people are given the laws first and only then the land in which they were to become operative. The inversion of the process suggests that the laws of the Torah are not merely the means for establishing and maintaining a viable national existence, but the very purpose for which it exists.[178] In effect, in this statement, Moses sets forth the rationale for the existence of Israel as a nation; to serve as a model for emulation by others, exemplifying in practice the ultimate divine wisdom revealed in the Torah bequeathed to them at Mount Sinai. He does not speak here of proselytizing, of reaching out to others, but rather becoming a national society that can be the envy of and inspiration of others. As one modern writer put it, "The essential nature of the people of Israel is not in the function that it carries out for others, but in its very own existence. Yet the stronger and more complete its existence, the more it also creates a light for others . . . The burning torch does not give light because it wishes to do so. It blazes because that is its existence, that is the way it expresses itself, and by so doing it also gives light to others."[179]

> *[4.9] Only take heed to thyself, and keep thy soul diligently lest thou forget the things which thine eyes saw, and lest they depart from thy heart all the days of thy life; but make them known unto thy children and thy children's children; [4.10] the day that thou stoodest before YHVH thy Elohim in Horeb, when YHVH said unto me: 'Assemble Me the people, and I will make them hear My words, that they may learn to fear Me all the days that they live upon the earth, and that they may teach their children.'*

In this passage, Moses attempts to confront the problem of the lack of deep conviction on the part of large numbers of Israelites, which led to rebellions against God earlier and would probably continue to do so in the future, unless steps were taken to reinforce personal commitment to the covenant. Each member of the community must undergo honest introspection: *take heed to thyself, and keep thy soul diligently*, an assertion that has been understood in different ways. Most simply put, it has been understood as a warning that if they choose to forget the past, they should on no account forget what they witnessed in Horeb, as explained in the rest of the passage.[180] Alternatively, it may be read as stating that each person is to take personal responsibility for his own moral welfare and the seriousness with which the demands of the covenant must be complied. It also has been read as insisting that each person has an obligation to do what is necessary for their physical well being, "for the body houses the soul."[181] Another interpretation suggests that, although others may see them as wise and understanding, as pointed out above, he cautions them to be on guard against ideas emanating from their wise men that contradict the monotheistic conception of God.[102] In the same vein, it has been understood as a caution against hubris. That is, when they establish a just and moral society, outsiders who have no knowledge of God may assume that the Israelites have created all these laws out of their own wisdom. Moses therefore warns against being seduced into believing their perceptions to be the truth, when if fact all these laws were given to them by God.[183]

Moses admonishes that this self-critical examination must be done *lest thou forget the things which thine eyes saw.* What was it that they saw that Moses is calling their attention to? Presumably, he is referring to the extraordinary events that they witnessed in Egypt prior to and during the exodus, as well as the other extraordinary events they witnessed in the wilderness, all of which attested to divine sovereignty over the universe and His special engagement with the children of Israel. His evident concern is that forgetting those things will in turn lead to the neglect of the divinely conceived role which Abraham and his descendents were chosen to play on the stage of world history. This is a point that Moses will mention repeatedly to emphasize that acceptance of the Torah by Israel in post-exilic times is grounded not in metaphysical speculation, as it almost certainly was for Abraham, but on the actual experience of God's presence in history. "The essence of Jewish religious thinking does not lie in entertaining a concept of God but in the ability to articulate a memory of moments of illumination by His presence. Israel is not a people of definers but a people of witnesses: 'Ye are My witnesses' (Isaiah 43:10)."[184]

Moreover, he insists, *make them known unto thy children and thy children's children.* He imposes an obligation on parents to convey the experience of Mount Sinai to succeeding generations so that they too may share it vicariously. That is essential, because as the rabbis put it, "In every generation a man must so regard himself as if he

came forth himself out of Egypt."[185] The obligation this text places
on parents "is the most pervasive expression of the biblical conviction
that religion is not simply a personal, individual concern," but extends
from one generation to another "so that they, too, may share in the
experiences, learn their responsibilities, and enjoy the benefits of faith
and observance."[186]

Moses cautions, all this is necessary *lest they depart from thy heart
all the days of thy life,* that is, should the spirit of rebellion against God
cause you to reject the implications of your own experience for the rest
of your life, you are nonetheless obligated to ensure that knowledge
of the divine role in Israel's history that you personally witnessed is
transmitted to your descendents. Thus, God commanded Moses on
Mount Sinai to assemble all the people in order to *make them hear My
words, that they may learn to fear Me all the days that they live upon the
earth, and that they may teach their children.* In recalling the events at
Sinai, Moses speaks to the children of Israel as though they were all
present at the event, when in fact only a small number of the people
between the ages of twenty and sixty could have made up his present
audience. The adjuration *that they may learn to fear Me all the days
that they live upon the earth* suggests that the proper fear of God may
be achieved only as the result of a lifelong learning process.[187] By
contrast, at Sinai, the evident intent of the revelatory spectacle was that
the palpable presence of God among the people would in itself instill a
sense of awe and fear among the generation present that they would in
turn convey to their descendents.[188]

> *4.11 And ye came near and stood under the mountain; and
> the mountain burned with fire unto the heart of heaven,
> with darkness, cloud, and thick darkness. 4.12 And YHVH
> spoke unto you out of the midst of the fire; ye heard the
> voice of words, but ye saw no form; only a voice. 4.13 And
> He declared unto you His covenant, which He commanded
> you to perform, even the ten words; and He wrote them
> upon two tables of stone. 4.14 And YHVH commanded me
> at that time to teach you statutes and ordinances, that ye
> might do them in the land whither ye go over to possess it.*

Moses reminds those who were present at the great assembly at Mount Sinai, and informs those who were too young or not yet born at the time, of the awesome spectacle of the mountain aflame while shrouded in deep darkness, out of which the *voice of words* of God was heard. The biblical assertion that God spoke to the children of Israel raises a number of conceptual issues that I have addressed at some length in my *The Ten Commandments*, which, for considerations of space will not be repeated here.[189] With regard to this passage, suffice it to note, as one commentator pointed out, "It does not say *ye heard the words*. Thus every time when their hearing words is mentioned, it is their hearing the *voice* that is meant, *Moses* being the one who heard words and reported to them."[190] That is, the people merely heard the sounds of an indistinct but powerful voice that seemed to emanate from the fire that flared on the top of the mountain.

It is noteworthy that some are troubled by the notion that the divine presence could be shrouded in darkness rather than by brilliant light that would dispel the darkness. Thus, it has been argued that the expression of this notion in the text be treated as a parable alluding "to our incapacity to apprehend Him." The notion of divine manifestation in a dark cloud "draws attention to the fact that the apprehension of His true reality is impossible for us because of the dark matter that encompasses us and not Him, may He be exalted."[191] However, it has also been suggested that the verse should be understood as saying that the deep darkness covered the entire area of the mountain, where the people stood, and "only the place from which God wishes His Word to be directed to Israel was lit up by fire."[192]

Most importantly, Moses emphasized, *ye heard the voice of words, but ye saw no form, only a voice.* What they saw at Mount Sinai was a visual spectacle so extraordinary that it riveted their attention, but its purpose was to prepare them for the revelation that was to come, which most emphatically was not visual but aural. They did not and could not see the incorporeal God, but they did hear the divine voice, which *declared unto you His covenant, which He commanded you to perform*, the essence of which was contained in the *ten words*, the Decalogue, which

God wrote *upon two tables of stone*, to indicate their permanence; any attempt to change them would result in defacing the covenant.

Although the text specifies that the Decalogue was written on *two tables of stone*, it does not indicate how the ten pronouncements were distributed among them. In some sources the rabbis give special emphasis to the tradition that each tablet contained five pronouncements, while noting that there was a controversy among them over the matter, some arguing that although there were two stone tablets, the entire Decalogue was recorded on each tablet.[193] However, another source similarly records a controversy over the matter, but in this instance the majority favored the view that all ten were placed on each of the tablets.[194] In other words, many of the rabbis maintained that the Decalogue was issued in duplicate. It is not clear why they took this position, although it may have been the simple fact that recording the first five on one tablet and the latter five on another would have resulted in a significant imbalance between the tablets, given that the first tablet would contain a hundred and forty-six Hebrew words and the second tablet a mere twenty-six. Nonetheless, the opinion that the Decalogue was evenly divided on the two tablets prevailed, and artistic representations of the Decalogue since the thirteenth century depict the Decalogue as evenly distributed between two tablets, compensating for the textual imbalance by inscribing only the opening words of each commandment, thereby making it appear balanced. However, notwithstanding the common notion that the Decalogue was written partly on one tablet and concluded on the other, it is far more likely that each tablet would have contained all of the Decalogue, consistent with "the normal practice of the suzerainty treaties under which one copy was retained by the suzerain and the other given to the vassal for deposit in the temple of his god. In Israel's case both copies were placed in the Ark (Deut. 10:1-5; 31:9, 26)," thereby symbolizing the permanent presence of God with his vassal Israel.[195]

However, these easily remembered precepts that were delivered directly to the children of Israel were by no means the totality of what the covenant stipulated. Indeed, Moses avers, God *commanded me at that time*, that is, during the many days I spent alone at the summit of the mountain, *to teach you statutes and ordinances* that God revealed to me to convey to you, *that ye might do them in the land whither ye go over to possess it.* In other words, the Decalogue was in effect the preamble to the covenantal constitution that was to serve as the basis for the civilization to be founded in the land promised to their forefathers and to them.

It is noteworthy that the text *And YHVH commanded me at that time to teach you statutes and ordinances,* coupled with the earlier text, *Behold, I have taught you statutes and ordinances, even as YHVH my Elohim commanded me,* appears to be the source, according to some,[196] of the ancient rabbinic doctrine regarding the impropriety of receiving payment for teaching Torah, except in special circumstances. Thus the rabbis maintained that, in these passages, Moses is saying, in effect, "just as I [taught you] gratuitously, so you must teach gratuitously."[197] This doctrine is also seen as implicit in the biblical teaching, *Buy the truth, and sell it not* (Prov. 23:23), which at least one commentator has understood as saying, if you cannot find someone to teach you gratis, then pay to learn but do not say that because you had to pay to learn you will have to be paid to teach.[198]

It should be noted that some commentators have struggled with the statement, *ye heard the voice of words, but ye saw no form [temunah],* whereas we were informed in an earlier text with regard to Moses that *the similitude [temunah] of YHVH doth he behold* (Num. 12:8), which suggests that God does have a form, but that only Moses could see it. A number of explanations have been offered in an attempt to deal with the idea of an incorporeal God having a visible form, most failing to deal with the problem satisfactorily. Perhaps the most plausible of the various suggestions is that the term *temunah* in these texts "refers to the inner Voice which was not seen at all."[199] That is, the term translated as "seeing" would be better rendered as "perceiving," which need not connote visual experience. That is, the people heard *the voice of words,* but did not experience the inner voice, as did Moses alone.

> [4.15] *Take ye therefore good heed unto yourselves—for ye saw no manner of form on the day that YHVH spoke unto you in Horeb out of the midst of the fire—[4.16] lest ye deal corruptly, and make you a graven image, even the form of*

> *any figure, the likeness of male or female,* [4.17] *the likeness of*
> *any beast that is on the earth, the likeness of any winged*
> *fowl that flieth in the heaven,* [4.18] *the likeness of any thing*
> *that creepeth on the ground, the likeness of any fish that*
> *is in the water under the earth;* [4.19] *and lest thou lift up*
> *thine eyes unto heaven, and when thou seest the sun and*
> *the moon and the stars, even all the host of heaven, thou*
> *be drawn away and worship them, and serve them, which*
> *YHVH thy Elohim hath allotted unto all the peoples*
> *under the whole heaven.* [4.20] *But you hath YHVH taken*
> *and brought out of the iron furnace, out of Egypt, to be*
> *unto Him a people of inheritance, as ye are this day.*

Once again, Moses calls upon the people to take *good heed unto yourselves,* which may be understood in the present context as an adjuration for them to build the equivalent of a protective wall around their minds, to divert from entrance any influences destructive to their spiritual well being. The land they are about to enter will abound with idolatrous temptations that must be resisted, and everyone must do this for their own sakes. Moses declared, in effect, should you forget everything else, you must remember this; that *ye saw no manner of form on the day that YHVH spoke unto you in Horeb out of the midst of the fire.* God is creator and sovereign of the universe, and as such is necessarily incorporeal. To visualize God is to deny His essence, since by definition He cannot be delimited within the universe that He created. Accordingly, it is categorically forbidden to insult God by attempting to give Him physical representation in any human or animal form, in *the likeness of male or female,* possibly a clear reference to the Baal and Astarte cults that pervaded the region. Moreover, it is equally forbidden to worship any celestial object, sun, moon, or stars, a prohibition that reflects many of the common forms of pagan worship in antiquity. All of these existents, astral and terrestrial, were created by God, to whom it would be an insult for humans, created in the image of God, to consider them as possessing divinity.

It has been suggested that in this passage Moses is concerned primarily with idolatrous practices resulting from spiritual confusion.

The people have been inspired by the revelatory event at Sinai, and may wish to maintain the sense of elation they experienced there, "to perpetuate that connection by representation of God with images . . . Here we are not talking about a danger from the outside [which will be raised by the text later], but rather an inherent danger embedded within the very experience of perceiving God." In this case, the text is not speaking about the worship of other gods, but rather the inappropriate worship of the one true God. This, it is suggested, is what is meant by the expression *avodah zarah* or strange worship.[200] All this was stated, *lest ye deal corruptly* and commit any such folly. That is, any such idolatrous act with regard to anything created will place one in the camp of those who reject the uniqueness and singularity of God.

Moses acknowledges that other peoples worship not only a variety of creatures found in the animal world but also the visible heavenly bodies. However, he points out that all of these *YHVH thy Elohim hath allotted unto all the peoples under the whole heaven*, presumably for purposes of worship, which seems to suggest that idolatry as such is itself part of the divine plan for mankind. That is, as one rabbi put it, this teaches that God effectively gave the typical objects of idolatry the power to deceive and seduce men, who are intrinsically capable of resisting their attractions. Thus, "if one comes to defile himself he is granted facilities for so doing."[201] The implication of this teaching is that, although polytheism is intrinsically an affront to God, He is not directly engaged in a campaign to wipe out paganism as such, which is in itself represents the consequence of human failure to understand the nature of the universe and the divinely assigned role played by the heavenly bodies in it. Thus, this text has been understood as meaning "that He made the spheres intermediaries for the governance of the created beings and not with a view to their being worshipped."[202] It is noteworthy in this regard that, according to the rabbis, the original Septuagint translation of the text into Greek (which is not found in contemporary editions of the work) rendered the text as, "Which the Lord thy God hath allotted unto all the peoples to give light under the whole heaven," the addition of "to give light" evidently intended to make the point that it was not so that these bodies should be worshipped.[203]

However, at least one major medieval commentator read the text as explicitly intending that God had no concern about providing for the worship of His creations by the other nations, but absolutely forbade it to Israel, for whom only He alone was to be worshipped.[204] Indeed, it has been argued by a later commentator that the Torah does not indicate that non-Israelites were commanded to accept monotheism.[205] However, it should not be concluded that because God did not specifically enjoin the other nations from polytheism it is therefore acceptable; all this text indicates is that the other nations were not given a specific prohibition in this regard.[206] In this vein, it has been suggested that God interposes no objection to the worship of His created intermediaries by the other nations because, once they reach that stage, they may ultimately be led by Israel's example to conclude that there is but one God, and thus generalize what occurred in the exceptional case of Abraham by his own force of intellect.[207]

The point is that Abraham, who by force of his own intellect came to the realization that there was but a one and only true God, was subsequently chosen to be the progenitor of a nation and civilization based on this understanding that would serve as a model for other peoples to emulate. Accordingly, the children of Israel, whom God had *taken and brought out of the iron furnace, out of Egypt, to be unto Him a people of inheritance*, the metaphor of *the iron furnace*, which was employed to purify valuable metals by burning out their impurities, suggests that their experience in Egypt should have served the same purpose for the children of Israel by ridding them of any predisposition towards idolatry. Accordingly, by entering into the divine covenant, any subsequent regression to idolatry on their part would be considered treason against their divine sovereign.

Nonetheless, the reality is that the primitive belief in the influence of the heavenly bodies has characterized much of mankind, including many among the children of Israel, throughout recorded history to this day, and the text under discussion has served as a prooftext for the idea that the stars and planets exercise significant influence in the world. Thus one important medieval commentator wrote that the phrase *hath allotted unto all the peoples* means that God assigned the constellations to the various nations and assigned specific angels to rule over them.[208]

In this regard, it is noteworthy that even among the rabbis there were those that believed strongly in astrological influences. Thus, one rabbi maintained: "The planetary influence gives wisdom, the planetary influence gives wealth, and Israel stands under planetary influence." His colleagues, however, demurred, insisting that "Israel is immune from planetary influence," while implicitly agreeing that this was an exceptional case because of Israel's special relationship with God.[209] As explained by one medieval commentator, according to the planetary influences, it was Israel's destiny to remain in servitude, but that God, out of His love for the Patriarchs, intervened in the celestial order and removed Israel from under the influence of the zodiac *to be unto Him a people of inheritance.*[210] Accordingly, the text asserting that God *hath allotted unto all the peoples under the whole heaven* thus specifically excludes Israel.[211]

It should be noted, however, that the general understanding of this text must be modified in one regard if it to be found consistent with fundamental biblical teaching. It is one thing to assert that Israel alone is "immune from planetary influence," and quite another to imply that this extends to individual free will, that is, that only the children of Israel have it, a proposition that clearly flies in the face of the concept of man being created in the divine image. Accordingly the text under consideration, at best, must be understood as not applying to man's inherent moral autonomy, the belief in which is critical to all biblical thought.[212]

> *4.21 Now YHVH was angered with me for your sakes, and swore that I should not go over the Jordan, and that I should not go into that good land, which YHVH thy Elohim giveth thee for an inheritance; 4.22 but I must die in this land, I must not go over the Jordan; but ye are to go over, and possess that good land.*

One again Moses voices his disappointment at not being permitted to accompany the people across the Jordan, reiterating that he was being punished in this manner because God *was angered with me for your sakes*, the meaning of which was discussed earlier at the beginning of this chapter, notwithstanding that the Hebrew text employs a different term, better translated as *because of your deeds*.[213] He also indicates that the divine decision in this regard was irrevocable because God *swore that I should not go over the Jordan*. It would appear that Moses felt the need to explain to the people why he, who had led them for some forty years, would not be crossing the Jordan with them, perhaps primarily out of concern that they might misunderstand his reason for not doing so and therefore hesitate to cross the river themselves.[214] His raising the issue was therefore not simply to complain publicly about his personal situation but rather to emphasize what a great privilege God was extending to them by allowing them to enter the land, while he alone was being denied that same privilege because of divine anger at him *for your sakes*. It has been suggested that there might have been another reason for his public explanation, namely that he wanted to preclude the emergence of a personality cult centered on him. Thus, he pointed out, despite all the extraordinary things that he did, especially his ability to communicate with God, he was nonetheless a mortal like they, completely under God's control and as unworthy of adoration as the sun, moon, or stars.[215]

Moses also states, *I must die in this land, I must not go over the Jordan*, assertions that appear to be out of sequence because if Moses is to die in Transjordan, it would not be possible for him to cross the Jordan. Accordingly, the rabbis read these statements as Moses saying that not only must he die without first crossing the Jordan, but that even his bones will not be permitted to cross it even just to be buried in the promised land.[216] The reason for this extreme position is not made clear in the biblical texts. However, at least one interpretation suggests that the divine pique at Moses reflected here went back to the very beginning of the Moses narrative, when he fled from the wrath of Pharaoh, eventually winding up in Midian where he assisted the daughters of Jethro. Thus, according to one midrashic commentary, when Moses prayed that he be allowed to cross the Jordan, he argued:

"If Joseph's bones were permitted to be carried into the promised land, why not mine?" God replied, "whosoever acknowledges his country shall be buried therein, but whosoever does not acknowledge his country shall not be buried therein. Joseph pledged allegiance to his country when he said, 'For indeed I was stolen away out of the land of the Hebrews,' and therefore also does he deserve to have his bones brought to the land of Israel, but thou didst in silence hear the daughters of Jethro say to their father, 'An Egyptian delivered us out of the hands of the shepherds,' without correcting them by saying, 'I am a Hebrew'; and therefore shall not even thy bones be brought into the land of Israel."[217]

Moses thus cautions the people to learn from his experience not to do anything to antagonize God, which will result in His not being there to intervene on their behalf in a crisis. Moreover, Moses also will not be there to intercede on their behalf. It has been suggested, as indicated above, that what concerned Moses at this point was that, in his absence, the people might repeat the sacrilege of the golden calf, which was originally intended as a substitute for him, and make a statue of him that they might be able to revere, as implicitly suggested by the following admonishment.[218]

> [4.23] *Take heed unto yourselves, lest ye forget the covenant of YHVH your Elohim, which He made with you, and make you a graven image, even the likeness of any thing which YHVH thy Elohim hath forbidden thee.* [4.24] *For YHVH thy Elohim is a devouring fire, a jealous God.* [4.25] *When thou shalt beget children, and children's children, and ye shall have been long in the land, and shall deal corruptly, and make a graven image, even the form of any thing, and shall do that which is evil in the sight of YHVH thy Elohim, to provoke Him;* [4.26] *I call heaven and earth to witness against you this day, that ye shall soon utterly perish from off the land whereunto ye go over the Jordan*

> to possess it; ye shall not prolong your days upon it, but
> shall utterly be destroyed. [4.27] And YHVH shall scatter
> you among the peoples, and ye shall be left few in number
> among the nations, whither YHVH shall lead you away.
> [4.28] And there ye shall serve gods, the work of men's hands,
> wood and stone, which neither see, nor hear, nor eat, nor
> smell.

First and foremost, he warns them, they must never forget or neglect the cardinal principle of the covenant they have entered into, which demands a total unwavering commitment to *YHVH*, who is their one and only *Elohim*. Moses understands the difficulty of accepting the idea of an all-powerful incorporeal deity, but there can be no compromise in this regard. They are categorically prohibited from making *a graven image, even the likeness of any thing which YHVH thy Elohim hath forbidden thee*, which, as suggested above, would include any such portrayal of him. Remember, he warns, *YHVH thy Elohim is a devouring fire, a jealous God*, who will not tolerate any idolatrous assault by them on His divine integrity. Moses implicitly acknowledges that, given their collective memory of the golden calf affair and its aftermath, as well as other events in the wilderness, that such recidivism is unlikely in the near future. However, what will happen afterward, once the present generation is well established in its own land and has raised children and grandchildren to whom the events and commitments of the past are no longer vivid memories, is less certain. The point of danger will come when they begin to assume that they possess the land as a matter of right, one established by their own initiative. It is noteworthy that Moses says *when* this happens, not *if* it happens. That is, it is phrased as both a forewarning and a prophecy, and not merely as a possibility. However, it is insisted that this should not be construed as inevitable but rather as likely to occur unless the children of Israel take steps to avoid falling into that trap.[219] One of the rabbis thus taught, "The land of Israel was not laid waste until seven Courts of Justice had sanctioned idolatry." When questioned about the source for this assertion, the response was that it is to be found intimated in the text, *When thou shalt beget children, and children's children.*[220]

Moses is keenly aware that the land the Israelites are about to enter and conquer is populated with people that worship a variety of gods in representational forms, and there is a strong likelihood, if not a certainty, that some among them may be seduced to emulate their pagan neighbors. This, he warns them, would be an ultimately fatal mistake for them as a nation; *I call heaven and earth to witness against you this day* that you have been forewarned. It has been suggested that the reason for Moses' invocation of *heaven and earth* is that he expected to die soon but heaven and earth would be eternal witnesses that the people were fully forewarned regarding the consequences of malfeasance with respect to their God.[221] It has also been observed that the invocation of *heaven and earth* as witnesses "reflects the suzerainty treaty form in which both divine and natural phenomena are cited as witnesses to the treaty"[222] a form that would have been recognized by the elders of the people. However, since the Decalogue precluded the invocation of any divine phenomena as witnesses, *heaven and earth* in this and other instances must refer to the created universe, which is considered eternal.

The pursuit of idolatry in any form, as well as to act in a manner that *is evil in the sight of YHVH thy Elohim*, is to court disaster. Moses assures them that divine forbearance is limited, and *ye shall soon utterly perish from off the land whereunto ye go over the Jordan to possess it; ye shall not prolong your days upon it, but shall utterly be destroyed.* However, Moses immediately clarifies this statement to mean that it is the nation of the children of Israel living in its own territory that *shall utterly be destroyed.* If your inclination is toward idolatry, God will accommodate you by scattering the survivors of the destruction among the nations where you will be free to *serve gods, the work of men's hands, wood and stone, which neither see, nor hear, nor eat, nor smell;* but He will not permit you to do this in the land promised to your forefathers. It has been observed that this description of the sensual incapacities of what idolaters worship omits the sense of touch, which may be considered as subsumed by the ability to eat, both representing physical functions common to all sentient beings. However the remaining three senses are all considered as spiritual senses, which by contrast to the objects of idolatry, are spoken of, metaphorically to be sure, as senses that the biblical texts attribute to God. Thus it states, *And YHVH saw the wickedness* (Gen. 6:5), *And YHVH smelled the sweet savor* (Gen. 8:21), *and when YHVH heard it* (Num. 11:1).[223] As one medieval philosopher explained: "Now these two senses, I mean the sense of taste and the sense of touch, do not apprehend the things sensed by them before they are in contact with them. On the other hand, the sense of sight, that of hearing, and that of smell, can apprehend from a distance the qualities sensed by them as well as the bodies that are bearers of those qualities. It is, therefore, according to the imagination of the multitude, permitted to ascribe them to God."[224]

It is noteworthy that to the biblical writers, being sent into exile was equivalent to being told to go and serve other gods. Thus, fleeing from King Saul, David complained, *they have driven me out this day that I should not cleave unto the inheritance of YHVH, saying: Go, serve other gods* (1 Sam. 26:19). The rabbis suggested that the intention of this text was "to tell you that whoever lives outside the Land may be regarded as one who worships idols."[225]

> [4.29] *But from thence ye will seek YHVH thy Elohim; and thou shalt find Him, if thou search after Him with all thy heart and with all thy soul.* [4.30] *In thy distress, when all these things are come upon thee, in the end of days, thou wilt return to YHVH thy Elohim, and hearken unto His voice;* [4.31] *for YHVH thy Elohim is a merciful God; He will not fail thee, neither destroy thee, nor forget the covenant of thy fathers which He swore unto them.*

However, Moses assures the people that God is always open to sincere repentance, which he predicts will take place when circumstances will force them to the realization that only God can help them; that He will never *forget the covenant of thy fathers which He swore unto them.* It is noteworthy that the text switches from the plural *ye will seek* to the singular *and thou shalt find*, indicating that, notwithstanding the importance of communal prayer, ultimately the burden of repentance always ultimately rests on the individual.[226]

It has been suggested that the passage seems to refer to two distinct types of repentance, spontaneous and externally driven. Thus the first verse speaks of the spontaneous desire to seek and find God *if thou search after Him with all thy heart and with all thy soul*, a desire prompted by one's heart and soul. The remainder of the passage reflects a rather different perspective; the seeking is motivated by distress of helplessness, at which time one will seek divine assistance and succor. Although the first type of repentance is the clearly more desirable and meritorious, the second is no less acceptable because its appeal for divine mercy, coupled with the anguish suffered, makes it comparable to the former.[227]

> [4.32] *For ask now of the days past, which were before thee, since the day that Elohim created man upon the earth, and from one end of heaven unto the other, whether there hath been any such thing as this great thing is, or hath been heard like it?* [4.33] *Did ever a people hear the voice of Elohim speaking out of the midst of the fire, as thou hast heard, and live?* [4.34] *Or hath Elohim assayed to go and take Him a nation from the midst of another nation, by trials, by signs, and by wonders, and by war, and by a mighty hand, and by an outstretched arm, and by great terrors, according to all that YHVH your Elohim did for you in Egypt before thine eyes?* [4.35] *Unto thee it was shown, that thou mightest know that YHVH, He is Elohim; there is none else beside Him.* [4.36] *Out of heaven He made thee to hear His voice, that He might instruct thee; and upon earth He made thee to see His great fire; and thou didst hear His words out of the midst of the fire.*

Moses adjures the people to think clearly and remember what took place before, during, and after the exodus, singular events that are unique in human history. It is especially noteworthy that Moses' remark, *Or hath Elohim assayed to go and take Him a nation from the midst of another nation*, thus demonstrating the impotence of the gods of Egypt to prevent it,[228] also implies that Israel is in a sense a divine experiment in history, one that may or may not succeed, the decision in this regard is placed in Israel's hands, not in God's. By contrast, Moses' assertion, *YHVH, He is Elohim; there is none else beside Him*, which asserts that God alone is omnicompetent and omnipotent, is an unequivocal declaration of monotheism, one that will be repeated a number of times later in the text.

Although this surely is the point at which Moses was driving, some have read his opening statement in this passage as having other significant implications. Thus, it has been argued that *ask now of the days past . . . since the day that Elohim created man upon the earth* clearly suggests that legitimate inquiry into origins may begin only with the creation narrative, but not with speculation regarding what preceded creation, about which Scripture has nothing to say.[229] As one ancient sage put it, "What is too sublime for you, seek not; into things beyond your strength, search not. What is committed to you, attend to; what is hidden is not your concern. With what is beyond you, meddle not; more than enough for you has been shown you. Indeed, many are the speculations of human beings—evil and misleading fancies."[230]

It has been suggested with regard to the assertion, *Unto thee it was shown, that thou mightest know that YHVH, He is Elohim*, that the essence of Judaism may be found in this phrase. That is, "it is through *seeing* that you have been brought to *knowing*." Knowledge of God and affirmation of His engagement with Israel are not founded on belief alone but also on the personal experience of what our ancestors witnessed in the wilderness, as recorded in the biblical texts.[231] Moreover, the statement that God *made thee to hear His voice, that He might instruct thee* implies that, at least for that precious moment they were all elevated to the status of prophet to receive directly the divine word.[232]

> [4.37] *And because He loved thy fathers, and chose their seed after them, and brought thee out with His presence, with His great power, out of Egypt,* [4.38] *to drive out nations from before thee greater and mightier than thou, to bring thee in, to give thee their land for an inheritance, as it is this day;* [4.39] *know this day, and lay it to thy heart, that YHVH,*

He is Elohim in heaven above and upon the earth beneath; there is none else. [4.40] *And thou shalt keep His statutes, and His commandments, which I command thee this day, that it may go well with thee, and with thy children after thee, and that thou mayest prolong thy days upon the land, which YHVH thy Elohim giveth thee, for ever.*

Moses emphasizes once again, indeed he cannot repeat it often enough, that Israelite nationhood is not a natural social development but one fashioned by God for His own purposes. It came about because *He loved thy fathers, and chose their seed after them.* The translation of the second clause in this citation, *vayivhar bezaro aharav*, rendered as *and chose their seed after them*, is not faithful to the Hebrew text, which is in the singular and not the plural, as shown in the ArtScroll translation. Presumably, early translators saw a need to correct the text by making the second clause consistent with the first, which is given in the plural. This, it has been pointed out is an error, because to do so would suggest that all of the many nations that emerged from the Patriarchs were also chosen to inherit the land, which would include the Ishmaelites as well as the other descendents of Abraham and Ketura, which the text specifically excluded as his heirs (Gen. 25: 1-6). Moreover, the text also made it quite clear that for purposes of inheritance, only *in Isaac shall seed be called to thee* (Gen. 21:12). Thus, when the text is properly translated as, *and chose his seed after him*, the reference is to Jacob, thus excluding, in addition to Ishmael and the six other sons of Abraham and Ketura, also Isaac's other son Esau.[233]

God also gave Israel a covenant by adherence to which they were expected to create the just and moral civilization that could serve as the model for other nations. It is for this purpose, Moses asserts, that God is making it possible for you *to drive out nations from before thee greater and mightier than thou,* and to establish your control of the lands they now occupy, *as it is this day,* following the victories over the Amorite kings in Transjordan.[234] After considering all this, *know this day, and lay it to thy heart* that the key to your future is your unwavering acknowledgment *that YHVH, He is Elohim in heaven above and upon the earth beneath, there is none else.* It is noteworthy that in the Hebrew phrase *vahashevota el levavekha*, translated as *and lay it to thy heart*, the term *vahashevota* actually means *and return it*. Accordingly the phrase has been understood as saying that, after considering all the aspects of past experience and present promises, select and internalize that aspect which is the truth, namely that concerning belief in the oneness of God.[235]

It has been argued that the oneness of God has been affirmed in four different ways, depending on an individual's personality and ability to grasp complex abstractions. The first is simply to state that God is One. The second is to affirm the oneness of God on the basis of what may be considered reliable tradition. The third is to affirm the truth of the proposition on the basis of their "being able to derive proofs for His existence on their own, but who do not know the difference between 'true' and 'circumstantial' Oneness." That is, they know their goal but are not able to reach it because they are confused by detours on the road. "The fourth category is composed of those who say and feel God is One after deriving logical proofs for it on their own, and who are firm in their belief in the truth of it. Theirs is the best, most complete form of, and it is the level the prophet advised us to arrive at when he said, *know this day, and lay it to thy heart, that YHVH, He is Elohim.*"[236] However, another hastens to caution, the knowledge that God is One is effectively the limit of what one can know of God; the intrinsic nature of God is beyond the grasp of the human mind, as it states, *It is the glory of Elohim to conceal a thing* (Prov. 25:2).[237] That is, "God's government of the universe is mysterious and baffles human understanding. This fact redounds to His *glory* in that it points to the working of a mind of infinite wisdom which is inscrutable by man."[238]

But, Moses insists, acknowledgment of the reality of God is not a matter of merely intellectual affirmation; it requires that *thou shalt keep His statutes, and His commandments, which I command thee this day.* If you and your descendents do this, then and only in this manner will you assure your future as a nation in your own land. Once again, Moses drives home the point that the essence of proper understanding and knowledge is that it should result in proper behavior.

This exhortation concludes the first of Moses' final discourses to the people of Israel. Before beginning the presentation of his second and longest discourse, the text inserts the following passage describing an action that Moses took, which appears as being out of any discernible context here. It has been suggested, however, that Moses had expected to designate all six cities of refuge after the Israelites crossed over the Jordan and took control of the land; now that he was told definitively that he was not going to cross the river, he undertook to designate the cities of refuge in Transjordan, to do whatever he could for Israel before he passed from the scene.[239]

> *4.41 Then Moses separated three cities beyond the Jordan toward the sunrising; 4.42 that the manslayer might flee thither, that slayeth his neighbor unawares, and hated him not in times past; and that fleeing unto one of these cities he might live: 4.43 Bezer in the wilderness, in the tableland, for the Reubenites; and Ramoth in Gilead, for the Gadites; and Golan in Bashan, for the Manassites.*

According to divine instructions received earlier, as soon as the land came under Israelite control, six cities of refuge were to be established, three of which were to be located on each side of the Jordan, places to which someone accused of unintentional manslaughter might flee for safety from vengeance *until he stand before the congregation for judgment* (Num. 35:12). Now that the territories formerly held by the Amorite kings in Transjordan were firmly in Israel's grip, Moses proceeding to designate three cities of refuge to serve the tribes of Reuben, Gad, and the clans of Manasseh that settled there. It has been suggested that it was Moses' original intention to dedicate all six cities simultaneously, which was predicated on the expectation that he would lead the invasion across the Jordan and oversee the conquest of the land. Now that it was clear that he was not going to be allowed to cross the river, he undertook to do as much as he could under the circumstances and therefore named the cities of refuge in Transjordan. It has been suggested that Moses did this "not only to give the land on that side its full consecration, and thoroughly confirm the possession of the two Amoritish kingdoms on the other side of the Jordan, but also to give the people in this punctual observance of duty devolving upon it an example for their imitation in the conscientious observance of the commandments of the Lord, which he was about to lay before the nation."[240] This decision thus relates this seemingly out of place passage to the opening of this entire section, *And I besought YHVH at that time* (Deut. 3:23), to plead for permission to cross the river with the rest of the children of Israel, permission that was refused.[241]

The rules concerning the use of these cities as refuges are outlined later (Deut. 19), but their mention at this point may be a reflection of Moses' intense personal interest in their establishment because of his own experience as a fugitive when still a very young man. It will be recalled that Moses intervened when he saw an Egyptian beating an Israelite, his intervention causing the death of the Egyptian, for which he felt compelled to flee the country for safety from summary judgment and execution.

Having concluded the first discourse, the text now turns to the second discourse, which it prefaces by the following introductory statement.

> [4.44] *And this is the Torah which Moses set before the children of Israel;* [4.45] *these are the testimonies, and the statutes, and the ordinances, which Moses spoke unto the children of Israel, when they came forth out of Egypt;* [4.46] *beyond the Jordan, in the valley over against Beth-peor, in the land of Sihon king of the Amorites, who dwelt at Heshbon, whom Moses and the children of Israel smote, when they came forth out of Egypt;* [4.47] *and they took his land in possession, and the land of Og king of Bashan, the two kings of the Amorites, who were beyond the Jordan toward the sunrise;* [4.48] *from Aroer, which is on the edge of the valley of Arnon, even unto mount Sion—the same is Hermon—* [4.49] *and all the Arabah beyond the Jordan eastward, even unto the sea of the Arabah, under the slopes of Pisgah.*

The meaning of the opening assertion in this passage, *this is the Torah which Moses set before the children of Israel*, is far from clear. At issue is what the text implies as included within *the Torah which Moses set before the children of Israel.* The difficulty, of course, is that the word *Torah* has multiple meanings. At one end of the range of meanings, *Torah* is taken to refer to the entirety of the five books of Moses, the Pentateuch. Thus, the opening assertion traditionally is recited in the synagogue when the Torah scroll is raised following a reading from it. At the other end of the range, *Torah* is understood as "teaching." In the present instance, *Torah* is often translated as "law," with the following clause, *these are the testimonies, and the statutes, and the ordinances*, taken as defining its content.

The *edot* or *testimonies* or "attestations," have been understood by some to refer to "solemn declarations of God's will on matters of moral and religious duty."[242] Others have considered *edot* to refer to those biblical requirements that attest to divine immanence, such as the laws concerning the Sabbath and the various festivals.[243] The new JPS version translates *edot* as *decrees*. Etymologically, considering cognate terms in other ancient languages, *edot* "refers to the terms or stipulations of a treaty (*edut*) imposed by a suzerain on a vassal."[244] In a similar vein, it has been suggested that *edot* is best understood as written commandments and admonitions, the purpose of which is to bear testimony against those who violate them. The Decalogue etched in stone is a prime example of such *edot*, often referred to as *luhot ha'edut* or "tablets of the testimony," and the written Torah itself is just such a testimony, as it states later, *Take this book of the Torah, and put it by the side of the ark of the covenant . . . that it may be there for a witness against thee* (Deut. 31:26).[245] However, it remains uncertain as to precisely what Moses had in mind when he made use of this term; any of those noted above would fit the context of the passage.

The rabbis of the talmudic period generally understood the categories of ordinances and statutes to reflect the distinction between those biblical precepts considered to be in accord with human reason and those that do not comport with that criterion. Thus, the rabbis asserted that the biblical ordinances proscribing idolatry, immorality, bloodshed, robbery, and blasphemy are the sort of "commandments which, if they were not written [in Scripture], they should by right have been written." That is to say, these prohibitions are the kinds of constraints that would be placed by any ordered society on conduct negatively affecting the public welfare. Statutes, on the other hand, were considered by the rabbis to be the sort of "commandments to which Satan objects."[246] The statutes, which have no evidently rational bases, at least none that are accessible to the unaided human intellect, presumably would be found to be objectionable by persons inclined to reject the legitimacy of any rule or regulation that does not serve as a rational response to a societal need. Assuming such a position obviously places one in direct opposition to divine authority, a posture the rabbis considered satanic.

The remainder of the passage contains a brief recapitulation of the events that took place following the thirty-eighth year of their forced sojourn in the wilderness, when the Israelites crossed into Transjordan, bypassed Moab, and defeated the Amorite kings, asserting control over their territories that they had themselves only recently conquered. It also outlines the dimensions of the territory settled by the tribes of Reuben, Gad, and clans of Manasseh on the east bank of the Jordan.

It would seem that this and the previous biblical passage concerning the cities of refuge that were established in Transjordan are intended to emphasize that it was the original divine intention that the territory of the new nation include the indicated lands on the east bank of the Jordan. Presumably, this was considered important because the territories involved might be considered as transcending the divine commitment to Abraham when he was located in the heights between Bethel and Ai in Canaan. God said to him, *Lift up now thine eyes, and look from the place where thou art, northward and southward and eastward and westward; for all the land which thou seest, to thee will I give it, and to thy seed for ever* (Gen. 13:14-15). Arguably, from the place where Abraham stood during that revelation, one could see a substantial part of the territory in Transjordan conquered by Moses and settled by Reuben, Gad, and part of Manasseh, which would legitimize Israelite settlement there. Having made this point, the text returns to the presentation of Moses' second discourse.

5.1 And Moses called unto all Israel, and said unto them: Hear, O Israel, the statutes and the ordinances which I speak in your ears this day, that ye may learn them, and observe to do them. 5.2 YHVH our Elohim made a covenant with us in Horeb. 5.3 YHVH made not this covenant with our fathers, but with us, even us, who are all of us here alive this day. 5.4 YHVH spoke with you face to face in the mount out of the midst of the fire (5.5 I stood between YHVH and you at the time, to declare unto you the word of YHVH; for ye were afraid because of the fire, and went not up into the mount) saying:

The statement that Moses' call on this occasion was to *all Israel* seems to imply that the audience for his earlier addresses was more limited. Thus, it has been suggested that this time he insisted on addressing everyone including all the children, even the oldest of which was born long after the events at Horeb, that were now to be brought into the covenant as were their elders at the time. He would repeat for their benefit the Decalogue that their parents and grandparents heard directly from God some four decades earlier.[247]

It is of interest to note that, contrary to the biblical preface to his second discourse, Moses omits the category of *testimonies*, which presumably are subsumed under the categories of *the statutes and the ordinances*. The assertion *that ye may learn them, and observe to do them* makes an important point, that knowledge is a prerequisite to appropriate performance.[248] However, the text also has been read as implying that knowledge without performance is insufficient, that "mere intellectual knowledge without practical fulfillment has no value."[249] This was an issue of some concern to the rabbis, who decried those who professed an interest in studying the Torah as an end rather than as a means to better performance.[250]

It has been argued by many if not most commentators that the assertion that God *made not this covenant with our fathers* must be understood as saying that this covenant was not made only *with our fathers*.[251] That is, the revelation of the covenant at Horeb was not exclusive to the older generation now deceased, but continues to apply to their present and future descendents. This, of course, raises the broader question of how those who were born after the events at Horeb could become bound to a covenant to which they had not assented, an issue that will be discussed later when Moses reasserts this position in even clearer terms near the conclusion of his discourses. Moreover, by stressing that the covenant was made *with us, even us, who are all of us here alive this day*, he makes it clear that with respect to the covenant and its requirements, Moses includes himself as merely another one of the people, that he has no special status with respect to the Torah. In effect, Moses may be understood as asserting implicitly the principle of the equality of all before the law.

Moses thus explains, parenthetically, that the only reason that *I stood between YHVH and you at the time* when God *spoke with you face to face* was because you were too awestruck to deal with it, and not because I am any different from you with respect to God's word. Nonetheless, the notion that God *spoke with you face to face* would seem to be incompatible with the later assertion that Moses was the only one that God knew *face to face* (Deut. 34:10). It should be noted, however, that the Hebrew in the latter case is *panim el panim*, whereas in the former it is *panim befanim*. The distinction, in one opinion, is that the latter formulation does not imply the same kind of interpersonal communication as that which took place between God and Moses. It is more analogous, as one rabbi put it, to "a statue—a thousand men look at it, each and every one of them of whom says, 'It is looking at me.' Even so the Holy One, blessed be He, made each and every man in Israel feel that He was looking at him." Others suggested that the slight difference between the phrases implied different meanings, and understood *panim befanim* to mean not *face to face* but *face after face*. That is, God spoke to them with one face after another, each one seeing something different.[252] In other words, what they each saw was what their imaginations presented to them; they visualized but did not actually see God.

The text continues with Moses' restatement of the Decalogue.

> *5.6 I am YHVH thy Elohim, who brought thee out of the land of Egypt, out of the house of bondage. 5.7 Thou shalt have no other gods before Me. 5.8 Thou shalt not make unto thee a graven image, even any manner of likeness,*

of anything that is in the heaven above, or that is in the earth beneath, or that is in the water under the earth. ^{5.9} *Thou shalt not bow down unto them, nor serve them; for I YHVH am a jealous God, visiting the iniquity of the fathers upon the children, and upon the third and upon the fourth generation of them that hate Me,* ^{5.10} *and showing mercy unto the thousandth generation of them that love Me and keep My commandments.* ^{5.11} *Thou shalt not take the name of YHVH thy Elohim in vain; for YHVH will not hold him guiltless that taketh His name in vain.* ^{5.12} *Observe the sabbath day, to keep it holy, as YHVH thy Elohim commanded thee.* ^{5.13} *Six days shalt thou labor, and do all thy work;* ^{5.14} *but the seventh day is a sabbath unto YHVH thy Elohim, in it thou shalt not do any manner of work, thou, nor thy son, nor thy daughter, nor thy man-servant, nor thy maid-servant, nor thine ox, nor thine ass, nor any of thy cattle, nor thy stranger that is within thy gates; that thy man-servant and thy maid-servant may rest as well as thou.* ^{5.15} *And thou shalt remember that thou wast a servant in the land of Egypt, and YHVH thy Elohim brought thee out thence by a mighty hand and by an outstretched arm; therefore YHVH thy Elohim commanded thee to keep the sabbath day.* ^{5.16} *Honor thy father and thy mother, as YHVH thy Elohim commanded thee; that thy days may be long, and that it may go well with thee, upon the land which YHVH thy Elohim giveth thee.* ^{5:17} *Thou shalt not murder. Neither shalt thou steal. Neither shalt thou bear false witness against thy neighbor.* ^{5.18} *Neither shalt thou cover thy neighbor's wife: neither shalt thou desire thy neighbor's house, his field, or his man-servant, or his maid-servant, his ox, or his ass, or anything that is thy neighbor's.*

It may be noted that there are a number of differences between this text of the Decalogue and that originally recorded in the book of Exodus, the most important of which concerns the Sabbath. However, because I have already published a comprehensive discussion of the Decalogue from a Judaic perspective in my *The Ten Commandments*, and have addressed there the differences between the two renditions, I would refer the reader to that work rather than burden this study with a lengthy repetition of already published material. Suffice to note for present purposes that the Decalogue should be considered an epitome of the vast body of biblical legislation, that presented in the book of Exodus being a concise statement of a mere one hundred and seventy-two Hebrew words that was published as a credo that could easily be memorized and serve as a basic list of essentially easily understandable general rules. It was not expected that the ordinary citizen would remember or fully understand the plethora of commandments found in the Torah that demand compliance and observance by the children of Israel, their descendents, and those who chose to cast their lot in life with them. To understand the meaning and significance of the Ten Commandments in Judaic thought, it is therefore necessary to correlate them with the body of legislative enactments set forth in the Torah dealing with the same subject matter, much of which will be discussed in the following pages.

> 5.19 *These words YHVH spoke unto all your assembly in the mount out of the midst of the fire, of the cloud, and of the thick darkness, with a great voice, and it went on no more. And He wrote them upon two tables of stone, and gave them unto me.* 5.20 *And it came to pass, when ye heard the voice out of the midst of the darkness, while the mountain did burn with fire, that ye came near unto me, even all the heads of your tribes, and your elders;* 5.21 *and ye said: 'Behold, YHVH out Elohim hath shown us His glory and His greatness, and we have heard His voice out of the midst of the fire; we have seen this day that Elohim doth speak with man, and he liveth.* 5.22 *Now therefore why should we die, for this great fire will consume us; if we hear the voice of YHVH our Elohim any more, then we shall die.* 5.23 *For who is there of all flesh, that hath heard the voice of the living Elohim speaking out of the midst of*

the fire as we have, and lived? [5.24] *Go thou near, and hear
all that YHVH our Elohim may speak unto thee; and we
will hear it, and do it.'*

It has been observed that Moses stated *These words YHVH spoke unto
all your assembly,* but did not say *all these words,* the omission implying
that the repetition of the Decalogue by Moses was not verbatim, but
modified somewhat, presumably to enhance comprehension.[253] What
the people heard was *the voice of the words* of the Decalogue proclaimed
by God, *and it went on no more.* That is, the public revelation ended
with the Decalogue, which God inscribed on two stones thus clearly
indicating that the precepts contained therein were intended to be
permanent, fixed in stone for all time. The theophany was overwhelming
and the people as a whole were terrified by it, fearing that the exposure
could cost them their lives. In this vein, it has been suggested that
what they were afraid of was not that contact with God would result
in their deaths, but rather that they feared the *great fire* out of the
midst of which the divine voice spoke to them might consume them
physically.[254] Since Moses alone seemed able to communicate directly
with God without fear, the tribal elders and other leaders pleaded with
Moses that he serve as their interlocutor with God. *Go thou near, and
hear all that YHVH our Elohim may speak unto thee; and we will hear it,
and do it.* They thus acknowledged Moses as their legislator, trusting
that whatever laws he might subsequently proclaim would have divine
sanction.

> [5.25] *And YHVH heard the voice of your words, when ye
> spoke unto me; and YHVH said unto me: 'I have heard
> the voice of the words of this people, which they have
> spoken unto thee; they have said well all that they have
> spoken.* [5.26] *Oh that they had such a heart as this always,
> to fear Me, and keep all My commandments, that it might
> be well with them, and with their children for ever!* [5.27]
> *Go say to them: Return ye to your tents.* [5.28] *But as for
> thee, stand thou here by Me, and I will speak unto thee all
> the commandment, and the statutes, and the ordinances,*

> *which thou shalt teach them, that they may do them un*
> *the land which I give them to possess it.'*

God was pleased with the response of the people but observed that their responsiveness was the result of the emotions stirred by the awesome spectacle to which they were witness, and not the consequence of careful reflection. It would be wonderful if *that they had such a heart as this always*, but God knew this would not always be the case, notwithstanding that it would be greatly to their advantage, and to that of their descendents, for all time were they to *keep all My commandments*. God had given them the opportunity to secure their future, but also gave them the free will to reject Him. Only time would tell what they and their descendents would choose to do. As a rabbi put it in a classic formulation, "Everything is in the hand of heaven except the fear of heaven."[255]

In the meantime, He instructed Moses to have the people return to their tents from the base of Mount Sinai to resume their normal family life. As for Moses, he was to remain on the mount to be instructed with regard to the precepts that should be the foundation of their civilization as well as the statutes and ordinances that should govern their model society in what would now be their national patrimony, their homeland.

> *5.29 Ye shall observe to do therefore as YHVH your Elohim hath commanded you; ye shall not turn aside to the right hand or to the left. 5.30 Ye shall walk in all the way which YHVH your Elohim hath commanded you, that ye may live, and that it may be well with you, and that ye may prolong your days in the land which ye shall possess.*

Having received divine instruction, Moses admonished the people to conduct their lives *as YHVH your Elohim hath commanded you*. These divine commandments or precepts were not to be considered as general guidelines that might arbitrarily be amended. On the contrary, they were not to be deviated from either to make them more stringent or less onerous. God had set forth a path for them to follow that would assure their well being as a society, and thereby enable them to meet and overcome the vicissitudes they would inevitably confront *in the land which ye shall possess*, which was the landbridge between Asia and Africa and the great empires and pagan civilizations of the ancient Middle East.

> *6.1 Now this is the commandment, the statutes, and the ordinances, which YHVH your Elohim commanded to teach you, that ye might do them in the land whither ye go over to possess it (6.2 that thou mightest fear YHVH your Elohim, to keep all His commandments, which I command thee, thou, and thy son, and thy son's son, all the days of thy life; and that thy days may be prolonged. 6.3 Hear therefore, O Israel, and observe to do it; that it may be well with thee, and that ye may increase mightily, as YHVH, the Elohim of thy fathers, hath promised unto thee) a land flowing with milk and honey.*

Having concluded the historical introduction outlining the central elements of the divine plan for them, Moses proceeded to present them with the divine commandments or precepts and the specific legislation reflected in the statutes and ordinances that were to regulate their lives as a nation, and without which they would be unlikely to survive in the land, proverbially *a land flowing with milk and honey.* The parenthetical statement is especially noteworthy because, even though the discourse generally is directed to the people as a community, it is directed specifically to the children of Israel as individuals; each is personally responsible for becoming sufficiently acquainted with the laws being revealed to them so that they guide the individual's conduct. What stands out here is the assertion that *thou mightest fear YHVH your Elohim,* which suggests that Moses is cautioning the people that it would be an error to expect reward for following God's commandments. Although such beneficence may or may not be forthcoming, the laws should be followed out of fear simply because God commanded them. In other words, observance and performance of the divine legislation cannot be made contingent on divine reciprocity.[256] Moreover, each individual is responsible for transmitting this knowledge to his descendents, and they to theirs, and so on throughout the course of history.[257]

The phrase *a land flowing with milk and honey* is widely assumed to refer to large quantities of milk to be derived from the many flocks of goats to be found there, since the breeding of milk cows was never a major industry in the country in antiquity and the honey is assumed to refer the nectar of dates, figs, and pomegranates rather than to the produce of bees, which although available was not a product for which the land was noted. What has puzzled many is why the text chose to speak of the country as one abounding with *milk and honey* when it could have spoken of it as a land flowing with wine and olive oil, or other more typical products of the country. Indeed, the text later describes the country as *a land of wheat and barley, and vines and fig trees and pomegranates, a land of olive trees and honey* (Deut. 8:8), but not as *a land flowing with milk*.

It is noteworthy that the rabbis saw a rather different significance in the biblical description of the promised land as *a land flowing with milk and honey*, which relates to the Torah's sumptuary laws. The text had already stipulated that *flesh with the life thereof, which is the blood thereof, shall ye not eat* (Gen. 9:4), which has been understood as eating anything from a living animal. Milk, of course, does come from a living animal and would therefore, so it would seem, be banned under the same prohibition. With regard to bees, there is also the biblical injunction, *All winged swarming things . . . are a detestable thing unto you* (Lev. 11:20, 23), and may not be eaten with the exception of those specified, among which bees are not included. Since honey, without further description as in our text, is normally associated with bees, and there is an implicit presumption that "that which goes forth from the unclean is unclean," the eating of honey should be forbidden as well. However, because the biblical text states, *a land flowing with milk and honey*, one may deduce that both milk and honey may be consumed as exceptions to the general rule since it would be unreasonable to assume that the text would laud products that were forbidden.[258]

Moses then proceeded to issue a declaration of faith that has reverberated throughout the course of Jewish history from that moment to the present day.

⁶.⁴ Hear, O Israel: YHVH our Elohim, YHVH is One.

It has been argued that Israel's basic knowledge of God derives from seeing and not from hearing, as it states, *Unto thee it was shown, that thou mightest know that YHVH, He is Elohim; there is none else beside Him* (Deut. 4:35). "They saw God with their own eyes breaking their chains in Egypt leading and feeding them through the wilderness and bringing them to the Promised Land." Of course, what they saw were the footprints of divine intervention in history. However, perception of the divine presence itself in a visual manner only occurred once, at Mount Sinai, and was never to be repeated. From that point on, divine revelation is aural rather than visual. Thus Moses commands: *Hear, O Israel.*[259] Henceforth, knowledge will come through tradition and its transmission from generation to generation. It has been suggested that Moses chose to begin his declaration in this manner because of his abiding concern that most of the generation of Israelites standing before him had not been eyewitnesses to the divine interventions of behalf of Israel and might be prone to forget the past and follow the temptations before their eyes as they enter into a new phase of their history. Accordingly, he placed critical emphasis on *Hear*, on orally received tradition and teaching. It is noteworthy in this regard that, when reciting the declaration in the liturgy, it is a longstanding tradition to cover one's eyes to avoid visual distractions while focusing one's thoughts on it.[260]

Somewhat surprisingly, this declaration, which is generally held to be the preeminent faith affirmation of Judaism, is not entirely clear about what it intends to convey. Indeed, it has been argued, "the syntax of this cardinal sentence, which proclaims the unique oneness of God presents a logical difficulty. If, as it is affirmed here, God is one, absolute and universal, how may we designate Him as our God, attaching a possessive pronoun, which particularizes Him as merely our God, the God of Israel, but not of other people?"[261] Indeed, it was asked what the significance of the assertion *YHVH our Elohim* can be, since the same sentence declares that God is one, which states in effect that God is the God of everyone. The rabbis concluded that the implicit message of the phrase God of Israel is not intended to be exclusionary but rather to assert that Israel has a special responsibility to profess the oneness of God.[262] In this vein, it has been suggested that it is intended to emphasize once again that *YHVH* is still only Israel's *Elohim* because He is not yet accepted as the God of all.[263] That is, His divine oneness clearly is still not manifest to all at present, but is destined to become so eventually.

It is noteworthy in this regard that the rabbis did not as a rule concern themselves with the statement's theological content. They simply designated an individual's recitation of the formula as *kabbalat ol malkhut shamayim* (acceptance of the yoke of the Kingdom of Heaven). As one rabbi taught: "Why does the section *Hear, O Israel* precede *And it shall come to pass if ye shall hearken?*—so that a man may first take upon him the yoke of the kingdom of heaven and afterward take upon him the yoke of the commandments."[264] Indeed, it has been suggested that, as far as the rabbis were concerned, the formula "is not a confession of belief in God's existence, His unity, or His incorporeality, but rather an expression of our allegiance to God and our readiness to obey Him."[265] Supportive of this is the opinion that the text should be understood as affirming that "*YHVH* alone is our *Elohim*, and we have no other god."[266] In other words, as one writer put it, Moses was not "making a speculative statement about the reality of the universe. Instead, he was asserting a claim to the people's loyalty," admonishing them that "this is the exclusive Power that you may worship and obey."[267] Indeed, it has been argued, this reading of the text best conforms to the context in which the declaration is given. "God is very much afraid that the Jews will not obey his commandments . . . In this context, a statement about the metaphysical indivisibility of God is of no help."[268] It is noteworthy that the verse is translated in this manner in the New Jewish Publication Society edition of the Bible.

Moreover, some have taken strong issue with the usual English rendition of the biblical verse as cited above, arguing that it obscures the deeper theological meaning of the statement. It is maintained that the biblical declaration is concerned principally with affirming that *YHVH*, the transcendent sovereign of the universe, is identical with *Elohim*, the immanent deity more familiar to man. Accordingly, the verse might better be translated as, *Hear, O Israel, YHVH is our Elohim; YHVH is one.* Rendered in this fashion, it becomes a vital statement about God in which there is no redundancy. "It asserts that *YHVH* is identical with our Elohim. The transcendent Creator is also the immanent Preserver. God who in his absoluteness is far removed is also near; the King and Ruler is also the Father and Sustainer." In sum, it asserts, *YHVH* who is also Elohim, is nonetheless One.[269]

The declaration has also been understood as conveying two different albeit closely related and compatible concepts of deity. In the opinion of some medieval commentators, the declaration should be interpreted as propounding the idea of God's *uniqueness.* Thus, after reviewing the implications of the grammatical structure of this declaration of faith in the original biblical Hebrew, it was concluded that it should be understood as if it stated: "Hear, O Israel: YHVH our Elohim alone is YHVH," thereby emphasizing the absolute uniqueness of God.[270] Alternatively, it has been suggested that the intent of the declaration was to proclaim God's essential *unity*, as one poet-philosopher wrote: "You are One; the wise wonder at the mystery of Your unity, because they do not know what it is. You are One; and Your unity cannot be detracted from or added to. You are One; not like the one of dimension or number, because neither multiplication nor change, neither attribute nor quality, can be predicated of You."[271] Similarly, writing in a later period, another understood the declaration to mean that God, in Himself, is an irreducible reality, without any form of plurality, whether of substance or attribute.[272] Or, as another writer put it more recently, the concept of unity, of irreducible reality, is inapplicable to material things, which are infinitely reducible. "Only what is above the physical can be truly one. And when we say God is one, we declare that He is outside all the considerations which govern the realm of the physical."[273]

Others have sought to bridge these interpretations with the assertion that the *unity* of God is *unique*. In this view, the application of the idea of unity with respect to God is necessarily distinct from any other possible use of the concept of unity to describe particular aspects of the universe. As one modern writer put it most succinctly, "He is One, because there is no other God than He; but He is also One, because He is wholly unlike anything else in existence. He is therefore not only One, but the Sole and Unique God."[274] An early expression of this position is may be seen in an ancient work written some two millennia ago.

> God is alone, a single being: not a combination: a single nature: but each of us, and every other animal in the world, are compound beings . . . But God is not a compound Being, nor one which is made up of many parts, but one which has no mixture with anything else; for whatever could be combined with God must be either superior to Him, or equal to Him. But there is nothing equal to God, and nothing superior to Him, and nothing is combined with Him which is worse than himself; for if it were, He himself would be deteriorated; and if He were to suffer deterioration, He would also become perishable, which it is impious even to imagine. Therefore God exists according to oneness and unity.[275]

In similar fashion, it was suggested that the intrinsic unity of God should be conceived as radically different in character from the unity of a species composed of discrete members, or from the unity of an organism that is made up of interrelated yet relatively distinct elements. The unity of God, it is argued, cannot be conceived as either an aggregate or a synthesis, because the absolute singularity of God does not allow for the coexistence of other divine beings. If one were to conceive the existence of other divinities, they would have to be delimited in some manner since it would be possible to differentiate one from another only if each were considered to be inherently finite in form, dimension, or quality. But such constraints cannot apply to the true God since He is, by definition, boundless. It is therefore logically impossible, in this view, that God should be conceived as anything other than a unique infinite unity.[276] This argument has recently been recapitulated in the following formulation.

G-d is a unity, and His unity is singular in nature.
His unity, however, is not to be construed as a unity
composed of separate entities or powers; He is not to
be viewed as a genus composed of distinct beings. The
unity of G-d is not the unity of collectivity. Similarly,
the unity of G-d is not the unity of an aggregate. G-d
is not a compound that may be separated into discrete
elements; His unity is not the unity of a composite
divisible into its component parts. G-d's unity is not
the unity of a magnitude. It is a unity that cannot
admit of any division whatsoever. Clearly, G-d's unity
is unique and unparalleled.[277]

It has been suggested that the unique infinite unity of God is a
logical necessity when considered from a Judaic theological perspective.
"Two, or more, gods cannot be absolute. Two, according to the nature
of the concept, are relative . . . Two, or more, cannot be incorporeal,
because there must be limits separating one from another, and limits
belong to the world of corporeality. If there are two, or more, there
can be no basis for the concept of omnipotence, because each must
necessarily be limited in power and activity."[278]

This argument has been taken a step farther by asserting that the
idea of divine uniqueness incorporates the concepts of both God and
existence. That is, as one modern philosopher put it, "only God has
being. Only God is being. And there is no unity that would be an
identity between God and the world, no unity between world and
being. The world is appearance . . . only God is being. There is only
one kind of being, only one unique being: God is this unique being.
God is the Unique One." In this view, this idea is of fundamental
theological importance and is given expression in the "Hear, O Israel"
proclamation. Moreover, it is suggested, "throughout the development
of religion unity was realized as uniqueness, and this significance of
the unity of God as uniqueness brought about the recognition of the
uniqueness of God's being, in comparison with which all other being
vanishes and becomes nothing. Only God is being."[279]

The affirmation of the unique unity of God may justifiably be considered the pivotal doctrine of Judaism because virtually everything else in Judaism derives from it. It has been characterized as "a rich idea," one that means and implies a great deal. "The Unity of God may be said to range over, and include, almost all the parts of our faith respecting God's dealings and relations with mankind. Everything seems to turn upon it; all goes back to it; all flows out from it. No wonder, then, that our forefathers felt that this doctrine of God's unity was so central and so sacred that sooner than abandon it, sooner than admit any weakening or impoverishment of it, they would suffer, and they would die."[280] Thus, the doctrine of the unique unity of God precludes "every form of multiple and distributed divinity," at the same time that "it implies the unity of the universe, the fraternity of all men, and the unity of history."[281]

The idea of the unity of God was given perhaps its most poignant and most popular expression in the beautiful *Song of Glory (Shir haKavod)*, attributed to a twelfth century pietist, that was subsequently incorporated into the Sabbath liturgy. "I shall relate Your glory, though I see You not; I shall allegorize You, though I know You not. Through the hand of Your prophets, through the counsel of Your servants; You allegorized the splendorous glory of Your power . . . They allegorized You, but not according to Your reality, and they portrayed You according to Your deeds. They symbolized You in many varied visions; yet You are a Unity containing all the allegories."[282]

It has been emphasized that the declaration "is made about *Yahweh in particular*, not just about *deity in general . . .* It is not being said simply that there is ultimately only one divine reality . . . A philosophical monotheism that leaves the divine reality unnamed and characterless is alien (both unknown and hostile) to the OT faith. It is vital to see that, in OT terms, *it is Yahweh who defines what monotheism means*, not a concept of monotheism that defines how Yahweh should be understood."[283]

> [6.5] *And thou shalt love YHVH thy Elohim with all thy heart, and with all thy soul, and with all thy might.*

To begin to comprehend what this adjuration intends it is essential to clarify what we understand by the term "love." One definition proposes that love "is the feeling of striving to get the closest attachment to the other by completely giving oneself up to him and endeavoring to make him attached to you," which makes love "the most intimate bond between two beings."[284] With regard to what constitutes proper love for God, another suggests that one "should love the Lord so strongly that his spirit is bound to the love of God and drawn to it always like a lovesick person, whose mind is never free from the love of a certain woman and is drawn to her always whether he is standing or sitting, eating or drinking. More than this should be the love for the Lord continually in the heart of those who love Him all the time."[285] It also has been asserted, "One can say that love as an emotion is the anticipation of the reunion which takes place in every love-relation. Love, like all emotions, is an expression of the total participation of the being which is in an emotional state."[286] Moreover, it is argued that the consequence of rejecting this understanding of love as *eros* with respect to God "is that love towards God becomes an impossible concept to be replaced by obedience to God. But obedience is not love. It can be the opposite of love. Without the desire of man to be reunited with his origin, the love towards God becomes a meaningless word."[287] Alternatively, it has been argued, "nothing would be more erroneous than to limit these expressions to instinctive sensual desires which could also be directed to human persons. The whole man out of his innermost self, out of all the directions of his consciousness, must bring forth the love of God. How could sensual love be intended, how could it be thought of in this connection? In no way is this love for God a duty of the heart only, but it is the duty of the unity of man, and therefore primarily of the spirit."[288]

Do these arguments suggest that the culmination of love towards God rests in a mystical union in which the individual human is completely subsumed or annihilated? Not necessarily! It has also been argued, "love is the rational demand for wholeness, human integrity, and correlation; it is the quest for a union of our own half-worlds with what fulfills us as persons . . . The 'commandment to love' is thus not an impossible imperative demanding an unnatural emotional response but rather an expression of the fundamental, irreplaceable human need for personal integrity."[289] The problem with this, of course, is that it obscures the simple meaning of the biblical text by transmuting "commandment" into an "expression" of human need, essentially ignoring the clear imperative of the text.

It is noteworthy that this may well be "the first instance in human history that the *love* of god was demanded in any religion."[290] However, if one understands "love" to be an emotion or sentiment, the biblical demand defies comprehension. How can one be commanded to have a particular emotion or sentiment? It therefore seems clear that the love spoken of in this text must have a rather different meaning. Moreover, the text will later speak of *this commandment which I command you, to do it, to love YHVH your Elohim* (Deut. 11:22), raising the question of how an expression of action *to do it* can be applied to love, which is a matter of the heart. One response to this is that the love of God takes two forms, the first of which "is the natural yearning of the soul to its Creator. When the rational soul prevails over the grossness [of the body], subdues and subjugates it, then [the love of God] will flare and blaze with a flame which ascends of its own accord."[291] Or as a medieval writer put it, "The love of God is the demonstration of the soul's longing and inherent affinity for the Creator that gives it the capacity to cling to His supernal light . . . When the soul senses the presence of something that could augment its own light and power, if focuses its attention upon it, clings to it in thought, dwells on it, and desires and yearns for it. And that is an instance of pure love."[292] The second type "is a love which every man can attain when he will engage in profound contemplation in the depths of his heart on matters that arouse the love of G-d . . . Thus, there can be applied to this second type of love an expression of charge and command, namely, to devote one's heart and mind to matters which stimulate love. However, an expression of command and charge is not at all applicable to the first kind of love which is a flame that ascends of its own accord."[293]

With regard to the first kind of love described above, it has been suggested that "when man contemplates God's works and His great and marvelous creations, and sees from them wisdom that is without estimate or end—he immediately loves and praises and marvels and hungers to know the great Name, even as David said, *My soul thirsteth for Elohim, the living God* (Ps. 42:3)."[294] It would thus appear that a key ingredient to loving another is selflessness. "*To love God* is to be so imbued with the love of God that we are impelled, of our own accord, to give Him pleasure, so to speak, in the same way as a child sometimes feels moved to give pleasure to his father and mother."[295] It has been suggested that love of God is the highest form of love, as typified by Job, who could declare, *Though He slay me, yet will I trust in Him* (Job. 13:15). The implication of this is, as one modern writer puts it: "When I am aware that You, God, are there, everything is all right—not because the world is perfect, or all is well with my life, or because this makes me richer or happier. Life is all right because You exist, and that in itself provides all the satisfaction I need. Job's extreme statement defines the most unconditional kind of love."[296]

The implications of the demand that love of God should be *with all thy heart, and with all thy soul, and with all thy might* have been the subject of a great amount of speculation through the centuries. Thus, parsing the Hebrew term *levavkha* (*thy heart*), the rabbis inferred two alternate meanings. One deconstructed the term to *lev* (heart) and *bekha* (within you), yielding the meaning that you should love God "with all the heart that is within you," that is, you should be wholehearted with regard to your love.[297] As one writer put it, "*To be whole-hearted* is to serve God with pure motive, that is, for the sake of worship itself, and without any ulterior aim. The service of God demands whole-heartedness. That excludes both hesitancy and mechanical observance."[298]

Another interpretation considered the term *levav* as implying the plural of *lev*, and reading the text as demanding that you love God *with all thy hearts*, that is, with both of your natural inclinations, "the inclination to good and the inclination to evil."[299] How would one demonstrate his love for God with his evil inclination? It should be noted in this regard that, in the rabbinic view, the evil inclination is not inherently evil but merely represents those natural inclinations that, when overindulged in, can lead to evil. Such overindulgence is subject to man's conscious control, if he chooses to exercise it. As one commentator put it, even when you are engaged in following your evil inclination, redirect it to a good purpose, and in this manner you will change its character from evil to good.[300] It has been argued, however, that none of our inclinations are intrinsically good or bad. They only become good or bad according to whether they are used for divinely sanctioned purposes. Accordingly, "to love God with the whole of our heart means—to keep our whole mind—with all inclinations and in every direction—dedicated exclusively to accomplishing the Will of God."[301] In this regard it has been suggested that *heart* in this text means *mind*, which in the present context is a synonym for an "enlightened spirit."[302] Alternatively, it has been understood as saying that to love God with your whole heart means with a willingness to subordinate your most fervent desires to Him.[303] In this same vein, it has been suggested that *with all thy heart* is an allusion to man's moral autonomy and his inherent ability to choose freely.[304] It has also been suggested that *with all thy heart* is a logical corollary to the idea that *YHVH* alone is *Elohim*; that is, because there are no other gods, there is no reason for man's heart or mind to be diverted from total commitment to the One and Only God, as would be the case were he to come to believe in the existence of a pantheon.[305]

The Hebrew term *nefesh*, often translated as 'soul', usually refers to the life of each individual living creature both human and animal, and most likely it is in this sense that the term is used in the present text. Thus, the rabbis generally understood the adjuration to love God with all your soul as meaning to love God even if He takes your life, or as one rabbi put it, "love Him until the last drop of life is wrung out of you."[306] It is related in this regard that when he was about to be brutally executed by the Romans, the sage Rabbi Akiba recited the present text, explaining to his disciples: "All my days I have been troubled by this verse, *with all thy soul*, [which I interpret,] 'even if He takes my soul.' I said:: When shall I have the opportunity of fulfilling this? Now that I have the opportunity shall I not fulfill it?" He thus recited, *Hear, O Israel: YHVH our Elohim, YHVH is One*, prolonging the word One until he expired.[307] It is noteworthy that some have understood *with all thy soul* to mean that one should submit to martyrdom in sanctification of the divine name when circumstances call for it.[308]

The translation of the Hebrew phrase *bekhol me'odekha* (lit. 'with all your very-muchness') as *with all thy might* has been understood as meaning that one should love God with the "full concentration of feeling and power."[309] Another view takes it to refer to one's power of reason, that which distinguishes man from the rest of creation.[310] However, many render the phrase as *with all your possessions*, suggesting that one should be prepared to sacrifice one's wealth, if necessary, for the sake of the love of God. As explained by the rabbis: "There are men whose bodies are more precious to them than their wealth, and *with thy soul* is directed to them. There are other men whose wealth is more precious to them than their bodies, and *with all thy might* is directed to them."[311]

> *6.6 And these words, which I command thee this day, shall be upon thy heart; 6.7 and thou shalt teach them diligently unto thy children, and shalt talk of them when thou sittest in thy house, and when thou walkest by the way, and when thou liest down, and when thou risest up.*

Moses adjures the people to take the words that he is conveying to them seriously, for they are critical to the unique civilization and society they are to found in the land that they are about to enter. Moreover they each have a responsibility to assure continuity of adherence through *diligently* teaching them to the following generations. Implicit in this passage is a concern that these teachings are apt to be forgotten unless continually emphasized, discussed, and invoked whenever an opportunity presented itself. In this manner they would remain always fresh and vital. Moreover, it has been argued, the emphasis on *shalt talk of them* suggests that the basic formulation be repeated verbatim, without paraphrase, for the latter may easily introduce erroneous concepts; the integrity of the declaration of faith must always be maintained.[312] Accordingly, the words are to be recalled and discussed *when thou sittest in thy house*, that is, when you are home, perhaps with your family, a provision understood by some as indicating that "a man should conduct himself with due propriety in his house, so as to set an example to his household."[313] The words and the precepts of the Torah they imply are also to be recalled *when thou walkest by the way* engaged in conversation. Moreover, you should remain cognizant of them *when thou liest down, and when thou risest up.* That is your final thoughts before going to sleep should be of these words and their implications. It has been suggested that filling one's mind with noble thoughts will enable one to face the hours of darkness with greater confidence that he will pass the night untroubled.[314] Similarly, they should constitute your very first thoughts upon awakening, setting the religious tone and moral context for the mundane affairs that will preoccupy you throughout the day.

> [6.8] *And thou shalt bind them for a sign upon thy hand, and they shall be frontlets between thine eyes.*

These words are to be written and placed in devices that can be bound to one's hand as well as worn on the forehead, as constant reminders of the covenant into which the children of Israel have entered. As one commentator explained, "we are to bind on our hands as a symbol of 'binding duty,' and bind on our forehead as a symbol of 'directing our eyes and thoughts'."[315] It has been suggested that the *frontlets* refer to a headband, which was commonly worn in the region in biblical times.[316] Presumably, the bound words would have been attached to this headdress. The *sign* and *the frontlets* spoken of in this text were subsequently transformed into the *tefillin* or phylacteries, as we know them to this day, some of the knotting of which is traditionally held to have been revealed to Moses at Sinai.[317] Against this traditional view, it has been suggested that these requirements may originally have been meant to be taken figuratively rather than literally, to keep these teachings readily at hand and before one's eyes.[318]

> [6.9] *And thou shalt write them upon the door-posts of thy house, and upon thy gates.*

The text seems to be saying that the words should be directly inscribed on the doorposts. However, if the number of words that were to be inscribed corresponded to later tradition, it would have made such direct inscription impractical. Pursuant to a textual analysis, the rabbis concluded that the requirement *thou shalt write them* intended that the writing be on a scroll that would subsequently be attached a door post.[319] The rabbis also interpreted *upon thy gates* to include the gates of houses, courts, provinces, and cities.[320] The procedure followed was to place selected passages, written on parchment, in a variety of containers that could be attached to the doorposts of a house as well as at the point of entry into gated properties, a practice that continues to this day. The presence of these containers on one's doorposts serves as a reminder of the covenant whenever one enters or leaves the house or gated property. In effect, they serve as markers indicating the separation between the covenant-bound and the unbound outer world.

> *6.10 And it shall be, when YHVH thy Elohim shall bring thee into the land which He swore unto thy fathers, to Abraham, to Isaac, and to Jacob, to give thee great and goodly cities, which thou didst not build, 6.11 and houses full of all good things, which thou did not fill, and cisterns hewn out, which thou didst not hew, vineyards and olive trees, which thou did not plant, and thou shalt eat and be satisfied, 6.12 then beware lest thou forget YHVH, who brought thee forth out of the land of Egypt, out of the house of bondage.*

This passage reflects an evident concern on Moses' part about the future steadfastness of the children of Israel with regard to the covenant. They had exhibited recidivist tendencies in the past, when they still were under Moses' strong hand, and he was troubled by the prospect of their acting more impulsively in this regard once he no longer was on the scene. Indeed, he had good reason to be worried about their stubbornness coupled with short memory, which could prove to be a disastrous combination. Moses thus took the occasion to forcefully remind the Israelites that their very existence as a free people and nation, now and in the future, was contingent on their compliance with the covenant. He implicitly reminds them that the land they are about to inherit is one that they themselves, because of their perfidy, did not deserve. They are being given the land solely because God had promised it to the Patriarchs, a land rich with cities, houses, cisterns for storing rainwater, vineyards and forests, all of which were built and planted by others. They themselves had contributed nothing to the wealth they were about to inherit, and thus had no claim to any of it; it was being given to them only as a consequence of the covenant with God that they accepted unequivocally. Accordingly, Moses warns them not to forget their obligations to God, who alone liberated them from Egypt, an event to which they essentially contributed little if anything.

> *6.13 Thou shalt fear YHVH thy Elohim; and Him shalt thou serve, and by His name shalt thou swear. 6.14 Ye shall not go after other gods, of the gods of the peoples that are round about you; 6.15 for a jealous God, even YHVH thy Elohim, is in the midst of thee; lest the anger of YHVH thy Elohim be kindled against thee, and He destroy thee from off the face of the earth.*

Earlier, Moses spoke of the commandment *thou shalt love YHVH thy Elohim*, now he addresses the obverse side of the coin, presumably because he has little confidence that the people are truly ready for such a positive relationship. If they cannot as yet love God, they had better fear Him, for they are well aware, or at least should be, of the peril in provoking His wrath. They were not freed from the clutches of Pharaoh to be able to do as they please; they were liberated so that they would be enabled to live in consonance with the covenant into which they entered at Sinai. The price of their liberation from abject slavery in Egypt was voluntary servitude to a benign divine sovereign. That divine sovereign, however, is *a jealous God* and will not tolerate perfidy towards Him on the part of the children of Israel. He alone is their God, and just as the pagans commonly swear by the names of their various gods, the Israelites are to swear only by His name, a name not to be invoked improperly, and a name to be treated with the greatest respect if one is not to be guilty of sacrilege.

126

It is noteworthy that some have understood the phrase *by His name shalt thou swear* as establishing a positive obligation "to swear only by His Name (exalted be He), whenever we are required to confirm or deny something on oath, because by so doing we exalt, honor and magnify Him . . . Just as we are forbidden to take an oath for which there is no necessity, and this is a Negative Commandment, so we are commanded to take an oath when necessary, and this is a Positive Commandment."[321] However, it should be noted, others argue categorically that there is no such biblical obligation to swear for any reason, but if one should elect to take an oath he may do so only in His Name.[322]

Moses is implicitly also reminding the people that the pagan societies they will encounter in the promised land will appear quite different from the ragged and unsophisticated children of Israel. As had recently occurred, with their seduction by the Midianite women to participate in the orgy-worship of Baal-peor, they will face many similar temptations once they cross the Jordan. These, he warns them, must be avoided at all costs, because they will provoke God to *destroy thee from off the face of the earth.* In other words, they must always remember that their welfare is contingent on observance of the requirements of the covenant; any serious malfeasance on their part can lead to its nullification and their annihilation.

> *6.16 Ye shall not try YHVH your Elohim, as ye tried Him in Massah. 6.17 Ye shall diligently keep the commandments of YHVH your Elohim, and His testimonies, and His statutes, which He hath commanded thee. 6.18 And thou shalt do that which is right and good in the sight of YHVH; that it may be well with thee, and that thou mayest go in and possess the good land which YHVH swore unto thy fathers, 6.19 to thrust out all thine enemies from before thee, as YHVH hath spoken.*

Moses cautions the people against repeating the error of trying God's patience as they did some four decades earlier at Rephidim, renamed Massah (trying) because of the incident that occurred there when they experienced a shortage of water. They murmured against

Moses, *Wherefore hast thou brought us up out of Egypt, to kill us and our children and cattle with thirst* (Ex. 17:3), knowing that it was God and not Moses who had brought them out of Egypt. They thereby displayed not only a lack of gratitude but also of trust, something that God tolerated at the time but would do so no longer. However, he tells them, they can demonstrate their gratitude and trust by diligently complying with the variety of precepts and imperatives God has commanded them to obey.

In addition, Moses warns, *Ye shall not try YHVH your Elohim*, the meaning and intent of which are not entirely clear. In one opinion, this admonition constitutes a negative precept that prohibits a person from arrogantly asserting that he will perform one of the commandments and see if a blessing is forthcoming, in effect testing whether God will respond *quid pro quo*.[323] Alternatively, this text has been understood as an admonition not to once again ask, even implicitly, that God intervene supernaturally in their behalf, as was done repeatedly earlier. In effect, Moses advised them that the time of miracles that were needed to proclaim the reality of the divine presence in the world had passed and no new miracles were to be expected.[324] If this latter understanding of the text is correct, the historical implication is far-reaching, suggesting that Israel as a nation had now reached the point of maturity where it had to assume full responsibility for its future, without expectation that God would intervene to compensate for its misjudgments. This is not to suggest that God will not intervene in Israel's history in some manner but only that Israel may not assume that such intervention will in fact occur, or if it does take place that it will be in a preferred manner. Presumably, the character of future providential intrusions into history will be determined by how and to what extent Israel is deemed to have complied with the terms of its covenant with God.

Moreover, because not everything Israel should do as individuals and as a society can be encapsulated in a code of conduct, *thou shalt do that which is right and good in the sight of YHVH*. This has been understood broadly as asserting that it is not sufficient to do *that which is right*, what is permitted under law; the act must also be *good in the sight of YHVH*, that is, it should also be just, which may require going beyond the strict letter of the law. This has been interpreted as meaning, depending on circumstances, we should not be overly insistent on demanding our rights according to the law, but be prepared to accept a reasonable compromise when vital interests are not at stake, "where the advantage we forego is small and out of proportion to the advantage which the other party would gain by our relinquishment."[325] Thus, Moses adds that this should be done *that it may be well with thee.* What God wants the Israelites to construct in the land they are about to inherit is a just and moral society, not one that is merely legally correct. If you understand and accept this, then *thou mayest go in and possess the good land which YHVH swore unto thy fathers, to thrust out all thine enemies from before thee, as YHVH hath spoken.* The implication of the latter is that if the Israelites enter the land that awaits them to build a society on any other basis than what *is right and good in the sight of YHVH*, they will not have divine support.

As already indicated, the Israelites are not only to acknowledge and accept the divine commandments, they are also to transmit them to succeeding generations both through thought and deed. Thus,

> [6.20] *When thy son asketh thee in time to come, saying: 'What mean the testimonies, and the statutes, and the ordinances, which YHVH our Elohim hath commanded you?'* [6.21] *then shalt thou say unto thy son: 'We were Pharaoh's bondmen in Egypt; and YHVH brought us out of Egypt with a mighty hand.* [6.22] *And YHVH showed signs and wonders, great and sore, upon Egypt, upon Pharaoh, and upon all his house, before our eyes.* [6.23] *And He brought us out from thence, that He might bring us in, to give us the land which He swore unto our fathers.* [6.24] *And YHVH commanded us to do all these statutes, to fear YHVH our Elohim, for our good always, that He might preserve us alive, as it is at this day.* [6.25] *And it shall be righteousness unto us, if we observe to do all this commandment before YHVH our Elohim, as He hath commanded us.'*

Moses instructs that when your child asks you about the origin and significance of the panoply of observances and practices that characterize your society, you shall explain that their origin and basis is in the experience of their forefathers in Egypt, where they were enslaved by the Egyptian state, a status that they themselves could not alter or reverse. There they witnessed both the natural and supernatural blows that God inflicted on their oppressors, delivering them from their bondage, and ultimately giving them the land long ago promised to the Patriarchs. And, to ensure our future in the land, God ordained that we live by a special code of laws, and fear Him *for our good always,* that is, in our own self-interest, *that He might preserve us alive,* as evidenced by our continuing presence. And, when we are in compliance with that code of laws, *it shall be righteousness unto us,* that is, "it will be accounted to us as meritorious, and deserving of God's approval."[326] That is, even though we live by the commandments in our own self-interest, it nonetheless will be considered meritorious because we thus give testimony to our voluntary bending to the divine will.[327]

It is noteworthy that the various categories of law, the testimonies, understood broadly as commemorative practices relating for the most part to the exodus from Egypt, the ordinances, and the statutes mentioned at the beginning of the passage are subsequently subsumed under the category of statutes. The intent of this is not clear, although one commentator has asserted that its purpose is to indicate that just as statutes are understood to refer to those things that are between man and God, so too are the other categories "as the immoveable spheres drawn by God within which the whole of our spiritual, sexual and social lives are to unfold. The obligation rooted in the history of our origin makes them all into *hukim* [statutes], and ensures them eternal inviolable fulfillment."[328]

In this regard, it has been argued that, although from the standpoint of God all the various forms of laws and commandments are *hukim* [statutes], there is a significant difference between commandments and statutes from the standpoint of the people that are commanded to comply with them. Thus, in the penultimate sentence in the passage we are told that God *commanded us to do all these statutes, to fear YHVH our Elohim, for our good always, that He might preserve us alive.* By contrast, the final sentence asserts, *it shall be righteousness unto us, if we observe to do all this commandment.* That is, we are commanded *to do* the statutes, but it will be considered meritorious if we *observe to do* the commandments, the difference in language begging for explication. It is argued that the phrase *observe to do* is not used with regard to the statutes because, as the text clearly indicates, the statutes are divine laws that should be obeyed out of fear of God. Accordingly, it is sufficient to demand of us *to do* them, notwithstanding that there is also a *quid pro quo* for complying with them, namely *that He might preserve us alive.* By contrast, the commandments are divine laws that are complied with out of love for God and not because of any expectation of reward for obedience. Accordingly, we are urged to *observe to do* them, that is, to do them not because we must but because we choose to do so out of reverence for God. Such observance shall be considered *righteousness unto us.*[329]

It has also been suggested that what the child may be asking regarding the *testimonies* is why there are no new ones, only those relating to the increasingly distant past. Why, he may want to know, are there no longer such miracles and divine signs now, and why is the world so different from what it was in the past when God was so directly involved in the life of the people? Understood from this perspective, the appropriate response to the query is that the miracles and signs occurred only at the time of the exodus; subsequently it is conformity with God's law that determines our collective future.[330]

From what Moses says next it seems clear that he had an abiding concern about the steadfastness of substantial segments of the children of Israel and their susceptibility to assimilation into the cultures of the various peoples and nations they will confront in the land.

> *7.1 When YHVH your Elohim shall bring thee into the land whither thou goest to possess it, and shall cast out many nations before thee, the Hittite, and the Girgashite, and the Amorite, and the Canaaanite, and the Perizzite, and the Hivite, and the Jebusite, seven nations greater and mightier than thou; 7.2 and when YHVH thy Elohim shall deliver them up before thee, and thou shalt smite them; then thou shalt utterly destroy them; thou shalt make no covenant with them, nor show mercy unto them; 7.3 neither*

> shalt thou make marriages with them: thy daughter thou
> shalt not give unto his son, nor his daughter shalt thou
> take unto thy son. [7.4] *For he will turn away thy son from*
> *following Me, that they may serve other gods; so will the*
> *anger of YHVH be kindled against you, and He will*
> *destroy thee quickly.* [7.5] *But thus shall ye deal with them:*
> *ye shall break down their altars, and dash in pieces their*
> *pillars, and hew down their Asherim, and burn their*
> *graven images with fire.*

Moses tells the people that there are seven nations occupying the land promised to them, and that God will cast them out to be replaced by the children of Israel. That is, the Israelites will invade the land, but their ability to overcome the resistance of the nations there will be a direct consequence of providential assistance. True, they will have to fight hard, but their efforts alone will not assure victory, until God *shall deliver them up before thee, and thou shalt smite them.* Because victory ultimately will be contingent on the divine will, the usual rules of war will not apply. Whereas a defeated nation would be compelled to become a vassal of the victor, paying tribute and providing slaves, this was not to happen in this case. Instead, with regard to the seven nations that you will challenge for control of the land, *thou shalt utterly destroy them; thou shalt make no covenant with them, nor show mercy unto them.* That is, you shall destroy them entirely as political entities in the land; there are to be no suzerainty treaties with them and no concessions that would allow them to retain a semblance of nationhood. However, these demands only apply to the seven nations as nations. It does not apply to the individual members of those nations that survive the wars, as is made clear in the remainder of the passage.

The principal concern of the text here is with a second kind of idolatry, the kind arising from cultural tensions. "Here we are not talking about an idealistic, 'higher' attraction to idolatry [of the sort resulting from spiritual confusion discussed earlier]. It is not the ideas or ideals of a particular religion . . . instead, it is the desire to associate with a particular nation, or cultural experience—the need to belong, to merge with the cultural expressions of another group."[331] In short, what is at issue here is idolatry via assimilation, and to prevent this, dramatic steps needed to be taken. In antiquity, there was no distinction between the secular and the religious. Accordingly, the national identity of the polytheistic peoples of the land could not be sustained in any organized sense alongside that of Israel; it had to be eliminated completely.

Thus, once you have destroyed them as political entities, you are forbidden to *make marriages with them: thy daughter thou shalt not give unto his son, nor his daughter shalt thou take unto thy son.* By inference, the Israelites are permitted to live peaceably with the peoples of these former nations, as they do with the "mixed multitude" of non-Israelites that accompanied them during the exodus from Egypt. However, there is to be no integration with them through marriage. This prohibition is not based on ethnic grounds; mixed marriages as such are not categorically excluded. Thus, later law specifically permitted marriage with a female captive taken in war (Deut. 21:10-14). "What was ruled out here was the kind of intermarrying that involved the social bonding of families and joint religious rituals."[332] Although the original prohibition (Ex. 34:16) mentioned only the marriage of sons to alien women, here the injunction is expanded to apply equally to mixed marriages of sons as well as daughters, there being an implicit expectation that there would be a surplus of such marriage-eligible females because of the large number of men killed in the wars. The change has also been interpreted as a "reassessment of women, whereby they were treated as equal partners with men within the covenant community,"[333] although the evidence for this is rather skimpy. In either case, as before, the larger concern is with the marriage of an Israelite son to the daughter of a non-Israelite, Israelite men having already proven their greater susceptibility to the seductions of pagan cultic practices. As the text expresses it, presumably because of the strong ties of daughters to their fathers, the non-Israelite father in-law *will turn away thy son from following Me, that they may serve other gods.* This will infuriate God, especially since it negates the very purpose for allowing the Israelites to dispossess the other nations, and the divine anger will *be kindled against you, and He will destroy thee quickly.*

To prevent such religious perversion from taking place, *ye shall break down their altars, and dash in pieces their pillars, and hew down their Asherim, and burn their graven images with fire.* That is, you shall eliminate any public vestige of paganism in the land. The pagans among you may continue to believe what they will, but a condition of their continued residence among you is that there be no overt pagan practices, every vestige of which must be entirely destroyed. The reason why this harsh approach must be taken, Moses assures them, is because of the special role assigned to the children of Israel in the divine scheme.

> *7.6 For thou art a holy people unto YHVH thy Elohim: YHVH thy Elohim hath chosen thee to be His own treasure, out of all peoples that are upon the face of the earth. 7.7 YHVH did not set His love upon you, nor choose you, because ye were more in number that any people, for ye were the fewest of all peoples, 7.8 but because YHVH loved you, and because He would keep the oath which He swore unto your fathers, hath YHVH brought you out with a mighty hand, and redeemed you out of the house of bondage, from the hand of Pharaoh king of Egypt.*

Moses reminds them that they have been chosen to be *a holy people unto YHVH thy Elohim*, the term *holy* understood here as meaning set aside for God's purposes, a unique privilege granted only to them *out of all peoples that are upon the face of the earth.* Why did God do this? Clearly, it was not because they were the largest in number of the distinct peoples of the world; in fact they were among smallest in population. They were chosen, not because of any special aptitude or characteristic that made them superior to any other people, but only because God *loved you*, a love that you actually may not have merited, *and because He would keep the oath which He swore unto your fathers*, which was therefore irrevocable. This suggests that the divine love for Israel, notwithstanding their considerable faults, was a consequence of His commitment to the Patriarchs, which alone explains why He *brought you out with a mighty hand, and redeemed you out of the house of bondage.* In a sense, Moses may be understood as saying that because of His love for Abraham, Isaac, and Jacob, He was saddled with their descendents whom He loved because of their ancestors. In this regard, it has been observed that the Hebrew term used for "love" in this passage is *heshek*, which is normally used to describe blind, non-rational love. "This love is like the love (*heshek*) which has no reason, but is due solely to the will of the lover. And it is this love which was promised to the people at the time of the Sinaitic revelation, as a reward for accepting the Torah."[334] However, this unconditional love does not mean that God would not show 'tough love' for the Patriarchs' often-wayward offspring, when called for by their inappropriate actions.

> *7.9 Know therefore that YHVH thy Elohim, He is Elohim; the faithful God, who keepeth covenant and mercy with them that love Him and keep His commandments to a thousand generations[335]; 7.10 and repayeth them that hate Him to their face, to destroy them; He will not be slack to him that hateth Him, He will repay him to his face. 7.11 Thou shalt therefore keep the commandment, and the statutes, and the ordinances, which I command thee this day, to do them.*

This section of Moses' second discourse concludes with the warning that God's unconditional love for Israel should not be abused, for there are positive long-lasting consequences for them *that love Him and keep His commandments*. It has been suggested that *love Him* refers to those who act out of love for God, whereas *keep His commandments* refers to those whose observance derives from the fear of God.[336] Although acting out of love clearly would be preferred, acting out of fear will well serve those incapable of the former. In the final analysis, the main thing is to act in accordance with the terms of the covenant, for there will be dire consequences for those *that hate Him . . . He will not be slack to him that hateth Him, He will repay him to his face.* That is, according an early commentary, God will repay those who hate Him, during their lifetimes, for whatever good they have done, and exact retribution from them later.[337] Accordingly, prudence alone urges compliance with the range of laws that Moses will set before them.

3

EKEV

(7:12-11:25)

Moses continues his discourse, turning momentarily from the preceding admonitions to a brief account of the blessings to be realized from faithful compliance with the requirements of the covenant.

> *7.12 And it shall come to pass, because ye hearken to these ordinances, and keep, and do them, that YHVH thy Elohim shall keep with thee the covenant and the mercy which He swore unto thy fathers, 7.13 and He will love thee, and bless thee, and multiply thee; He will also bless the fruit of thy body and the fruit of thy land, thy corn and thy wine and thine oil, the increase of thy kine and the young of thy flock, in the land which He swore unto thy fathers to give thee. 7.14 Thou shalt be blessed above all peoples; there shall not be male or female barren among you, or among your cattle. 7.15 And YHVH will take away from thee all sickness; and He will put none of the evil diseases of Egypt, which thou knowest, upon thee, but will lay them upon all them that hate thee.*

The rabbis assumed that Moses is now repeating what he originally said to the children of Israel at the time of the exodus to assuage their concerns about whether the land they were going to might be economically inferior to Egypt, where they were able to sustain themselves notwithstanding the forced labor and other indignities to which they were subjected. The point of the oration was to affirm that

136

the land to which they were going was superior in many respects to the one they were leaving behind.[338]

Moses chooses his words here very carefully, saying *ekev tishme'un et hamishpatim haeleh* or *because ye hearken to these ordinances*, the term *hearken*, meaning hearing in the sense of internalizing what one hears, taking it to heart or imbedding it in one's mind. In effect, Moses is teaching that such conceptual internalization is a critical precursor to keeping or preserving the teachings and then proceeding to *do them*. The question has been asked as to why the text states *because ye hearken* rather than "because you carry out or do," which is after all what is desired? The rabbis responded by pointing out that at the revelation at Mount Sinai, Moses *took the book of the covenant, and read in the hearing of the people; and they said: 'All that YHVH hath spoken will we do [naaseh], and obey [or hearken--venishma]* (Ex. 24:7), placing *doing* before *hearkening*. However, it only took a few days before they negated their *doing* with respect to God's commandments, as it states, *they have made them a molten calf, and have worshipped it, and have sacrificed to it* (Ex. 32:8), leaving them only with *hearkening*. For this reason, from that point on Moses only instructed them with regard to *hearkening*, such as *Hear, O Israel* (Deut 6:4), *if ye shall hearken* (Deut. 11:13), *hear all these words which I command thee* (Deut. 12:28) in the hope that *hearkening* might once again result in actually *doing*.[339]

It should be noted at this point that the traditional rabbinic interpretation of *keep, and do them* understands *keep* as observing those laws that call upon one to desist from a forbidden action, and *do* as referring to those laws that demand action.[340] His message would thus appear to be that God is not interested in mindless pro forma compliance with His laws. Presumably those who act in such a manner are always readily susceptible to external influences that will cause them to act in an unacceptable manner. Moreover, it has been argued that *because ye hearken to these ordinances* implies that the benefits described later are a direct consequence of taking these ordinances to heart, that is, self-enforcing them as a matter of your own will to follow God's will, and not because your reason finds them appropriate.[341]

Moses again makes clear that the promises of beneficence made to the Patriarchs regarding their descendents are conditional on the latter actually meriting them. That is, the promise to the Patriarchs that their descendents will inherit the land is irrevocable; however, the ability of the present generation of the children of Israel to enjoy it in prosperity is contingent on their complying with the terms of the covenant. Should they fully comply with the terms, it will evoke divine love and the blessings that flow from that love will be showered upon them. Should they fail to do so, the promised blessings will be given to a later generation.[342]

These assertions raise the question as to whether these blessings are "in exchange for" or *quid pro quo* for obedience,[343] or whether there is a cause and effect relationship at work, as many commentators maintain. Thus adopting the former understanding, the ArtScroll translation renders the text *This shall be the reward when you hearken to these ordinances*.[344] Arguing in favor of the latter proposition, it is noted that Moses speaks here only of *mishpatim* or *ordinances*, evidently subsuming the *mitzvot* (commandments), the *edut* (testimonies), and the *hukim* (statutes) spoken of earlier under the general rubric of *mishpatim* (ordinances). It has been suggested that *mishpatim* in this text should be understood in the sense that *mishpat* is employed in the teaching of the biblical sage, *The king by justice [mishpat] establisheth the land* (Prov. 29:4).[345] In other words, *mishpatim* in this text should be understood as 'acts of justice' rather than 'ordinances' in the conventional sense. As one commentator put it: "At rock bottom they are all nothing but 'legal maxims' with which the most varied conditions and relationships of the spiritual and material life of the individual and state have to be carried out, so that they are in accordance with the yardstick *tzedek* [justice], the Divine ideal for all conditions of the world. As such, as the duty we owe to what is right, for which no thanks and no reward can be claimed, are they to be carried out." But, because they conform so harmoniously with "the nature and purpose of things and men . . . by their being faithfully carried out by the nation, a condition of the richest blessings of a national existence on earth emerges."[346] In other words, it is argued, the blessings that Moses speaks of are not *quid pro quo* for compliance, but will follow automatically *ekev* (on the 'heel' of) as cause and effect of such compliance. Moreover, subsuming the various types of rules and regulations under a single rubric, as Moses does here, suggests that no general distinction is to be made between them in terms of relative importance or priority. In principle, all have equal weight, even though specific circumstances may require ad hoc prioritization.

As a consequence of compliance, they are assured *thou shalt be blessed above all peoples.* In what way will they be so blessed? It has been suggested that the meaning of this assertion is simply that the peoples of the land currently are able to pursue their livelihoods and welfare with comparative ease, whereas the Israelites can only look forward to long periods of war. Nonetheless, Moses asserts, the children of Israel will ultimately become more prosperous than those they displace.[347] Not only will their numbers increase through the fruit of the womb, the fertility of the land itself will yield large quantities of its natural commodities, corn or grain, wine, and oil, and their livestock, calves and lambs, will multiply as well, assuring their prosperity, as promised.

The blessing of fertility, of both humans and livestock, will surpass that of all the other peoples found in the land, something that will be achieved by direct divine intervention that will inure you to the diseases common to the region, especially those that typically afflicted Egypt, such as elephantiasis, opthalmia, and dysentery,[348] with which you are quite familiar. In this regard it has been suggested that the phrases *kol holi,* translated as *all sickness,* and *kol madvei mitzrayim harayim,* translated as *none of the evil diseases of Egypt,* but better rendered as *all the bad maladies of Egypt,* refer to acute and chronic conditions, respectively.[349] Instead of afflicting you, they will be diverted to your enemies, who will thereby be diverted from attempting to take steps to harm you.[350] It has been suggested that Moses said this because the Israelites earlier expressed concern that they had been brought to the wilderness to die. Not so, he now assures them, not only does God not have any evil in mind for you, He will even divert from you those diseases that are endemic in the region, and which there was much greater fear of contracting in Egypt.[351] This appears to suggest that though some of these diseases may be naturally contagious, Israel nonetheless will remain unaffected by them.[352]

With regard to the latter text, one cannot but ask whether these assertions are to be taken literally or figuratively. It would appear that at least some of the rabbis read the text from the latter perspective, evidently being troubled by the implication that the Israelites would thrive only because they were unnaturally protected against diseases that afflicted their neighbors or even strangers living among them. Accordingly, they sought alternative non-miraculous explanations of the text. They thus interpreted these statements as referring to psychosomatic illnesses resulting from fear and worry about life's uncertainties, which might exacerbate the consequences of other natural illnesses. Alternatively, the statements were understood as referring to weakened immunity to disease brought about by succumbing to unhealthful desires; "the evil inclination being sweet at the beginning and bitter in the end."[353] Presumably, alleviation of such concerns or behaviors because of faith in divine beneficence and enhanced self-control would have the positive health effects mentioned.

> [7.16] *And thou shalt consume all the peoples that YHVH thy Elohim shall deliver unto thee; thine eye shall not pity them; neither shalt thou serve their gods; for that will be a snare unto thee.*

The idea of 'consuming' the peoples of the land, spoken of in the opening verse of this passage, probably should be understood as suggesting the destruction of their collective national identities, as ruthlessly as necessary, but not necessarily as figuratively devouring their individual remnants. Moses had already informed the Israelites more than once that they were not to intermarry with them, even though they were allowed to remain under Israel's domination, a demand that would be pointless if there was any expectation of annihilation of the alien population. Accordingly, given the most recent experience of the sacrilegious behavior of many Israelites that were induced to worship Baal-peor, Moses explicitly warns them once again about the danger inherent in serving the gods of the peoples they would conquer, *for that will be a snare unto thee.* To be enticed into so doing would be to court the same sort of disaster that struck those Israelites who earlier had the temerity to affront God with their perversion to idolatry.

Accordingly, Moses insists, *thine eye shall not pity them.* One may ask why Moses here associates the trait of mercy with the eyes rather than with the heart, as one might have expected. It has been argued that this is indeed an anomaly because, in biblical writing generally, it is the heart that is the repository and source of emotions such as pity. However, in this instance, the emphasis on the eyes is more *a propos.* God commands the children of Israel to annihilate the forces of the nations in the land, and this command may resonate in one's heart as appropriate because God so willed it. However, when one actually confronts the enemy in combat and sees him as another fellow human being, he may find it very difficult to kill that person once he no longer poses an imminent threat. Because of this, Moses insists, *thine eye shall not pity them.*[354] That is, if "you let your feelings of pity rule you, thinking that you will be more merciful than Heaven itself, know that this is the sort of logic used by idolaters."[355] In this matter you must rely on divine judgment rather than on your own conception of propriety, which may deceptively lead you into the great danger of defiance of God.

It is noteworthy that the term *pity* has more than one connotation; on the one hand it may mean heartfelt sympathy or compassion, and on the other hand it may refer to a sense of regret at the apparent waste involved in seeing something useful being neglected or destroyed. The Hebrew term in our text translated as *shall not pity* is *lo tahos*, which is used to convey the latter meaning rather than the former, which would more like be *lo terahem.* In other words, Moses is cautioning the Israelites not to constrain their destruction of the nations in the land by pitying the loss of productive manpower that could be subjected to slavery if the enemy were captured rather than killed.[356] That is, in this instance they must go against the grain of their natural inclinations and act mercilessly toward the nations they will encounter in the land; not to do so out of either genuine pity or pragmatic considerations will put them at great future risk. However, the extreme approach called for in this instance is to be treated as "an exception, expressly commanded by God, to be done at His bidding because of special circumstances."[357] The demand also reflects the view that to fail in this regard would be the same as attempting to thwart divine justice. Since the tenure of nations is divinely determined, it is not proper for the Israelites to second-guess God's historical determinations. As one commentator put it, "through the pity of judges all justice may be lost."[358]

> *7.17 If thou shalt say in thy heart: 'These nations are more than I; how can I dispossess them?' 7.18 thou shalt not be afraid of them; thou shalt well remember what YHVH thy Elohim did unto Pharaoh, and unto all Egypt: 7.19 the great trials which thine eyes saw, and the signs, and the wonders, and the mighty hand, and the outstretched arm, whereby YHVH thy Elohim brought thee out; so shall YHVH thy Elohim do unto all the peoples of whom thou art afraid. 7.20 Moreover YHVH thy Elohim will send the hornet among them, until they that are left, and they that hide themselves, perish from before thee. 7.21 Thou shalt not be affrighted at them; for YHVH thy Elohim is in the midst of thee, a God great and awful.*

Implicitly recalling what took place thirty-eight years earlier, when the Israelites were poised to enter the land from Kadesh-barnea and were deterred from so doing by the destruction of their morale by their tribal leaders, Moses warns them against repeating the error of the earlier generation. Even if they never dare to express openly their potentially debilitating fears that the enemy awaiting them across the frontier may be more powerful than they, and that the Israelites may not be able to dislodge them, Moses adjures them to *remember what YHVH thy Elohim did unto Pharaoh, and unto all Egypt*, which surely were more powerful than the aggregate of all the minor kingdoms they would encounter across the Jordan. In other words, Moses is well aware that, in the aggregate, the seven nations they will encounter in the land may indeed be greater in number both of population and military forces than Israel. Acknowledgment of this by the people may engender thoughts of perhaps only trying to take part of the country, thereby limit the opposition to them, and to make peace with the rest.[359] This might be a sound assessment of the situation under normal circumstances, but this was not a normal situation because it did not take into account that God was on their side, thus giving the Israelites effective power beyond what they could otherwise muster. Accordingly, Moses tells them, *thou shalt not be afraid of them.* Of course, Moses' command in this regard is intrinsically meaningless, given that fear is an involuntary emotion that cannot be turned off because Moses so insisted. What gives his command authority is the assertion that God is on their side. Accepting that they have such a powerful ally with them should significantly diminish if not eliminate their fear entirely, and to impress this on them Moses invokes their memory of God's interventions on their behalf.[360]

It is curious that Moses made reference to *the great trials which thine eyes saw, and the signs, and the wonders, and the mighty hand, and the outstretched arm, whereby YHVH thy Elohim brought thee out; so shall YHVH thy Elohim do unto all the peoples of whom thou art afraid,* when in fact only the surviving elders among the Israelites, as children, would have witnessed any of those signs and wonders. It would seem that a more *a propos* reminder would have been their recent defeat of the Amorite kings in Transjordan and their conquest and occupation of the territories of Gilead and Bashan. Indeed, Moses had earlier reminded them of his command to Joshua: *Thine eyes have seen all that YHVH your Elohim hath done unto these two kings; so shall YHVH do unto all the kingdoms wither thou goest over. Ye shall not fear them; for YHVH your Elohim, He it is that fighteth for you* (Deut. 3:21-22). One might speculate that Moses made this reference deliberately to remind the younger generation that it was not the successful wars against the Amorites, in which they played an active role, that was the basis for the covenant by which they were obligated to abide, but the events of the exodus, in which the people as a whole played a virtually completely passive role.

In any case, Moses assured them that they would be victorious, no matter the odds against success, because God would be with them. Indeed, their victory would be so overwhelming that even those remnants of the armies of the nations that took refuge in caves would be forced out into the open to be destroyed, thus eliminating any potential threat of a protracted guerrilla war. Indeed, if necessary to accomplish this, God *will send the hornet among them* to drive them out of their hiding places, an assertion that clearly appears to be a bit of morale-raising hyperbole. In sum, Moses assured his audience, there was no reason whatever to be concerned about the enemy that awaited them across the Jordan *for YHVH thy Elohim is in the midst of thee, a God great and awful.* If they are to be afraid of anything, it should be of God and nothing else.

> *7.22 And YHVH thy Elohim will cast out those nations before thee little by little; thou mayest not consume them quickly, lest the beasts of the field increase upon thee. 7.23 But YHVH thy Elohim shall deliver them up before thee, and shall discomfit them with a great discomfiture, until they be destroyed. 7.24 And he shall deliver their kings into thy hand, and thou shalt make their name to perish from under heaven; there shall no man be able to stand against thee, until you have destroyed them.*

However, Moses forewarns them, they are not to expect that once they invade the land the resistance of their enemies will collapse suddenly. It will not happen this way. Instead, God *will cast out those nations before thee little by little.* Accordingly, you will *not consume them quickly, lest the beasts of the field increase upon thee.* It has been suggested that the meaning of this is that if the conquest were to be completed too quickly, "large areas would be left desolate, in which wild beasts would multiply."[361] This implies that the Israelites were too few in number to occupy the entire country, and that God would therefore initially give them only as much of the territory as they could effectively occupy, doling out the remainder as their population grew.[362]

However, a more compelling argument can and has been made that the text should be understood as alluding to something rather different and politically more realistic. If the Israelite invasion of Cisjordan were to be seen as a common threat to all the disparate and routinely quarreling nations there, it might compel those nations, metaphorically *the beasts of the field*, to form a defensive alliance that could make the ultimate conquest more difficult, forcing the Israelites to delay settlement of the country until it was conquered entirely. By attacking one national entity at a time, the threat to all would not appear imminent, and the likelihood of a common defense among normally contending rulers would be greatly diminished, facilitating incremental conquest and settlement of the country.[363] As a practical matter, the conquest had to be done piecemeal because the Israelites were neither equipped nor able to attack multiple fortified cities simultaneously, nor to challenge powerful chariot forces and cavalry in open field combat. Thus, incrementally, God *shall deliver them up before thee, and shall discomfit them with a great discomfiture, until they be destroyed.* It has been argued that the phrase *until they be destroyed* should not be construed as commanding a war of total annihilation, for if this were the case, as noted earlier, there would be little point in prohibiting intermarriage with them. The phrase therefore can relate only to their men at arms.[364]

Moreover, Moses asserts, *He shall deliver their kings into thy hand, and thou shalt make their name to perish from under heaven.* It has been observed that this adjuration suggests that on no account should the heirs to the throne of a defeated nation be spared, because history demonstrates that they will tend to become a thorn in one's side as they vie to recover their lost power. In this regard, we are told elsewhere what occurred later when this advice was ignored: *And YHVH raised up an adversary unto Solomon, Hadad the Edomite; he was of the king's seed in Edom. For it came to pass, when David was in Edom, and Joab the captain of the host . . . had cut off every male in Edom that Hadad fled, he and certain Edomites of his father's servants with him, to go into Egypt; Hadad being yet a little child* (1 Kings 11:14-18). After David died and Solomon succeeded him, Hadad emerged as a force that Solomon had to deal with.[365] Related to this is the assertion *there shall no man be able to stand against thee, until you have destroyed them,* which may be understood as stating that with the disappearance of the royal line in these nations, there will be no rallying point around which to reconstitute an armed force capable of challenging the Israelites, and those that do attempt such a challenge would easily be eliminated.[366] This interpretation reflects a reasonable assessment of the situation in the ancient world, in which popular national liberation movements simply did not exist.

The intentional delay in the total conquest also comports with the divine scheme as laid out in the texts. Thus, God originally told Abraham that his *seed shall be a stranger in a land that is not theirs . . . four hundred years . . . And in the fourth generation they shall come back hither; for the iniquity of the Amorite is not yet full* (Gen. 15:13-16). Jacob and his sons subsequently went to Egypt, where they ultimately became enslaved. *And it came to pass in the course of those many days that the king of Egypt died; and the children of Israel sighed by reason of the bondage, and they cried, and their cry came up unto Elohim by reason of their bondage. And Elohim heard their groaning, and Elohim remembered His covenant with Abraham, with Isaac, and with Jacob* (Ex, 2:23-24). This text suggests that Israel's servitude was so harsh that God decided that they should leave their exile in Egypt long before the four centuries He had foretold Abraham, many believing the period of servitude to have been no more than two hundred and ten years. The problem this early termination entailed was that, as Abraham had been told, *the iniquity of the Amorite* was still *not yet full*. Accordingly, by Israel conquering the land piecemeal, a process that took about two hundred years, during which *the beasts of the field* never united against them in common cause, both *the iniquity of the Amorite* and the *four hundred years* of homelessness would have reached their respective limits.

> *7.25 The graven images of their gods shall ye burn with fire; thou shalt not covet the silver or the gold that is on them, nor take it unto thee, lest thou be snared therein; for it is an abomination to YHVH thy Elohim. 7.26 And thou shalt not bring an abomination into thy house, and be accursed like unto it; thou shalt utterly detest it, and thou shalt utterly abhor it; for it is a devoted thing.*

When they defeat the various rulers in the land and conquer their territories, Moses insists, they must take steps to assure that there remain no visible appurtenances of polytheistic worship. *The graven images of their gods shall ye burn with fire.* That is, they must be totally destroyed or effaced beyond recognition. This, Moses asserts, is necessary to preclude leaving them intact because of the value of

their silver or golden contents, *lest thou be snared therein*, and become a
victim of divine wrath. Presumably, ancient idols were frequently made
of wood but overlaid with precious metals, and those who come across
them might be tempted to benefit from the value of those coverings.
Therefore he admonishes, *thou shalt not covet the silver or the gold that
is on them*, which might cause you to delay destroying them.[367] The
stringency of this prohibition is such, that according to one rabbinic
legal authority, "Even if they have been broken and melted down or
sold to a *Gentile*, it is forbidden to draw profit from the price obtained
for them."[368] There are to be no trophies of this sort, for their very
presence in land under Israel's control would constitute *an abomination
to YHVH thy Elohim.* Indeed, they are forbidden even to allow such
objects into their homes, which will result in their being *accursed like
unto it.* In short, such objects are to be abhorred and detested--*for it
is a devoted thing*; that is, it is *herem*, a proscribed thing with which
contact is categorically forbidden.

> [8.1] *All this commandment which I command thee this day
> shall ye observe to do, that you may live, and multiply, and
> go in and possess the land which YHVH swore unto your
> fathers.* [8.2] *And thou shalt remember all the way which
> YHVH thy Elohim hath led thee these forty years in the
> wilderness, that He might afflict thee, to prove thee, to
> know what was in thy heart, whether thou wouldest keep
> His commandments, or no.* [8.3] *And He afflicted thee, and
> suffered thee to hunger, and fed thee with manna, which
> thou knewest not, neither did thy fathers know; that He
> might make thee know that man doth not live by bread
> only, but by every thing that proceedeth out of the mouth
> of YHVH doth man live.* [8.4] *Thy raiment waxed not old
> upon thee, neither did thy foot swell, these forty years.*
> [8.5] *And thou shalt consider in thy heart, that, as a man
> chasteneth his son, so YHVH thy Elohim chasteneth thee.*

Moses again reminds his audience that there is an indissoluble
contingent relationship between observance of the requirements of the

covenant and the ability of the children of Israel to *possess the land which YHVH swore unto your fathers.* Moreover, Moses stipulates, *All this commandment which I command thee this day shall ye observe to do.* That is, he is not providing them with a menu of commandments from which they are free to choose which ones they will observe and do; they must observe and do *all* of them.[369]. Moses' point is that God has not intervened in history to liberate the Israelites and give them a national homeland in order for them to do as they please. He wants them to create a new civilization characterized by morality and justice, and toward this end has given them clear guidelines for building that civilization. Of course, like all humanity, they have been granted moral autonomy and can choose to act contrary to those divine guidelines. However, should they so choose to do, Moses puts them on notice that God is under no obligation to assist or even allow them to prosper in *the land which YHVH swore unto your fathers.* It has been suggested that Moses mentions *that you may live, and multiply* to draw the contrast between the present and the preceding generation that was doomed to die in the wilderness because of their essential faithlessness.[370] Therefore, if you want to *live, and multiply, and go in and possess the land,* you should bear in mind the experience that you, as a nation, underwent for forty years in the wilderness.[371]

It should be noted that the Hebrew term translated as *shall ye observe* is *tishmerun*, rather than *tishmeru*, which is the way the plural imperative would normally be stated. Some have taken the anomalous addition of a final letter *nun* as indicating a diminution. That is, the addition of the final *n* is understood to suggest that the extent of the commanded observation is not absolute but relative to circumstances. Thus, it has been argued that the term implies that not all of the commandments that Moses will unveil are immediately applicable; some will be actionable only after the conquest and settlement. Nonetheless, they are to be safeguarded in memory so that they may be applied when circumstances permit.[372] While this is an interesting homiletic gloss on Moses' statement, it is not clear how this interpretation would apply to the other numerous instances in which the term *tishmerun* or other words bearing a seemingly superfluous final *nun* appear in the biblical text.

In this presentation, perhaps for the first time, Moses undertakes an exposition of the divine purpose behind the four decades-long tribulations in the wilderness, which was *that He might afflict thee, to prove thee, to know what was in thy heart, whether thou wouldest keep His commandments, or no.* The purpose, he asserts, was to determine whether the children of Israel were able to become trustworthy partners to the covenant, meriting the fulfillment of the divine commitment to the Patriarchs through them. It has been suggested that the statement *to know what was in thy heart* is an oblique reference to the notion that man inherently embodies two inclinations, one that directs him to the good and the other to the contrary, the bad or the evil. The question is whether the children of Israel have the will to subordinate their naturally evil inclinations to the good inclination, which will lead them to observe and carry out the divine laws that are being bequeathed to them.[373] This will determine what takes place next. They must bear in mind that there was a point earlier, during the incident of the golden calf, when God indicated that He was prepared to wipe out the children of Israel and fulfill His promise through Moses and his direct descendents alone. *And YHVH said unto Moses: 'I have seen this people, and, behold, it is a stiff-necked people. Now therefore let Me alone, that My wrath may wax hot against them, and that I may consume them; and I will make of thee a great nation* (Ex. 32:9-10).

As for Moses himself, God made it clear that no harm would befall him personally, but that a new attempt to create a nation to serve God would be undertaken and that Moses would continue to play a major role in its unfolding, including the identical promise originally made to Abraham, *I will make of thee a great nation* (Gen. 12:2). According to one opinion, this assurance surely troubled Moses, who understandably was concerned that his calm acceptance of such an assurance could justifiably be perceived as self-serving. As one of the rabbis put it, Moses countered by deferentially arguing that if "a stool with three legs [that is, the three Patriarchs] cannot stand before Thee in the hour of Thy wrath, how much less a stool with one leg. And moreover, I am ashamed before my ancestors, who will now say: See what a leader He has set over them, one that sought greatness for himself, but did not seek mercy for them."[374] Moses pleaded for the children of Israel and was successful in dissuading God from actualizing His wrath, but it took some time before God was willing to engage fully with the people once again.

Nonetheless, the relationship between Israel and God remained testy at best, with the Israelites constantly trying His patience, culminating in the popular complicity in the perfidy of the spies that caused the people to be condemned to remain in the wilderness for an additional thirty-eight years. During that long period, *He afflicted thee, and suffered thee to hunger, and fed thee with manna, which thou knewest not, neither did thy fathers know.* That is, He made you hunger and then fed you in a unique manner to demonstrate that life is in God's hands, *that He might make thee know that man doth not live by bread only, but by every thing that proceedeth out of the mouth of YHVH doth man live.* "The sharpest learning curve and the most significant lesson to be learned came through the most basic and universal form of human need—hunger."[375] The assertion that *man doth not live by bread only* does not negate the importance or bread, because the fact is that man requires bread to live. "*All* life on earth needs bread (or its equivalent); *human* life needs the mouth of God that first breathed into our nostrils. For while bread will keep us physically alive, it is the word of God that uniquely gives human life its meaning, shape, purpose, and value."[376] The implication of this, of course, is that one must not pursue solely material ends, but must make room for spirituality as well, always bearing in mind that while man may devote his energies to some achievement, effort alone will not assure success.

It may be asked, in what manner did the *manna*, which was gathered without great difficulty, constitute an affliction? Upon reflection, although the *manna* was made available every day, it could not be stored. This meant that the people were totally dependent on God for their sustenance, which also meant that for those unable to have unquestioning faith in God's providential concern for Israel there was daily anxiety as to whether the *manna* would be there for them the following morning. "As long as trust in Hashem for the daily manna did not become ingrained in the mind, the ordeal did not yet achieve its principal objective."[377] The *manna* they received was intended not only to nourish their bodies but also to instill in them a profound understanding of the critical relationship between man and God. Because of that relationship, they were able to survive their long sojourn in a most inhospitable environment.

The statement, *Thy raiment waxed not old upon thee, neither did thy foot swell, these forty years,* has been understood by some as pointing out another aspect of beneficent divine intervention throughout the course of the four decades long sojourn in the wilderness. What was the nature of that intervention? The rabbis clearly wrestled with this question but could not come up with a definitive conclusion. Thus, one asked if, when the children of Israel were going out of Egypt, they brought looms with them to make new clothing. Another responded that the "ministering angels" provided them with new clothes when necessary. Evidently rejecting this answer, the first sage pointed out that many children were involved in the exodus and over time those children surely grew out of the clothes they had been wearing. Where did their new clothes come from? The response was, "Go out and learn from the snail: all the while that he grows, his shell grows with him," again implying miraculous divine intervention. Undeterred, the first sage pointed out that the statement, *Thy raiment waxed not old upon thee*, suggests that they wore the same clothes for forty years, and asked what they did when they had to wash those clothes. The response was, "The cloud of fire cleansed their garments, and made them shine," again invoking the idea of a miracle. This answer was challenged with the question of why the garments were not burned by the fire. The response was that the clothes were woven from a form of asbestos "which is cleansed only by fire." The first sage then raised the question of whether the children of Israel had vermin from wearing the same clothes for so many years, and received the response, "Since worms and maggots have no power over the dead children of Israel, how much less have they got over living children of Israel!" Finally, the challenger asked, " Since the children of Israel did not change their garments, did they not reek with sweat?" The reply was: "The well of living waters brought up certain plants and certain spices for the children of Israel, and in these they were made to lie down, as it is said *He maketh me to lie down in green pastures; He leadeth me beside refreshing waters* (Ps.

151

23:2), and so the fragrant smell of them was carried from the world's end to world's end."[378]

The tongue-in-cheek character of this exchange makes it obvious that the rabbis did not know quite what to make of the biblical text under discussion. Attempts to explain the text without resort to the supernatural, such as the notion that their clothes *waxed not old* because they brought wardrobes with them,[379] also are not compelling. With regard to the assertion *neither did thy foot swell*, it may be understood the result of a divine intervention that prevented swelling, which would have been problematic for a people repeatedly moving by foot over the trackless wilderness.[380] Although it may be possible to posit scenarios to account for these assertions without resort to the supernatural,[381] it should be borne in mind that such surely would not have been what Moses intended by these remarks, the purpose of which was to illustrate that the welfare of the people was in divine hands and contingent on their full acceptance of His commandments.[382]

Alternatively, the statement may be understood as a rhetorical flourish that never was meant to be taken literally; that it simply was intended as a metaphor for God's providential concern for their welfare during that long period of tutelage. The people, Moses avers, should reflect on this experience as a manifestation of divine concern rather than as retribution, *And thou shalt consider in thy heart, that, as a man chasteneth his son, so YHVH thy Elohim chasteneth thee*, or as the biblical sage later put it, *He that spareth his rod hateth his son; but he that loveth him chasteneth him betimes* (Prov. 13:24). It has been suggested that the implication of *thou shalt consider in thy heart* is that they should reflect on what Moses is telling them now until it becomes rooted in their hearts so that it need neither to be repeated nor considered anew.[383] Alternatively, the closing words of the passage may be understood as an implicit response to the question of "why me?" or, "why us?" After all, it is not apparent that God is paying much attention to other nations that are engulfed in polytheism, why is He so hard on us? It is because, as Moses' clearly implies, there is a paternal relationship between God and Israel, and just as a father will be more concerned with deviant behavior on the part of his own son than with that of someone else's son, so too does God demand more from Israel than from others.[384]

It is noteworthy that what is described here is the transfiguration of suffering into what the rabbis would later term 'chastisements of love.' Accordingly, it was taught: "If a man is visited by affliction, he should be grateful to God for it, because suffering draws man to God."[385] The psalmist reflected this view when he wrote: *Before I was afflicted, I did err; but now I observe Thy word. . . . It is good for me that I have been afflicted, in order that I might learn Thy statutes. . . . I know, O Lord, that Thy judgments are righteous, and that in faithfulness Thou hast afflicted me* (Ps. 119:67, 71, 75). The people needed discipline in order to reliably carry out the provisions of the covenant, and the ordeals they underwent in the wilderness served the purpose of instilling a significant degree of discipline in most of the people.[386]

> [8.6]*And thou shalt keep the commandments of YHVH thy Elohim, to walk in His ways, and to fear Him.* [8.7]*For YHVH thy Elohim bringeth thee into a good land, a land of brooks of water, of fountains and depths, springing forth in valleys and hills;* [8.8]*a land of wheat and barley, and vines and fig-trees and pomegranates; a land of olive trees and honey;* [8.9]*a land wherein thou shalt eat bread without scarceness, thou shalt not lack any thing in it; a land whose stones are iron, and out of whose hills thou mayest dig brass.* [8.10]*And thou shalt eat and be satisfied, and bless YHVH thy Elohim for the good land which He hath given thee.*

Turning from the troubled past to the promise of the future, Moses adjures them not to repeat the errors of the past, but to *keep the commandments of YHVH thy Elohim, to walk in His ways, and to fear Him,* the prerequisites for enjoying the blessings of the land they are about to inherit. It is noteworthy that here, by contrast with earlier descriptions of the country as a land of milk and honey, the land is described as *a land of wheat and barley, and vines and fig-trees and pomegranates; a land of olive trees and honey,* as a virtual paradise as compared to the wilderness they had known for forty years, and in which many were born never knowing any other environment. It may also be observed in this regard that in this passage the *land* is mentioned seven times, coinciding with the enumeration of its natural food products.[387] Moreover, because the products listed are all agricultural, the reference to *honey* is most likely to the nectar of dates and figs rather than the secretion of bees.

The land will not only yield an abundance of various foods that will sate the appetite, but it will also contain natural deposits such as iron-stone, probably referring to volcanic black basalt, and copper. Alternatively, the text has been interpreted as saying that what your eyes perceive as stones will turn out to be iron.[388] However, and perhaps reflecting awareness that there was little iron or copper to be found in the land of Israel, the early Aramaic paraphrases of the biblical texts interpreted this text in non-literal fashion. Thus one metaphorically renders *a land whose stones are iron, and out of whose hills thou mayest dig brass* as "a land whose sages will enact decrees unalloyed as iron, and whose disciples will propound questions weighty as brass."[389] Of greater immediate interest, the fragment of another work renders the text as a land "whose stones are pure as iron, and whose hills are firm as brass."[390] The latter statement has been interpreted as suggesting that the Israelites will find quarries of great and heavy stones that can be used to build solid homes and towers and walls, as compared to the primarily clay dwellings they left behind in Egypt, which are subject to becoming graves for those who live in them, presumably because of their inherent structural weakness.[391]

In any case, the point Moses is making is that the land abounds with natural blessings of which they will be able to make good use. Once settled, they will forget the struggles that they had to undertake to conquer the land; they will be content and shall *bless YHVH thy Elohim* for the blessing they received by the award of this good land to be their patrimony. In this regard, tradition treats this latter statement as a command, demanding such a blessing whenever *thou shalt eat and be satisfied*, understood as mandating blessings after eating in addition to blessings for the food prior to eating. Thus, although it is quite understandable that a person who is hungry would bless God for the food he is about to consume, blessing God after eating is probably unique to Mosaic teaching. It is precisely when one has eaten and satisfied his hunger that he is commanded to bless God, in effect, as an acknowledgement of debt to Him and a reminder of his dependence on divine favor. The command to bless God for the fertility of the land also serves as a reminder to avoid pursuing the practices of the previous polytheistic inhabitants of the land that linked the fertility of the land to the worship of Baal and Astarte.

The question that this text evokes is what does it mean for a human to bless God? To express one's gratitude is certainly appropriate, but what significance can a person's blessing have for God, especially when the beneficence of a blessing descends from the higher to the lower, from God to man rather than the reverse?[392] In this regard, it may be suggested that although blessing God may not be meaningful in a strict sense, it nonetheless has the effect of engaging God in one's thoughts and efforts and thereby increases the potential for providential concern.[393]

Having made this point, Moses admonishes them once again never to forget why they were given this land and what was demanded of them as a prerequisite for keeping it and enjoying its blessings.

> [8.11] *Beware lest thou forget YHVH thy Elohim, in not keeping His commandments, and His ordinances, and His statutes, which I command thee this day;* [8.12] *lest when thou hast eaten and art satisfied, and hast built goodly houses, and dwelt therein;* [8.13] *and when thy herds and thy flocks multiply, and thy silver and thy gold is multiplied, and all that thou hast is multiplied;* [8.14] *then thy heart be lifted up, and thou forget YHVH thy Elohim, who brought thee forth out of the land of Egypt, out of the house of bondage;* [8.15] *who led thee through the great and dreadful wilderness, wherein were serpents, fiery serpents, and scorpions, and thirsty ground where was no water; who brought thee forth water out of the rock of flint;* [8.16] *who fed thee in the wilderness with manna, which thy fathers knew not; that He might afflict thee, and that He might prove thee, to do thee good at thy latter end;* [8.17] *and thou say in thy heart: 'My power and the might of my hand hath gotten me this wealth.'* [8.18] *But thou shalt remember YHVH thy*

> *Elohim, for it is He that giveth thee power to get wealth;*
> *that He may establish His covenant which He swore unto*
> *thy fathers, as it is this day.*

Moses warns them most emphatically about the danger of forgetting who brought them here and for what reason. It is noteworthy that Moses earlier also admonished the people *Beware lest thou forget YHVH* (Deut. 6:12) when they would be engaged in the struggle to establish their control in the land. Here he reissues the admonishment with respect to the period following the conquest when normalization of their situation takes place.[394] The key to remembering God is through purposive activity, *keeping His commandments, and His ordinances, and His statutes, which I command thee this day*. Doing so will serve as a constant reminder of their relationship with God. Just what is intended by *mitzvot* or *commandments* in this passage as distinct from *ordinances* and *statutes* is unclear, although it has been suggested that it refers to the "employment of one's forces and means for God's purposes," whereas *ordinances* and *statutes* "express the demands of justice and equity and morality as the boundaries for our efforts to obtain possessions and enjoyments." Accordingly, it is suggested, this is the reason why *mitzvot* or *commandments* is given priority in the listing.[395]

Moses correctly anticipates that once they begin to enjoy the blessings of the land, *then thy heart be lifted up*, putting out of their mind how downtrodden they were when still in servitude, and how they experienced hunger and thirst in the wilderness.[396] Many will tend to *forget YHVH thy Elohim, who brought thee forth out of the land of Egypt, out of the house of bondage* and the miracles He performed for them, enabling them to survive the hardships of wilderness life. The danger point will be reached when they begin to forget the past and begin to imagine that they achieved the wealth they enjoy by stint of their own power and effort. Not so, he declares, the power to create the wealth that they celebrate is that which God instilled in them for one purpose, namely to fulfill His commitment to the covenant that He originally made with the Patriarchs, a covenant that was remade and ratified by them, and to which they will be held accountable for compliance.

The assertion, *for it is He that giveth thee power,* may be understood as asserting that the very aspects of one's abilities critical to success in one's endeavors are divine gifts, as are the complex of circumstances that make success possible.[397] By contrast, the assertion was understood by some in the context of the strong belief of many, in ancient as well as modern times, in the divinely empowered influence of the celestial bodies on what takes place on earth. Thus, it was assumed that the *power* in this text refers to the power of the constellations. That is, that God transfered the astrological powers to the children of Israel, who were thus freed from their influence and able to set their own courses in life. This, it is argued, is the meaning of the assertion *for it is He that giveth thee power that He may establish His covenant which He swore unto thy fathers.* It was this freedom that God promised Abraham for his descendents when *He brought him forth abroad, and said: 'Look now toward heaven . . . So shall thy seed be* (Gen. 15:5). That is, Abraham's descendents were to be on the same level as the constellations, and therefore free of their influence.[398] Although this opinion may strike the modern reader as farfetched, who can say with confidence that such an interpretation does not reflect the mindset of the biblical writers.

> [8.19] *And it shall be, if thou shalt forget YHVH thy Elohim, and walk after other gods, and serve them, and worship them, I forewarn you this day that ye shall surely perish; because ye would not hearken unto the voice of YHVH thy Elohim.* [8.20] *As the nations that YHVH maketh to perish before you, so shall ye perish; because ye would not hearken unto the voice of YHVH your Elohim.*

Moses warns them not to labor under the delusion that once they have established firm control of the territory, they will be in a position to declare their independence of their sovereign, God. Not so! If they should have the temerity to turn their backs on God, and follow other less demanding gods, such as those they will encounter among the nations presently in the country, they will unleash divine wrath against them and will quickly lose everything, including many of their lives. The nation of Israel, which is just becoming a reality, will disappear from the stage of history, as will the nations they are about to dispossess or displace.

> *9.1 Hear, O Israel: thou art to pass over the Jordan this day, to go in to dispossess nations greater and mightier than thyself, cities great and fortified up to heaven, 9.2 a people great and tall, the sons of Anakim, whom thou knowest, and of whom thou hast heard say: 'Who can stand before the sons of Anak?' 9.3 Know therefore this day, that YHVH thy Elohim is He who goeth over before thee as a devouring fire; He will destroy them, and He will bring them down before thee; so shalt thou drive them out, and make them to perish quickly, as YHVH hath spoken unto thee.*

Once again, Moses admonishes the people not to lose perspective regarding their own power and abilities, as they invade the land and confront their enemies there. It is ironic that Moses now repeats, in effect, the precise arguments raised by ten of the twelve scouts sent to assess the military situation in the country thirty-eight years earlier, arguments that triggered a rebellion that resulted in the protracted stay in the wilderness. Thus, he warns them, they are about to invade and *dispossess nations greater and mightier than thyself, cities great and fortified up to heaven, a people great and tall, the sons of Anakim*, the giants that terrified their immediate ancestors, *whom thou knowest, and of whom thou hast heard*. This last statement has evoked two questions. If one *knows* something, what is the significance of adding what he *has heard said* about it? And, if it is significant for some reason, why does the text not simply say *whom thou knowest, and hast heard say*, omitting the second *thou*? It has been suggested that Moses makes his statement in this manner because he is actually addressing two different audiences. The first consists of Joshua and Caleb, the only surviving members of the ill-fated reconnaissance mission, and the only ones who had a real appreciation of the so-called *sons of Anakim*, and their actual strength, *whom thou knowest* from firsthand experience. The second audience is the mass of the people who have not benefitted from any first hand exposure to the *sons of Anakim*, about *whom thou hast heard*.[399]

How are they going to achieve this? They certainly will not accomplish this because of their own power. It will be only because God will fight with them, preceding them *as a devouring fire* that will rage through the enemy's ranks and fortifications, a rhetorical flourish intended to spur the people on to face the enemy without fear. At the same time, however, Moses reminds them that although they will be battling the enemy with all their strength, they should bear in mind that their success will be contingent on divine assistance. That is, it will not be their unaided efforts that will crush the enemy, but God who *will destroy them* and *bring them down before thee*, destroying their morale and weakening their will to resist, as it states later: *And it came to pass, when all the kings of the Amorites, that were beyond the Jordan westward, and all the kings of the Canaanites, that were by the sea, heard how that YHVH had dried up the waters of the Jordan from before the children of Israel, until they were passed over, that their heart melted, neither was there spirit in them any more, because of the children of Israel* (Josh. 5:2). Once God does this, it will be their task to *drive them out, and make them to perish quickly*. It may be suggested that the latter assertion is not necessarily in conflict with the earlier statement that the conquest of the land will be piecemeal over a protracted period, for the reasons discussed above. Here the statement *make them to perish quickly* surely refers to the main Canaanite/Amorite forces that will try to block the initial Israelite invasion. The victory over your enemies will thus be the result of their partnership with God; it will not be the result solely of their own power and abilities, a truth they should not forget even for a moment.

> *9.4 Speak not thou in thy heart, after that YHVH thy Elohim hath thrust them out from before thee, saying: 'For my righteousness YHVH hath brought me in to possess this land'; whereas for the wickedness of these nations YHVH doth drive them out before thee. 9.5 Not for thy righteousness, or for the uprightness of thy heart, dost thou go in to possess their land; but for the wickedness of these nations YHVH thy Elohim doth drive them out from before thee, that He may establish the word which YHVH*

swore unto thy fathers, to Abraham, to Isaac, and to Jacob.
9.6 Know therefore that it is not for thy righteousness that
YHVH thy Elohim giveth thee this good land to possess it;
for thou art a stiff-necked people.

Moses cautions them further against hubris and self-delusion in thinking that all this is happening, their victories and their enemy's defeats, because they have merited such because of their righteousness and the lack thereof of the enemy. If they come to think this, he tells them, they are only half-right. It is because of the *wickedness of these nations YHVH thy Elohim doth drive them out from before thee.* As God foretold to Abraham, his descendents will return to the land after four centuries of exile *for the iniquity of the Amorite is not yet full* (Gen. 15:16). That is, divine governance will not permit their destruction until their iniquity has reached the point where their existence as a nation in the land becomes completely dysfunctional. Therefore, *not for thy righteousness, or for the uprightness of thy heart, dost thou go in to possess their land.* On the basis of comparative righteousness, Moses assures them, they are not much better than those they are displacing. Accordingly, they are not being enabled to conquer and settle the land because of their moral superiority, but only so *that He may establish the word which YHVH swore unto thy fathers, to Abraham, to Isaac, and to Jacob.* Except for that solemn obligation, they would not merit the land because *thou art a stiff-necked people,* obstinate, rebellious, disobedient, and prone to faithlessness. Moreover, it has been argued that it is nigh impossible to attain justice and contentment with people who are stiff-necked and who tend to do whatever comes into their mind even though it is wrong and ultimately counterproductive or even destructive.[400] And, to emphasize the latter point, Moses recounts some of the more egregious instances of their stubbornness and rebelliousness.

9.7 Remember, forget thou not, how thou didst make
YHVH thy Elohim wroth in the wilderness; from the day
that thou didst go forth out of the land of Egypt, until
ye came unto this place, ye have been rebellious against
YHVH. 9.8 Also in Horeb ye made YHVH wroth, and

YHVH was angered with you to have destroyed you. ^{9.9}
*When I was gone up into the mount to receive the tables of
stone, even the tables of the covenant which YHVH made
with you, then I abode in the mount forty days and forty
nights; I did neither eat bread nor drink water.* ^{9.10} *And
YHVH delivered unto me the two tables of stone written
with the finger of Elohim; and on them was written
according to all the words, which YHVH spoke with you
in the mount out of the midst of the fire in the day of the
assembly.* ^{9.11} *And it came to pass at the end of forty fays
and forty nights, that YHVH gave me the two tables of
stone, even the tables of the covenant.* ^{9.12} *And YHVH said
unto me: 'Arise, get thee down quickly from hence; for thy
people that thou hast brought forth out of Egypt have dealt
corruptly; they are quickly turned aside out of the way
which I commanded them; they have made them a molten
image.'* ^{9.13} *Furthermore YHVH spoke unto me, saying:
'I have seen this people, and, behold, it is a stiff-necked
people;* ^{9.14} *let Me alone, that I may destroy them, and blot
out their name from under heaven; and I will make of
thee a nation mightier and greater than they.'*

As a general proposition, Moses tells them that they angered God
repeatedly from the very outset of the exodus to the present day. Even
at Horeb, where they received and ratified the covenant, their conduct
was so outrageous and so infuriated God that He was on the verge
of destroying them completely. Moses recalls that the unforgiveable
incident took place while he had *gone up into the mount to receive the
tables of stone, even the tables of the covenant which YHVH made with
you.* He spent forty days and nights on the mountain, at the end of
which he received the tablets of the Decalogue, only to be informed by
God at the same time that below, the Israelites were busy committing
the ultimate sacrilege of worshipping a molten image. Moses pointedly
notes that during that entire period of his encounter with God, while
they were entertaining the idea of treason and subsequently carrying it
out, "he was beyond human needs and concerns."[401] *I did neither eat*

bread nor drink water, while they were engaged in a wild pagan orgy below. That was the point at which God informed him that He was prepared to annihilate them completely, and begin anew the historical process of creating a nation worthy of the Patriarchs exclusively out of the descendents of Moses, as discussed above.

In the earlier version of the story, Moses immediately pleaded with God to desist from carrying out His expressed intention. In principle, the Israelites should have been destroyed for their perfidy. However, God evidently preferred to give Moses the opportunity to bring them back from their folly, if he so chose to do. Accordingly, He said to Moses, *Now therefore let Me alone, that My wrath may wax hot against them, and that I may consume them* (Ex. 32:10). By asking Moses to desist from arguing with him about it, so that He could go about the business of putting an end to the budding nation, God was subtly suggesting that Moses could actually successfully intervene in their behalf, if he was so inclined; if he were not so disposed, they would be doomed. It has been pointed out in this regard that, "though at times He seems on the point of annulling the contract and fulfilling His promises through the seed of Moses alone (Exod. 32:10), God never actually abandons His people, for, legally speaking, He has bound Himself to them for eternity."[402]

The implication of the statement, *Now therefore let Me alone,* as understood by some, would appear to be that Moses was in fact defending the people so vigorously that it led God to ask him to relent. That is, according to one opinion, "this teaches that Moses took hold of the Holy One, blessed be He, like a man who seizes his fellow by his garment and said before Him: Sovereign of the Universe, I will not let Thee go until Thou forgivest and pardonest them."[403] In the earlier and fuller account it states:

> *And Moses besought YHVH his Elohim, and said: 'YHVH, why doth Thy wrath wax hot against Thy people, that Thou hast brought forth out of the land of Egypt with great power and with a mighty hand? Wherefore should the Egyptians speak, saying: For evil did He bring them forth, to slay them in the mountains, and to consume them*

*from the face of the earth? Turn from Thy fierce wrath,
and repent of this evil against Thy people. Remember
Abraham, Isaac, and Israel, Thy servants, to whom Thou
didst swear by Thine own self, and saidst unto them: I
will multiply your seed as the stars of heaven, and all this
land that I have spoken of will I give unto your seed, and
they shall inherit it for ever.' And YHVH repented of the
evil which He said He would do unto His people* (Ex.
32:11-14).

The passage cited above[404] begins with a puzzling statement, that
Moses besought YHVH his Elohim, the one and only time in the Torah
that the phrase *his Elohim* is used with respect to Moses. Why did the
text not say simply that *Moses besought YHVH*? It has been suggested
that the text reflects a reaction to the divine intention to disassociate
completely from the wayward children of Israel, to whom He would
no longer be their *Elohim*. However, Moses was not disavowed and
God remained his *Elohim*, and the text seems to attest to this.[405] It has
been pointed out by many that the phrase *vayehal moshe*, translated as
Moses besought, may also be read as "Moses became ill," that is, Moses
pleaded on behalf of Israel until he became ill from it.[406] Alternatively,
the phrase has been understood as saying that he became ill because of
what they did,[407] and the resulting perceived divine anger at the people
of Israel and the prospect of divine disavowal of them. Moreover, the
translation ignores the fact that the text actually states *vayehal moshe et
pnei YHVH elohav*, the phrase *et pnei YHVH elohav*, meaning *the face
of YHVH his Elohim*. Thus, the text could be rendered as "And Moses
became ill because of the *face of* God, that is, his perception of God's
disposition towards the children of Israel.[408] Sickened by what he was
afraid might happen, Moses proceeded to plead that God not disavow
the people that he had come to care for so deeply. This text also seems
to mark a fundamental change in Moses' attitude toward the people,
whom he heretofore tended to view as a burden imposed on him by
God, who would not allow him to demur from the task of leading them
out of Egypt. Notwithstanding their obstinacy and seemingly inherent

rebelliousness, he had come to identify with them so completely that he was prepared to challenge God on their behalf.

The divinely granted opportunity to intervene in behalf of the Israelites did not escape Moses, and he pursued it with alacrity. Emulating his distinguished ancestor Abraham, who had the courage to challenge God directly over the planned destruction of Sodom and Gomorrah, Moses rose to the challenge and confronted God over His determination to wipe out the people because of what was happening in the Israelite camp at the base of the mountain. It is noteworthy that Moses does not even attempt to defend in any way what the people have done; he too considers it reprehensible and unworthy of the beneficence shown them by God. Nonetheless, he cannot but try to convince God to recant His disavowal of them, and he attempts to do this by turning the attention away from their deserved punishment to the implications of it for God's purpose.

Why, he asked God, *doth Thy wrath wax hot against Thy people, that Thou hast brought forth out of the land of Egypt with great power and with a mighty hand?* Whereas God previously referred to the Israelites as the people that Moses brought out of Egypt, thus implicitly disassociating from them, Moses now reminds God that it was He that brought the children of Israel out of Egypt. This assertion has been understood as pointing out that they were just recently liberated from a society and culture saturated with idolatry and that should be considered a mitigating factor in their momentary recidivism, which perhaps should not be treated as though it were a carefully thought through repudiation of God. It would take time before the people truly internalized a view of the world and themselves that negated virtually everything they had been exposed to over a course of generations.

Moses also reminded God that the people had not volunteered to be liberated but had to be *brought forth out of the land of Egypt with great power and with a mighty hand*, and therefore needed time to adapt to the new circumstances in which they found themselves.[409] In this regard it should be noted that some understand the phrase *with a mighty hand* as meaning "against their will." That is, it took God's *mighty hand* to virtually compel the children of Israel to overcome their lethargy and fear of change and join in the exodus. The children of

Israel subsequently made their view in this regard quite plain when they stated to Moses, *Is not this the word that we spoke unto thee in Egypt, saying: Let us alone, that we may serve the Egyptians?* (Ex. 14:12) Moreover, since they were not prepared for the dramatic change in religious perspective that was to be demanded of them, it was only reasonable to expect that there would be occasional lapses in this regard, including some serious ones such as that which was taking place below at the very moment that Moses was receiving the tablets of the Decalogue at the summit of the mountain.

Continuing with his plea on behalf of the children of Israel, Moses argued that since God had already gone to so much trouble on their behalf to liberate them, and at the same time causing the Egyptians to feel the brunt of divine power, from which it would take them a long time to recover, why would God want to squander that which had been achieved thus far? *Wherefore should the Egyptians speak, saying: For evil did He bring them forth, to slay them in the mountains, and to consume them from the face of the earth?* At the end, the Egyptians were being compelled to acknowledge the supremacy of God over all the imagined gods of Egypt. Why would God want to undo what He had accomplished by now doing something that would be perceived in the pagan world as completely arbitrary and heartless? Moses thus pleaded, *Turn from Thy fierce wrath, and repent of this evil against Thy people*, which would prove counterproductive to the divine purpose.

If this argument was not sufficiently persuasive, Moses offered an alternate reason for God not to do what He intended, namely the promises He had made to the patriarchs Abraham, Isaac, and Jacob. Moses implored God to *Remember Abraham, Isaac, and Israel, Thy servants, to whom Thou didst swear by Thine own self, and saidst unto them: 'I will multiply your seed as the stars of heaven, and all this land that I have spoken of will I give unto your seed, and they shall inherit it for ever.'* He implicitly suggested that even if the people merited punishment for their perfidy, they might be forgiven the extremely harsh punishment of which God spoke on the basis of the merit of their ancestors, to whom God had repeatedly made the indicated promise. It is noteworthy that in making this argument Moses referred to *Abraham, Isaac, and Israel*, rather than Jacob, suggesting that the promise God made was not only to Abraham, Isaac, and Jacob as individuals, but also to Jacob in his role as the eponymous ancestor of the children of Israel, which He was now proposing to disavow.[410]

Moreover, it has been pointed out that Moses asserts that God made this promise to the Patriarchs *by Thine own self,* the meaning of which is not self-evident, but surely does not mean to assert that God did this freely without external compulsion. In one opinion, what this meant was that Moses argued, in effect, that had God sworn to them by the heaven and the earth, he would agree that just as the heaven and the earth can pass away, so too could even a divine oath that invoked them pass away. But, since God swore to them by His own name, circumstances changed. Just as God's great name endures forever, so too does God's vow to the Patriarchs remain in effect forever.[411] However, this argument could not in itself be very persuasive since God had already indicated that His commitment to the Patriarchs could be fulfilled through Moses alone, to whom He asserted, *I will make of thee a great nation.*

Nonetheless, God evidently was pleased with Moses' spirited defense of the children of Israel and He responded favorably to Moses' plea on their behalf, and He *repented of the evil which He said He would do unto His people.* As the psalmist wrote: *Therefore He said that He would destroy them, had not Moses His chosen stood before Him in the breach, to turn back His wrath, lest He should destroy them* (Ps. 106:23). However, this only attests that when God *repented of the evil which He said He would do unto His people,* it spoke only of His intent to destroy them. It did not necessarily imply that He forgave their perfidy with regard to the golden calf affair. Moreover, God's repentance may have taken place only with regard to those among the people that had not participated in the sacrilege, but not with those who did participate either actively or passively; the latter would still be dealt with later.[412]

Why did God change His mind? The very notion of God threatening to act precipitously and being talked out of it by Moses is truly mind-boggling and would seem to challenge some fundamental ideas regarding divine omniscience and omnipotence. It may well be that what the text is telling us is that God informed Moses, albeit implicitly, that unless he was prepared to accept responsibility for assuming control over the stiff-necked and unruly children of Israel and deal forcefully with their sacrilegious outrage, *My wrath may wax hot against them, and that I may consume them.* In other words, God did not tell Moses what He was going to do but rather what He might do unless Moses interceded on their behalf, such intercession being deemed equivalent to assuming personal responsibility for dealing with them.

It was at this point that Moses fully understood, perhaps for the first time, that his role did not end with bring the people out of Egypt and then to Horeb where they would receive the divine word. Henceforth, he would have to be both teacher and disciplinarian of the children of Israel. In effect, he would have to act as uncrowned monarch of the Israelites, ruling in accordance with divine guidance whenever it was provided and by his own best judgment when it was not.

> *9.15 So I turned and came down from the mount, and the mount burned with fire; and the two tables of the covenant were in my two hands. 9.16 And I looked, and, behold, ye had sinned against YHVH your Elohim; ye had made you a molten calf; ye had turned aside quickly out of the way which YHVH had commanded you. 9.17 And I took hold of the two tables, and cast them out of my two hands, and broke them before your eyes. 9.18 And I fell down before YHVH, as at the first, forty days and forty nights; I did neither eat bread nor drink water; because of all your sin which ye sinned, in doing that which was evil in the sight of YHVH, to provoke Him. 9.19 For I was in dread of the anger and hot displeasure, wherewith YHVH was wroth against you to destroy you. But YHVH hearkened unto me that time also.*

Why did Moses destroy the tablets, along with the golden calf, as described below, which was itself the handiwork of God? There certainly is no indication in the text that he did this in accordance with any divine instruction. Was this not in itself an act of sacrilege? Could it be that Moses simply went berserk with anger for a moment?

If not, what was it that impelled Moses to do this on his own initiative? It has been suggested that Moses broke the tablets because, by their actions, the people showed that they did not merit them.[413] That is, since the purpose of presenting the Decalogue to the people was to bring them ceremoniously into the covenant and to commit them to the observance of the strictures contained therein, their idolatrous acts effectively violated and therefore nullified the covenant, thereby making the tablets superfluous.[414]

A similar approach to answering the question suggests that Moses smashed the tablets in order to preserve the integrity of the covenant epitomized in them. If Moses had not destroyed the tablets, those who had participated in the worship of the golden calf might have concluded that they could violate the terms of the covenant with impunity. As one commentator put it, when Moses saw what the people were doing he thought to himself, "my mission had come to an end, that it would be acting treacherously to the treasure entrusted to me were I to hand it over to you and make you its depository," and he chose to smash the tablets rather than give them to the people who were undeserving of them.[415] By smashing them, Moses sent the people the strongest possible signal that their violation of the commandments effectively nullified the covenant and they would have to face the consequences that entailed. Just as they failed to observe the Second Commandment, so too would God fail to honor the promise to give them the land originally promised to their ancestors.[416] That meant, in effect, that they had no place to go and would have to spend the rest of their lives in the wilderness without divine assistance, which at a minimum meant ultimate death from starvation even if they survived attacks from hostile forces competing for control of the limited natural resources of the wilderness.

The weakness of these explanations is that Moses did not have to break the tablets in order not to give them to the people; he could simply have put them aside and not arbitrarily undertaken to destroy something that the text tells us was the direct work of God, an act that was itself sacrilegious. Accordingly, and upon further reflection, it would seem that his shattering of the tablets was not the result of uncontrollable rage, something that would have been completely out of character for Moses, but that it was a deliberate and calculated act on his part, the purpose of which justified destroying the tablets prepared by the divine hand.

Having been raised as an Egyptian prince, Moses had to be fully aware of the symbolism of the golden calf in Egyptian culture. Thus, when he saw that the children of Israel had not only constructed one, even if only by contributing their gold, but were celebrating before it, he clearly understood the difficulty they were having in fully internalizing the concept of an invisible God that might not be represented in some tangible fashion by something in nature or made by man. Of course, the golden calf had to be destroyed and the people made to feel in their stomachs that they had committed a grievous sin against the God who had liberated them from servitude in Egypt and was leading them to the establishment of their own free nation in the land promised to their ancestors. However, Moses may have feared that destroying the calf and then presenting the people with the stone tablets that *were the work of God* might cause them to perceive the tablets as a substitute for the golden calf, which would effectively transform them into idolatrous paraphernalia. Accordingly he destroyed both the tablets and the golden calf in public view, thus making it clear to all that even the divine handiwork has no intrinsic sanctity if used for non-sanctioned purposes; only carrying out the will of God constituted the essential approach to the adoration and sanctification of God.

In the earlier account of the incident, as soon as he learned from God what was happening below, Moses immediately pleaded with God not to carry out His threat to annihilate the children of Israel, and we are told, *And YHVH repented of the evil which He said He would do unto His people* (Ex. 32:14). In the present text, after Moses smashed the tablets, he prayed to God a second time not to carry out His threat to annihilate the people, which is not mentioned in the earlier account. Is there not an obvious inconsistency between the two texts? In an effort to reconcile the two descriptions of what took place, it has been argued that before Moses smashed the tablets, he prevailed upon God to reverse His decision regarding destruction of the people. However, although God rescinded His earlier decision, divine anger at the children of Israel was not assuaged. Essentially, what Moses achieved was a divine decision not to take immediate retribution against the people, which left open the possibility of this taking place later. Accordingly, Moses records that he pleaded with God a second time, after he smashed the tablets, *for I was in dread of the anger and hot displeasure, wherewith YHVH was wroth against you to destroy you. But YHVH hearkened unto me that time also.*[417]

> [9.20] *Moreover YHVH was very angry with Aaron to have destroyed him; and I prayed for Aaron also the same time.*

Aaron's role in the affair of the golden calf is essentially ignored in these discourses, but is presented in detail in the earlier and fuller account. *And Moses said unto Aaron: 'What did this people unto thee, that thou hast brought a great sin upon them?' And Aaron said: 'Let not the anger of my lord wax hot; thou knowest the people, that they are set on evil* (Ex. 32:21-22). Moses' first concern upon descending to the camp was to deal with the golden calf, his outraged appearance stunning the people, who made no attempt to interfere with his actions. Once this was being done, he next turned to Aaron, bewildered that his brother and faithful companion had allowed himself to be drawn into the travesty that took place with his help. He demanded an explanation of how he had become a party to the outrage. *What did this people unto thee, that thou hast brought a great sin upon them?* This question has been understood in two diametrically opposed ways. On the one hand, it has been read as an expression of sympathy for Aaron, implying that he must have been placed under horrendous pressure to make him a party to what happened.[418] On the other hand, it has been interpreted as a harsh criticism of Aaron, suggesting that he should not have yielded to the mob no matter what pressure they placed on him. As a result of his failure, not only did he commit a sin by creating the golden calf but also must bear the responsibility for causing others to sin through worshipping it,[419] notwithstanding that Aaron personally was not accused of the latter, presumably because Moses could not conceive that his brother would do such a thing himself.

Aaron offered no defense of his actions, which he understood were indefensible, and as Moses did earlier with respect to God, he now similarly pleaded with Moses, whom he addressed as *my lord*, because Aaron had to explain to him what happened in his absence since Moses left the camp in his charge.[420] *Let not the anger of my lord wax hot; thou knowest the people, that they are set on evil.* That is, he told Moses that there was no point in getting angry. Moses knows how stubborn the people are, and that once they decide on something, even if reason says it is wrong, they are so stiff-necked that they will do it anyway. Accordingly, when the people became distraught over the protracted absence of Moses, they demanded that he make them something symbolic that could be placed before them in lieu of Moses. Since they were not asking for an idol to be worshipped but only something that could be taken as a substitute for Moses, he acceded to their demand, asking them to gather gold from the people, *and I cast it into the fire, and there came out this calf* (Ex. 32:24). By any measure this is a rather bizarre statement. Aaron seems to be asserting that all he did was to melt down all the gold, which somehow emerged from the smelter in the form of a golden calf, and that when this occurred the people saw it as an expression of the divine will and therefore worshipped it.

It is noteworthy that the rabbis were so troubled by this passage that they ruled that when it was read publicly in the synagogue it should not be accompanied by a translation into the vernacular, as was common practice in early times when Hebrew virtually became exclusively the language of scholars.[421] They evidently preferred not to have to explain it to those who would not otherwise be aware of and troubled by its possible implications.

Some commentators, beginning in antiquity, assuming the role of apologists for Aaron, have proposed a variety of fanciful explanations for his behavior and the account of the seemingly spontaneous formation of the golden calf, most of which explain virtually nothing that would be found acceptable to a modern reader and will therefore not be considered here, with one exception.[422] One apologist for Aaron suggested that what he meant by his statement was not that the golden calf mysteriously emerged from the fire, but rather that the calf that he created for legitimate purposes was somehow transformed by the people into *this calf,* that they treated as an idol.[423] Suffice it to note that in Moses' present recounting of the episode, he ignores Aaron's incomprehensible explanation and states unequivocally, *YHVH was very angry with Aaron to have destroyed him,* something that did not happen because of Moses' prayers on his behalf (Deut. 9:20). There is a presumption that Moses was successful in interceding on behalf of Aaron by arguing that although he was indirectly responsible for the affair, and should have been punished severely for his failure in leadership, the mitigating factor was that he was gulled into assisting in the very perpetration he sought to impede. God's subsequent appointment of Aaron to serve as high priest, something that surely would not have happened if He had not completely forgiven him for his unfortunate misjudgment, is clear evidence of divine exoneration of his role in the bizarre affair.[424]

> [9.21] *And I took your sin, the calf which ye made, and burnt it with fire, and beat it in pieces, grinding it very small, until it was as fine as dust; and I cast the dust thereof into the brook that descended out of the mount.* ([9.22] *And at Taberah, and at Massah, and at Kibroth-hattavah, ye made YHVH wroth.* [9.23] *And when YHVH sent you from Kadesh-barnea, saying: 'Go up and possess the land which I have given you'; then ye rebelled against the commandment of YHVH your Elohim, and ye believed Him not, nor hearkened to His voice.* [9.24] *Ye have been rebellious against YHVH from the day that I knew you.)*

Moses recalls how he destroyed the idolatrous calf, effectively eradicating it to the extent that not a single piece of it remained. He then, parenthetically, reminded his audience that what he just described at length was no an isolated incident, but perhaps just the most egregious among the numerous examples of faithlessness and rebellion that took place repeatedly even after the incident of the golden calf, suggesting that the people never fully or truly repented for it.[425] The most notable of their subsequent lapses was the failure to follow God's instructions at Kadesh-barnea to enter the promised land, a failure that caused them to await the demise of an entire generation before being permitted to go into the land, as they were about to do. In sum, Moses points out that they have been a rebellious lot for as long as he knows them, repeatedly turning their backs on God. Returning to his earlier recapitulation of the near-disastrous events at Horeb, Moses recalls what took place atop Sinai after the destruction of the golden calf and the tablets containing the Decalogue.

> *9.25 So I fell down before YHVH the forty days and forty nights that I fell down; because YHVH had said He would destroy you. 9.26 And I prayed unto YHVH, and said: 'O Adonai YHVH, destroy not Thy people and Thine inheritance, that Thou hast redeemed through Thy greatness, that Thou hast brought forth out of Egypt with a mighty hand. 9.27 Remember Thy servants, Abraham, Isaac, and Jacob; look not unto the stubbornness of this people, nor to their wickedness, nor to their sin; 9.28 lest the land whence Thou broughtest us out say: Because YHVH was not able to bring them into the land which He promised unto them, and because He hated them, He hath brought them out to slay them in the wilderness. 9.29 Yet they are Thy people and Thine inheritance, that Thou didst bring out by Thy great power and by Thy outstretched arm.*

Moses relates once again the point made earlier, that he returned to the mount for another forty days and nights during which he pleaded incessantly for divine forgiveness for the people to avert their destruction, concocting every argument he could think of to assure the preservation of the children of Israel. Of particular interest here is the concluding verse of the passage, which states in effect that when all is said and done, God is stuck with the children of Israel because *they are Thy people and Thine inheritance, that Thou didst bring out by Thy great power and by Thy outstretched arm.* God surely knew from the outset that, as descendents of the Patriarchs, they were stiff-necked, yet He chose to free them from servitude in Egypt and to make a new covenant with them. Accordingly, as might have been expected under the circumstances, Moses' intervention was successful.

The story of the second ascension of the mount described here does not fit well with the narrative in the book of Exodus; however, their harmonization, which has been attempted by many commentators, is not at all critical to understanding what Moses is trying to achieve through these discourses and will not be pursued any farther in this study of them.

> [10.1] *At that time YHVH said unto me: 'Hew thee two tables of stone like unto the first, and come up unto Me into the mount; and make thee an ark of wood.* [10.2] *And I will write on the tables the words that were on the first tables which thou didst break, and thou shalt put them in the ark.'* [10.3] *So I made an ark of acacia wood, and hewed two tables of stone like unto the first, and went up into the mount, having the two tables in my hand.* [10.4] *And He wrote on the tables, according to the first writing, the ten words, which YHVH spoke unto you in the mount out of the midst of the fire in the day of the assembly; and YHVH gave them unto me.* [10.5] *And I turned and came down from the mount, and put the tables in the ark which I had made; and there they are, as YHVH commanded me.*

It does not seem reasonable to suppose that *at that time* refers to the time immediately following the smashing of the first tablets; Moses surely would have had to obtain divine forgiveness for the people before he would be instructed regarding a second set of tablets. According to some, this suggests that Moses' pleading on behalf of the people took place while he was in the Israelite camp below, before he ascended the mountain a second time.[426] However, whether the opening verse of this passage refers to the second ascension, as the above comment suggests, or to yet a third ascension is a matter of contention among commentators and is a question to which I do not have a useful response, and as already suggested, resolution of that issue is not critical to understanding the substance of the text.

Some commentators are perplexed by the command that, in addition to carving the stone tablets, Moses is told to *make thee an ark of wood* to house the tablets, something that was not ordered for the first set of tablets, even though it seems obvious that they would have to be kept in some sort of receptacle. Moreover, Moses is specifically instructed with regard to the second set, *thou shalt put them in the ark.* It has been argued that this element of the passage implicitly reflects some irritation with him for having smashed the first set of tablets, albeit that he did so for good reason, as discussed above. In any case, by specifically instructing him to build an ark for the tablets and to place them therein, God seems to be making it clear that He does not want to see this second set destroyed, the instruction regarding the ark serving as an implicit warning to Moses not to dare once again to destroy the tablets to which God effectively affixed his imprimatur by inscribing His words thereon.[427]

The text informs us that Moses was instructed to carve two blank tablets and bring them with him to the summit of the mount, where they were to be inscribed, *according to the first writing.* The question, of course, is why this procedure was necessary. The first time, the tablets were taken from the mountain itself. Why does Moses, for whom the climb itself must be exhausting, have to cut the stone tablets below and carry them up to the summit, compounding the difficulty? Perhaps it was done deliberately so that word should spread through the camp that Moses was ascending the mountain once again to see God, and to re-inscribe the tablets with the words that had earlier been conveyed to them and to which they declared their acceptance, before publicly transgressing the Second Commandment.

That the second set of tablets was to be prepared *according to the first writing* has been understood as indicating most emphatically, "God does not alter His Law to accommodate the lapses of man," thus emphasizing that "the Torah is something fixed and unalterable." It is noteworthy that this text has been used polemically to argue, "Not reform of the Torah, our reform to the Torah remains for all times the one task."[428]

It also has been suggested that there was a deeper purpose behind the command that Moses prepare the stone tablets and bring them to the summit of Sinai, where God would inscribe the Decalogue on them once again. In the case of the original tablets, both the tablets and the Decalogue inscribed on them came directly from God. Moses ascended the mountain empty-handed and returned with the inscribed tablets. There was, however, a danger in this, namely that the tablets themselves be transformed into an idol or a fetish, given the proven disposition of the people to worship such. "The golden calf convinced God that this people, with their deeply rooted attachment to idolatry and fetishism were not the appropriate recipients for heavenly tablets." They might have concluded that both the stone tablets and the writing on them were equally sacred, whereas they should have understood that only the writing, reflecting the voice of God was divine, not the stones on which they were written. It was for this reason that Moses was asked to prepare the second set of tablets so that the people would know that it was he who shaped them and took them, smooth-faced without writing on them, up the mountain to God, and that the writing alone that could be seen on them when he returned was divine in origin. Accordingly, it was argued, the true significance of this story is that "Only the voice, the thought, the word, the commandment, that which had been written, should have been reckoned as heavenly and the work of God."[429]

> (*[10.6]* And the children of Israel journeyed from Beeroth-benejaakan to Moserah; there Aaron died, and there he was buried; and Eleazar his son ministered in the priest's office in his stead. *[10.7]* From thence they journeyed unto Gudgod; and from Gudgod to Jotbah, a land of brooks of water. *[10.8]* At that time YHVH separated the tribe of Levi, to bear the ark of the covenant of YHVH, to stand before YHVH to minister unto Him, and to bless in His name, unto this day. *[10.9]* Wherefore Levi hath no portion nor inheritance with his brethren; YHVH is his inheritance, according as YHVH thy Elohim spoke unto him).

Moses' discourse is interrupted with a parenthetical statement primarily concerning Aaron and his sons, noting the location of the burial site of Aaron, and the succession of his son Eleazar to his position of high priest. It would appear that the author or editor of the text introduced this information because he wanted to make it clear to the reader that the place of the priests and Levites in the community of Israel was divinely ordained, and there was no better place to do so in the book because of the mention here of the ark that contained the tablets of the Decalogue, which the Levites were charged with caring for and carrying when necessary.[430]

It has been noted by many commentators that the indication that Aaron died and was buried at Moserah does not comport with the earlier statement that he died at Mount Hor (Num. 20:28), some contending that as was the case with Horeb and Mount Sinai, Moserah is the name of the mountainous area in which Mount Hor is located. In any case, what is most noteworthy is not the location of where Aaron died but the reason given for his demise at this point in time. God said, *Aaron shall be gathered unto his people; for he shall not enter into the land which I have given unto the children of Israel, because ye rebelled against My word at the waters of Meribah* (Num. 20:24).

However, the assertion *ye rebelled* is directed at both Aaron and Moses for their evident impatience with the people who were complaining about the lack of water, and Moses' consequent act of striking the rock to cause water to gush forth, instead of merely speaking to the rock as God instructed him, thereby evoking divine anger. *And YHVH said unto Moses and Aaron: 'Because ye believed not in Me, to sanctify Me in the eyes of the children of Israel, therefore ye shall not bring this assembly into the land which I have given them'* (Num. 20:12). As noted earlier with respect to this verse, the sin entailed that by striking the rock it made it appear that it was Moses' act that was causing the water to flow, whereas it would have been clear that if the water came forth as a result of waving his rod and speaking to the rock, that it was divine intervention that was the cause. Accordingly, Moses too should have been refused entry into the land on this same basis, as many traditional commentators contend; yet Moses himself stated seemingly unequivocally more than once, as discussed earlier, that it was because of the affair of the spies that he was denied entry. And, if this is the case, it must be assumed that Moses was forgiven for his actions *at the waters of Meribah*, whereas Aaron, who merely assisted him in assembling the people, was not forgiven, a distinction that begs for explication. However, since the episode *at the waters of Meribah* took place after the affair of the spies, as discussed earlier, if Moses was already denied entry into the land because of the latter, there would not be much point in re-imposing denial of entry because of his smiting the rock, which would suggest that Moses was not forgiven for what he did *at the waters of Meribah* but that since the punishment of dying in exile had already been imposed, any additional punishment would have faded in importance for the aging leader.

The statement, *at that time*, is ambiguous and may be interpreted in at least two ways. One is that it refers to the period following the death of Aaron, when the tribe of Levi, in accordance with the divine wish, was assigned the exclusive responsibility for the *ark of the covenant* and the tabernacle and effectively all matters of a sacral nature. Alternatively, *at that time* may be understood as referring to the time of the incident of the golden calf and its immediate aftermath, when the tribe of Levi stood apart from the rest of the people, and joined Moses in executing those who actively participated in the sacrilege. *And the sons of Levi did according to the word of Moses; and there fell of the people that day about three thousand men. And Moses said: 'Consecrate yourselves today to YHVH . . . that He may also bestow upon you a blessing this day'* (Ex. 32:28-29). The presumption then, is that from that point on, the Levites were consecrated to God and given charge of the sanctuary and everything pertaining thereto.[431] And subsequently, once the tabernacle was constructed and there was work for them to do with regard to it, to facilitate their total engagement with sacral matters, the entire tribe was denied its own portion of the land that was to be distributed among the tribes to preclude its distraction by mundane agricultural concerns.[432] In effect, their needs were to be satisfied through assignment of a portion of the sacrifices brought to the tabernacle, and the establishment of a system of tithing in their behalf.

> [10.10] *Now I stayed in the mount, as at the first time, forty days and forty nights; and YHVH hearkened unto me that*

time also; YHVH would not destroy thee. ^10.11^ *And YHVH*
said unto me: 'Arise, go before the people, causing them
to set forward, that they may go in and possess the land,
which I swore unto their fathers to give unto them.

This passage is a continuation of Moses' accounts of his intercession on Mount Sinai, which the text interrupted with the passage about Aaron. Moses states that he remained on the mountain for another forty days and nights to receive the second set of tablets, and successfully interceded on behalf of the people to avert the unleashing of divine wrath that would have eradicated them. And God told him at that time to lead the people to the land promised to their forefathers. Of course, this did not happen at the time because of the problem of the spies. Now, thirty-eight years later, Moses can cite the same divine command to the new generation that will shortly cross the Jordan to fulfill the divine commitment to the Patriarchs.

^10.12^ *And now, Israel, what doth YHVH require of thee,*
but to fear YHVH thy Elohim, to walk in all His ways,
and to love Him, and to serve YHVH thy Elohim with all
thy heart and with all thy soul; ^10.13^ *to keep for thy good*
the commandments of YHVH, and His statutes, which
I command thee this day? ^10.14^ *Behold, unto YHVH thy*
Elohim belongeth the heaven, and the heaven of heavens,
the earth, with all that therein is. ^10.15^ *Only YHVH had a*
delight in thy fathers to love them, and He chose their seed
after them, even you, above all peoples, as it is this day.

Moses concludes his second discourse or sermon with a final review of why Israel owes God obedience and the beneficence God is prepared to shower upon them in their land. He begins with an assertion of what he considers to be the essence of the covenant between God and Israel. What, he asks, *doth YHVH require of thee?* This rhetorical question seems intended to suggest that, in the final analysis, there is nothing that God is asking of you that is so unreasonable and burdensome that you are constantly rebelling against Him. Of course, God had already conveyed to the people a host of specific rules and regulations that were to be followed, but these are not what Moses is getting at with this rhetorical question. As he understands it, the essence of what God wants from the children of Israel is "nothing impossible or extraordinary, but what is simple, and within the people's duty—fear, love, service and fulfillment of commandments."[433]

But is it really so simple? It is one thing, and rather simple at that, to fear someone or something that can cause you bodily harm, or to love those such as parents or spouses who love you and help you deal with the problems of life. The objects of fear and love are more often than not tangible and visible, reflecting an existing or potential physical relationship. However, it is extraordinarily difficult to relate in this manner to an incorporeal God, whose very existence is beyond human comprehension, and with whom only a Moses can communicate face to face. Nonetheless, Moses is telling the people, this can be done, if they put their minds and wills to it, notwithstanding that "the mind finds it most difficult to form a true conception of God, since it is not aided by the senses. Yet any man of normal intelligence can come to feel that he is actually communing with God, let him but give thought and attention to the matter."[434]

Viewed from another perspective, what Moses is doing in this passage is explaining the extraordinary kindness of God, while effectively acknowledging that it is very difficult for a person to attain the requisite degree of fear, love, and service with all one's heart and soul. God therefore made it easier for man, commanding him merely to observe His statutes and commandments, and to attain thereby attain the equivalent of what he would garner from service with all his heart and soul. "The meaning of the above passage is therefore this: Now, Israel, consider the wonderful kindness of God. What does He ask of you? Instead of the fear of God, instead of walking in His ways and loving Him, instead of serving Him with all your heart and soul, all of which you are obliged to do—He asks merely to keep the commandments of God and His statutes which I command you this day, for your good."[435]

It is noteworthy that a later prophet would pose the same question regarding what God wants of man, and offer a somewhat different response: *Only to do justly, and to love mercy, and to walk humbly with thy Elohim* (Micah 6:8). However, the problem that Moses faced was different from the widespread deterioration of values that were of primary concern to the later prophet. For Moses, the key problem was that the people had not fully internalized the nature of their relation to the unseen and un-seeable God who intervened in their lives whenever He saw it fit to do so. Although acting out of love of God would certainly be considered the more appropriate motivation, under the circumstances motivation from fear of God seemed more attainable in the short run, and might indeed ultimately lead to love of God.[436] Moses thus gave priority in his response to the *fear* of God. Fear is a powerful motive for compliance with rules that one may neither understand nor choose to follow on his or her own initiative. This unruly stiff-necked people needed discipline, and a healthy fear of God would well serve all but the most recalcitrant as an incentive to heed the divine word. Indeed, the biblical sage would later observe that *the fear of YHVH is the beginning of knowledge* (Prov. 1:7), or as the psalmist put it, *the fear of YHVH is the beginning of wisdom* (Ps. 111:10). The later rabbinic sages taught: "Every man who possesses learning without the fear of Heaven is like a treasurer who is entrusted with the inner keys but not with the outer: how is he to enter?"[437]

The question that may be asked is the meaning of *fear* in the present text, given that the Hebrew term *yirah* may be understood to mean "awe" or "reverence" as well as "fear" in its usual connotation. *Yirah* as fear would imply acting in appropriate ways out of concern of what might happen if one failed to do so. Alternatively, *yirah* as awe or reverence implies acting appropriately out of acceptance of divine wisdom, which is reflected in the concern that one might not be acting in a manner that one ought.[438] Some have suggested that the latter notion of *yirah* as awe or reverence is the essence of faith, "the demand of total surrender to the subject of ultimate concern," that is, "the state of being ultimately and unconditionally concerned" about God and what He asks of us.[439] It seems most likely that this is the intended meaning of the term in the present text.[440]

The statement, *what doth YHVH require of thee, but to fear YHVH thy Elohim*, has also been understood to affirm one of the principal teachings of the Torah, namely, that man has been granted moral autonomy, as a famous rabbinic adage puts it, "Everything is in the hand of heaven except the fear of heaven."[441] If this were not the case, God would not have to ask for it. Returning to the preceding point, the implication of this is that what Moses is interested in is not some primal fear of the unknown but a conscious fear of the known, of the omnipotent God who brought the children of Israel out from servitude in Egypt, the omnipotent God who fed them in the wilderness, and the omnipotent God who is giving them the land they are about to enter. To maintain a rational fear of offending such a God places one, as the ancient authors noted, on the road to true knowledge and wisdom.

The requirement, *to walk in all His ways*, seems to imply the concept of *imitatio Dei*, the conscious emulation of God. In this regard, it has been asserted: "Because the moral is divine, therefore you shall be moral, and because the divine is moral, you shall become like unto God. It may be said that the highest form and ultimate purpose of human life is likeness to God, and the ethical ideals are conceived as attributes of God, in whose image man was created, and whose copy and image it is man's task to strive to become."[442] However, the notion of man being urged to imitate God may strike one as rather problematic, given that we have virtually no knowledge of God or His nature, which may explain why there is no Hebrew term equivalent to *imitatio Dei*. Indeed, it has been suggested that the concept of *imitatio Dei* "is the central paradox of Judaism. A paradox, for how should man be able to imitate God, the invisible, incomprehensible, unformed, not-to-be-formed? One can only imitate that of which one has an idea--no matter whether it be an idea springing from the imagination or the memory; but as soon as one forms an idea of God, it is no longer he whom one conceives, and an imitation founded on this conception would be no imitation of him."[443]

How does one characterize the moral likeness of God so as to permit man to emulate it? The concept of imitating God has traditionally been understood to refer to man's imitation of the acts of divine beneficence, as these are presented both explicitly and implicitly in Scripture. Thus, the rabbis taught: "The Holy One, blessed be He, who is called righteous and upright, created man in His image only that he might be righteous and upright like Him."[444] In another source, the rabbis elaborated further on this theme by identifying additional divine attributes for emulation: "As God is called merciful, so should you be merciful; as the Holy One, blessed be He, is called gracious, so too should you be gracious. . . . As God is called righteous . . . so too should you be righteous. As God is called kind . . . so too should you be kind."[445]

The rabbis observed that Scripture also offers implicit examples of providential deeds that merit emulation by man:

> What means the text *Ye shall walk after the Lord your God*
> [Deut. 13:5]? Is it, then, possible for a human being to
> walk after the *Shekhinah*; for has it not been said, *For
> YHVH thy Elohim is a devouring fire* [Deut. 4:24]? But
> the [meaning is] to walk after the attributes of the Holy
> One, blessed be He. As he clothes the naked, for it is
> written, *And YHVH Elohim made for Adam and for his
> wife coats of skin, and clothed them* [Gen. 3:21], so do
> thou also clothe the naked. The Holy One, blessed be
> He, visited the sick, for it is written, . . . [Gen. 18:1],
> so do thou also visit the sick. The Holy One, blessed
> be He, comforted mourners, for it is written, . . . [Gen.
> 25:11], so do thou also comfort mourners. The Holy
> One, blessed be He, buried the dead, for it is written, .
> . . [Deut. 34:6], so do thou also bury the dead.[446]

The clear implication of all this is that man should aspire to emulate those divine deeds which by their very nature will contribute to the enhancement of man's moral stature and the further enrichment of his essential humanity. By making such imitation of God a principal teaching of Judaism, the rabbis effectively established it as a foundation of Israel's moral law.[447]

It is especially noteworthy that the focus in these teachings is on man's affective behavior; his practical activity that directly and positively touches the lives of others. There is neither implication nor suggestion that one should seek to imitate those attributes of God that may have other evidently less favorable consequences for man. "The teachers of Judaism set bounds to this call to imitate God. We may only imitate His mercy and His love, not His sternness. The sterner aspects of God's providence, those deriving from His role as Judge, are not invoked by the Rabbis as models for man's imitation."[448] Similarly, it has been observed "that this God-likeness is confined to his manifestations of mercy and righteousness, the Rabbis rarely desiring the Jew to take God as a model in His attributes of severity and rigid justice, though the Bible could have furnished them with many instances of this latter kind."[449]

Moreover, "it is distinctly taught that man should not imitate God in the following four things, which He alone can use as instruments. They are, jealousy, revenge, exaltation, and acting in devious ways."[450] With regard to jealousy, it is written: *For I YHVH thy Elohim am a jealous God* (Ex. 20:5). This was interpreted as meaning: "A God above jealousy: I rule over jealousy, but jealousy has no power over me."[451] The evident implication of this is that it is only God, and not man, who can remain unaffected by jealousy.[452] Accordingly, this is one divine attribute that man is not to attempt to emulate because jealousy will pervert sound judgment. With regard to revenge, the divine proscription is patent: *Thou shalt not take vengeance, nor bear any grudge against the children of thy people* (Lev. 19:18). *Vengeance is Mine* (Deut. 32:35). With regard to "exaltation" and "acting in devious ways," their implications seem self-evident; self-exaltation will lead to unmitigated arrogance and moral indifference, and deviousness will pervert morality and ethics. Similarly, with respect to the divine exercise of stern judgment, it is God alone who has unerring knowledge of the universe and can truly judge the merits of the men He has created. Because of man's basic limitations in this regard, he is adjured to function in strict accordance with the concepts of justice that are set forth for him in the Torah, and not on the basis of any self-styled analogy to his Creator. The idea that the ways of God become the laws of God for mankind "applies only to the extent to which those ways may be projected to the human scene. Insofar, however, God's way is God's *mishpat* [justice] as the cosmic order of God envisaged appropriateness, no *imitatio Dei* is possible."[453]

With regard to the requirement *to love Him*, Moses places this third in his order of priority, presumably because it is more difficult to achieve than the two preceding requirements; whereas fear can be brought on instantaneously, love, rather than mere infatuation, requires maturation over time. Because the issues concerning the idea of the love of God have been discussed at some length with regard to the text *And thou shalt love YHVH thy Elohim* (Deut. 6:5) in the preceding chapter, that discussion will not be repeated here.

Moses also adjures the people *to serve YHVH thy Elohim with all thy heart and with all thy soul*. What does it mean *to serve* God? It is assumed by some that this refers to service in the form of prayer.[454] Why would Moses specify prayer as something that God asks of us? Although we cannot know for a certainty what Moses had in mind by this stipulation, it seems reasonable to assume that heartfelt sincere prayer to God will tighten the connection between the God of Israel and man, leaving no room for polytheistic deviances, a matter of primary concern to Moses given the recent history of such. In this regard, Moses earlier admonished the people to beware that if they lapsed into idolatry, they would be turned out of the land, *But from thence ye will seek YHVH thy Elohim; and thou shalt find Him, if thou search after Him with all thy heart and all thy soul* (Deut. 4:29). What Moses is telling them here is that if they *serve* God wholeheartedly, they will avoid lapsing into error and sin in the first place and thus preclude the undesirable consequences that may be expected to follow such violation of the covenant. "The biblical God demands a relationship of exclusivity. You must serve Him *with all your heart* so that no room is left therein for worship of anything else."[455]

Conspicuous by its absence in the statement, *with all thy heart and with all thy soul*, is the third element demanded earlier in the text, *And thou shalt love YHVH thy Elohim with all thy heart, and with all thy soul, and with all thy might.* Could it be that Moses came to the conclusion that the extent of self-sacrifice implied by *with all thy might* was beyond the ability of most people, and therefore was reluctant to restate it here? Interestingly, he does not assert that all this must be done because of its intrinsic value and significance, but rather *to keep for thy good the commandments of YHVH, and His statutes, which I command thee this day*, which would seem to emphasize the primary role of fear in assuring compliance with God's instructions. These commandments and statutes should be carried out and followed, he says, in your own self-interest. "It is not for the benefit of the Lord that he asks this of you. Unlike the gods of the pagans, He is self-sufficient, totally autonomous. He needs neither your offerings nor your praise."[456]

Moreover, if God did not think these commandments and statutes were good for Israel, He would not have issued them. God surely does not require compliance with His commandments and statutes for His sake; He is after all, sovereign of the universe, as it states, *unto YHVH thy Elohim belongeth the heaven, and the heaven of heavens, the earth, with all that therein is*, of which Israel in its entirety is like a speck of dust. Why does God bother with Israel? *Only YHVH had a delight in thy fathers to love them, and He chose their seed after them, even you, above all peoples, as it is this day.* God, beginning with Abraham who sought Him out, took a special interest in how he and his descendents Isaac and Jacob made constructive use of the moral autonomy granted to mankind to reject the prevailing pagan beliefs of their time and to seek attachment to the one and only true God. The children of Israel, Moses tells them, through no special merit of their own, continue to be the recipients of divine beneficence because of their forefathers. However, although this divine commitment to the Patriarchs and the descendents of Jacob/Israel remains intact irrespective of whether or not those descendents merit such consideration, fulfillment of that commitment in any particular generation is indeed contingent on whether it is deserved. It therefore becomes incumbent on the people to establish their worthiness, and this requires action, beginning with serious introspection and behavioral change.

> [10.16] *Circumcise therefore the foreskin of your heart, and be no more stiff-necked.* [10.17] *For YHVH your Elohim, He is Elohim of gods, and Lord of lords, the great God, the mighty, and the awful, who regardeth not persons, not taketh reward.* [10.18] *He doth execute justice for the fatherless and the widow, and loveth the stranger, in giving him food*

and raiment. [10.19] *Love ye therefore the stranger; for ye were strangers in the land of Egypt.*

In effect, Moses tells them that just as circumcision of the foreskin marks one as a party to the covenant, as it did Abraham, so too will removing the hard crust of stubbornness covering their hearts, that seems to make them "impervious to Divine influence," now make them open to God's instruction.[457] However, this notion cannot be generalized. Moses surely wants them to open their hearts to the divine word, but just as surely wants them to remain as stiff-necked as possible with regard to other contrary influences, thus transforming their intrinsic stubbornness from a vice to a virtue. Moreover, he tells them once again that they must do this because by doing otherwise they are challenging the master of the universe. *For YHVH your Elohim, He is Elohim of gods, and Lord of lords, the great God, the mighty, and the awful.* This statement should not be construed as admitting the existence of other gods. The term *elohim,* translated here as *gods* is also used in Scripture to refer to non-divine human entities endowed with authority such as judges, or to celestial agents such as angels.[458] Similarly, it has been argued, *Lord of lords* refers to God's mastery over the constellations and the zodiac that others consider as "lords."[459]

As the one and only almighty God, He *regardeth not persons,* for compared to Him none is worthy of distinction, nor does He *taketh reward;* He does not show favoritism in judgment and cannot be placated or corrupted by gifts, as is the case with some human judges. The implication of this is that Israel makes a grievous error if it believes it can sin and rely on the merits of their ancestors to assure their forgiveness. On the contrary, they were chosen precisely so that they could be held to a higher standard than others. Thus the later prophet could declaim in the name of God: *You only have I known of all the families of the earth; therefore I will visit upon you all your iniquities* (Amos 3:2).

Moses follows up on this point by providing an indication of the higher standard of conduct God expects of them, singling out two aspects in which the Israelites evidently were deemed deficient, social justice and hospitality, two values that were difficult to cultivate sufficiently during centuries of oppression and servitude. Now that they were free, it behooved them to learn from God and emulate His beneficence. Thus, Moses asserts, *He doth execute justice for the fatherless and the widow, and loveth the stranger, in giving him food and raiment. Love ye therefore the stranger; for ye were strangers in the land of Egypt.* One may infer from this latter adjuration that Moses was concerned about the attitude of many of the children of Israel toward the *mixed multitude* that joined them in the exodus, the grandchildren of which now found themselves as an alien minority, whose presence among the children of Israel had been problematic from the start. The implicit presumption of Moses' assertion appears to be that many of the problems resulting from the alien presence among them might have been averted if the Israelites had been more welcoming to them and thereby ultimately absorbing them into the body of the nation. Thus, it has been suggested, we are adjured to love the stranger among us because he does not have recourse to the merit of our forefathers as a mitigating factor.[460] It has also been suggested that the rationale provided for such love, that *ye were strangers in the land of Egypt*, indicates that "the required new feeling is made vivid on the basis of historical consciousness. As little as the memory of the slavery in Egypt should be frightening, so little is it permissible to ask about the stranger's moral qualities, let alone his religious convictions. Only the fellowman is to be discovered in him."[461]

> [10.20] *Thou shalt fear YHVH thy Elohim; Him shalt thou serve; and to Him shalt thou cleave, and by His name shalt thou swear.* [10.21] *He is thy glory, and He is thy Elohim, that hath done for thee these great and tremendous things, which thine eyes have seen.* [10.22] *Thy fathers went down into Egypt with threescore and ten persons; and now YHVH thy Elohin hath made thee as the stars of heaven for multitude.*

The context of this passage suggests that the adjuration *Thou shalt fear* should be taken literally as a matter of prime importance. When the Israelites cross the Jordan they will begin engaging in a seemingly endless series of conflicts with the peoples whose nations they are intent on displacing, and in the proverbial fog of war much exhortation and teaching will be cast aside unless the fear of God remains foremost in their minds. Nonetheless, numerous commentators consider fear in this passage to relate to awe and reverence.

In periods of stress, when things are not going as desired and there is an urge to seek assistance, Moses cautions them not to turn to the gods of the pagans, emphasizing *Him shalt thou serve,* and no other. No matter what hardships may have to be faced and experienced, *to Him shalt thou cleave*; only He will not abandon you. And, when the need arises for you to make a firm and true commitment, only *by His name shalt thou swear.*

The meaning of the Hebrew phrase *hu tehillatkha,* translated as *He is thy glory,* is ambiguous and lends itself to a variety of interpretations. Two possible meanings are "to Him alone is thy praise due" or "He is the cause of thy fame,"[462] because He *hath done for thee these great and tremendous things, which thine eyes have seen.* To emphasize this point, Moses directs their attention to the fact that when their ancestor Jacob descended to Egypt with his sons and their families, they numbered only seventy souls, and that despite their later enslavement and the harsh conditions of their daily lives they nonetheless blossomed into the large population that is about to find their new home in the land promised to their forefathers and to them.

> [11.1] *Therefore thou shalt love YHVH thy Elohim, and keep His charge, and His statutes, and His ordinances, and His commandments, always.*

For the reasons just stated, Moses tells them, they should not only fear God because of His power but that they should love God because He has shown them repeatedly His love for them. And the way to manifest that love in practice is by keeping *His charge*; that is, by living in consonance with the general precepts He has set forth for their guidance. In addition, they must always observe the variety of specific rules and regulations that are to underpin the unique society they are to create in their old-new homeland.

> *^{11.2} And know ye this day; for I speak not with your children that have not known, and that have not seen the chastisement of YHVH your Elohim, His greatness, His mighty hand, and His outstretched arm, ^{11.3} and His signs, and His works, which He did in the midst of Egypt unto Pharaoh the king of Egypt, and unto all his land; ^{11.4} and what He did unto the army of Egypt, unto their horses, and to their chariots; how He made the water of the Sea of Reeds to overflow them as they pursued after you, and how YHVH hath destroyed them unto this day; ^{11.5} and what He did unto you in the wilderness, until ye came unto this place; ^{11.6} and what He did unto Dathan and Abiram, the sons of Eliab, the son of Reuben; how the earth opened her mouth, and swallowed them up, and their households, and their tents, and every living substance that followed them, in the midst of all Israel; ^{11.7} but your eyes have seen all the great work of YHVH which He did. ^{11.8} Therefore shall ye keep all the commandment which I command thee this day, that ye may be strong, and go in and possess the land, whither ye go over to possess it; ^{11.9} and that ye may prolong your days upon the land, which YHVH swore unto your fathers to give unto them and their seed, a land flowing with milk and honey.*

Moses now directs his remarks specifically to the older generation, that is, those between the ages of forty and sixty, many of whom who were alive and below the age of twenty at the time of the exodus. Although his remarks may not have made sufficient impression on their children, who did not personally witness the awesome power of God, the older generation that did witness those events has no excuse whatever for deviating from the path that God had marked out for them. They personally experienced the chastising hand of God as He lashed out against those who defied Him, humiliating the king of Egypt, destroying the elite forces of his army, and how He dealt with the rebels within the Israelite camp, most specifically with Dathan and

Abiram of the tribe of Reuben, who were co-conspirators in a plot to undermine Moses' authority and were severely punished for it (Num. 16). Conspicuous by its absence is any reference here to the leader of the plot, Korah, who was from Moses' own tribe of Levi. The reason for this, it has been suggested, is because, as the text informs us, by contrast with the families of Dathan and Abiram that were killed along with them (Num. 16:32), the *sons of Korah did not* (Num. 26:11). "It was consequently from consideration of their feelings that he omitted the name of their father."[463] It is noteworthy that in a later recounting of the episode of the plot against Moses, it states, *The earth opened and swallowed up Dathan, and covered the company of Abiram* (Ps. 106:17), but no mention is made of Korah, presumably because the compiler of Psalms was sensitive to the fact that the descendents of Korah served as ministers in the sanctuary, as evidenced by the numerous psalms chanted there that bear their names.

Moses concludes his brief historical review with the admonition *Therefore shall ye keep all the commandment which I command thee this day.* That is, if you fail to do this you too will experience the chastising hand of God. Accordingly, it is in their self-interest to have God on their side rather than against them so that they may not only succeed in conquering the land, but also in remaining in control of it, *that ye may prolong your days upon the land, which YHVH swore unto your fathers to give unto them and their seed.* Once again Moses makes the point that although the land, in a sense, is theirs by default as a result of God's promise to their ancestors, it is one thing to hold title to the land and quite another to able to actually possess it. Their ability to do the latter will be contingent on their remaining in God's good graces and this will require that they pay heed to what He requires, indeed demands, of them.

> [11.10] *For the land, whither thou goest in to possess it, is not as the land of Egypt, from whence ye came out, where thou didst sow thy seed, and didst water it with thy foot, as a garden of herbs;* [11.11] *but the land, whither ye go over to possess it, is a land of hills and valleys, and drinketh water as the rain of heaven cometh down;* [11.12] *a land*

*which YHVH thy Elohim careth for; the eyes of YHVH
thy Elohim are always upon it, from the beginning of the
year even unto the end of the year.*

Moses pointedly reminds them that in Egypt, whose agricultural production is wholly dependent on the regular annual flooding of the Nile; its fields had to be watered *with thy foot,* that is by foot-powered water wheels that distributed the water derived from the river, an arduous task that made each plot of land into the equivalent of a well cared for *garden of herbs.* By contrast, the land into which they were about to enter did not require such intense labor for it was provided with water by the annual periods of rain from heaven. It is a land to which God pays special attention throughout the year, determining when and where the rains shall fall. It is noteworthy that some of the rabbis read *the eyes of YHVH thy Elohim are always upon it, from the beginning of the year even unto the end of the year* as asserting that at the beginning of the year God determines how much rain and dew, how much sunshine, and how much wind will take place in the land throughout that year,"[464] all presumably predicated on His evaluation of Israel's performance the preceding year.

> *11.13 And it shall come to pass, if ye shall hearken diligently
> unto My commandments which I command you this day,
> to love YHVH your Elohim, and to serve Him with all
> your heart and with all your soul, 11.14 that I will give the
> rain of your land in its season, the former rain and the
> latter rain, that thou mayest gather in thy corn, and thy
> wine, and thine oil. 11.15 And I will give grass in thy fields
> for thy cattle, and thou shalt eat and be satisfied. 11.16 Take
> heed to yourselves, lest your heart be deceived, and ye turn
> aside, and serve other gods, and worship them; 11.17 and the
> anger of YHVH be kindled against you, and He shut up
> the heaven, so that there shall be no rain, and the ground
> shall not yield her fruit; and ye perish quickly from off the
> good land which YHVH giveth you.*

If they pay heed to what God demands of them, *to love YHVH your Elohim, and to serve Him with all your heart and with all your soul;* if they do all this, God promises that He *will give the rain of your land in its season, the former rain and the latter rain, that thou mayest gather in thy corn, and thy wine, and thine oil.* In effect, God will water all their crops, their vineyards, and their olive groves—all they will have to do is harvest it all, and thus reap the benefits of divine providence, as they did with regard to the *manna* that God provided for them all these years in the wilderness.

As before, again conspicuous by its absence in the statement, *with all your heart and with all your soul,* is the third element demanded earlier in the text, *And thou shalt love YHVH thy Elohim with all thy heart, and with all thy soul, and with all thy might* (Deut. 6:5). It has been noted that the earlier statement is given in the singular, whereas the present statement is given in the plural. Therefore, it is argued, because there may be individuals whose property is more dear to them than their very lives, the statement directed to the individual demands *And thou shalt love . . . with all thy might.* However, because Moses is now directing his remarks to the people as a whole, it is unreasonable to assume that the majority of the people would similarly consider their property more dear to them than their lives, and since Moses is calling upon the people here to *serve him with all your heart and with all your soul,* the latter makes mention of *with all thy might* unnecessary.[465] Nonetheless, the problem that this interpretation presents, as logical as it seems, is that what it does not address is the fact, mentioned above, that it states that what God asks of the children of Israel is to serve Him *with all thy heart and with all thy soul* (Deut. 10:13), omitting *with all thy might,* even though the text is stated in the singular. One possible explanation of the omission of *with all thy [your] might* is that it might be misconstrued as commanding voluntary impoverishment, a notion that would clearly be rejected by Mosaic teaching.

Moses reminds the people that this promised blessing is contingent upon their meriting God's providential concern. Noting that "satiety easily indices forgetfulness,"[466] he warns them that should they allow themselves to come to believe that the rains will arrive as regularly as the Nile overflowed, and *turn aside, and serve other gods, and worship them*, divine beneficence will cease. God will block the heavenly outlets so *that there shall be no rain, and the ground shall not yield her fruit; and ye perish quickly from off the good land which YHVH giveth you.* He does not say what will happen then, but it surely was clear to them that they would be put in the same position as their ancestor Jacob, when the resulting famine in the land prompted his relocation to Egypt, and they all know quite well what happened to them there.

> *11.18 Therefore shall ye lay up these My words in your heart and in your soul; and ye shall bind them for a sign upon your hand, and they shall be for frontlets between your eyes. 11.19 And ye shall teach them your children, talking of them, when thou sittest in thy house, and when thou walkest by the way, and when thou liest down, and when thou risest up. 11.20 And thou shalt write them upon the door-posts of thy house, and upon thy gates; 11.21 that your days may be multiplied, and the days of your children, upon the land which YHVH swore unto your fathers to give them, as the days of the heavens above the earth.*

To help prevent any such possibility, Moses insists that these words of admonition be taken to heart, committed to writing, and that the material on which they are written shall be bound *for a sign upon your hand, and they shall be for frontlets between your eyes.* You are to teach them to your children and thus assure continuity, and to talk about them whenever the opportunity arises, and *thou shalt write them upon the door-posts of thy house, and upon thy gates*, demands that were made earlier, and discussed earlier, with regard to the declaration *Hear O Israel* (Deut. 6:6-9). This, Moses warns, is essential if they wish to survive as a nation in their own land.

> *11.22 For if ye shall diligently keep all this commandment which I command you, to do it, to love YHVH your Elohim, to walk in all His ways, and to cleave unto Him, 11.23 then will YHVH drive out all these nations from before you, and ye shall dispossess nations greater and mightier*

than yourselves. ^{11.24} *Every place whereon the sole of your foot shall tread shall be yours: from the wilderness, and Lebanon, from the river, the river Euphrates, even unto the hinder sea shall be your border.* ^{11.25} *There shall no man be able to stand against you: YHVH your Elohim shall lay the fear of you and the dread of you upon all the land that ye shall tread upon, as He hath spoken unto you.*

With regard to the assertion, *which I command you, to do it,* the rabbis asked, rhetorically, to be sure, why this is stated, given that it already said *for if ye shall diligently keep all this commandment,* which seems to make it redundant. Their response was: "I might think that once one has kept the words of Torah [understood in the sense of not forgetting them], he may stop with that and need not perform them; therefore Scripture goes on to say, *to do it*—the purpose is *to do it.*"⁴⁶⁷ What Moses is primarily concerned with is performance; right thinking alone will not create the moral society that is the goal of God's engagement with Israel. To achieve this, they must learn *to walk in all His ways.* What are God's *ways* that are to be followed? The rabbis singled out the following: mercifulness and compassion, graciousness, and righteousness, all of which are traits essential to fostering social harmony.⁴⁶⁸

Moses assures them that if they fully accept and diligently observe God's demands, and their acting out fear of God becomes transformed to acting out of love for God, then God will respond accordingly and will *drive out all these nations from before you, and ye shall dispossess nations greater and mightier than yourselves.* The symbiotic relationship between God and Israel will be such as to empower the latter to conquer the entire land from the wilderness in the south as far as the Euphrates in the north, and from that river westward to the Mediterranean Sea. They will be able to do this because the awareness that God is with Israel will demoralize their enemies, who will be unable to prevent Israel from dispossessing them.

With regard to the matter of borders, the rabbis read the text, *Every place whereon the sole of your foot shall tread shall be yours: from the wilderness, and Lebanon, from the river, the river Euphrates, even unto the hinder sea shall be your border*, as dealing with two distinct but related considerations. If the purpose of the text was to define the boundaries, as indicated by the assertion, *from the wilderness, and Lebanon, from the river, the river Euphrates, even unto the hinder sea shall be your border*, what is intended by *every place whereon the sole of your foot shall tread shall be yours?* Since it obviously refers to places outside the specified borders, it was inferred that what it was intended to convey was that although any territory conquered outside those borders would become subject to the covenant, priority was to be given to the conquest of the territories within the initially specified borders. Thus, the text states, "*Ye shall dispossess nations greater and mightier than yourselves* (11:23). And afterwards, *Every place whereon the sole of your foot shall tread*, thus indicating that the Land of Israel must not remain contaminated by idols while you turn back and conquer other lands; rather, only after you have conquered the Land of Israel will you be permitted to conquer places outside of it."[469]

Finally, Moses assures his audience, God *shall lay the fear of you and the dread of you upon all the land that ye shall tread upon.* The sentence appears redundant since *fear of you* and *dread of you* seem to say the same thing. The rabbis, however, drew a distinction between the two terms, suggesting that *fear* was imminent whereas *dread* is anticipatory, "*fear* is felt by those who are nearby, and *dread* is felt by those who are far off."[470]

4

RE'EH

(11:26-16:17)

The section begins with a concise summarization of the purpose and intent of Moses' second discourse, sets forth the religious foundations of the covenant, and concludes with that part of the code of laws dealing with worship and related matters.

> ^{11.26} *Behold, I set before you this day a blessing and a curse:* ^{11.27} *the blessing, if ye shall hearken unto the commandments of YHVH your Elohim, which I command you this day;* ^{11.28} *and the curse, if ye shall not hearken unto the commandments of YHVH your Elohim, but turn aside out of the way which I command you this day, to go after other gods, which ye have not known.*

It should be noted that this passage opens with the word *re'eh* or *behold*, a synonym for *see*, raising the question of why Moses uses this term rather than *shema* or *hear*, as he does repeatedly in previous texts, where he calls out *Hear, O Israel*. After all, he is not showing them something that they need to see; he is telling them something that they need to hear. It has been suggested that the choice of *hear* or *see* depends on the particular kind of attention the text wishes to convey to different kinds of messages. Thus it is proposed that the use of *shema* or *hear* indicates that what is being asked for is an intellectual commitment. By contrast, the use of *re'eh* or *behold* indicates that what is being asked for is an emotional commitment. "To 'hear' requires a greater and deeper understanding, and to 'see' requires a greater reaction to an understanding that is already present . . . 'Hearing' requires a greater and deeper understanding because when we are able to hear someone we are able to truly communicate well with them . . . 'Sight' is used to garner our emotions to a great reaction for an understanding that we already have because sight is our strongest and most reliable sense. Seeing really is believing and I can commit to something much more easily when I see it rather than if I only hear it."[471] Although most would probably agree with the notion that sight is our strongest sense, the notion of its being the most reliable sense is a matter of contention and is hardly supportable by the biblical texts.[472] Nonetheless, the distinction drawn between the use of 'hear' and 'see' or 'behold' in the biblical text seems on point. Moses is asking for their commitment to something that can only take place at a later time, and this calls for an emotional conviction in addition to an intellectual one.

Moses, in effect, invites Israel to *behold*, to take note of, and reflect on the retrospective he has presented covering their moral history from the exodus to the present day, when they now find themselves preparing to cross the Jordan to begin the struggle for their God-given homeland. Everything he has said should have led to the conviction that God has given them the ability to shape their own future; their destiny as a nation is in their own hands. God has already told them what He wants and expects from them, and Moses has set forth the rewards of compliance and the punishments that may be expected for non-compliance. What Moses wants to address now is their need to make a deep commitment to their future as a nation under God and decide how to proceed to its realization.[473] The fundamental choice that has been set before them, that is, the choice they must now make before they cross into the land promised to them, is whether to pursue the path of *blessing*, the condition of progressive development and prosperity, or that of the *curse*, the condition of stagnation and deterioration.[474]

It has been suggested that there is another nuance embedded in the text. That is, Moses also is telling them that they are destined to be different from all other nations; for them there can be no middle road of mediocrity. They must excel or fail disastrously. God has not gone through the trouble of bringing them out of Egypt and tolerated their stubbornness and rebelliousness these past forty years for them to become a nation like all others. They will not be permitted that choice. They have but two options: to pursue the course that will lead to *blessing*, success beyond all reasonable expectation, or to pursue the path that will lead to *curse*, the course that will lead to an existence beneath mediocrity.[475] In this same vein, it has been suggested that the blessing and the curse may be understood in the context of the beginning of the following passage, which speaks of conquering and settling the land. That is, if Israel chooses the way of blessing, the gift of the land to them will prove a blessing; they will conquer and settle the land and live in peace. However, if they choose the alternate course, the land will turn out to be a curse for them, for they will be constantly engaged in a struggle for survival in it.[476]

Thus, the passage begins with an implicit affirmation of the fundamental biblical principle of moral autonomy, as Moses will reassert later: *I call heaven and earth to witness against you this day, that I have set before thee life and death, the blessing and the curse; therefore choose life* (Deut. 30:19).[477] It has also been suggested that, contrary to the view that although man is endowed with the freedom to choose from his youth he becomes ensnared by habit and social pressures and effectively loses it, Moses is here insisting unequivocally that man always has the power of moral choice and, accordingly, the children of Israel, individually as well as collectively, have the option of choosing whether or not to *hearken unto the commandments of YHVH your Elohim*, who will hold them accountable for their choice.[478] As indicated, it will be *the blessing, if ye shall hearken unto the commandments of YHVH your Elohim*. However, it should be noted that this translation obscures an important nuance in the Hebrew text, which does not actually say *im tishme'u* or *if ye shall hearken*, but rather *asher tishme'u* or *that ye shall hearken*. In other words, the *hearkening* itself constitutes an essential element of the blessing. As one commentator put it, "The mental and moral act which is accomplished every time we faithfully obey the Torah is itself a blessed progress, a step forward of our whole being."[479] In other words, the text may be understood as suggesting that conforming to the tenets of the covenant is in itself an ennobling and enriching experience.

By contrast, the text does say with regard to the curse, *if ye shall not hearken*, again clearly indicating that one may choose to do otherwise. Thus, Moses cautions, each choice entails rather different consequences, a certain blessing for compliance and the probability of a curse for non-compliance, especially if the latter involves turning away from God *to go after other gods, which ye have not known*, or as the New JPS translation has it, *other gods whom you have not experienced or who have not proved themselves to you.*[480] That is, as one prophet put it, *I am YHVH thy Elohim from the land of Egypt; and thou knowest no Elohim but Me, and beside Me there is no savior* (Hos. 13:4). No other god has done anything for you, and to go after such a god would be the equivalent of treasonous betrayal of your sovereign lord, a crime that will not go unpunished. By employing the phrase, *which ye have not known*, Moses again raises the argument of Israel's obligation to God, whom they have known, either directly or by collective memory, through His interventions in their recent history. In effect, what Moses is saying is that mere belief in the existence of God is insufficient; it is acceptance of God as our sovereign lord and our submission to His law that He demands.

It has also been observed that there is a significant difference in the way the text deals with the notion of the blessing and the curse. As a general proposition, wherever the text mentions *hearken*, it is immediately followed by some verb indicating action, such as *to do*, indicating that understanding a commandment is not sufficient in itself unless it results in proper action. Thus, when the text says, with regard to the curse, *if ye shall not hearken unto the commandments of YHVH your Elohim*, it is immediately followed by the negative action, *but turn aside out of the way which I command you this day*. There is no sin until there is an actual violation of the commandment. But, in this passage, with regard to the blessing, it simply states, *if ye shall hearken unto the commandments of YHVH your Elohim*, it does not say anything about actually doing them, which is clearly an anomaly. It is therefore suggested that what the text is intimating is that in this instance, the blessing begins to take effect as soon as the intention to carry out the divine commandments becomes internalized, thus enabling the person to resist attempts at subversion, whereas with regard to the curse, it does not take effect until after the subversion actually takes place, effectively leaving open only the opportunity for repentance and change of heart.[481]

Addressing the distinction between the treatment of the blessing and the curse, it also has been suggested that, with regard to the former, it states simply that the blessing will be yours *if ye shall hearken unto the commandments.* The implication of this is that there is but one path that leads to felicity and that is the path of *hearkening,* which is in itself a blessing. By contrast, the road to the curse has many bypaths, which starts out with one *not hearken[ing] unto the commandments,* thus stepping on to the slippery slope of increasing non-compliance leading you to *turn aside out of the way which I command you this day,* and ultimately *to go after other gods,* earning you the divine curse. That is, the typical pattern of those who choose not to *hearken* is to begin their rebellion by transgressing a minor restriction and, when nothing happens to them, they then proceed to increasingly more serious transgressions until they are in open revolt against God.[482]

> [11.29] *And it shall come to pass, when YHVH thy Elohim shall bring thee into the land whither thou goest to possess it, that thou shalt set the blessing upon mount Gerizim, and the curse upon mount Ebal. (* [11.30] *Are they not beyond the Jordan, behind the way of the going down of the sun, in the land of the Canaanites that dwell in the Arabah, over against Gilgal, beside the terebinths of Moreh?)* [11.31] *For ye are to pass over the Jordan to go in to possess the land which YHVH your Elohim giveth you, and ye shall possess it, and dwell therein.* [11.32] *And ye shall observe to do all the statutes and the ordinances which I set before you this day.*

The test of their intentions will come not now, when they are about to cross into the promised land, but as soon as they have established a foothold in the center of the land. At that time, before they complete the conquest and settlement of the entire land, they are to *set the blessing upon mount Gerizim, and the curse upon mount Ebal.* The latter statement appears to be saying that they are to bless one mountain and curse the other, which seems rather bizarre. Accordingly, the Aramaic translation of the text renders the Hebrew *venatata et haberakhah*, or *thou shalt set the blessing*, as *vetiten yat mevorkhaya* or *thou shalt set those who bless*,[483] a translation that unravels the mystery of the text. That is, according to this rendition of the verse, when they reach the center of the country, they shall assemble near the twin mountains of Gerizim and Ebal, and place those who are to deliver the blessing *if ye shall hearken unto the commandments*, and the curse *if ye shall not hearken unto the commandments*, on the slopes of Gerizim and Ebal respectively so that they can address the people from above.

It has been argued, however, that although this interpretation resolves some of the issues that may be raised with regard to the text, it does not conform to the actual wording of it. Accordingly, it is suggested that the word *venatata* may also be understood to mean "pronounce," which would then render the text as, *thou shalt pronounce the blessing upon mount Gerizim, and the curse upon mount Ebal*, which makes what is proposed more comprehensible.[484] That is, they are to conduct there a public ceremony of commitment to the covenant, with the mountains serving as physical metaphors of the blessing and the curse. According to the rabbis, when the blessings and the curses were pronounced, the people turned first to one mountain and then to the other, answering *Amen*, thereby affirming their acceptance of the challenge presented to them.[485] The ceremony is described in further detail later (Deut. 27:11-26).

It is noteworthy that when Joshua reached the area during the conquest, he positioned the priests in the valley between the mountains, and not on the mountains as suggested above, some facing Gerizim and some facing Ebal, where he assembled all the people, *half of them in front of mount Gerizim, and half of them in front of mount Ebal; as Moses the servant of YHVH had commanded at the first, that they should bless the people of Israel. And afterward he read all the words of the law, the blessing and the curse, according to all that is written in the book of the law* (Josh. 8:33-34). The rabbis both amplified and modified this description by adopting in part the description given later (Deut. 27:11-26), that six tribes went up the slope of each mountain as far as the top, with the priests and the Levites positioned between them with the ark. They then turned first toward Gerizim and began with the blessing, "Blessed be the man that maketh not a graven or a molten image," effectively reciting the curses in the form of blessings. They then turned toward Ebal and recited the actual curses, beginning with *Cursed be the man that maketh a graven or molten image* (Deut. 27:15).[486]

Because of their geological composition and orientation, the two opposing mountains, their peaks some three and a half kilometers apart, represent two extremes, Gerizim being lush with vegetation and Ebal appearing largely devoid of such, the former suggesting the blessing and the latter the curse. The implications of the differences between the mountains, and the symbolism attached to them should serve as a reminder to the children of Israel of the choice they must continually make. No further verbal elaboration regarding the choice of the site was deemed necessary; the visual perception said it all.[487] They are to do this because, in fact, they are about to cross the Jordan to conquer and settle the land *your Elohim giveth you.* By so doing, God fulfills His commitment to the covenant He entered into with their forefathers as well as with them. It remains for them to fulfill their part of the agreement and toward that end, Moses asserts, *ye shall observe to do all the statutes and the ordinances which I set before you this day.* It has been pointed out that this stipulation requires that the people generally be familiar with all the statutes and ordinances for which they are to be held accountable for compliance, which means they must study them in order to do them.[488] Presumably it was for this reason that the rabbis understood the phrase *ye shall observe* in the adjuration to mean you shall study.[489]

In lieu of a footnote, a literary contrivance unknown in antiquity, the text interrupts Moses' discourse to insert a parenthetical notice presumably for the benefit of those unfamiliar with the sites referred to, and specifies their location in Cisjordan, *in the land of the Canaanites,* along the main north-south route passing east of Shechem, alongside the *terebinths of Moreh,* a site associated with the life of Abraham; it was the site at which Abraham arrived when he entered Cisjordan and where God appeared to him, promising to give the land to his descendents

(Gen. 12:6). Now his descendents are returning to that very place to take possession of the land promised to Abraham.[490]

It should be noted that the specification of the location of the mountains as being *in the land of the Canaanites that dwell in the Arabah* is highly problematic because, in fact, the mountains are actually located some thirty miles west of the area presumably being described as the *Arabah* and thus nowhere near the biblical city of *Gilgal* mentioned later (Josh. 4:20), which is near the Jordan. Although scholars have addressed this issue, to date no compelling explanation of what appears to be a gross geographical error has been forthcoming.[491] Nonetheless, perhaps the most promising of proposed solutions is that which suggests that the *Arabah* mentioned here does not refer to the Jordan valley but rather to a valley in Samaria, and that the *Gilgal* mentioned here is another site about three kilometers south of Mount Gerizim bearing the same name in antiquity, where Joshua presumably established his headquarters in the heart of the country.[492] Indeed, another nearby *Gilgal* is purported to have been a Canaanite royal city located in the Sharon plain southwest of Shechem.[493] There is also a *Gilgal* mentioned later in connection with the story of Elijah that apparently was located in the hill country near Bethel (2 Kings 2:1). The text thus earlier indicated that the Amorites lived in the hill country, and the text here is pointing out that the Canaanites lived in the lowlands.[494]

Having set the stage, so to speak, Moses proceeds to lay out the code of laws that the children of Israel are to follow in fulfillment of their commitment to the covenant, beginning with the laws relating to matters of worship and other religious matters that will occupy the remainder of this section. Until this point in his discourse, Moses has spoken in terms of general principles regarding the need for conformance with the divine laws that are to be the basis for the unique society they are to build and the civilization they are to create. Now he turns to the specific precepts and laws that are to be put into practice, first and foremost, those concerning their exclusive loyalty to God as their sovereign lord.

12.1 These are the statutes and the ordinances, which ye shall observe to do in the land which YHVH, the Elohim of thy fathers, hath given thee to possess it, all the days that ye live upon the earth. [12.2] *Ye shall surely destroy all of the places, wherein the nations that ye are to dispossess served their gods, upon the high mountains, and upon the hills, and under every leafy tree.* [12.3] *And ye shall break down their altars, and dash in pieces their pillars, and burn their Asherim with fire; and ye shall hew down the graven images of their gods; and ye shall destroy their name out of that place.*

Moses begins by asserting that, in addition to those laws already announced that are to be observed in perpetuity wherever they find themselves, *all the days that ye live upon the earth*, the following relate specifically to the land *which YHVH, the Elohim of thy fathers, hath given thee to possess it.*[495] Indeed, observance of *the statutes and the ordinances* is a necessary condition for possessing the land *all the days that ye live upon the earth.*[496] As a matter of highest priority, they are to eliminate any public manifestation of the polytheism of the nations they are going to displace. This is essentially a reprise of the commandment in this same regard issued earlier (Deut. 7:1-5), the focus here being exclusively on the religious aspects of the conquest and settlement. The demand being made is harsh and unequivocal. All semblances of pagan worship are to be destroyed, all *altars* and *pillars*, the latter probably referring to phallic steles, although it has been suggested that the *pillars* were pedestals on which idols might be placed,[497] to be demolished, and sacred trees (*Asherim*) to be consumed by fire. It has been observed that the form of the verb used in the command, *Ye shall surely destroy*, indicates that the intent is that the people themselves undertake this chore directly, that it is to be a popular hands-on project. Therefore it does not say, "Ye shall cause to be destroyed."[498] Perceived from this standpoint, Moses deemed it important that the people participate directly in the elimination of all manifestations of paganism; passivity in this regard might reflect personal disinterest or indifference.

It is noteworthy that the rabbis asserted that the meaning of the passage is that what is to be destroyed are the manmade objects of worship to be found on the mountains and the hills, and not the mountains and hills themselves, which are not the creations of man. As for the sacred trees, although they are not creations of man, they were treated as an exception to the general rule. If the tree became a sacred site after it was planted, it was to be destroyed, but the trunk might be left intact. If, on the other hand, it was planted for the purpose of serving as an *Asherah*, it was to be burned to the ground.[499] It would seem that the special concern with sacred trees was their pervasiveness and ease of access, the *Asherah*, in the view of many, being a tree serving as a symbol of the goddess of fertility, Astarte.[500]

The command, *ye shall destroy their name out of that place*, seems to have been interpreted in part as requiring changing the names of places that were conquered if they included the names of gods, such a *Baal-meon* (Num. 32:38). It has also been suggested that the commandment applied to structures that served as pagan temples, requiring that any idolatrous sign or symbol be removed from them even if no longer used for such worship.[501] However, the rabbis interpreted the command as limiting the required destruction of shrines, altars, and other paraphernalia, to *that place*, that is, "in the Land of Israel you are commanded to pursue their destruction, outside the Land of Israel you are not commanded to do so."[502] The rationale for this position is that "the gentiles outside the land are not idolaters, they only continue the customs of their ancestors."[503] That is, despite their paganism, they are not considered guilty of any deliberate rebellion against God because they do not know of Him. Moreover, the fact that they follow the traditions received from their parents is considered meritorious. Indeed, traditions handed down from generation to generation is expected to be the means by which compliance with the covenant is to be inculcated in subsequent generations of Israelites.

In short, given the religiously unstable history of the Israelites during the relatively short period of four decades since the exodus, there was to be zero tolerance for anything that might to contribute to such errant behavior in the land that they were about to conquer and settle. There is no suggestion whatever that this policy extended to the homes of non-Israelites, or that any pressure was to be placed on non-Israelites to reject their traditional beliefs and modes of worship, as long as they were not done publicly. This policy of public religious intolerance evidently was deemed necessary because of Israelite weakness and susceptibility to religious assimilation rather than triumphalism. The full acceptance of the belief in a God that could not be seen or represented in any manner was an extraordinarily difficult challenge for people long conditioned to visual imagery, with which paganism abounded. It would take a long time before *hearkening* to the word of God would overcome decisively the notion that "seeing is believing," and until that happened the nation of Israel would remain susceptible to pagan cultural influences that placed the entire covenantal enterprise and therefore Israel itself in danger of divine abandonment. Accordingly, those influences in the Israelite homeland had to be minimized, and the demand that Moses makes of the people, as a matter of highest priority, is to do what was necessary to accomplish that goal.

It is noteworthy that some rabbis associated the next verse with the preceding demand that *ye shall destroy their name out of that place. Ye shall not do so unto YHVH your Elohim*, and understood it as saying that it constitutes an implicit prohibition against destroying or mutilating anything dedicated to the service of God, including erasing even a single letter from the written name of God, an act to be considered a violation of a negative commandment.[504] This subsequently led to the Jewish practice of burying books and letters containing the name of God rather than destroying them.

> *12.4 Ye shall not do so unto YHVH your Elohim. 12.5 But unto the place which YHVH your Elohim shall choose out of all your tribes to put His name there, even unto His habitation shall ye seek, and thither thou shalt come; 12.6 and thither ye shall bring your burnt-offerings, and your sacrifices, and your tithes, and the offering of your hand, and your vows, and your freewill-offerings, and the firstlings of your herd and of your flock; 12.7 and there ye shall eat before YHVH your Elohim, and ye shall rejoice in all that ye put your hand unto, ye and your households, wherein YHVH thy Elohim hath blessed thee.*

Having already noted that pagan worship took place *upon the high mountains, and upon the hills, and under every leafy tree*, Moses insists *Ye shall not do so unto YHVH your Elohim*. Whereas a plethora of various sorts of sacred sites served the purposes of paganism, it would not do for establishing monotheism as the sole and unique religion of the Israelites in their national homeland. Moses clearly was concerned that simply replacing the paraphernalia at the pagan sites with Israelite altars would prove counterproductive. Although he was strongly supportive of the tribal structure of the nation because of the need to rely on traditions being passed from father to son to assure adherence to the covenant, he also recognized the danger to the national purpose of unfettered diversity among the tribes, especially with regard to the worship of God. With respect to the latter, he was convinced that uniformity was required as the thread that would hold the diverse tribes together as a nation in service to God.

Accordingly, Moses called for the establishment of a single central national sanctuary at *the place which YHVH your Elohim shall choose out of all your tribes to put His name there*. By contrast with the practice of those they were displacing, which was to select places at which they would worship their gods, Moses insists that the children of Israel must seek the place that God will choose for them to worship, which the rabbis interpreted as saying that they should seek what they consider to be an appropriate place and see whether their judgment is confirmed by a prophet.[505] The central point being made here is that the place that God will choose is "to be a physical, visible expression of the principle of monotheism: one God, one place of worship," that is, the one and only sanctioned place where sacrifices may be offered.[506] Of course, as the text makes clear, the national sanctuary is only the place where God places His name; it surely cannot conceivably contain God. "The visible symbol of the presence of the divine name is the ark. And so every occurrence of this expression in Deuteronomy refers to the place where the ark is."[507]

It is noteworthy that with regard to the pagan sites of worship, their primary locations are *upon the high mountains, and upon the hills, and under every leafy tree*. Worship takes place at sites marked by their natural characteristics to which sanctity is attached. "The choice of mountains and hills for places of worship by most of the heathen nations, had its origin in the wide-spread belief, that men were nearer to the Deity and to heaven there. The green trees are connected with the holy groves, of which the heathen nations were so fond, and the shady gloom of which filled the soul with holy awe at the nearness of the Deity."[508] By contrast, the site where God is to be worshipped is *the place which YHVH your Elohim shall choose out of all your tribes to put His name there.* Wherever God deigns to permit His name to be associated with, that place attains sanctity, irrespective of location or natural features. *Unto His habitation shall ye seek, and thither thou shalt come;* the choice of site will be made by God and not by man. Presumably, the tribal leaders will propose potential sites, but the selection will be God's, which will be revealed in some unspecified manner,[509] perhaps by drawing lots or through prophetic confirmation.

As a practical matter, it goes without saying that the identification of a future site for the sanctuary will be a politically sensitive issue because of inter-tribal jealousies, and for this reason, if for no other, Moses defers the recommendation of such a site to his successors. Thus, to limit contention, he asserts that the site will be chosen by God and presumably revealed through a prophet, and not by any tribe or other individual.[510] Moreover, it would have made little sense for Moses to attempt to name a site before the Israelites even crossed the Jordan, not knowing what the pace of the conquest would be. As it turned out, a temporary national sanctuary was established at a variety of successive locations, depending upon the fortunes of war, the first to be so designated was to be at Mount Ebal, as indicated later (Deut. 27:4-7).

A permanent site was established in Jerusalem more than two hundred years later. In this regard, tradition asserts that King David was obsessed with finding an appropriate site for the erection of a permanent central sanctuary. Thus, the psalmist recalls David's vow: *Surely I will not come into the tent of my house, nor go up into the bed that is spread for me; I will not give sleep to mine eyes, nor slumber to mine eyelids; until I find out a place for YHVH, a dwelling place for the Mighty One of Jacob* (Ps. 132:3-5). It is noteworthy that David, with the assent of the prophet Gad, ultimately chose a site in Jerusalem to establish a permanent home for the altar (2 Sam. 24:16), Jerusalem being a Jebusite city that had never come under the control of any of the tribes and had been conquered by a force led by David himself, who claimed it as his personal fiefdom, independent of the kingdoms of Israel and Judah, of which he was the monarch, thus making Jerusalem the non-tribally based capital of his dual monarchy.

At this point, however, all Moses could do was to set forth the precept that there was to be one central sanctuary for the entire nation, and it was to that sanctuary that the nation was to come to render homage to God in the variety of authorized ritual practices, including *your burnt-offerings, and your sacrifices, and your tithes, and the offering of your hand, and your vows, and your freewill-offerings, and the firstlings of your herd and of your flock.* As understood by the rabbis, the *olah* or *burnt-offering* was a sacrifice wholly devoted to God, and as such was to be consumed entirely by fire; nothing of it was to remain for later human consumption. The *zevah* or *sacrifice* refers to that category of offerings that in most but not all cases were in large part made available to be consumed by those offering the sacrifice. These included thanksgiving offerings, as well as individual and communal peace offerings. The tithes, discussed below, were gifts or payments of ten percent of annual agricultural products and natural increase in cattle. The *offering of your hand* or contributions apparently refers to offerings of the first fruits.[511] The *vow* has been understood to refer to offerings promised in return for some divine beneficence such as the birth of a son or a safe return from war. The *freewill-offering* refers to an offering made simply as an expression of gratitude or devotion. The *firstlings of your herd and of your flock* refers to the firstborn male oxen, sheep, and goats during the course of the year, all of which are considered to devoted to God from birth. All of these categories are mentioned later in the text and will be discussed further where they appear. The text does not actually specify when these four categories of offerings, animal sacrifices, taxes on agricultural products, voluntary gifts, and the firstlings of cattle and sheep, were to be brought to the central sanctuary, although it seems likely that, as a practical matter, the most convenient occasions for this would have been the three mandatory pilgrimage festivals that were to be celebrated at the site of the national sanctuary, where *ye shall rejoice in all that ye put your hand unto, ye and your households, wherein YHVH thy Elohim hath blessed thee.* Moses insists that *ye shall rejoice* there as befits those who serve their master out of love rather than fear.[512]

> *12.8 Ye shall not do after all that we do here this day, every man whatsoever is right in his own eyes; 12.9 for ye are not as yet come to the rest and to the inheritance, which YHVH your Elohim giveth you. 12.10 But when ye go over the Jordan, and dwell in the land which YHVH your Elohim causeth you to inherit, and He giveth you rest from all your enemies round about, so that ye dwell in safety; 12.11 then it shall come to pass that the place which YHVH your Elohim shall choose to cause His name to dwell there, thither shall ye bring all that I command you: your burnt-offerings, and your sacrifices, your tithes, and the offering of your hand, and all your choice vows which ye vow unto YHVH. 12.12 And ye shall rejoice before YHVH your Elohim, ye, and your sons, and your daughters, and your men-servants, and your maid-servants, and the Levite that is within your gates, forasmuch as he hath no portion nor inheritance with you. 12.13 Take heed to thyself that thou offer not thy burnt-offerings in every place that thou seest; 12.14 but in the place which YHVH shall choose in one of thy tribes, there thou shalt offer thy burnt-offerings, and there thou shalt do all that I command thee.*

Having explained that once they are established in the land the worship of God will be centered in a single site chosen by God, Moses emphasizes *Ye shall not do after all that we do here this day, every man whatsoever is right in his own eyes.* He acknowledges that there is no current uniform system or organization to religious practice, everyone being free to give expression to their desire to communicate with God in accordance with their own predilections, and at a site of their own choosing. It is noteworthy that this appears to conflict with the earlier stipulation that all sacrifices had to be brought to *the door of the tent of meeting, unto the priest* (Lev. 17:5). One opinion suggests that the problem to which Moses is alluding was that many of the people simply were not sufficiently God-fearing to comply with the requirement, and chose to continue with sacrificial practices that were more familiar to them, either from observation or previous performance.[513] Evidence for this may be seen in the text, *and they shall no more sacrifice their sacrifices unto the satyrs, after whom they go astray* (Lev. 17:7). It has been noted that the worship of satyrs, or sylvan gods or demons in the shape of goats, "accompanied by the foulest rites," was common in Lower Egypt and evidently was practiced by many Israelites.[514]

It has also been suggested that deficiency in belief was not the problem, and that as a rule they did comply with the stipulation requiring them to bring the sacrifices to *the door of the tent of meeting*. However, the site of the *tent of meeting* was continually changing as the people moved about the wilderness, sometimes making compliance difficult, and if some were not inclined to eat meat, which could only come from their voluntary offerings, they could avoid going to the sanctuary at all.[515] Although it is unlikely that the author of this interpretation had this in mind, his argument opens the possibility that the problem was not that they had any difficulty bringing their sacrifices to the *tent of meeting*, but that the *tent of meeting* was not identified with a particular site that could serve as the rallying point for the nation as its capital.

However, it seems more likely that Moses was explaining the apparent conflict between the already existing law and actual practice in his assertion that this is because *ye are not as yet come to the rest and to the inheritance, which YHVH your Elohim giveth you.* The unsettled state of life in the wilderness made organized and ritualized religious practices impracticable, notwithstanding the stipulation that called for this to be done. As a practical matter it was made acceptable for everyone to worship as they pleased, a situation that was deemed more desirable than seeing large numbers of people neglecting their sacrificial obligations entirely. But, this was something that would no longer be tolerated once they conquered and settled the land. Then, when God *giveth you rest from all your enemies round about, so that ye dwell in safety*, a central sanctuary will be established at *the place which YHVH your Elohim shall choose to cause His name to dwell there.*

It is noteworthy that Moses refers to the national sanctuary as the place where God will *cause His name to dwell there*, that is, God's name but not God will dwell there, a significant distinction consistent with the general thrust of biblical thought, which rejects any delimitation of God. Once such a permanent sanctuary is established, which would not happen for more than another two centuries, the people are admonished once more that only to that place *shall ye bring all that I command you: your burnt-offerings, and your sacrifices, your tithes, and the offering of your hand, and all your choice vows which ye vow unto YHVH.*

The central sanctuary also is to serve as a place of pilgrimage for the families and households of the children of Israel, the site where they may celebrate divine beneficence at the place chosen by God for that purpose. This obligation of pilgrimage will also apply to those Levites who dwell in various places because they have *no portion nor inheritance with you.* That is, one might think that because the Levites are to be landless, they will have little reason to celebrate divine beneficence. Nonetheless, they too will be obligated to make pilgrimage to the site of the central sanctuary; perhaps to celebrate their selection to minister to the spiritual needs of the people. However, because the resources of the Levites are expected to be limited, *the Levite that is within your gates* is to be considered as though he were a member of your household, the implication being that householders have an obligation to facilitate the pilgrimage of the Levites among them.

Although it seems clear that, as discussed above, the statement *Ye shall not do after all that we do here this day, every man whatsoever is right in his own eyes* is related to the matter of centralization of the sacrificial rite in a national sanctuary, it may also have other significant implications. In this regard, it should be noted that the expression has been used in Scripture to denote a state of anarchy, as in the statement, *In those days there was no king in Israel; every man did that which was right in his own eyes* (Judg. 17:6, 21:25). Thus, diminishing his own leadership role, Moses appears to be asserting in effect that the people are without an authoritative leader, and without such everyone feels equal to everyone else and is disinclined to listen to anyone, including Moses. The idea that God is their sovereign, while perhaps accepted in principle, can only be manifested by worship of Him at a sanctuary bearing the divine designation. However, because that portable sanctuary has been moving from place to place, none more impressive than any other, the significance of the sanctuary has significantly diminished and some have undertaken to worship in a manner that they find meaningful, each in a manner *which was right in his own eyes.* In other words, not only is there an undercurrent of political anarchy in the Israelite camp but religious anarchy as well.[516] This, Moses tells the people, will have to cease once they cross the river, where unity of purpose and action will be critical to their viability as a nation.

Moses concludes his presentation of this commandment with a reiteration of its essence, namely that once the central sanctuary is established, they may no longer offer sacrifices to God anywhere other than *the place which YHVH shall choose in one of thy tribes.* And it is there that they are to carry out the instructions that Moses will give them relative to such pilgrimages. It should be borne in mind that this statement reflects the idea that all of the territory of Cisjordan would be subdivided among the tribes, which is not the same thing as saying that all the tribally assigned territories would necessarily be entirely under the actual control of the named tribes. Thus, Jerusalem, which arguably was in the tribal territory allocated to Benjamin, remained a Jebusite stronghold until conquered by David and made the site of the national sanctuary more than two centuries after the Israelites first crossed the Jordan and under took the conquest of the country.

It should be noted that there is a virtual consensus among modern biblical scholars that passages such as the one just discussed clearly were written centuries later, after the Temple in Jerusalem was built in the time of Solomon. Without going into a discussion of the merits of this conclusion, the only dubious evidence for which is the consensus among such scholars, which will contribute nothing to understanding the text as we have it, suffice it for present purposes to note that a reasonably plausible case can be made for the Mosaic origin of the passage and its message.

Perhaps the most difficult task confronting Moses as a political leader was molding a coherent nation out of a loosely connected albeit ethnically related group of independent and quarrelsome tribes. For this purpose, their common emancipation from slavery was a critically important factor for covenantal purposes, but was insufficient as a basis for national cohesion. Each tribe or even clan could acknowledge its debt to God in its own way, irrespective of how other tribes or clans did the same thing. However, Moses was well aware that unless they were united as a nation, they would not be able to survive as political entities in the hostile and volatile environment into which they were entering. The land they were going to conquer and settle was not in some relatively secluded area where they essentially would be free to develop their new civilization and national society without hindrance from alien forces. Indeed, the land they were about to invade was centrally located in the land bridge between Africa and Asia, which served in many instances as the frontier and sometimes as the battleground between the competing empires of Egypt and the succession of powers that dominated Mesopotamia and Asia Minor. Virtually none of the existing nations in the land were indigenous to it, being essentially un-repatriated remnants of earlier wars and population movements. Moses, who was raised and educated as an Egyptian prince was surely aware that the imminent invasion of Cisjordan by the Israelites was taking place at a time when there was a temporary hiatus in the Egyptian-Mesopotamian struggle for control of the trade routes along the Mediterranean littoral, routes that passed through the territories on both sides of the Jordan. There was no reason to assume that such a struggle could not resume at any time, as it did repeatedly over the next centuries, and unless the children of Israel were united as a coherent nation worthy of providential concern, they would not be able to survive politically once confronted by the major powers of the region.

Although, as discussed earlier, Moses was favorably disposed towards the tribal arrangement for purposes of transmitting the legacy of the covenant from generation to generation, he also understood that the time would come when such an arrangement, a loose tribal confederation, would become dysfunctional when confronted by powerful unitary states. It would therefore be necessary to set the stage for the ultimate transformation of the loose confederation of Israelite tribes into a nominal federation with a strong central government, and the glue that would hold it together was the centralization of the covenant-based religion. Accordingly, as soon as political and security conditions allowed, steps were to be taken to centralize the worship of God, which was primarily sacrificial, and to prohibit its diffusion. As will be seen later, Moses, acting in his capacity as a true prophet, also proposed other steps to consolidate the political structure of the nation: he foresaw the long-term consequences, both intended and unintended, of continuing with the present deficiencies in the sense of national purpose and societal cohesiveness, just as later prophets foresaw the destruction of what had become the dysfunctional kingdoms of ancient Israel and Judah.

Moses next turned to the issue of increasing the distinctiveness of the Israelites from the surrounding nations and populations through ordaining sumptuary laws that would make social integration and assimilation with the peoples of the region more difficult. At the same time, some of these laws would further strengthen the role of the central sanctuary in the lives of the people without regard to tribal identification. He begins with the matter of slaughtering of animals for food and a restriction on the consumption of their blood.

> [12.15] *Notwithstanding thou mayest kill and eat flesh within all thy gates, after all the desire of thy soul, according to the blessing of YHVH thy Elohim which He hath given thee; the unclean and the clean may eat thereof, as of the gazelle, and as of the hart.* [12.16] *Only ye shall not eat the blood; thou shalt pour it out upon the earth as water.*

While this passage may appear rather strange if not incomprehensible at a first reading, it seems reasonable to assume that its intent was clear to those to whom it originally was addressed. Thus, it has been argued that during the four decades spent in the wilderness, domesticated livestock, which represented a major portion of the wealth of the people, was slaughtered for food only on rare special occasions. As a general rule, the slaughter of an animal, even when portions of it were to be consumed by its owner, was carried out as a sacrificial act, and Scripture earlier declared: *Whatsoever man there be of the house of Israel, or of the strangers that sojourn among them, that offereth a burnt-offering or sacrifice, and bringeth it not unto the door of the tent of meeting, to sacrifice it unto YHVH, even that man shall be cut off from his people* (Lev. 17:8-9). This procedure, which surely was instituted for the purpose of imposing common practices on the diverse tribes, theoretically was practicable in the wilderness where the tent of meeting, which served initially as a central sanctuary, was physically located in the center of the tribes, allowing for reasonably easy access to it from every direction. However, as already suggested, it seems unlikely that this was actually done to any great extent during the repeated relocations that the nation underwent during the four decades of moving from place to place in the wilderness. Moreover, this requirement, even in theory, would be impracticable for a nation spread out over a relatively large territory.

The intent of the rule given in this passage seems murky, particularly with regard to its use of the term *notwithstanding*. The rabbis therefore imputed to it a special significance. Thus they asked, "To what does this verse refer? If to meat slaughtered for personal pleasure, it has already been mentioned elsewhere; if to the eating of sacrifices, this too has already been mentioned elsewhere. Therefore this must refer solely to animals dedicated but found unfit, which must be redeemed." The reference in this citation is to the divine command, stated earlier, *Sanctify unto Me all the first-born, whatsoever openeth the womb among the children of Israel, both of man and of beast, it is Mine* (Ex. 13:2) and later amplified by Moses, *All the firstling males that are born of thy herd and thy flock thou shalt sanctify unto YHVH thy Elohim; thou shalt do no work with the firstling of thine ox, nor shear the firstling of thy flock* (Deut. 15:19). Because of their special status such animals cannot be used for mundane purposes in the manner of other animals, but if the imperfection is considered permanent, *notwithstanding* that they were consecrated, they may be slaughtered for food.[517] Accordingly, Moses is instructing the people that, when they become established in the land, animals consecrated for sacrificial purposes but subsequently deemed permanently unsuitable because of some disqualifying defect, *thou mayest kill and eat flesh within all thy gates*, and not only at the central sanctuary. Moreover, *the unclean and the clean may eat thereof, as of the gazelle, and as of the hart*. That is, whereas those persons deemed ritually unclean were prohibited from partaking of a sacrifice, this prohibition does not apply when the animal deemed unsuitable for ritual sacrifice is to be slaughtered for its meat. Such animals may be eaten for food in the same manner that the gazelle and the hart, which exhibit the appropriate physical characteristics but are nonetheless deemed ineligible for ritual sacrifice because they are not considered domestic animals, may be eaten.

In addition, Moses commands, *ye shall not eat the blood; thou shalt pour it out upon the earth as water.* This categorical prohibition against the consumption of blood, which also is elaborated on below, is the basis for many of the dietary laws that distinguish the children of Israel from other nations and peoples. What, one may ask, is the significance of the simile, *pour it out upon the earth as water?* This may be understood as a response to the implicit question of what to do with the blood since one may not consume it. Instead of pouring it out where one disposes of waste, Moses instructs that it be poured out on the earth. The reason for this, according to the rabbis is that, "just as one is permitted to derive benefit from water, so is one permitted to derive benefit from blood." That is, because one may not eat it does not imply that one might not derive some benefit from it. Accordingly it was suggested that just as water "makes seeds fit, so does blood,"[518] that is, it was held that the blood as fluid should be used for constructive purposes rather than as mere waste.

Again emphasizing the importance of a central sanctuary as the point of convergence for the children of Israel, irrespective of tribal affiliation, Moses stipulates further,

> *12.17 Thou mayest not eat within thy gates the tithe of thy corn, or of thy wine, or of thine oil, or the firstlings of thy herd or of thy flock, nor any of thy vows which thou vowest, nor thy freewill-offerings, nor the offering of thy hand; 12.18 but thou shalt eat them before YHVH thy Elohim in the place which YHVH thy Elohim shall choose, thou, and thy son, and thy daughter, and thy man-servant, and thy maid-servant, and the Levite that is within thy gates; and thou shalt rejoice before YHVH thy Elohim in all that*

thou puttest thy hand unto. ^{12.19} *Take heed to thyself that thou forsake not the Levite as long as thou livest upon thy land.*

In this passage, Moses forbids the consumption of any of the named sacramental foods outside *the place which YHVH thy Elohim shall choose.* This stipulation effectively compels pilgrimage to the central sanctuary, where one's household may consume these things in celebration of divine beneficence. The text, *lo tukhal le'ekhol,* translated as *Thou mayest not eat,* actually says, "You will not be able to eat," which seems problematic since Moses surely is not suggesting that one will be physically incapable of eating, a problem the translation glosses over. The implication of the literal meaning of the text, however, is that once the people fully internalize the importance of complying with God's wishes in such regard, they will find themselves simply unable to eat elsewhere that which they are so permitted only at the site of the sanctuary; their inability will be psychological rather than physical.

Once again, Moses reminds the people not to neglect the needs of the Levites who must rely on public support for their needs because of their mandated exclusion from the agricultural economy. The admonition, *Take heed to thyself that thou forsake not the Levite as long as thou livest upon thy land,* suggests that the concern for the Levites reflects significant national implications. It is not only that they have to be supported because they are precluded from being landowners, but because they fulfill a critical role in the life of the nation. They are, as one commentator put it, "the living nerves and arteries coming out from the center point of the Sanctuary by means of which the members are kept in spiritual connection with the brain and heart of the nation."[519] It is precisely because they do not participate in the agricultural economy that they are able to serve as the intellectual elite of the nation, serving as teachers and moral guides for the people at-large. Their work is crucial to the spiritual and moral well-being of the nation, and it would be a tragic error not to be concerned for their welfare for *as long as thou livest upon thy land.*

Moses then announces additional new regulations that are to apply in the land into which they are about to enter.

12.20 *When YHVH thy Elohim shall enlarge thy border,*
as He hath promised thee, and thou shalt say: 'I will eat
flesh,' because thy soul desireth to eat flesh; thou mayest eat
flesh, after all the desire of thy soul. 12.21 If the place which
YHVH thy Elohim shall choose to put His name there be
too far from thee, then thou shalt kill of thy herd and of thy
flock, which YHVH hath given thee, as I have commanded
thee, and thou shalt eat within thy gates, after all the desire
of thy soul. 12.22 Howbeit as the gazelle and as the hart is
eaten, so thou shalt eat thereof; the clean and the unclean
may eat thereof alike. 12.23 Only be steadfast in not eating
the blood; for the blood is the life; and thou shalt not eat
the life with the flesh. 12.24 Thou shalt not eat it; thou shalt
pour it out upon the earth as water. 12.25 Thou shalt not
eat it; that it may go well with thee, and with thy children
after thee, when thou shalt do that which is right in the
eyes of YHVH.

It would appear that when Moses stated, *When YHVH thy Elohim shall enlarge thy border, as He hath promised thee*, he was not talking about expanding the borders of the future Israelite state, but rather reflecting about their immediate situation in Transjordan, where they were all clustered around the tent housing the ark of the covenant, and the altar that stood before it. At the time, all animals that were to be slaughtered were supposed to have been brought to the altar and slaughtered by the priests in a ritual manner. What Moses was concerned with was the change in this practice that might become necessary for many once they crossed the Jordan and dispersed to their allotted lands throughout Cisjordan.

It should be noted that it has also been maintained that the statement merely is a reference to God's earlier assertion, *For I will cast out nations before thee, and enlarge thy borders* (Ex. 34:24).[520] However, the latter statement was made in a rather different context, namely the need for all the males to make three annual pilgrimages to the national sanctuary. *Three times in the year shall all thy males appear before the Adon [Lord], YHVH the Elohim of Israel. For I will cast out nations before thee, and enlarge thy borders; neither shall any man covet thy land, when thou goest up to appear before YHVH thy Elohim three times in the year* (Ex. 34:23-24). The question that this raises is how all the males could leave their homesteads defenseless to appear before God at some selected location. The divine response is that *I will cast out nations before thee, and enlarge thy borders.* It would seem that the implicit notion here is that extending the borders of their territory beyond the areas of settlement will significantly reduce concern about external threats to the security of their unguarded homes and farms. Presumably, there should be little or no concern about internal threats that might take advantage of land left unguarded, because *neither shall any man covet thy land, when thou goest up to appear before YHVH thy Elohim three times in the year,* that is, because he too will be with you there. It may of course be argued that the presumption that expanded borders would preclude the necessity of some men being required to patrol those borders is unrealistic, making this explanation dubious and leaving the text open to an alternate interpretation yet to be put forward.

In this passage, Moses effectively announces cancellation of the general restriction on the private slaughtering of animals eligible for sacrificial purposes exclusively for food, and explains that the easing of the restriction on slaughtering such animals only at the sanctuary is being done in acknowledgment that the distance from where many people will live to the sanctuary may be so far as to make following the rule that held sway in the wilderness impracticable. Nonetheless, to assure the continuing significance of the central sanctuary, he does not relent and permit the erection of local altars. Instead, he effectively secularized the slaughter of animals for food. However, this secularization of the law with regard to the slaughter of domestic animals for food did not affect the other sacrificial obligations imposed by the covenant that henceforth could only be carried out at the central national sanctuary.

This announcement in itself adds nothing new to the previous text. However, the statement *thou shalt kill of thy herd and of thy flock, which YHVH hath given thee, as I have commanded thee* has been read as implying that Moses previously commanded them regarding the required ritual method to be used in slaughtering the animals. That is, whereas it was supposed to be the priests who slaughtered the animals in accordance with the methods revealed to them, now that slaughtering of animals for non-sacramental purposes by the general population was being allowed, Moses is stipulating that they must follow the same rules and methods of slaughter as employed by the priests with regard to sacrifices.[521] The rabbis thus concluded that the laws of ritual slaughter must have been conveyed to Moses at Mount Sinai and were subsequently transmitted orally from generation to generation, arguing, "the verse *And thou shalt slaughter . . . as I have commanded thee* teaches us that Moses was instructed concerning the gullet and the windpipe; concerning the greater part of one of these organs [that must be cut] in the case of a bird, and the greater part of each in the case of cattle."[522]

As a corollary to permitting the slaughter to take place away from the central sanctuary, Moses declares, *Howbeit as the gazelle and as the hart is eaten, so thou shalt eat thereof; the clean and the unclean may eat thereof alike.* It has been suggested that this statement contains an implicit warning against allowing the slaughter to appear as a sacrificial act, which would negate the purpose of the easing of the restriction. Accordingly, the animal to be slaughtered is to be consumed in a manner that will make it evident that it was not killed as a sacrificial act, and this was to be accomplished by authorizing those persons deemed ritually impure or unclean to participate in its consumption. Since the ritually unclean were precluded from eating of a sacrificial animal, allowing them to do so would be seen as asserting that the animal was not being sacrificed but merely slaughtered for food.[523] In this manner there would be no perception that the singularity of the national sanctuary was being compromised.

In discussing the prohibition regarding the consumption of blood, Moses begins with the admonition, *only be steadfast in not eating the blood,* which strongly suggests that the consumption of blood must have been pervasive in antiquity. It has been noted that the use of the phrase *be steadfast* in connection with a command not to do something is unusual if not entirely exceptional, and supports the assumption that this was something that the Israelites, or at least a considerable number of them, actually did routinely. Thus, as noted above, the text already mentioned that *they shall no more sacrifice their sacrifices unto the satyrs, after whom they go astray* (Lev. 17:7), the presumption being that this particular mode of pagan worship, which involved the consumption of the animal's blood, was common in Lower Egypt and evidently was practiced by many Israelites.[524] In this regard, it has been observed that even in modern times there are instances of people drinking the blood of their enemies.[525] However, one need not go that far; suffice it to note the continuing popularity of eating meat "rare," that is, meat that is still blood-soaked, a practice that is biblically abhorrent. This may account for the prohibition against eating blood being mentioned no fewer than seven times in the Torah.

Moses explains that the reason for the ban is that *the blood is the life; and thou shalt not eat the life with the flesh,* a prohibition made clear much earlier in Scripture, that *only flesh with the life thereof, which is the blood thereof, shall ye not eat* (Gen. 9:4). It has been suggested that the idea that *the blood is the life* is an obvious deduction from the fact that as the blood is drained from the body, its vitality diminishes until it ceases altogether. "Life, in every form, has in it an element of holiness, since God is the source of all life. Therefore, although permission is given to eat the flesh of an animal, this was done with one special restriction; *viz.* life must altogether have departed from the animal before man partakes of its flesh."[526] The expression *the blood is the life* has also been explained as follows: "To the Torah, the blood is the material which at every beat of the pulse circulates through the whole body, is the medium by means of which the soul exercises its ever-present mastery of the body. So that it is eminently the foremost bearer of the soul, and the Torah forbids animal blood, as the bearer of the animal soul, animal life, any entry into the realm—the holy morally free-willed realm—of the human soul, human life."[527]

Moses concludes his statement of the injunction by reasserting *thou shalt not eat it; that it may go well with thee, and with thy children after thee, when thou shalt do that which is right in the eyes of YHVH.* The final clause of this statement is repeated below, where it's meaning and implication will be discussed at some length. The repetition in the passage of the injunction *thou shalt not eat it,* which appears redundant, has been interpreted by the rabbis as signifying that even the residual blood found in the animal after the flow of blood has ceased is also prohibited. Accordingly, the dietary laws elaborated by the rabbis require that meat be heavily salted to drain whatever remaining blood there may be in the flesh before preparation for consumption.

The blood of animals slaughtered for domestic consumption is to be poured out on the earth and not to be preserved for any other purpose; that is, the blood is not to poured into containers for storage as is done with wine or olive oil and other liquids for later consumption.[528] However, as will be seen below, this rule does not apply to sacrificial animals, the blood of which is used as part of the sacrificial rite.

> [12.26] *Only the holy things which thou hast, and thy vows, thou shalt take, and go unto the place which YHVH shall choose;* [12.27] *and thou shalt offer thy burnt-offerings, the flesh and the blood, upon the altar of YHVH thy Elohim; and the blood of thy sacrifices shall be poured out against the altar of YHVH thy Elohim, and thou shalt eat the flesh.*

However, Moses emphasizes, the permission to slaughter *within thy gates* does not apply with regard to fulfillment of religious obligations. For the latter you must *go unto the place which YHVH shall choose,* the central sanctuary, and there make your sacrificial offerings *upon the altar of YHVH thy Elohim.* As for the blood of the animals that are sacrificial offerings, it is to poured against the altar, instead of on the ground as in the case of animals slaughtered exclusively for food, as earlier stated, *and Aaron's sons, the priests, shall present the blood, and dash the blood round about against the altar that is at the door of the tent of meeting* (Lev. 1:5). The symbolism of pouring the blood against the altar is unclear, although it has been suggested that it reflects the idea that "the blood is regarded as the seat of life, and is given back to God, who is the author of life."[529]

¹²·²⁸ Observe and hear all these words which I command thee, that it may go well with thee, and with thy children after thee for ever, when thou doest that which is good and right in the eyes of YHVH thy Elohim.

Moses repeats almost verbatim what he said a few lines earlier about the implications that complying with what he is commanding will have for them and their descendents *for ever, when thou doest that which is good and right in the eyes of YHVH thy Elohim.* The meaning of this statement is quite unclear. Is doing *good* in the eyes of God different from doing *right* in His eyes? The appropriate answer to this question was a matter of contention among the rabbis, who seem to have rejected the literal reading of the text as unedifying. Thus, essentially ignoring the syntax of the statement, according to one prominent rabbinic sage, the statement should be read as asserting, "that which is good in the sight of heaven and right in the sight of man." By doing both, as the biblical sage put it, *So shalt thou find grace and good favor in the sight of Elohim and man* (Prov. 3:4). Alternatively, it was suggested that the biblical text might also be understood as speaking of what is good in the eyes of man, and right in the eyes of God.[530]

The essence of the first position is that the idea of *good* fits better with matters between man and God, and *right* with matters between man and man. The rationale behind this is that knowledge of the *good* is a function of wisdom, and man is incapable of discerning between what is ultimately good or evil in the path he chooses. It requires a higher wisdom to discern this. Accordingly, man does *good* by following what God has determined to be the appropriate path and evil when he fails to conform with divine wisdom. By contrast, what is *right* or fair in any particular situation is something about which man can render sound judgment based on reason alone, if he has a sound mind and an open heart.

The contrary position argues that even though the preceding argument has a superficial validity, we have no choice but to associate the *right* with matters between man and God because it is essential that we consider them as rational commandments. At the same time, with regard to those matters between man and man, which we are able to determine what is right, we should nonetheless approach them as matters of *good* or evil that can only be determined by a higher divine wisdom.[531] The advocate of this opinion appears to be troubled by the notion that man can deal with matters between man and man on a rational basis, because man is fully capable of rationalizing his behavior to suit his predilections. He therefore interprets the biblical passage in a way that would place constraints on man's freedom to do as he pleases within the context of society.

However, and notwithstanding the profundity of the argument among the rabbis, it is unclear that this helps explain the immediate connection of the statement with the subject matter of the texts in which it is found. In the first instance it is stated in connection with the prohibition against the consumption of blood, and in the second in connection with the affirmation that sacramental matters must be dealt with at the central sanctuary. It may be suggested that the statement has implications for the children of Israel both as individuals and as a nation. With regard to the former, one implication of the statement is that in each such act of slaughter man is to be reminded of his individual place in the universe. A part of nature, yet transcending it, he must always remain cognizant of his purpose and mission in life. Man is intended by God to be above the rest of created nature, to care for it always, even when out of necessity he is compelled to destroy certain elements of it. He is to be sure that his shedding of animal blood does not become an end in itself, a thirst after bloodshed. Though he may kill for food like the animal, he must still not be animal-like in his demeanor. He must not, like the wild beast, tear his prey apart and eat its flesh while its heart is still pumping blood through its vessels. Man, who is capable of killing for the sake of killing, must learn to abhor blood, particularly the taste of fresh blood. He must differentiate himself from the animal as much as possible. It is noteworthy that the original injunction was addressed to mankind generally and not specifically to the children of Israel.

With regard to the implication of the statement for Israel as a nation, it suggests that its future will be assured only to the extent that it takes and retains its position on the stage of history as a nation unified under God, and that unity must transcend both ethnicity and tribalism. The unifying factor must be individual and collective obedience to God as Israel's sovereign lord and master, and this will be manifested by the convergence of all Israel on a single sanctuary that will serve as the portal for communication between man and God and between God and man, the former consisting of acts of devotion and the latter of acts of revelation. Religion, as manifested in the covenant, is to be the tie that binds the nation together to confront the challenges that will await it both in the present and in the foreseeable as well the unforeseeable future.

Moses predicts both in respect to the individual and the nation, *it may go well with thee, and with thy children after thee forever, when thou doest that which is good and right in the eyes of YHVH thy Elohim.* The key to that bright future is total and unequivocal fealty to God alone, and it is to this theme that Moses returns once again.

> *12.29 When YHVH thy Elohim shall cut off the nations from before thee, whither thou goest in to dispossess them, and thou dispossessest them, and dwellest in their land; 12.30 take heed to thyself that thou be not ensnared to follow them, after that they are destroyed from before thee; and that thou inquire not after their gods, saying:'How used these nations to serve their gods? even so will I do likewise.' 12.31 Thou shalt not do so unto YHVH thy Elohim; for every abomination to YHVH, which He hateth, have they done unto their gods; for even thy sons and their daughters do they burn in the fire to their gods.*

Moses cautions them once again to take all necessary steps to preclude being enticed into the trap of disloyalty to God. He points out that their greatest vulnerability in this regard will occur after they succeed, with God's help, in dispossessing the nations and settling in their former territories, where remnants of them will still be found. Feeling victorious, you may feel inclined to be solicitous of those remnants of the nations, who will privately continue to worship their gods. And because they will no longer pose a security threat, out of sheer curiosity you may become susceptible to their influence. Moses warns the people specifically not to be overly curious about the alien religions, saying: *How used these nations to serve their gods?* The danger in this is that you may be come ensnared by them, eventually saying, *even so will I do likewise.*

Why does Moses think the children of Israel are so vulnerable to such external religious influences even after having destroyed nations whose gods failed them? The most simple answer, as difficult as it may be for some to accept, is that Moses was far from convinced about the extent to which the belief in an invisible God had truly permeated the consciousness of many of the children of Israel. Their fairly abysmal record in such regard during the four decades following the exodus was hardly one that instilled confidence in him. Compared to the rituals and orgies of the fertility rites practiced by the Canaanites and others, the simple worship of God, even with its sacrificial rite, was essentially drab and unexciting. Indeed, much of the book of Leviticus is devoted to transforming the simple mode of Israelite worship into an impressive colorful ritual that could capture the imagination. But even though the plans for this were already laid out in detail, full implementation would not take place anytime soon in the foreseeable future; the land would have to be conquered and settled before a permanent central sanctuary could be established with all the pomp appropriate to it. In the meantime, the danger of assimilation and apostasy remained great, and Moses could not but repeatedly warn against such, as he does here.

As seems to be the case in this instance, he occasionally appears to be pleading with the people more than commanding them: *Thou shalt not do so unto YHVH thy Elohim; for every abomination to YHVH, which He hateth, have they done unto their gods; for even thy sons and their daughters do they burn in the fire to their gods.* Not only are the pagan practices abominable in principle, they have reached the peak of such abomination in practice with the ritual sacrifice of their own children, effectively recalling that God tested Abraham by asking him to sacrifice his son Isaac and then pointedly stopped him from doing so when it appeared that he was going to comply.

In light of all this, Moses outlines concrete steps that are to be taken to mitigate what he sees as a mortal threat to the nation, insisting,

13.1 All this word which I command you, that shall ye observe to do; thou shalt not add thereto, nor diminish from it.

What he is about to order them to do they are to carry out to the letter, without qualification or obfuscation. God's commandments, conveyed through him, are not to be carried in any manner that a person may be inclined to do, and this is especially the case in matters of ritual worship—He wants to be worshipped exclusively in the manner that He has commanded and that Moses will relay to them. Man should not presume to know what would please God with regard to worship simply because man's thoughts are not the same as those of God. Although there is no mention of it here, the text reflects an implicit allusion to what took place earlier with regard to Nadab and Abihu, the two oldest sons of Aaron, who were to have taken their father's place as leaders of Israel's priesthood after his demise. This did not come to pass because, as the biblical text informs us, they *took each of them his censer, and put fire therein, and laid incense thereon, and offered strange fire before YHVH, which He had not commanded them. And there came forth fire from before YHVH, and devoured them, and they died before YHVH* (Lev. 10:1-2). It is clear from this text that they, acting on their own initiative for unspecified reasons, deviated from the precise ritual that God had commanded and were severely punished for it. In matters between man and man, the divine principles of proper conduct leave great discretion to man, through the use of his reason, to apply principles in accordance with the circumstances of place and time. However, with regard to those things between man and God, much less leeway is permitted; and in matters relating to the ritual worship of God virtually none. Moses exhibits a continuing concern that laxity in this regard can easily lead to idolatrous practices.

Moses thus cautions that God does not want overzealousness in this regard, *thou shalt not add thereto*, broadening his instructions to cover matters he does not specifically mention, nor does he want anyone to *diminish from it*, deciding arbitrarily to soften its impact by qualifying its application. It has been intimated that perhaps what

Moses was particularly concerned about with regard to the sacrificial rites was that excessive zeal might lead some to wish to emulate the child-sacrifice practiced by some of the peoples they encountered.[532] What is at issue is the spiritual and moral well being of the nation, and as past experience has shown, threats to it must be dealt with harshly and decisively. In addition to foolish and misplaced nostalgia for the colorful religions of the previous inhabitants of the land, Moses sees three other basic sources of the threat to the moral well-being of the people, "the influence of spiritual conceit; the influence of members of one's own family; and the influence of one's fellow citizens,"[533] that he will now warn them against.

> [13.2] *If there arise in the midst of thee a prophet, or a dreamer of dreams, and he give thee a sign or a wonder,* [13.3] *and the sign or the wonder come to pass, whereof he spoke unto thee, saying: 'Let us go after other gods, which thou hast not known, and let us serve them';* [13.4] *thou shalt not hearken unto the words of that prophet, or unto that dreamer of dreams; for YHVH your Elohim putteth you to proof, to know whether ye do love YHVH your Elohim with all your heart and with all your soul.* [13.5] *After YHVH your Elohim shall ye walk, and Him shall ye fear, and unto His voice shall ye hearken, and Him shall ye serve, and unto Him shall ye cleave.* [13.6] *And that prophet, or that dreamer of dreams, shall be put to death; because he hath spoken perversion against YHVH your Elohim, who brought you out of the land of Egypt, and redeemed thee out of the house of bondage, to draw thee aside out of the way which YHVH your Elohim commanded thee to walk in. So shalt thou put away the evil from the midst of thee.*

The opening words of this passage, *If there arise in the midst of thee a prophet*, have been understood as asserting implicitly that the only kind of prophet that is of concern for Israel is one who emerges from *the midst of thee*, that is, an Israelite who claims to be a prophet.[534] This is not intended to minimize the danger of bad influences from the outside, but only to emphasize that the greater threat of subversion may come from within the community.

To appreciate the problem inherent in this passage one should recall an earlier episode in the biblical narrative that relates the conversation between Moses and God concerning his selection to be the one to lead the Israelites out of Egypt. Moses wanted to refuse the assignment on the basis that, because of his personal fortunes that caused him to have very little contact with his people for almost eighty years, he had no credibility with the elders of the people, who were unlikely to respond to him simply because he would claim that his mission was divinely conceived and ordered.

> *And Moses answered and said: 'But, behold, they will not believe me, or hearken unto my voice; for they will say: YHVH hath not appeared unto thee.' And YHVH said unto him: 'What is that in thy hand?' And he said: 'A rod.' And He said: 'Cast it on the ground.' And he cast it on the ground, and it became a serpent; and Moses fled from before it. And YHVH said unto Moses: 'Put forth your hand, and take it by the tail—and he put forth his hand, and laid hold of it, and it became a rod in his hand—that they may believe that YHVH, the Elohim of their fathers, the Elohim of Abraham, the Elohim of Isaac, and the Elohim of Jacob, hath appeared unto thee' (Ex. 4:1-5).*

The text assumed that performing this feat before the elders would surely cause them to believe that God appeared to him and instructed him to undertake leadership of the children of Israel. Some have seen this as problematic because of the tenuous nature of a belief predicated on what might be nothing more than an illusion or trick. In this regard, it was argued "Moses our teacher knew that whoever depends upon miracles has in his heart doubts, thoughts and reflections, just as he when he himself tried to avoid going to the people," because he feared they would not believe him.[535] Indeed, it would appear that it was anticipated that the belief that might be engendered by the signs with which Moses would dazzle the elders would not be stable or reliable, but that the theatricality of their performance was merely a temporary expediency for the purposes of advancing the redemption process. True belief would only come through an incontrovertible sign after the exodus from Egypt, as stated earlier, *this shall be the token unto thee, that I have sent thee: when thou hast brought forth the people out of Egypt, ye shall serve Elohim upon this mountain* (Ex. 3:12). That is, true belief will come later through the people's direct experience of God at Mount Sinai.

Now Moses finds himself in the unenviable position of finding it necessary to caution the people that another prophet like himself might appear before them and *give thee a sign or a wonder, and the sign or the wonder come to pass*, just as it came to pass when Moses presented himself before the elders of the people. A *sign* has been defined as a marker that signals something that will occur that in some way resembles the marker, and a *wonder* as a novel occurrence that seemingly involves an apparent aberration from the laws of nature.[536]

The question that troubled the rabbis and later commentators is whether this newly emerged prophet was a true prophet or a false prophet, and if he was a false prophet how was he able to *give thee a sign or a wonder, and the sign or the wonder come to pass*, which was to be considered proof of his prophetic legitimacy? The diametrically opposed positions on this question were set forth by the rabbis, as follows: "It has been taught: R. Jose the Galilean said: The Torah understood the extreme depths [of depravity inherent in] idolatry, that should he even cause the sun to stand still in the middle of the heavens, thou must not hearken to him. R. Akiba said: God forbid that the Almighty should cause the sun to stand still at the behest of those who transgressed His will, but [the Torah refers to one] as Hananiah the son of Azur, who was originally a true prophet and [only] subsequently became a false prophet (Jer. 28)."[537]

Later commentators proposed other possible solutions to the problem, none of them compelling, nor does the biblical text provide any clue to assist in resolving the question other than that the plain meaning of the text suggests that the person is a bona fide prophet, and not merely an illusionist or a trickster. In this case, the only basis for rejecting him cannot be on the basis of who he is but only by the character of his prophecy, and it is in this regard that Moses implicitly asserts the proposition that subsequently became an accepted doctrine in rabbinic Judaism, namely, that even miracles in themselves cannot be invoked as decisive in matters of reason and law, nor may seemingly or actual miraculous acts be considered as "an unerring attestation of a Divine mission."[538]

Accordingly, if the message of the self-proclaimed prophet deviates in any way from the covenant that was revealed to them through Moses in the past, and says to them *Let us go after other gods, and let us serve them*, which Moses assures them are gods *which thou hast not known*, indeed, for which there is no basis for concluding that they even exist,[539] they should not pay any attention to such a claimant to prophecy. Indeed, they are to consider the appearance of such *a prophet, or a dreamer of dreams*, the latter presumably referring to a lesser prophetic status, to be nothing more than a means by which God *putteth you to proof, to know whether ye do love YHVH your Elohim with all your heart and with all your soul.* It is another test of the extent of their faith in God, the same kind of test that they repeatedly failed in the past.

But why is such a test necessary? Does not an omniscient God know what is in their hearts and minds? Moreover, is it conceivable that God would set up someone to prophesy against Him and then have him executed just so He can test Israel's commitment to Him? The answer of course must be an emphatic 'no!' The prophet, whether originally true and subsequently false, or false from the outset, is possessed of the same moral autonomy as all other humans and chooses his path in accordance with his own inclination. The text itself states, *if there arise in the midst of thee a prophet* and not that such a prophet necessarily will arise. However, the emergence of such an enticer, which God will not prevent in order to test the response of the people, will present a challenge that will allow the people to see for themselves whether they have the ability to be strong and remain faithful in the face of enticement and temptation, even when such is offered by someone purporting to speak in the name of God.[540]

The point that Moses is making is that the covenant, which represents an eternal bond between God and Israel, cannot be subject to modification or even interpretation that nullifies any of its content, and any proposition to do so, no matter how authoritative it might appear, must be rejected categorically. It should be noted, however, that such categorical rejection apples specifically to the nullification of any of the terms of the covenant but, in the view of the rabbis, does not apply to the temporary suspension of a rule for exigent reasons. Thus it was taught: "In every matter, if a prophet tells you to transgress the commands of the Torah, obey him, with the exception of idolatry: should he even cause the sun to stand still in the middle of the heavens for you [as proof of Divine inspiration]. Do not hearken to him."[541]

Moses warns the people that any repetition of such failures in the future will have disastrous consequences, because God will not tolerate polytheism among the children of Israel. They are to remain constant in their exclusive loyalty to God, whom they would be wise to fear, and whose commandments they are to keep, listening only to His authentic voice, which speaks to them through Moses. It is to *YHVH your Elohim* that they are to remain steadfast in loyalty and to serve—no other! Moreover, *unto Him shall ye cleave.* "This hints at the idea of religious ecstasy, but its meaning is much broader. It is a perpetual condition of being-with-Hashem, an intimate togetherness, a total conformity of man's will to Hashem's will."[542]

One may ask, however, what the significance is of the caution against a *dreamer of dreams.* If one will not accept the word of a prophet, they surely would not accept that of a mere *dreamer of dreams.* It would appear, however, that the text may be asserting that the prophet of concern here is one who claims to be comparable to Moses, who directly experienced revelation while awake and on his feet, but cautions that there will not be another such prophet after Moses. All subsequent true prophets will have prophetic visions that they apprehend through their imaginative faculty while in a dreamlike state, in which they lose conscious control of their physical beings, and it is the latter type of prophet that the text is referring to as a *dreamer of dreams.*[543]

As for the prophet or *dreamer of dreams* that would mislead the people in the manner described and thereby pose a direct threat to the national well being, he is to be executed for treason, because *he hath spoken perversion against YHVH your Elohim*, and sedition, because he sought *to draw thee aside out of the way which YHVH your Elohim commanded thee to walk in.* Such harsh measures are necessary because of the historical proclivity of many of the children of Israel for essentially pagan notions and practices. In effect, until monotheism is so deeply engrained in them that they become immune as a people to the blandishments of paganism, there can be no tolerance for the public airing of such seditious propaganda. Only by adopting such harsh measures, Moses declares, *shalt thou put away the evil from the midst of thee.*

Moreover, Moses insists, this is such a serious and fundamental problem that the zero-tolerance rule regarding incitement to rebellion against God and His commandments is not confined to a prophet or *dreamer of dreams* but must be made applicable to anyone guilty of such incitement, including members of one's own family and personal friends.

> *13.7 If thy brother, the son of thy mother, or thy son, or thy daughter, or the wife of thy bosom, or thy friend, that is as thine own soul, entice thee secretly, saying: 'Let us go and serve other gods,' which thou hast not known, thou, nor thy fathers; 13.8 of the gods of the peoples that are round about you, nigh unto thee, or far off from thee, from the one end of the earth even unto the other end of the earth; 13.9 thou shalt not consent unto him, nor hearken unto him; neither shall thine eye pity him, neither shalt thou spare, neither shalt thou conceal him; 13.10 but thou shalt surely kill him; thy hand shall be the first upon him to put him to death, and afterwards the hand of all the people. 13.11 And thou shalt stone him with stones, that he die; because he hath sought to draw thee away from YHVH thy Elohim, who brought thee out of the land of Egypt, out of the house of bondage. 13.12 And all Israel shall hear, and fear, and shall do no more any such wickedness as this is in the midst of thee.*

It should be noted that there is a significant distinction between the rule given above concerning a prophet and that given here concerning a layman. With regard to the former, the capital crime of which he is held guilty is that of enticing one *to draw thee aside out of the way which YHVH your Elohim commanded thee to walk in,* whereas with regard to the layman the capital offense is limited to enticement to *go and serve other gods.* In other words, the layman may be found guilty of a capital offense by enticing one to apostasy, whereas the prophet is considered guilty of such an offense even for causing someone to violate permanently any provision of the covenant. The distinction between the two is the difference in the perceived authority of the propagandist. The actions of the prophet can undermine the society as a whole, whereas the impact of the layman is likely to be far less harmful, being much more limited in scope and effect, thus making his crime of enticement to transgression a non-capital offense, except of course with regard to apostasy.[544]

Moses tells the people that the true test of their commitment and loyalty to their divine sovereign will come when the perpetrator of incitement to paganism is someone very close to them, either by birth or by voluntary association, someone that they might naturally be inclined to protect from punishment. Conspicuous by its absence is any mention of the father or the mother in this listing of potential perpetrators, possibly suggesting the underlying assumption that the sense of responsibility of parents makes it improbable that they would serve as agents for the perversion of their children, what may have been a reasonable assumption in remote antiquity, albeit merely an aspiration in modern times. It is noteworthy in this regard that the rabbis, without explanation, interpreted the phrase *that is as thine own soul* as referring to a father.[545] It has been suggested, however, that the reason the text employs such veiled language with regard to a son bringing his father to trial is because of the requirement placed on the one reporting the transgression that *thy hand shall be the first upon him to put him to death,* something that a son cannot be compelled to do to his father.[546]

Some also have been puzzled by the mention of a *brother, the son of thy mother,* but not the son of one's father, and having assumed that it was an accidental omission render the text as *And if thy brother by thy father or thy mother*,[547] an interpretation also adopted by the rabbis.[548] However, it has been pointed out that such an emendation of the text tends to trivialize it by ignoring the consideration that "in the days of polygamy, the sons of the same mother were more intimate with one another than with the sons of their father by another wife,"[549] which argues against a brother by a different mother being considered an intimate. Indeed, Scripture itself provide the clearest evidence of this in the story of Joseph and his brothers, which clearly depicts the sibling rivalry and hatred among brothers of a common father but different mothers and the immeasurably greater intimacy and loyalty among the brothers of a common mother. It might also be suggested that, in light of the latter comments, the text may be obliquely intimating the undesirability of polygamous families among the children of Israel even if for no other reason than its potential effects on social harmony and political cohesion.

If any of such intimates should attempt to *entice thee secretly* to apostasy, Moses demands, not only are they not to be listened to or be allowed to carry on such proselytizing, it is incumbent upon you not to spare them because of your intimacy, or to conceal their perfidy, but rather to expose them without pity, *lo tahos einkha alav velo tahmol*, translated as *neither shall thine eye pity him, neither shalt thou spare* [him]. It has been suggested that the biblical distinction between *tahos* and *tahmol*, both of which may be rendered as *pity*, is that *tahos* refers to a sense that one should not destroy or cause harm to a being or thing that can be useful, where *tahmol* refers to a desire not to destroy or cause harm to a being that is presumed to have intrinsic worth.[550] If this interpretation is correct, Moses may be understood as cautioning the people not to entertain ignoring the commandment and overlooking the crime on the basis of either type of independent judgment, but to defer to divine judgment in the matter.

Moreover, once the transgressor is found guilty and sentenced to death, presumably on the basis of the testimony of corroborating witnesses, the process resulting from your initial denunciation of him, *thou shalt surely kill him*; you personally shall not only take part in his execution; *thy hand shall be the first upon him to put him to death*, *and afterwards the hand of all the people.* This anticipates the rule set down later that requires the convicting witnesses in a capital case to bear the initial responsibility for carrying out the sentence, without regard to the personal anguish this may entail (Deut. 17:7). Some two millennia ago it was asserted that such a perpetrator "should be punished as a public and common enemy, and we should think but little of any relationship, and one should relate his recommendations to all the lovers of piety, who with all speed and without any delay would hasten to inflict punishment on the impious man, judging it a virtuous action to be zealous for his execution."[551] This early reading of the text seems to understand it as a call for vigilantism, an approach rejected by the rabbis, who insisted on a more cautious and deliberate process of conviction and punishment. Thus, acknowledging the extraordinary seriousness of such a crime, the rabbis concluded, "they may not place witnesses in hiding against any that become liable to the death-penalties enjoined in the Law save in this case alone. If he spoke [after this fashion] to two, and they are such that can bear witness against him, they bring him to court and stone him."[552]

It is noteworthy that the text itself explains the enormity of the transgression inherent in the statement, *Let us go and serve other gods.* What follows is the text's interpolation of what this means, namely the worship of gods, *which thou hast not known, thou, nor thy fathers; of the gods of the peoples that are round about you.* First, the gods that are to be worshipped are completely alien to you, so why would you so easily transfer your loyalty? Second, they also were unknown to your ancestors, which makes this shameful because "the nations of the world do not abandon the tradition handed over to them by their fathers, but Israel do abandon the tradition handed over to them by their fathers in order to go and worship idols."[553] Finally, the transgressor is not even coming up with something new on the basis of his original thought, but is mindlessly proposing to mimic what he sees other people do in preference to what God, to whom he owes loyalty, asks of him.[554]

Moses sums up this legislative item by clarifying the indictment and the purpose of imposing capital punishment. The capital charge is sedition, *because he hath sought to draw thee away from YHVH thy Elohim, who brought thee out of the land of Egypt, out of the house of bondage*, and thereby undermining the very foundation of the nation and society. The primary rationale for the extreme penalty thus seems to be not retribution for sin against God, as some maintain,[555] but rather to discourage others from attempting to likewise: *And all Israel shall hear, and fear, and shall do no more any such wickedness as this is in the midst of thee.*

Having presented the law of sedition against God as it applied to individuals, Moses turns to the law as it applies to entire communities within cities, that is, within organized political entities.

> [13.13] *If thou shalt hear tell concerning one of thy cities, which YHVH thy Elohim giveth thee to dwell there, saying:* [13.14] *'Certain base fellows are gone out from the midst of thee, and have drawn away the inhabitants of their city, saying: Let us go and serve other gods, which ye have not known';* [13.15] *then shalt thou inquire, and make search, and ask diligently; and, behold, if it be truth, and the thing certain, that such abomination is wrought in the midst of thee;* [13.16] *thou shalt surely smite the inhabitants of that city with the edge of the sword, destroying it utterly, and all that is therein and the cattle thereof, with the edge of the sword.* [13.17] *And thou shalt gather all the spoil of it into the midst of the broad place thereof, and shalt burn with fire the city, and all the spoil thereof every whit, unto YHVH thy Elohim; and it shall be a heap forever; it shall not be built again.* [13.18] *And there shall cleave nought of the devoted thing to thy hand, that YHVH may turn from the fierceness of His anger, and show thee mercy, and have compassion upon thee, and multiply thee, as He hath sworn unto thy fathers;* [13.19] *when thou shalt hearken to the voice of YHVH thy Elohim, to keep all His commandments which I command thee this day, to do that which is right in the eyes of YHVH thy Elohim.*

This passage should not be misconstrued as licensing witch-hunts. Quite to the contrary, its provisions only go into effect *If thou shalt hear tell concerning one of thy cities* that is has succumbed to mass apostasy; that is, only if reports of such misconduct have come to your attention. To who does the pronoun *thou* in this passage refer? Although it is unstated, it presumably is being addressed particularly to those bearing national authority, but at the same time also to the public at-large so that they should understand fully the gravity of the subject transgression. The wording of the Hebrew text, *yotzu anashim bnei velial*, translated as, *certain base fellows are gone out*, would be better rendered literally as the ArtScroll version has it, *men, sons of lawlessness have emerged*. The rabbis, questioning why the text apparently is redundant, *men* and *sons* being effectively synonymous, concluded that the purpose of specifying *men* was to exclude women and minors.[556] That is, in their reading of the text, Moses is saying that if it is women that are enticing people to apostasy, the collective punishment called for in the text does not apply. In such a case, "where women or children beguiled the city . . . they count only as single idolaters."[557] That is, they are held individually liable for the crime of sedition, and subject to execution if found guilty on the word of credible witnesses. This leaves open the question of the rationale for this distinction in this case of what is perhaps the most serious of capital crimes, the perversion of large number of people, especially in view of the consideration that it was women, albeit Midianite women, that caused the defection to idolatry reported earlier in the incident at Beth-peor, with such disastrous consequences. Nonetheless, one of the few commentators to discuss the issue has suggested that "the defection is only judged as a crime of communal nature if the enticement thereto was made by the solicitation of people who in general are justified in having influence in civic circles . . . otherwise the crime is looked on only as being committed by so and so many individuals."[558] That is, since women and children generally were not considered to be people of communal influence in antiquity, it seemed unreasonable to assume that their influence could be so great in this matter as to precipitate the destruction of a city and the annihilation of its inhabitants.

Should such complaints or information regarding assimilation to paganism in a particular city come forward, *then shalt thou inquire, and make search, and ask diligently*. Only after such information is made known are you to undertake a thorough investigation to determine the validity of the allegation. If the investigation reveals unequivocally that the charges are true, and a tribunal upholds them, *thou shalt surely smite the inhabitants of that city with the edge of the sword, destroying it utterly.* Indeed every living being in that city is to be annihilated, both man and beast. In addition, no one is to profit in any manner from the destruction, that is, no booty is to be taken. Instead, *thou shalt gather all the spoil of it into the midst of the broad place thereof, and shalt burn with fire the city, and all the spoil thereof every whit.* In effect, the city and everything within it is to be incinerated, *and it shall be a heap forever; it shall not be built again.*

Omitted here is any mention of the additional step introduced into the process by Moses' successor Joshua, namely that of formally appealing to the offending parties to repent. As a case in point, when the central sanctuary was located at Shiloh, the tribes of Reuben, Gad, and half of the tribe of Manasseh returned to their lands in Transjordan and *built there an altar by the Jordan, a great altar to look upon . . . And when the children of Israel heard of it, the whole congregation of the children of Israel gathered themselves together at Shiloh, to go up against them to war* (Josh. 22:10, 12). However, they first sent a high-powered delegation to plead with them to repent from the rebellion implicit *in building you an altar besides the altar of YHVH our Elohim* (22:19). The response they received was that the altar they built was not for the purposes of offering sacrifices but rather as a monument to remind their descendants that the altar they see is a mere replica of that which is to be found in the national sanctuary and that it is only upon the latter that sacrifices may be offered. The purpose of the altar was to memorialize the unbroken connection between the tribes settled in Transjordan with the rest of the nation of the Israel across the river. The explanation was found acceptable, *and the children of Israel blessed Elohim, and spoke no more of going up against them to war* (22:33).

The rationale offered for the stipulated punishment is appeasement of divine anger, so *that YHVH may turn from the fierceness of His anger, and show thee mercy, and have compassion upon thee, and multiply thee, as He hath sworn unto thy fathers.* Moses' message here is that God wants to do all these things, but will do them only *when thou shalt hearken to the voice of YHVH thy Elohim, to keep all His commandments which I command thee this day, to do that which is right in the eyes of YHVH thy Elohim.*

It is especially noteworthy that Moses speaks regarding *one of thy cities*, and the rabbis read this as asserting implicitly, "One city may be declared condemned, but three cities may not be so declared."[559] The logic behind this assertion is that when apostasy pervades a single city, it merits destruction before its contaminant spreads to other places. However, if it already pervades other towns the destruction of one will not abate the problem and must not be carried out. When such apostasy becomes widespread the ordinary citizen will be deluded into seeing it as something that is acceptable, and those led astray should no longer be considered as criminally liable.[560]

It seems clear that this entire passage reflects a demand for collective punishment that understandably will trouble many modern readers, as it did ancient and medieval students of the texts, especially with regard to the children of the condemned city. It has been pointed out in this regard that the Torah distinguishes between the sins between man and man, and those between man and God. The former "are judged in terms of the individual person's actions, and the person's intent is taken into account." The latter "are judged in terms of *groups* and *zones*, and intent is not an issue." The worship of other gods is the ultimate sin against God, and if it is an entire city that is guilty, it must be eliminated in its entirety.[561] However, before leaping to any conclusions about the matter, it may prove best to consider the relationship of this passage to the much earlier story of the virtually complete destruction of the known world in the great Deluge in the time of Noah and the later total destruction of the ancient cities of Sodom and Gomorrah.[562]

In the story of the Deluge, we were told that *the earth was corrupt before Elohim, and the earth was filled with violence . . . And Elohim said unto Noah: The end of all flesh is come before Me; for the earth is filled with violence through them; and, behold, I will destroy them with the earth* (Gen. 6:11, 13). Only Noah and his family were to survive along with representatives of the diverse animal species, presumably those required to reestablish the environmental conditions necessary for human survival and development. The societies of the earth are depicted as corrupt and violent and are therefore to be destroyed, because, it would seem, they had become dysfunctional within the context of the divine plan.

But, we may ask, is the biblical author to be understood as suggesting that *all* the people of the earth, with the exception of Noah and his family, were corrupt and violent and therefore deserving of the collective fate that awaited them? Were there no gradations of culpability? Might there not be a milder punishment for the less corrupt than for the more corrupt? In this regard, is it just to punish unequals equally? Moreover, can we even conceive of a violent and corrupt society in which there are no victims? And, if there are victims, can we conceive of a concept of justice that will condemn the victims of oppression to the same fate as their victimizers? From the standpoint of any rational conception of justice, the biblical story of the Deluge cannot but leave us bewildered. The intrinsic problem with the biblical portrayal of divine justice at work is brought into even sharper relief by the story of the impending destruction of Sodom and Gomorrah and Abraham's attempt to intercede on their behalf (Gen. 18).

> *And YHVH said: "Shall I hide from Abraham that which I am doing; seeing that Abraham shall surely become a great and mighty nation, and all the nations of the earth shall be blessed in him? For I have known him, to the end that he may command his children and his household after him, that they may keep the way of YHVH, to do righteousness and justice; to the end that YHVH may bring upon Abraham that which He hath spoken of him." And YHVH said: "Verily, the cry of Sodom and Gomorrah is great, and, verily, their sin is exceeding grievous."* (Gen. 18:17-20)

The dilemma that the biblical writer conceives God as debating with himself concerns the purpose for which Abraham was selected, namely, *that he may command his children and his household after him, that they may keep the way of the Lord, to do righteousness and justice* (Gen. 18:19). What comes through to the reader in these passages is the biblical notion of a sort of partnership between God and Abraham, predicated on the covenant, in which both parties will work in tandem to transform the world of man from its present state to one characterized by righteousness and justice. The ideal society to be created by Abraham and his descendants is intended to be the institutional embodiment of the principles of righteousness and justice. But, righteousness and justice may not always seem compatible, and this is a problem which will likely trouble Abraham. How will Abraham, who repeatedly shows intense concern for the welfare of others and already exemplifies the later biblical adjuration, *thou shalt love thy neighbor as thyself* (Lev. 19:18), reconcile this idea with the destruction of an entire society in the name of justice? Abraham is surely aware of the reprehensible conduct of the Sodomites, but undoubtedly believes that the Sodomites are ultimately redeemable through moral suasion, a notion that divine judgment had already rejected in favor of the justice of meting out collective punishment for their transgressions. The critical question is whether Abraham will comprehend the necessity for setting aside righteousness, as manifested in active compassion for one's fellow man, to satisfy the need for justice as determined in accordance with divine judgment.

Accordingly, it is crucial that Abraham come to understand and appreciate the overriding importance of justice as a social value when it appears to conflict with the principle of righteousness. The pursuit of justice is demanded of Abraham's covenantal heirs, the children of Israel, as the very justification for their collective existence as a distinct nation. The biblical imperative in this regard is explicit and unequivocal: *Justice, justice shalt thou follow, that thou mayest live, and inherit the land which YHVH thy Elohim giveth thee* (Deut. 16:20). Possession of the national patrimony is thus made contingent on the collective pursuit of justice.

Although the biblical narrator does not make clear the precise nature of the transgressions of which the two ill-fated societies were guilty, we are told that *the cry of Sodom and Gomorrah is great, and, verily, their sin is exceeding grievous*. Presumably, the level of corruption in the cities had reached the point where their continued existence could no longer be justified as acceptable within the divine plan for the universe. In other words, the biblical writer is implicitly asserting that there has always existed a universal moral law that all men are obligated to obey, irrespective of their religious beliefs, a "natural" law intended to assure the viability and stability of human society. When that law is violated consistently, creating an outcry that is heard in heaven, the offending society will ultimately be held accountable for its offenses. What this suggests is that from the standpoint of divine justice, the people are to be held collectively accountable for character of the society in which they live. Corrupt leaders can exist only with the complicity of public passivity. Unless there is clear evidence of attempts to reform society, or to take even stronger action to eliminate corruption, even the victims become culpable for the sins of their society. This was the case in the time of Noah and it was the case now with Sodom and Gomorrah, which were therefore marked for total obliteration; a punishment that evidently was considered appropriate retribution for their crimes in accordance with the requirements of divine justice.

The divine judgment of Sodom and Gomorrah is not presented by the biblical author as a legal proceeding concerning application of the law, but as a political one concerning the broader concept of justice; whether a society merits destruction is not a legal question, and the attempt to force a legal interpretation of the biblical terms seems to miss the point of the whole passage. The biblical writer is dealing with the matter of righteousness and wickedness as it applies to an entire society and not to the innocence or guilt of individuals within it.[563] What is at issue here is not the guilt or innocence of individuals but the broader question of whether a society that has become so dysfunctional as to be irredeemable should be permitted to continue to exist, and at what degree of dysfunction a negative response is appropriate.[564] Innocence and righteousness are not synonymous. Innocence is passive, whereas righteousness is active. Abraham evidently understands that there will always be innocent people in even the most corrupt society, and that in the course of historical events the innocent often get caught up in a web of circumstances that leads to their unwarranted suffering and death. But he also understands that the suffering of the innocent is not what is at issue in determining whether a society has become dysfunctional to the extent that its continued survival cannot be justified. The mere presence of even large numbers of innocent people does not in itself contribute to reforming a corrupt society. To do that requires righteous people who are prepared to act to improve their society. It requires that righteous people *within the city* be actively engaged in attempting to bring about the necessary change, if there is to be any hope for redeeming the society.[565]

It is noteworthy that the biblical author did not have Abraham argue that collective punishment is unjust even if there were only a single righteous person who would unjustifiably be affected by it. Presumably, Abraham agreed, at least from the standpoint of divine but not necessarily human justice, that if a community did not have a critical mass of good people it might be considered irredeemable. Without at least a given minimum of active virtuous people upon which to build, the essential basis for progressive improvement of the society simply would not exist. Under such circumstances divine collective punishment of the offending societies could conceivably be justified, even though it might involve what we in modern times have come to call "collateral damage," that is, inadvertently subjecting innocent persons to unwarranted suffering. In effect, divine justice overrode divine compassion, for to spare the city even if it did not contain a saving minority would be tantamount to condoning the outrages that led to the original determination that the city had become irredeemably dysfunctional.

What Moses is asserting here, in effect, is that the very existence of a city in Israel that has gone over to paganism is an intolerable affront to God, and must be dealt with accordingly. In the case of the Deluge and the cities of Sodom and Gomorrah, God intervened directly and dealt with them, as discussed above. However, in the case of the nation Israel, which was intended to be the embodiment of the virtues of Abraham, Moses insists that the nation itself was to assume responsibility for its moral integrity and to police itself, and *to do that which is right in the eyes of YHVH thy Elohim*; what is right in God's eyes, and not in accordance with what man may think is right in his own eyes. The existence of a body of Israelite pagans in the midst of Israelite society would threaten the very foundations of the covenant, which was the sole justification for national existence in the first place. To permit such a city to continue to thrive in Israel would be to nurture a cancer that would eat away at its integrity as a nation devoted to God, and this had to be prevented at all costs. And so Moses ordained that such a city must be wiped out in its entirety.

It is noteworthy, in this regard, that there is no record of the Mosaic law regarding the seditious city ever having been invoked in practice, presumably because Israel's faith in God was never challenged by more than a small fraction of its people in biblical times, and thus never reached the critical mass that would have made an Israelite city irredeemable. As the rabbis put it: "An apostate city never was and is not ever going to be. And why was the matter written? To say: Expound it and receive a reward."[566] By causing the reader to ponder the text, it remains an eternal reminder of the true basis of Israel's national existence, as understood from the biblical perspective.

Moses then turned to a series of prohibitions on individual as well as collective behavior that appear clearly designed to differentiate between Israel and the nations with respect to daily life, restrictions that presumably were deemed necessary to constantly remind the children of Israel of who they were and their special relationship with God.

> [14.1] *Ye are the children of YHVH your Elohim: ye shall not cut yourselves, nor make any baldness between your eyes for the dead.* [14.2] *For thou art a holy people unto YHVH thy Elohim, and YHVH hath chosen thee to be His own treasure out of all peoples that are upon the face of the earth.*

It has been suggested that the present text begins with *Ye are the children of YHVH your Elohim* as a reminder of divine concern for them, notwithstanding the extremely harsh collective punishment spoken of in the preceding section.[567] The initial wording of this passage also appears to be a reflection of God's instruction as to what Moses was to say to the king of Egypt, in asking for the release of the Israelites. *And thou shalt say unto Pharaoh: Thus saith YHVH: Israel is My son, My first-born* (Ex. 4:22). Thus, although all men are God's children, Israel is His spiritual first-born son. The implication of this that comes to mind is that since the first man, Adam, was fashioned by God according to His specifications, it is inappropriate for one to attempt to alter that configuration artificially, presumably unless necessary to sustain life and health. It is noteworthy that the rabbis were divided over the implications of the statement *Ye are the children of YHVH your Elohim*, one opinion suggesting that this is the case only when Israel conducts itself in a manner appropriate to children of God. The alternate view was that Israel remained children of God no matter what their behavior, just as children of a father remain such irrespective of whether their father can be proud of them.[568] In support of the latter opinion, it has been suggested that the reason the statement is given here, in connection with the injunction against following the mourning practices of the peoples they will conquer in the land, is because God has compassion for Israel as a father has for his children. What you perceive as tragic in someone's death may actually be for the best, and God does not want you to go to extremes in mourning their loss.[569]

Accordingly, Moses indicates that the children of Israel are not to imitate the mourning practices common to the surrounding peoples, particularly self-mutilation and shaving one's forehead. "The prohibition against this practice signifies that our obedience to the Divine Law is not to weaken even when very deep feelings are involved."[570] It is noteworthy that these prohibitions were previously included among those specifically given to the priests, *They shall not make baldness upon their head, neither shall they shave off the corners of their beard, nor make any cuttings in their flesh* (Lev. 21:5), and to the people at-large, *Ye shall not round the corners of your heads, neither shalt thou mar the corners of thy beard. Ye shall not make any cuttings in your flesh for the dead, nor imprint any marks upon you* (Lev. 19:27-28), the last clause stating a clear prohibition against tattooing, which in antiquity frequently represented the deity worshipped by the bearer of the tattoo.[571]

It should be noted, however, that some of the rabbis read this text in a political manner as saying, "Do not split yourselves up into several factions but rather be one faction."[572] In other words, Moses is calling for national unity in the tribal and clan-based society. This interpretation is based on the difference in verbs used in this text and that found in the earlier one. Thus, *ye shall not make any cuttings in your flesh* employs the verb *sarat* meaning scratch or incise, whereas *ye shall not cut yourselves* employs the verb *gadad* which also means cut but is often used in the sense of subdivide. It is presumed by advocates of this interpretation that the change in verb is significant in that the earlier statement is explicitly related to grieving practices whereas this is less clear in the present one.[573] A number of later commentaries also express a preference for this interpretation, which clearly is not the plain meaning of the text.

The children of Israel are not to adopt the heathenish practices of other peoples, *for thou art a holy people unto YHVH thy Elohim,* the entire verse being a repetition of what Moses stated earlier in his discourse in connection with the demand that they take serious steps to avoid any cultural assimilation to the peoples they will conquer when they cross the Jordan (Deut. 7:6). In this regard, Moses proceeds to set forth a series of specific guidelines concerning what may and may not be eaten. It has been pointed out, "The Torah regards limitations on man's appetite as fundamental to a proper way of life."[574] In this regard it might be noted that the very first commandment of God to man in the Garden of Eden concerned food. After it states, *And out of the ground made YHVH Elohim to grow every tree that is pleasant to the sight, and good for food* (Gen. 2:9), including the tree of the knowledge of good and evil, God then commanded: *Of every tree of the garden thou mayest freely eat; but of the tree of the knowledge of good and evil, thou shall not eat of it* (Gen. 2:16-17). Thus, although that particular tree was *pleasant to the sight, and good for food,* man was to restrain from eating of its fruit for no other obvious reason than that he had to learn that man must place divine judgment above his own, that there are desires that man must forego simply because God so instructed him. The object lesson of this was that because man failed this first and most important test, the tree was designated as *the tree of the knowledge of good and evil,* the latter being what man learned by violating the divine commandment. The Israelites too must learn to subordinate certain desires to the divine will, and the educational vehicle for this are the rationally inexplicable dietary statutes that Moses now sets before the people.

^{14.3} Thou shalt not eat any abominable thing. ^{14.4} These are the beasts which ye may eat: the ox, the sheep, and the goat, ^{14.5} the hart, and the gazelle, and the roebuck, and the wild goat, and the pygarg, and the antelope, and the mountain sheep. ^{14.6} And every beast that parteth the hoof, and hath the hoof wholly cloven in two, and cheweth the cud, among the beasts, that ye may eat. ^{14.7} Nevertheless these ye shall not eat of them that only cheweth the cud, or of them that only have the hoof cloven: the camel, and the hare, and the rock-badger, because they chew the cud but part not the hoof, they are unclean unto you; ^{14.8} and the swine, because he parteth the hoof but cheweth not the cud, he is unclean to you; of their flesh ye shall not eat, and their carcasses ye shall not touch.

Moses begins by essentially declaring that the animals that the children of Israel are not permitted to eat are to be considered *toevah* or *abominable*. The implication of the use of this term is that these animals are unsuitable for consumption by the children of Israel not because they are physically unhealthy but rather because they are spiritually unsuitable. In this regard it may be recalled that when Moses was negotiating with the king of Egypt about allowing the Israelites to go into the wilderness in order to sacrifice to their God, Pharaoh told them they did not have to go away but could do so where they were. Moses responded: *It is not meet so to do; for we shall sacrifice the abomination [toevah] of the Egyptians . . . lo, if we sacrifice the abomination of the Egyptians before their eyes, will they not stone us?* (Ex. 8:22). That is, the sacrifice of these animals would have been unpardonable, not because anything physically inherent in them but because of the religious significance that the Egyptians attached to them. For this reason their slaughter and consumption would have been an *abomination* to the Egyptians, just as the slaughter and consumption of the forbidden animals on Moses' list would be an *abomination* to Israel, something to be avoided assiduously. For the Egyptians, the religious significance attached to the animals that prohibited their consumption was that they reflected a divine spirit; for Israel the religious significance in avoiding the proscribed animals rested in the consideration that the prohibition was a divine statute, for which no reason was given, but which had to be obeyed because God demanded it. As it states: *And YHVH spoke unto Moses and to Aaron, saying unto them: Speak unto the children of Israel, saying: These are the living things which ye may eat among all the beasts that are on the earth* (Lev. 11:1-2). Here Moses is simply reiterating what God already had ordained as *hukim* or statutes.

It has been argued that the reason for the dietary restrictions is to emphasize Israel's mission to become *a kingdom of priests and a holy nation* (Ex. 19:6). Just as the priests of the other nations were distinguished from the general population by special laws and personal constraints, so too was it intended that Israel be made distinct from the heathen nations. This would serve to elevate the spirit of the people and discourage them from emulating their neighbors and cause them to cleave to the God of their ancestors and the proper and holy paths set before them.[575] It should be noted, however, that this opinion is strongly rejected by others on the basis that it is demeaning to suggest that the complex of dietary restrictions have no intrinsic meaning other than to differentiate Israel from its neighbors, notwithstanding that one cannot infer such meaning from the biblical texts, perhaps other than that they serve as a disciplinary device to accustom Israel to obeying God's will even when it is beyond human comprehension.[576]

The prohibition against even touching the carcass of one of the prohibited animals was evidently for the benefit of the children of Israel because coming into contact with them entailed entering a state of defilement that required ritual purification, which was not the case with the carcasses of permitted animals slaughtered in accordance with traditional methods.[577] Omitted from mention here is the earlier stipulation that *whatsoever goeth upon its paws, among all beasts that go on fours, they are unclean unto you; whoso toucheth their carcass shall be unclean until the even* (Lev. 11:27). It should be noted that there is a good deal of uncertainty about the identity of some of the animals named in the Hebrew text, although we must assume that they were known to the ancients, and the various translations of the text offer a variety of possibilities.

251

> *14.9 These ye may eat of all that are in the waters: whatever hath fins and scales may ye eat; 14.10 and whatsoever hath not fins and scales ye shall not eat; it is unclean unto you.*

The statement of this regulation given earlier is rather more detailed and merits restatement in part here. *And all that have not fins and scales in the seas, and in the rivers, of all that swarm in the waters, and of all the living creatures that are in the waters, they are a detestable thing unto you, and they shall be a detestable thing unto you; ye shall not eat of their flesh and their carcasses ye shall have in detestation* (Lev. 11:10-11). In this text, the *living creatures that are in the waters* are understood to refer to maritime animals such as seals that do not come under the category of fish. The prohibition of *all that have not fins and scales in the seas* has been understood to suggest that if they have scales and fins in the water that may not be discernible out of the water they would be considered edible. "The Rabbis were of the opinion that every fish which has scales also has fins, although these may be of a very rudimentary kind and not discernible to the eye. Therefore in actual practice they permit fish with scales only, but not fish with fins only."[578] It is noteworthy that, by contrast with forbidden animals, forbidden fish do not defile by touch.

> *14.11 Of all clean birds ye may eat. 14.12 But these are they of which ye shall not eat: the great vulture, and the bearded vulture, and the osprey; 14.13 and the glede, and the falcon, and the kite after its kinds; 14.14 and every raven after its kinds; 14.15 and the ostrich, and the nighthawk, and the sea-mew, and the hawk after its kinds; 14.16 the little owl, and the great owl, and the horned owl; 14.17 and the pelican, and the carrion-vulture, and the cormorant; 14.18 and the stork, and the heron after its kinds, and the hoopoe, and the bat. 14.19 And all winged swarming things are unclean unto you; they shall not be eaten. 14.20 Of all clean winged things ye may eat.*

With regard to fowl, all the prohibited birds are members of the class designated as birds of prey or scavengers,[579] the ones named being those familiar to the people of the Middle East; the list is not intended to be definitive. *All winged swarming things are unclean unto you*; this refers to the wide variety of winged insects; *they shall not be eaten.* It is noteworthy that the latter prohibition was elaborated earlier as, *All winged swarming things that go upon all fours are a detestable thing unto you* (Lev. 11:20), going *upon all fours* being understood not literally but as an expression conveying that the insects in question move more or less like quadrupeds. Omitted here is the qualifying statement, *Yet these may ye eat of all winged swarming things that go upon all fours, which have jointed legs above their feet, wherewith to leap upon the earth; even these of them ye may eat: the locust after its kinds, and the bald locust after its kinds, and the cricket after its kinds, and the grasshopper after its kinds* (Lev. 11:21-22). However, such creatures that do not *have jointed legs above their feet* are clearly prohibited, and their carcasses defile by touch for the remainder of the day until evening (Lev. 11:24).

Completely omitted by Moses in his discourse is the earlier stipulated prohibition regarding *the swarming things that swarm upon the earth: the weasel, and the mouse, and the great lizard after its kinds, and the gecko, and the land-crocodile, and the lizard, and the sand-lizard, and the chameleon* (Lev. 11:29-30). Moreover, the prohibition also applies to *whatsoever goeth upon the belly* and *whatsoever hath many feet* (Lev. 11:42).

> *14.21 Ye shall not eat of any thing that dieth of itself; thou mayest give it unto the stranger that is within thy gates, that he may eat it; or thou mayest sell it unto a foreigner; for thou art a holy people unto YHVH the Elohim. Thou shalt not seethe a kid in its mother's milk.*

Moses here prohibits the eating of anything that dies from natural causes, however, the Hebrew term *nevelah*, translated as *any thing that dieth of itself*, is also applied to any animal that is not slaughtered in the traditionally prescribed manner, because *thou art a holy people unto YHVH the Elohim.* However, there is no prohibition against selling it to a non-Israelite who lives with you or to a non-Israelite who dos not reside in your community. Once again, the presumption is that there is nothing essentially wrong with the animal other than the manner of its death. If it were death from natural causes and therefore posed a health risk, selling it to a stranger would surely be prohibited as well. However, if the animal were killed, perhaps during a hunt or by through an unacceptable manner of slaughter, it is perfectly acceptable to sell it to someone not bound by the covenant.

The injunction, *Thou shalt not seethe a kid in its mother's milk*, evidently was a matter of serious concern since it was mentioned twice earlier (Ex. 23:19 and 34:26). One suggested interpretation is the unattested allegation that since at the time of the final harvest of the year it was a custom of the local people in Canaan to celebrate by cooking a kid in its mother's milk in the belief that this would bring a blessing to their livestock, Israel was specifically forbidden to follow this pagan custom.[580] In this regard, it has been suggested that the laws concerning the roasting of the Paschal sacrifice (Ex. 12:8-9) "may consciously seek to differentiate Israelite practice from the indigenous Canaanite ritual with which it must on no account be associated."[581] It also has been noted that the time of the final harvest is also the time when the breeding season comes to fruition,[582] some of the rabbis considering it to be the time of the year when it is appropriate to tithe cattle.[583] In any case, the rationale for the injunction remains a matter of inconclusive speculation.

One isolated but notable interpretation is that the usual translation of the Hebrew term *lo tevashel* as *thou shalt not seethe* misconstrues the intent of the injunction. It is argued that the root of the term may also be understood as meaning "finished" or "ripe." Accordingly, the text should be understood as saying that, with regard to the sacrificial animal, one should not delay selecting a kid until it has finished nursing with its mother's milk.[584] The implication of this is that it may have been expected that a shepherd might be reluctant to take a young animal away from its nursing mother until it was weaned; this commandment would require him to go against his better judgment to meet the divine demand. This interpretation leaves much to be desired with regard to the grammar and syntax of the sentence. Moreover, it should be noted that it runs counter to the accepted interpretation of the text and the consequent restriction in traditional Judaism against mixing of meat and dairy foods and consuming them concurrently. In sum, the rationale behind this commandment is unknown and remains a matter of speculation.

Moses now turns to imposing a rather unique obligation, the evident intention of which is to build national solidarity among the tribally based children of Israel.

> *14.22 Thou shalt surely tithe all the increase of thy seed, that which is brought forth in the field year by year. 14.23 And thou shalt eat before YHVH thy Elohim, in the place which He shall cause His name to dwell there, the tithe of thy corn, and of thy wine, and of thy oil, and the firstlings of thy herd and of thy flock; that thou mayest learn to fear YHVH thy Elohim always. 14.24 And if the way be too long for thee, so that thou art not able to carry it, because the place is too far from thee, which YHVH thy Elohim shall choose to set His name there, when YHVH thy Elohim shall bless thee; 14.25 then thou shalt turn it into money, and bind up the money in thy hand, and shalt go unto the place which YHVH thy Elohim shall choose. 14.26 And thou shalt bestow the money for whatsoever thy soul desireth, for oxen, or for sheep, or for wine, or for strong drink, or for whatsoever thy soul asketh of thee; and thou shalt eat there before YHVH thy Elohim, and thou shalt rejoice, thou and thy household. 14.27 And the Levite that is within thy gates, thou shalt not forsake him; for he hath no portion nor inheritance with thee.*

Moses demands that every year, each landholder will be morally obligated to gather ten percent of the annual produce of his agricultural yield in grain, wine, and olive oil, in addition to the new firstborn of his cattle and sheep, and bring them to the site of the national sanctuary, whenever and wherever such is established, to be consumed there *before YHVH thy Elohim*, so that *thou mayest learn to fear YHVH thy Elohim always.* This tithe is identified as the second tithe, the first tithe being that dedicated annually to God, which in turn has been awarded to the Levites. *And unto the children of Levi, behold, I have given all the tithe in Israel for an inheritance, in return for their service which they serve* (Num. 18:21). Accordingly, the first tithe is to be provided annually to the Levites and the second tithe must be consumed at the place where the national sanctuary is to be found.

If it turns out that the location of the sanctuary is too far from your home for you, as a practical matter, to be able to transport all of the tithe and the firstborn cattle and sheep because of the amount involved *when YHVH thy Elohim shall bless thee* with such abundance, then you are to sell it all locally and take the money and go to the site of pilgrimage along with your household, and there spend *the money for whatsoever thy soul desireth, for oxen, or for sheep, or for wine, or for strong drink, or for whatsoever thy soul asketh of thee; and thou shalt eat there before YHVH thy Elohim, and thou shalt rejoice.* The wording of this text is such that it should be understood that the requirement that the money is to be spent *for whatsoever thy soul desireth* applies only to that which can be consumed *there before YHVH thy Elohim,* and this evidently means what can be eaten, food and drink, and not to other goods that might be purchased at the site.[585]

By any measure this tithe and its accompanying obligation must be considered an extraordinary imposition. Nonetheless, confronted by the problem of tribal and clan particularity, and the lack of a true sense of national identity on the part of the children of Israel, Moses mandates a compulsory annual pilgrimage for one's entire household to the central national sanctuary, which will in effect become the capital of the nation, to celebrate God's beneficence by consuming there ten percent of the annual yield of produce and firstborn cattle and sheep. And, of course, to the extent that it may be impracticable for some to actually bring all that is demanded with them, they are to bring the equivalent in disposable income to be spent in the capital, thereby contributing to its economy and thus strengthening its position as the center of the nation.

Since fulfillment of this obligation on the part of householders is entirely voluntary, there being no effective way of enforcing compliance, one must wonder whether Moses seriously expected everyone to carry out this mandate. It seems safe to assume that, knowing the people as he did, he could not realistically expect this to happen on a national scale. However, to the extent that some initially did as charged, it would begin to have the desired effect, incrementally to be sure, of impressing upon the broad public that it was God's desire that they think and act as a nation, an idea that would be strengthened by the centralization of divine worship in a central sanctuary.

Once again, Moses also reminds the people not to forget the Levites, who have little independent income, and to carry out what in the present day might be called an 'adopt a Levite' program, by including them as members of their households, aside from providing them with the annual first tithe. And in this same regard, Moses ordains yet another provision to help keep the Levites as well as others without reliable income out of abject poverty.

> [14.28] *At the end of every three years, even in the same year, thou shalt bring forth all the tithe of thine increase, and shalt lay it up within thy gates.* [14.29] *And the Levite, because he hath no portion nor inheritance with thee, and the stranger, and the fatherless, and the widow, that are within thy gates, shall come, and shall eat and be satisfied; that YHVH thy Elohim may bless thee in all the work of thy hand which thou doest.*

Every third year, each landholder is to gather a tenth of his agricultural produce and make it available for the Levites, strangers living in your community, orphans, and widows, to partake of it. And this should be done if you desire that God *may bless thee in all the work of thy hand which thou doest.* Here again, compliance is voluntary, however, the visible presence of the potential recipients of the tithe at one's doorstep would surely prick the conscience of anyone in the community who might be disinclined to comply with the mandate. In addition, peer pressure from one's neighbors and fear of embarrassment might also effectively urge compliance by the recalcitrant.

In effect, considering this and the previous mandates for tithing, some have argued that the Israelite householder would be required to set aside thirty percent of his yield every third year, the first tithe for the support of the Levites, the second tithe for his celebratory visit to the national sanctuary and a third tithe to meet the needs of the locally impoverished.[586] This provision has therefore been interpreted by others as saying that in the third year the second tithe normally taken to the national sanctuary and consumed there by the householder and his family should instead be put aside for the poor and consumed by them, thereby keeping the annual tax burden at twenty percent. It has been suggested that the opening of the passage, *at the end of every three years*, implies that this should take place at the time of the last of the annual pilgrimages, which the rabbis presumed to take place at Passover, at which time the householder is obligated to attend at the sanctuary, albeit without the tithe that he otherwise would bring with him to be consumed there.[587]

Alternatively, in a rather different simple reading of the passage, it has been suggested that the text *thou shalt bring forth all the tithe of thine increase, and shalt lay it up within thy gates* should be understood as implying that if it were not possible, perhaps because of illness or other circumstance, to fulfill one's obligation with regard to the second tithe completely in any one year, it would be permissible to consume it later, as long as it was done within the three-year period. In the third year, however, the householder is obligated to assemble whatever was not consumed from the second tithe for that year in addition to whatever may have been held over from the tithes of the preceding two years, which together constitute *all the tithe of thine increase*, and make them available to the poor. On this reading of the text, the landholder would remain obligated to eat the second tithe at the national sanctuary in the third year as well.[588]

It should be noted that the law of tithes promulgated by Moses here differs in a number of respects from what was ordained in earlier texts, as well as with what the accepted practice was in Israel's later history. Some have argued that the tithing in the earlier texts was intended to be voluntary, whereas those announced here by Moses are mandatory. In any case, the subject is complex as well as controversial

The Book of Deuteronomy in Political Perspective, Part One

and will not be pursued here, primarily because its resolution is not likely to contribute to any better understanding of the text before us. Continuing with the theme of dealing with issue of legislating to achieve the goal of social harmony essential to a stable society, Moses announces some additional measures in such regard.

> [15.1] At the end of every seven years thou shalt make a release. [15.2] And this is the manner of the release: every creditor shall release that which he hath lent unto his neighbor; he shall not exact it of his neighbor and his brother; because YHVH's release hath been proclaimed. [15.3] Of a foreigner thou mayest extract it; but whatsoever of thine is with thy brother thy hand shall release.

In the biblical paradigm, human rights take precedence over property rights.[589] The Torah thus imposes certain infringements on private property designed to reduce the gap between economic classes to a degree that effectively militates against both extreme wealth and extreme poverty. One of these infringements is the law of the Sabbatical Year, which was introduced perhaps primarily to attack the problem of gross economic inequalities within the context of the predominantly agricultural society of ancient Israel. This law quite clearly and explicitly impinges on one's rights to one's own property. Thus, in earlier biblical legislation, it states, *And six years thou shalt sow thy land, and gather in the increase thereof; but the seventh year thou shalt let it rest and lie fallow, that the poor of thy people may eat . . . In like manner thou shalt deal with thy vineyard, and with thy oliveyard* (Ex. 23:10-11). Every seventh year, the produce of the land is denied to its owner and made available to the poor who may help themselves to it without hindrance. In effect, the owner of the property temporarily loses some of his rights over the usufruct of the land. As a result of this provision, there are no tithes to be paid in the seventh year.

The second aspect of the law of the Sabbatical Year, presented in the passage under consideration, applies the basic concept to matters of finance. In the agricultural society of ancient Israel, for which the biblical legislation was originally intended, every family had its own normally self-sufficient homestead, and debts were contracted only in times of crop failure. Under such circumstances, loans to tide them over to the next growing season were considered acts of philanthropy rather than simple business transactions. Accordingly, *every creditor shall release that which he hath lent unto his neighbor; he shall not exact it of his neighbor and his brother; because the Lord's release hath been proclaimed.*

It has been suggested that the rationale behind the biblical passage is that the required debt release is in deference to the honor of God whose blessing provided the creditor with the money to lend in the first place.[590] Here again, the creditor effectively loses control of his assets through the mandatory cancellation of unpaid debts, an arrangement that gives the impoverished who needed to go into debt to survive an opportunity to start afresh every seventh year and thereby hopefully work their way out of chronic poverty.

However, over time, the economy of the society included a growing commercial sector in which loans were incurred as a normal part of business transactions, and the biblical ordinance was increasingly seen as anachronistic in the non-agricultural sector of the economy. There was an understandable reluctance on the part of lenders to make loans the repayment of which would extend beyond the Sabbatical Year. To ease the burden on those who needed such loans for the viability of their enterprises, the rabbis adopted a legal fiction, the *prosbul*, designed for the purpose by the sage Hillel at the beginning of the first century C.E. Because the requirement to cancel debts in the Sabbatical Year was addressed to the individual lender, the legal fiction concocted by Hillel formally transferred the debt to the courts, which as collective bodies were not bound by the biblical injunction. They were therefore able to collect the debt on behalf of the lender, notwithstanding the biblical stricture. The text of the *prosbul* stated, "I hand over to you, so-and-so, the judges in such-and-such a place, [my bonds], so that I may be able to recover any money owing to me from so-and-so at any time I shall desire."[591] This effectively secured the loans and permitted normal financial transactions to take place, to the great benefit of those who needed to borrow funds for a period that extended beyond the Sabbatical Year. In this way, the rabbis employed rigorous textual analysis to interpret the biblical law in a manner that fulfilled its beneficent intent under circumstances not dealt with specifically in the biblical text.

Pursuing the theme of the importance of ameliorating poverty in the national interest, Moses declares:

> *15.4 Howbeit there shall be no needy among you—for YHVH will surely bless thee in the land which YHVH thy Elohim giveth thee for an inheritance to possess it—15.5 if only thou diligently hearken unto the voice of YHVH thy Elohim, to observe to do all this commandment which I command thee this day. 15.6 For YHVH thy Elohim will bless thee, as He promised thee; and thou shalt lend unto many nations, but thou shalt not borrow; and thou shalt rule over many nations, but they shall not rule over thee.*

In this passage, Moses makes an impassioned argument that the problem of extreme economic disparity, which characterized all known nations, could be dealt with fairly if, and only if, *thou diligently hearken unto the voice of YHVH thy Elohim, to observe to do all this commandment which I command thee this day.* God, he assures the people, will surely bless them in the land He is giving to them. Indeed, diligently following His word will lead to unprecedented success as a nation. Not only need they not have any needy, they will become so wealthy as to be in a position to lend to other nations and never have to borrow. In this way they will be able to impose demands on others, while able to resist any such demands made on them. In effect, Moses is promising them complete autarky, if only they will heed what he is commanding them in the name of God.

In this same regard, it has been argued that the assertion, *Howbeit there shall be no needy among you* is directly linked with the preceding statement, *of a foreigner thou mayest extract it; but whatsoever of thine is with thy brother thy hand shall release.* That is, Moses was concerned that the requirement regarding the release of debts in the seventh year would cause people to prefer to make loans close to that time to strangers from who they could exact repayment. He therefore said they could do this if, and only if there were *no needy among you*. That is, preference would always have to be given to the needy among you regardless of your ability to reduce your financial risk by lending to non-Israelites.[592]

However, given man's inconstancy, Moses acknowledges that it is likely that *the needy shall never cease out of the land* (Deut. 15:11). The apparent contradiction between these almost adjacent passages may be resolved through a careful parsing of the earlier statement. It has been observed that the phrase *among you* may also be understood more literally as "in you." That is, there should not be "in you," or because of you, any reason for the poverty of others. That is to say, even in the ideal state there will always be people who cannot work and therefore will be unable to earn income. Nonetheless, it is the responsibility of every member of the society to make sure that no poverty should result from one's business decisions, because "when we are responsible for existing poverty, we are guilty of evil."[593] The Torah therefore sets forth a number of social laws that are designed to prevent the disparity between the "haves" and the "have-nots" in society from reaching a point that will produce social instability, a problem that modern progressive societies have continued to attempt to deal with not very successfully.

Since Moses' teaching, Judaism has consistently refused to make a virtue of poverty, and for that reason among others does not encourage asceticism. It does not accept the notion that voluntary poverty, ridding oneself of worldly goods, is the way to true piety. On the contrary, as one rabbi taught, "if there is no meal there is no Torah."[594] That is, without the necessary material resources to adequately satisfy his needs, man will not have the peace or presence of mind to devote himself to a concern about his spiritual wellbeing. It has been observed in this regard: "The common saying 'Poverty is no disgrace' may offer consolation—to those who are well off. As a statement of morality, an ethical imperative, it would have much to commend it—'Poverty *should* be no disgrace.' As a statement of fact, however, it is totally inaccurate. Poverty *is* a disgrace—for those who are poor. Poverty is destructive to the human personality."[595] And it should be borne in mind that the human personality is a reflection of the image of God, and that which is destructive of it is an affront to God. Indeed, as the biblical sage wrote, *Whoso mocketh the poor blasphemeth his Maker* (Prov. 17:5).

Poverty is considered to be an unmitigated disaster for a person. As the biblical sage put it, *the ruin of the poor is their poverty* (Prov. 10:15). The later rabbis taught: "Three things deprive a man of his senses and of a knowledge of his creator, and these are, idolatry, an evil spirit, and oppressive poverty."[596] Moreover, they pointed out: "Nothing is harder to bear than poverty; for he who is crushed by poverty is like one to whom all the troubles of the world cling and upon whom all the curses in Deuteronomy have descended. Our Teachers have said: If all the troubles were assembled on one side and poverty on the other, poverty would outweigh them all."[597] Poverty also causes a person to become insignificant in his own eyes, as well as an object of derision by others. Poverty leads to embarrassment and humiliation. The rabbis observed, "As soon as a man needs the support of his fellow creatures his face changes color."[598] Humiliation is the prelude to dehumanization, and Mosaic teaching demands, acknowledging the improbability of eliminating poverty entirely, that steps be taken to mitigate the severity of the problem. As one writer put it, "To aid the poor is to 'rehumanize' children of God."[599]

With this purpose in mind, although the Torah strongly affirms the principle of a right to private property, it does not consider that right absolute and inviolable. Indeed, no man is considered to have absolute control over what is conventionally considered to be his property. This view is a necessary corollary to the psalmist's assertion that *The earth is the Lord's and the fullness thereof* (Ps. 24:1). It has been argued in this regard: "The social attitude of Hebraic religion holds it to be the will of God that the resources of nature and the fruits of human creativity, which are a divine gift, should be used for the satisfaction of human needs and the enhancement of human welfare." Thus, while the Torah does not posit any preferred economic system, it does profess criteria for assessing the social adequacy and appropriateness of particular economic arrangements at a particular place and time. The ultimate criterion is the extent "to which humans are treated as ends in themselves, of equal worth and dignity as children of God and bearers of the divine image."[600]

Ideally, as Moses put it, *there shall be no needy [evyon] among you . . . if only thou diligently hearken unto the voice of the Lord thy God, to observe to do all this commandment which I command thee this day.* What Moses appears to be asserting is that if one follows the guidelines set forth in the Torah, the state of the society will be such that it will no longer contain a social and economic class of the "*needy.*" The Torah, however, does not provide a definition or the characteristics of what constitutes the "needy," something that is not as self-evident as it might appear at first glance. It is therefore important to note at the outset of this discussion that Moses does *not* say "there shall be no poor [*ani*] among you," but only *there shall be no needy [evyon] among you.* The use of the term *evyon* in the biblical passage is significant because there appears to be a critical substantive distinction in biblical terminology between *ani*, meaning "poor" or "low income" and *evyon*, translated as "needy."[601]

Based on conclusions drawn from their interpretation of the biblical texts in which the terms appear, traditional commentators have tended to define an *evyon* as one who is worse off than an *ani*, as one who desires everything but can attain nothing.[602] What they have not done is explain how one becomes an *evyon* in the contexts that the term is applied in the various biblical provisions in which it appears. Upon close examination of those texts, it becomes clear that, in the biblical view, the *ani* is a person who for unspecified reasons has been chronically poor, whereas the *evyon* is one who has suddenly become acutely impoverished and destitute, presumably as a result of some disastrous turn of events such as a crop failure or commercial misadventure. The importance of the distinction can hardly be overemphasized if one is to fully understand the biblical approach to the questions of social justice and welfare. There may be many reasons for the chronic poverty of individuals and families, and the Torah makes provisions for ameliorating their condition to a limited extent, affording them critical relief through a variety of means. The *evyon*, however, is viewed as a special case, a person who is not one of the chronically poor but who has become impoverished and prospectively, with appropriate assistance, can raise himself from a current state of destitution to one of relative affluence. Accordingly, while the Torah does not envision an end to the chronic poverty of those who for any one of a number of possible reasons are unable to ascend the economic ladder, the biblical desideratum stressed in this passage is that no one should be allowed unnecessarily to wallow in the state of an *evyon*, and that certain steps, outlined in the biblical text, should be initiated to alleviate the problem in the properly ordered society.

Nonetheless, Moses acknowledges that, given the prevalence of both natural and man-made contingencies, it is likely that *the needy [evyon] shall never cease out of the land* (Deut. 15:11). It thus appears to take for granted that even under the best of circumstances there will always be people subjected to financial catastrophe, either as a consequence of poor judgment or events beyond one's control. The principal concern in this passage is therefore with the plight of the *evyon*, one who has fallen on hard times, rather than on the *ani* who is chronically impoverished. This is not to suggest, however, that the Torah is less concerned with the welfare of the chronically poor than it is with the bankrupt. There are in fact, as already indicated, a number of notable biblical provisions that specifically concern themselves with alleviating the distress of the chronically poor, that is, the *ani*.

Having set forth the general proposition regarding the amelioration of poverty in the national interest, Moses now sets forth in some detail what this entails for the children of Israel in order for them to realize it in their society.

> *15.7 If there be among you a needy man, one of thy brethren, within any of thy gates, in thy land which YHVH thy Elohim giveth thee, thou shalt not harden thy heart, nor shut thy hand from thy needy brother; 15.8 but thou shalt surely open thy hand unto him, and shalt surely lend him sufficient for his need in that which he wanteth. 15.9 Beware that there be not a base thought in thy heart, saying: 'The seventh year, the year of release, is at hand'; and thine eye be evil against thy needy brother, and thou give him nought; and he cry unto YHVH against thee, and it be*

sin in thee. ^{15.10} Thou shalt surely give him, and thy heart
shall not be grieved when thou givest unto him; because
that for this thing YHVH thy Elohim will bless thee in all
thy work, and in all that thou puttest thy hand unto. ^{15.11}
For the poor shall never cease out of the land; therefore I
command thee, saying: 'Thou shalt surely open thy hand
unto thy poor and needy brother, in thy land.'

First and foremost, the ultimate key to national prosperity is generosity. The opening of the passage, *If there be among you a needy man, one of thy brethren, within any of thy gates, in thy land,* has been interpreted as a clause setting priorities for the rendition of assistance. That is, for the individual dealing with the issue of poverty, family comes first, followed by the residents of your town or city, and finally your countrymen generally.[603] If *a needy man* is identified, *thou shalt not harden thy heart, nor shut thy hand . . . but thou shalt surely open thy hand unto him, and shalt surely lend him sufficient for his need in that which he wanteth.* Accordingly, when the seventh year approaches and the law of release takes effect, Moses cautions them against turning their backs on the needy because they would have to incur a loss by lending them money one day and having the debt cancelled the next. To do so would be sinful and counterproductive to their own interests because God is watching what they do as well as what they refuse to do. If you do what you ought, *for this thing YHVH thy Elohim will bless thee in all thy work, and in all that thou puttest thy hand unto,* with God's help you will succeed in all your legitimate endeavors.

The adjuration *thou shalt surely open thy hand unto him, and shalt surely lend him* has been understood by the rabbis as indicating that *open thy hand* means to offer the needy a grant to meet his needs. However, should he demur from accepting charity *thou . . . shalt surely lend him,* that is, offer it to him as a loan.[604] In other words, the offer of assistance should be made in a way that permits the recipient to choose the method by which it is given.[605] This acknowledges that for some accepting a needed gift may offend their sense of dignity and self-worth, and this needs to be taken into account. Moreover, the clause, *sufficient for his need in that which he wanteth,* appears redundant, *his need* and *that which he wanteth* being virtually synonymous. The rabbis therefore interpreted the latter phrase as implying that there is no objective predetermination of need, which will vary according to the situation of the individual. *"Sufficient for his need*—you are not commanded to make him rich—*in that which he wanteth*—be it even a horse or a slave."[606] That is, the obligation is to grant or lend him sufficient to maintain the minimum standard of living for a person of the economic status he had before falling on hard times. Once again, according to the rabbis, it is of crucial importance to help people maintain a modicum of dignity and sense of self-worth. Thus, a person who had been affluent will have a different threshold of need than someone who has always lived modestly.

It is noteworthy that this biblical provision applies specifically to the *evyon* and not to the *ani* or chronically poor, bearing in mind the distinction between them discussed above. Presumably, the notion of lending money to one who is chronically poor *sufficient for his need in that which he wanteth* would constitute a long-term open-ended commitment that would not only make little sense to the creditor, whom it could bankrupt, but would also place the *ani* in the embarrassing position of accepting loans that he and everyone else knows he will never be able to repay. This is not to suggest that there are no circumstances under which giving a loan to an *ani* is both charitable and reasonable. Thus it states: *If thou lend money to any of My people, even to the poor with thee, thou shalt not be to him as a creditor* (Ex. 22:24), that is, you should not hound him for repayment. The significant word in this text is *If*, a conditional term that is not applied to the *evyon*. Loans in general and to an *ani* in particular would therefore seem to be considered meritorious but optional, given that there are other biblical provisions for dealing specifically with the needs of the poor. With the *evyon*, however, a timely loan may make all the difference in changing his situation dramatically, even though he may not be able to repay the loan before it was cancelled in conformance with the biblical prescription.

It is important to note, however, that one of the major rabbis specifically challenged the literal reading of the latter biblical passage, that is, as making loans to the poor optional rather than mandated.

He argued: "Every 'if' in the Torah refers to a voluntary act except this and two others . . . And also here you interpret: '*If thou lend money*' as referring to an obligatory act. You interpret it to be obligatory. Perhaps this is not so, but it is merely voluntary? Scripture however says: '*Thou shalt surely lend him* (Deut. 15:18)—it is obligatory and not voluntary."[607] The prooftext that is adduced in support of this argument is, of course, the one that specifically addresses the lending of money to the *evyon* [*sufficient for his need in that which he wanteth*] and makes no mention of the *ani*. One possible explanation of this anomaly is that the rabbi would not agree with the distinction between the *ani* and the *evyon* that has been pointed out here, something that seems quite unreasonable given the nature of the other provisions that applied to the *evyon* that would have required a redistribution of wealth that would have economically wrecked any community if also applied to the chronically poor. It therefore seems more likely that the conflation of the two distinct biblical provisions was done consciously and deliberately in order to achieve a practical social purpose, namely to encourage assistance to those at the bottom of the economic ladder whose situation was becomingly increasingly severe because of the seemingly unending turbulence through which the Jewish people were struggling for survival.

In either case, the rabbi's reading of the biblical text was subsequently accepted as normative by Maimonides, who included it as one of the 613 precepts set forth in the Torah that form the basis of halakhah, after which it garnered broad rabbinical acceptance.[608] In his law code, Maimonides simply echoed the sage's teaching: "It is an affirmative commandment to lend to the poor of Israel. For it is written *If thou lend money to any of My people, to the poor with thee* (Ex. 22:24). From this passage one might infer that lending money to the poor is optional, but when we read in another passage *Thou shalt surely lend him* (Deut. 15:8), we know that it is obligatory."[609] Since Maimonides, the assertion of a biblical obligation to lend to the poor has been included in all major codifications of the halakhah, although the notion that such loans should be *sufficient for his need in that which he wanteth* is left unstated. To do otherwise would have been the equivalent of declaring a war on poverty that could not possibly be won. Thus, in the traditionally authoritative code of Joseph Caro, it states simply: "It is a positive precept to lend money to the poor of Israel, and it is a precept of greater weight than *tzedakah*."[610] The implicit presumption here is that an appropriate loan may assist more than charity in helping one to break out of the condition of chronic poverty.

The passage ends with the assertion that all this is vital for the national interest, *for the poor shall never cease out of the land; therefore I command thee, saying: 'Thou shalt surely open thy hand unto thy poor and needy brother, in thy land.'* The uniqueness of this clause is that it places the responsibility for taking the initiative in assisting those in need on the donor rather than the recipient. As noted by one commentator, "in the imagery of the Torah it is not the poor man who stretches forth his hand begging for alms, but the donor who opens his hand so that the needy may help themselves."[611] This is made clear in the biblical adjuration that, aside from the tithe obligations spoken of above, *when ye reap the harvest of your land, thou shalt not wholly reap the corner of thy field, neither shall thou gather the gleaning of thy harvest. And thou shalt not glean thy vineyard, neither shalt thou gather the fallen fruit of thy vineyard; thou shalt leave them for the poor and for the stranger* (Lev. 19:9-10). Similarly, *When thou reapest thy harvest in thy field, and hast forgot a sheaf in the field, thou shalt not go back to fetch it; it shall be for the stranger, for the fatherless, and for the widow* (Deut. 24:19).

Acknowledging that there was always likely to be both chronically "poor" and temporarily destitute "needy", one of the ways people sought to alleviate their condition was to indenture themselves as bonded servants, sometimes erroneously considered "slaves" in the sense of chattel slavery. The biblical regulations concerning bonded servitude imposed such heavy burdens on the master of an Israelite slave that it became an increasingly less attractive means of obtaining a dedicated labor force. Indeed, it may be argued that the Torah effectively nullified the idea of chattel slavery with the following demand: *And if thy brother be waxen poor with thee, and sell himself unto thee, thou shalt not make him to serve as a bondservant [slave]. As a hired servant, and as a settler, he shall be with thee* (Lev. 25:39-40). In other words, biblical law does not allow an Israelite to become a slave in the conventional connotation of the term. The rabbis went so far as to suggest, "Perhaps he should not be called 'slave' at all, it being a term of opprobrium?"[612]

> *15.12 If thy brother, a Hebrew man, or a Hebrew woman, be sold unto thee, he shall serve thee six years; and in the seventh year thou shalt let him go free from thee. 15.13 And when thou lettest him go free from thee, thou shalt not let him go empty; 15.14 thou shalt furnish him liberally out of thy flock, and out of thy threshing floor, and out of thy winepress; of that wherewith YHVH thy Elohim hath blessed thee thou shalt give unto him. 15.15 And thou shalt remember that thou wast a bondman in the land of Egypt, and YHVH thy Elohim redeemed thee; therefore I command thee this thing today. 15.16 And it shall be, if he say unto thee: 'I will not go out from thee'; because he loveth thee and thy house, because he fareth well with thee; 15.17 then thou shalt take an awl, and thrust it through his ear and into the door, and he shall be thy bondman forever. And also unto thy bondwoman thou shalt do likewise. 15.18 It shall not seem hard unto thee, when thou lettest him go free from thee; for to the double of the hire of a hireling hath he served thee six years; and YHVH thy Elohim will bless thee in all that thou doest.*

The reference here to *Hebrew man, or a Hebrew woman* is understood by all to be synonymous with "Israelite man, or an Israelite woman," the term Hebrew first being applied in Scripture to Abram (Gen. 14:13) and the phrase *eved ivri* or *Hebrew servant* or *slave* being first applied to Joseph (Gen. 39:17). It is not clear why this apparently archaic term is used here, and if it was a citation from another ancient document, it is not clear why the editor of the text did not change it. The phrase, *be sold unto thee*, apparently refers to a situation in which a person was sold into servitude by a court of law because he had committed a burglary and was unable to repay what had been stolen to the victim, as biblical law demands, *he shall make restitution; if he have nothing, then he shall be sold for his theft* (Ex. 22:2). Nonetheless, the Hebrew

(Israelite) slaves could only serve for six years and had to be released in the seventh.

It should be noted, however, that there is another biblical text, *And if thy brother be waxen poor with thee, and sell himself unto thee* (Lev. 25:39), which indicates that one also might sell himself into servitude. But in this instance, the text says nothing about a six-year limit or about piercing the slave's ear if he chooses to continue in servitude. It merely states that, if he is not redeemed by other means, *then he shall go out in the year of the jubilee* (Lev. 25:54). It would thus seem that, according to the majority opinion of the rabbis, the text draws a significant distinction between involuntary and voluntary indenture, which states in part. "He who sells himself may be sold for six years or more than six years; if sold by the court, he may be sold for six years only. He who sells himself may not be bored (through the ear); if sold by the court, he may be bored."[613] A minority view argues to the contrary that the laws specified in the text before us draw no such distinction between involuntary and voluntary servitude and that they apply to both categories of Hebrew slaves.[614] According to the latter opinion, "each source contributes its part to the *halakhah*: the law that a slave is set free after six years is learned from Exodus and Deuteronomy; the practice of piercing the ear, from Exodus and Deuteronomy, and the interpretation of "being his servant for life" as meaning until the jubilee year, from Leviticus."[615]

Moreover, *when thou lettest him go free from thee, thou shalt not let him go empty; thou shalt furnish him liberally out of thy flock, and out of thy threshing floor, and out of thy wine-press.* In other words, the slave was entitled to a substantial severance package of cash-equivalent in-kind benefits. Moreover, Moses insists, *It shall not seem hard unto thee, when thou lettest him go free from thee; for to the double of the hire of a hireling hath he served thee six years.* That is, the master should not begrudge giving the bondmen either their freedom or their severance benefits since he had benefitted significantly from getting their labor at a much lower cost than would have been the case if he had to hire workers to perform the same tasks. As one commentator observed: "When it comes to motivating its socioeconomic vision and program, Deuteronomy is rich in theological and emotional reasoning, but it can do the arithmetic as well. It can preach the message, but it can also present the cost-benefit analysis."[616]

The Torah also took into account the possibility that such a slave might be reluctant to leave his servitude *because he loveth thee and thy house, because he fareth well with thee.* The rabbis taught with regard to this last clause: "he must be with [i.e., equal to] you in food and drink, that you should not eat white bread and he black bread, you drink old wine and he new wine, you sleep on a feather bed and he on straw. Hence it was said, 'Whoever buys a Hebrew slave is like buying a master for himself.'"[617] In this regard, it has been suggested, "The principle which underlies these regulations is that only the product of the servant's labor belongs to the master. This alone the master pays for and has a right to demand. The personal honor and human dignity of the servant are his own sacred rights, which the master dare not infringe upon. The servant is to be treated as a fellow-man in all respects."[618] Indeed, the author of the biblical book of Job makes clear that the inherent dignity of one's servant is in every way equal to that of his master. *If I did despise the cause of my man-servant, or of my maid-servant, when they contended with me—What then shall I do when God riseth up? And when He remembereth, what shall I answer Him? Did not He that made me in the womb make him? And did not One fashion us in the womb* (Job 31:13-15)?

Nonetheless, if one should choose to remain an indentured servant rather that go free, *then thou shalt take an awl, and thrust it through his ear and into the door, and he shall be thy bondman forever.* There is an implicit presumption that the permanent bondman would wear an earring as a sign of opprobrium because he preferred servitude to freedom, an attitude toward life incompatible with biblical thought, which posited servitude to God alone and not to man. Although the statement, *And also unto thy bondwoman thou shalt do likewise,* would seem to suggest that the same awful procedure also was to apply to a woman who preferred to remain in servitude, the rabbis concluded otherwise on the basis that another text states, *But if the servant shall plainly say: I love my master, my wife, and my children; I will not go out free* (Ex. 21:5), the use of the masculine term for servant understood as clearly indicating that the provision applied only to bondman and not a bondswoman.[619] Accordingly, the option of remaining in servitude past the seventh year was not open to a woman, who had to go out free.[620]

With regard to the indentured servitude of women, it was noted above that one could be sold into servitude if one was a convicted thief and could not make restitution, *then he shall be sold for his theft* (Ex. 22:2). The rabbis, however, who exhibited almost an abhorrence of the notion of a woman being sold into servitude, read this text literally as referring to one being sold *for his theft*, but not for her theft, and established it as a rule of law that a woman could not be sold into servitude.[621] However, a simple reading of the text suggests that it refers to a woman without means of support who chose to indenture herself to relieve her dire situation.[622] Indeed, if this were not the case, to what does the statement *and also unto thy bondwoman thou shalt do likewise* refer? How does a woman come to be a bondwoman if she cannot sell herself or be sold by a third party? The rabbis, however, rejecting the straightforward reading of the text, concluded that the clause is referring to another biblical provision: *And if a man sell his daughter to be a maid-servant* (Ex. 21:7), which is understood to be referring to the common right in antiquity of a father to sell his minor daughter to be a maid-servant in the expectation that she would marry the person to whom she was sold, or his son, when she reached maturity. However, if the arrangement does not work out, *then shall she go out for nothing, without money* (Ex. 21:11), that is, without requiring that she be redeemed through paying off any outstanding debt for which she had been indentured in the first place. The rabbis applied the provision *unto thy bondwoman thou shalt do likewise* to this situation and understood it to mean providing her liberally with severance benefits.[623]

Summarizing the distinctions between them, the rabbis noted, "the law differentiates between a Hebrew man and a Hebrew woman. A Hebrew man goes free after (he has served the statutory six) years, or in the Jubilee year, or by paying the balance of his indebtedness, which is not so in the case of a Hebrew woman; while a Hebrew woman attains freedom upon reaching maturity, cannot be resold, and must be redeemed even against her will, this is not so in the case of a Hebrew man. Since different laws thus apply to the Hebrew man and to the

Hebrew woman, it was necessary to specify *a Hebrew man* and *a Hebrew woman.*"[624]

It will be observed that the biblical text here speaks only of the treatment to be accorded to an Israelite slave. The presumed reason for this is that it was the pervasiveness of chattel slavery in the ancient world that made it necessary for the Torah to draw certain distinctions between an Israelite and an alien slave. That is, Israel's legislation could demonstrate considerably greater liberality towards slaves from among its own people because the practice could be regulated in the context of domestic policy. This situation was quite different, however, in terms of interstate relations that demanded reciprocity. Given that the primary source of slaves in antiquity was prisoners taken in war, it was politically infeasible to have a policy towards enslaved captives that was radically different from that of other nations toward enslaved Israelite captives. It was essential to make it clear that harsh treatment of captured Israelite slaves would be reciprocated with regard to the slaves of the offending nation. There were no Geneva Conventions in antiquity, setting standards for international behavior. Nonetheless, Israel's laws concerning alien slaves were markedly more liberal than those of its neighbors.

It is noteworthy that after presenting the various laws and regulations concerning the poor, the needy, and Israelite slaves, the text turns abruptly to a matter relating to sacrificial animals, which is in effect a continuation of the laws concerning tithes (Deut. 14:22-29). One might suggest that the reason for this is that it is one way of making a point that cannot be overemphasized, namely that the Torah does not distinguish between what we in modern times commonly refer to as the religious and the secular. In the Torah, they are merely different aspects of a common system of law, the former concerning those things between man and God and the latter those between man and man. Thus, Moses now turns to certain rules governing the sacrificial rite and obligatory observances, matters that come under the category of those between man and God.

15.19 All the firstling males that are born of thy herd and of thy flock thou shalt sanctify unto YHVH thy Elohim;

thou shalt do no work with the firstling of thine ox, nor shear the firstling of thy flock. ^{15.20} *Thou shalt eat it before YHVH thy Elohim year by year in the place which YHVH shall choose, thou and thy household.* ^{15.21} *And if there be any blemish therein, lameness, or blindness, any ill blemish whatsoever, thou shalt not sacrifice it unto YHVH thy Elohim.* ^{15.22} *Thou shalt eat it within thy gates; the unclean and the clean may eat it alike, as the gazelle, and as the hart.* ^{15.23} *Only thou shalt not eat the blood thereof; thou shalt pour it out upon the ground as water.*

It was stated earlier, *And thou shalt eat before YHVH thy Elohim . . . the firstlings of thy herd and of thy flock* (Deut. 14:23). Moses now elaborates further on this statute, implicitly asserting that because God had ordained that *whatsoever openeth the womb among the children of Israel, both of man and beast, it is Mine* (Ex. 13:2), the *firstlings* are to be sanctified to God, and because they belong to God from birth, it is forbidden to make use of them prior to their sanctification; that is, the ox calf may not be put to work nor may the lamb be shorn for its wool. However, no animal may be sanctified through sacrifice if it be deformed or blemished in any manner. What is dedicated to God must be whole and pure. After all, one would not dream of presenting a marred gift to a human king and may do no less with regard to the divine king of kings. Accordingly, although it may not be sacrificed, it may be eaten *within thy gates* just as other animals such as the gazelle and hart may be eaten but not sacrificed. Moses concludes by cautioning the people once again not to eat the blood of the animal but to spill it out on the ground.

Now, in addition to the obligation of an annual pilgrimage to the central sanctuary with one's household to celebrate God's beneficence to them (Deut. 14:22-26), Moses summarizes the three other celebratory occasions on which a pilgrimage to the central sanctuary is required.

^{16.1} *Observe the month of Aviv, and keep the passover unto YHVH thy Elohim; for in the month of Aviv YHVH thy Elohim brought thee forth out of Egypt by night.* ^{16.2}

And thou shalt sacrifice the passover offering unto YHVH thy Elohim, of the flock and the herd, in the place which YHVH shall choose to cause His name to dwell there. [16.3] *Thou shalt eat no leavened bread with it; seven days shalt thou eat unleavened bread therewith, even the bread of affliction; for in haste didst thou come forth out of the land of Egypt; that thou mayest remember the day when thou camest forth out of the land of Egypt all the days of thy life.* [16.4] *And there shall be no leaven seen with thee in all thy borders seven days; neither shall any of the flesh, which thou sacrificest the first day at even, remain all night until morning.* [16.5] *Thou mayest not sacrifice the passover offering within any of thy gates, which YHVH thy Elohim giveth thee;* [16.6] *but at the place which YHVH thy Elohim shall choose to cause His name to dwell in, there thou shalt sacrifice the passover offering at even, at the going down of the sun, at the season that thou camest forth out of Egypt.* [16.7] *And thou shalt roast and eat it in the place which YHVH thy Elohim shall choose; and thou shalt turn in the morning, and go unto thy tents.* [16.8] *Six days thou shalt eat unleavened bread: and on the seventh day shall be a solemn assembly to YHVH thy Elohim; thou shalt do no work therein.*

It is curious that Moses calls for the people to *observe the month of Aviv* when the actual celebratory occasion begins on the evening of the fourteenth day of the month of Aviv, subsequently know as the month of Nissan. Moreover, although mention is made of the exodus haven taken place *by night*, it was stated earlier, *on the fifteenth day of the first month; on the morrow after the passover the children went out with a high hand in the sight of the Egyptians* (Num. 33:3). Presumably, what Moses intended to say was that the process of the deliverance began at night (Ex. 12:31), notwithstanding that the exodus itself did not take place until the following morning.

It is somewhat surprising that Moses here calls for the paschal sacrifice to be *of the flock and the herd*, whereas it earlier specified that it be a lamb (Ex. 12:3). It has been suggested that the earlier specification of a lamb only applied to that special occasion immediately preceding the exodus, whereas Moses was now establishing the ritual for subsequent celebrations commemorating the event. Alternatively, *of the flock and the herd* may be understood as referring to two separate sacrifices, *of the flock* for the paschal sacrifice and of *the herd* for the regular sacrifice offered an all festivals. The latter interpretation appears to be the one adopted in practice, as it states, *And they roasted the passover with fire according to the ordinance; and the holy offerings [the festival offering] sod they in pots, and in caldrons, and in pans* (2 Chron. 35:13).[625]

It is noteworthy that Moses' characterization of the unleavened bread as *lehem oni* or *bread of affliction* is problematic. For one thing, the characterization seems inappropriate given the way unleavened bread is used elsewhere in the biblical texts. The term *matzot*, meaning cakes of unleavened bread, is first used in connection with the story of Lot's entertaining the two angels who visited him--*and he made them a feast, and did bake unleavened bread [matzot], and they did eat* (Gen. 19:3). Similarly, when an angel visited Gideon, the latter prepared a feast for him. *And Gideon went in, and made ready a kid, and unleavened cakes of an ephah of meal* (Judg. 6:19). In a third instance, in which King Saul visited a woman of Endor, she *had a fatted calf in the house, and she made haste, and killed it; and she took flour, and kneaded it, and did bake unleavened bread thereof* (1 Sam. 28:24). In each of these cases, it does not appear that the matzah prepared for the distinguished guests was typical of bread commonly used on a daily basis. Instead, as one modern scholar suggests, it seems reasonable to suppose that the term '*matzot*' was applied to thin delicate wafers that were served as a delicacy at meals where the main courses were meat and drink.[626] Indeed, one could argue in support of the latter interpretation that the same amount of meal used in a cake of unleavened bread is considerably less filling than would be the case when it undergoes the leavening process, as anyone who has eaten unleavened bread for a week can readily testify.

It has also been suggested that there is a symbolic significance to unleavened bread that should betaken into consideration. "It is likely that the process of fermentation was associated with decomposition and putrefaction, and so became emblematic of corruption. Accordingly, it would be inappropriate to associate such a symbol with a sacrificial ritual whose function was to effect conciliation between man and God and raise man to a higher level of spirituality."[627] This explanation would help account for the biblical rules restricting the use of leavened bread or meal in connection with the sacrificial rites in the Tabernacle and later in the Temple (Ex. 23:18, Lev. 2:11, Lev. 6:9-10).

It would therefore appear that Moses used the term *bread of affliction* to commemorate that the people had to eat less satisfying unleavened bread during the process of the exodus, when they were under great stress and worry about what was going to happen to them, simply because it could be prepared quickly, which was not the reason for it being used during the festival being celebrated the evening prior to the exodus. For that occasion there was more than ample time to prepare leavened bread. However, they were instructed not to do so because the festive meal they were to have that night was to be a banquet of the kind enjoyed by the nobility, where they filled their stomachs with fine food rather than with normal leavened bread.

In concluding the rule Moses once again emphasizes *Thou mayest not sacrifice the passover offering within any of thy gates, which YHVH thy Elohim giveth thee; but at the place which YHVH thy Elohim shall choose to cause His name to dwell in.* Proper celebration of the exodus required them to sacrifice the paschal offering only at the central sanctuary, thus portraying the occasion as a national day of commemoration, forcing the celebrants to leave their tribal areas to celebrate in the national capital.

Finally, Moses commands, *Six days thou shalt eat unleavened bread,* which seems to contradict what he said just a few verses earlier, *seven days shalt thou eat unleavened bread.* However, it should be noted that the *six days* are intended to commence after the pilgrim returns to his home, after already having eaten unleavened bread for a day, thus making it seven days. The rabbis concluded from this passage that while leavened bread is forbidden categorically during the seven-day period, the actual obligation to eat unleavened bread only applied on the first day. That is, one could choose not to eat bread at all for the next six days without violating the stated commandment.

16.9 Seven weeks shalt thou number unto thee; from the time the sickle is first put to the standing corn shalt thou begin to number seven weeks. 16.10 And thou shalt keep the feast of weeks unto YHVH thy Elohim after the measure of the freewill offering of thy hand, which thou shalt give, according as YHVH thy Elohim blesseth thee. 16.11 And thou shalt rejoice before YHVH thy Elohim, thou, and thy son, and thy daughter, and thy man-servant, and thy maid-servant, and the Levite that is within thy gates, and the stranger, and the fatherless, and the widow, that are in the midst of thee, in the place which YHVH thy Elohim shall choose to cause His name to dwell there. 16.12 And thou shalt remember that thou wast a bondman in Egypt; and thou shalt observe and do these statutes.

The *hag shavuot*, the *feast of weeks*, which is to be celebrated seven weeks from the day *the sickle is first put to the standing corn*, is also referred to as *hag hakatzir* or *feast of harvest* (Ex. 23:16) as well as *yom habikkurim* or *the day of the first-fruits* (Num. 28:26). Needless to point out, the day *the sickle is first put to the standing corn* seems to be a rather imprecise starting point for determining when the festival is to take place. In another place it states, *And ye shall count unto you from the morrow after the day of rest, from the day that ye brought the sheaf of the waving; seven weeks shall there be complete; even unto the morrow after the seventh week shall ye number fifty days; and ye shall present a new meal-offering unto YHVH* (Lev. 23:15-16), which too is not very edifying. The *sheaf of the waving* in the latter text presumably refers to what is made available when *the sickle is first put to the standing corn*, and to the commandment *ye shall bring the sheaf of the first-fruits of your harvest unto the priest* (Lev. 23:10). Although nowhere stated explicitly in the biblical text, *the morrow after the day of rest* has since antiquity been associated with the day following the onset of the festival of Passover. Accordingly, since the day of the *feast of unleavened bread* is the fifteenth day of Nissan, which is a day of rest, *the sickle is first put to the standing corn* and *the first-fruits* are brought to the sanctuary on the sixteenth day of Nissan, the first working day after the *day of rest,* which provides a rather precise timeline for when the *feast of weeks* is to take place. Later rabbinic tradition associated the *feast of weeks* with the revelation of the covenant on Mount Sinai and typically refers to it as *zeman matan toratenu* or "the Season of Giving of our Torah."

As with Passover, the householder was obligated to bring his entire establishment along with him to the site of the national sanctuary, there to celebrate the occasion with joy. However, by contrast with Passover, on which occasion the offering was specified, on the *feast of weeks* Moses stipulated *the freewill offering of thy hand,* that is, one could give whatever he thought appropriate, given his means. Moreover, there was no specified ceremony associated with the holiday, although a number of traditions in this regard emerged over the centuries.

> *16.13 Thou shalt keep the feast of tabernacles seven days, after that thou hast gathered in from thy threshing floor and from thy winepress. 16.14 And thou shalt rejoice in thy feast, thou, and thy son, and thy daughter, and thy man-servant, and thy maid-servant, and the Levite, and the stranger, and the fatherless, and the widow, that are within thy gates. 16.15 Seven days shalt thou keep a feast unto YHVH thy Elohim in the place which YHVH shall choose; because YHVH thy Elohim shall bless thee in all thine increase, and in the work of thy hands, and thou shalt be altogether joyful.*

The timing of the *hag hasukkot* or *feast of tabernacles* was given more precisely earlier, when it stipulated: *Howbeit on the fifteenth day of the seventh month, when ye have gathered the fruits of the land, ye shall keep the feast of YHVH seven days; on the first day shall be a solemn rest, and on the eighth day shall be a solemn rest* (Lev. 23:39). The name of the holiday derives from the stipulation *Ye shall dwell in booths [sukkot] seven days; all that are homeborn in Israel shall dwell in booths; that your generations may know that I made the children of Israel to dwell in booths, when I brought them out of the land of Egypt* (Lev. 23:42-43). A *sukkah* or booth (the term *tabernacle* being a misnomer suggesting that the *sukkah* was some sort of sacred site for worship, which it is not) "represents a hastily-constructed and unsubstantial edifice, such as the Israelites must have set up during the wanderings in the wilderness."[628] The festival is also known as *hag haasif* or *feast of ingathering* (Ex. 23:14, 34:22).

Having outlined in brief the three pilgrim festivals, Moses concludes this part of his discourse with a summary of the key points.

> [16.16] *Three times in a year shall all thy males appear before YHVH thy Elohim in the place which He shall choose: on the feast of unleavened bread, and on the feast of weeks, and on the feast of tabernacles; and they shall not appear before YHVH empty;* [16.17] *every man shall give as he is able, according to the blessing of YHVH thy Elohim which He hath given thee.*

On these three occasions, *all thy males*, with or without their families, if the latter cannot accompany them for unspecified reasons, are to attend the celebrations at the site of the national sanctuary. It should be noted, however, that the adjuration *thou shalt rejoice in thy feast* is stated only with regard to the festivals of *Shavuot* and of *Sukkot*, which are in essence agricultural festivals, but not with regard to Passover, the essence of which is commemoration of the miracle of deliverance in the exodus and its aftermath.[629] On all of these occasions, the people are not to come to the national sanctuary empty-handed, but with gifts appropriate to the state of their well being, that is, commensurate with the divine beneficence shown to them. Conformance with these requirements would contribute significantly to a sense of national cohesion, and this is something that was among Moses' greatest concerns for what would happen after he was no longer on the scene to cajole the diverse tribes and clans into a semblance of a national entity.

5

SHOFETIM

(16:18-21:9)

In the following passages Moses lays out the constitutional provisions for the structure of the Hebrew commonwealth that is to be founded in the land they are about to enter. It has been suggested that the state envisioned in the following texts is expected to reflect "a harmonious combination of the two necessities for any organized society: freedom and authority." The balance between these two elements "is assured by a system of checks and balances, long before such terms were popularized by western political philosophers." The role of the national executive leadership is balanced and kept within bounds by the judiciary with respect to the law, by the priesthood with regard to sphere of belief and worship, and by the prophets with regard to morals and ethics.[630]

Moses begins with the establishment of a judiciary to assure justice for its citizens. It has been suggested that what follows is connected to what preceded in that the latter spoke of the requirement to make pilgrimages to the national center where they would also go to learn from the priests, the guardians of the Torah, about the statutes and ordinances that were to establish the parameters for the conduct of their lives. Now, Moses makes the point that learning about the ordinances and statutes are not sufficient because the written law cannot deal with all contingencies and determinations of justice and fairness. For this purpose there must be a judicial system that can resolve the interpersonal issues that arise in all societies.[631]

However, it has been pointed out that a full appreciation of what follows requires recognition that the biblical concept of judgeship is not identical to how the term is understood in modern society. Whereas in contemporary legal systems a judge basically deals with events or actions already concluded, the biblical judge not only does that but also bears some responsibility for endeavoring to prevent such events or actions from taking place. In other words the judge has both a juridical and an educational task; it is part of his responsibility to foster social harmony in the public interest, and in doing so he must assume the role of moral guide for the people, a responsibility he will share with both priest and prophet.[632]

The priority Moses thus accords to the judiciary as the preeminent institution of government reflects his overriding concern for justice as the key to creating the sort of society envisioned by the covenant. The following texts appear to presuppose that the judicial system discussed earlier (Deut. 1:13-17), which was designed to meet the immediate needs, both military and civil of a people trekking through the wilderness, would be superseded by a system more appropriate to a settled and growing society such as was expected to emerge soon after the children of Israel crossed the Jordan and undertook the conquest of the territories divinely designated as their inheritance.

16.18 Judges and officers shalt thou make thee in all thy gates, which YHVH thy Elohim giveth thee, tribe by tribe; and they shall judge the people with righteous judgment.

This text, notwithstanding its brevity, is replete with nuances that beg for explication, and as a result has generated a substantial body of interpretation that will be explored here only to a limited extent; fuller treatment of this and the following texts concerning the organization of the state envisioned by Moses may be found in my *The Judaic State: A Study in Rabbinic Political Theory*, from which the analyses of the several components discussed below are derived in part.

To begin with, since the text announces the need to appoint *judges and officers* for each of the enumerated jurisdictions, one may ask how many are to be appointed; that is, how many judges are required to constitute a court? The rabbis concluded on the basis of an earlier biblical text (Ex. 22:7-8), which employs the term *elohim* in the sense of "authority" three times, that the minimum number required to constitute a court is three judges.[633] Alternatively, it has been suggested that the present text speaks of the appointment of *judges* in the plural, which grammatically requires that there be at least two. However, in case of a disagreement among the judges, a court of two would be dysfunctional, therefore logic dictates that a third judge be appointed to a court, if it is to be able to decide non-capital cases by majority rule.[634]

Another question of even greater significance concerns the meaning of the pronoun *thou* in the citation. Is Moses directing his charge to the people as a whole or is it intended for the tribal elders and other members of the leadership cadre as a collective body? Up till now, it was Moses who made the appointments upon the recommendations of the tribal elders. Who would do it later, and how would the recruitment and appointment be conducted? These questions are left unanswered by the text, and remain open to speculation. I would suggest that the most plausible answer is that it would be the existing leadership group that would take the initiative in this regard, notwithstanding the temptation to read into this a democratic impulse that would have the people as a whole make the choice, an approach that is probably overly anachronistic for the period under consideration.

In any case, it has been observed that this passage is worded in a rather awkward manner: *Shofetim veshotrim titen lekha . . .veshoftu et ha'am mishpat tzedek*, translated as *Judges and officers shalt thou make thee . . . and they shall judge the people with righteous judgment.* For one thing, *veshoftu* is not an imperative to be rendered as *and they shall judge*; it is a form that merely describes what may be expected to occur. Moreover, the sense of the phrase *titen lekha* or *shalt thou make thee* is that you should place such appointees over you. The meaning of the text would then become that if you appoint judges over you, that is, select people to be completely independent of you once they are appointed, and they are in no way further obligated to you, you will eliminate cronyism and nepotism, and if this is done you may rest assured that the judges will be in a position to render justice to all.[635]

With regard to the jurisdiction of the courts, the text makes it clear that although the other major institutions are all to be centralized in the national capital, the judiciary and the *officers* associated with it are to be decentralized in a manner that will best suit the needs of the society. Accordingly, judges and officers are to be appointed *in all thy gates*, which may be understood as referring to every village, town, and city. The notation *tribe by tribe* in the context of this prescription seems to suggest that it was Moses' intention that since the country was to be divided among the tribes, each tribal area would in effect become a quasi-independent province in a federation the center of which would be located at the site of the national sanctuary, when that location was determined. Another implication of this is that Moses held that justice would be best served if the judges were from the same tribe as those who came before them; pubic acceptance of their decisions was more likely if they came from fellow tribesmen than from outsiders. In this regard, it was asserted, "it is the duty of each tribe to judge its own members."[636] This is yet another indication of Moses' attempt to retain the tribal character of the nation at the same time that he emphasized the importance of establishing a national center that would serve as the point of convergence for the children of Israel as equal descendents of Jacob/Israel, their eponymous ancestor.

One is left wondering at this point, since there is no clear mention of it, whether Moses intended that there also be a court established at the tribal or provincial level to deal with matters that extended beyond the jurisdiction of the municipalities, unless one assumes that the municipal boundaries were to be such that they encompassed the entire tribal area. But even in the latter case, a tribal court might be needed to resolve matters that arose between the municipalities. In anticipation of this concern, it was taught: "Whence do we learn that courts should be appointed for every tribe? From the verse *Judges . . . tribe by tribe.*"[637] Thus, although the text is not clear on this point, it may be arrived at by exegetical inference. "It therefore appears to be the case that, aside from the court that is appointed for every city, a court is also appointed for every tribe irrespective of location, and its members are the supervisors of the affairs of their tribe even though the tribe is spread out among several cities. And we find, accordingly, that every person in Israel has two judges, one from his city and the second from his tribe."[638]

It may be argued that, in some respects, the relation of a municipality to the tribe within whose borders it is situated is typical of federal systems, as we know them today. The citizen of a municipality would also simultaneously be subject to the jurisdiction of the tribe. Thus, as one commentator put it, under the system suggested by the biblical text, no litigant could compel another to appear for judgment in a city other than his own. However, the tribal court could compel all members of the tribe to appear before it. And, "even if they were already judged in their city, one may say: Let us go before the tribal high court . . . If the court finds it necessary to correct or enact something for its tribe, it proceeds to do so."[639] The tribal high court is thus envisioned as having primary responsibility for the affairs of the tribe as a composite political entity.

A question that this raises is what happens when some of the people living in a municipality within a tribal area are members of a different tribe? One suggestion is that, "if there is found in a single city residents from two tribes, they establish two municipal courts."[640] The implication of this is that the requirement to provide judges for every municipality is not to be understood as implying the existence of an intrinsically autonomous political status for the municipality, which is considered a composite element within the tribal jurisdiction. Thus, where the population of a municipality is not homogeneous, municipal courts are to be established there along tribal lines. In effect, this might give a tribe an extraterritorial right in the territory of another tribe. Accordingly, if a judicial proceeding involved members of different tribes, the case would probably have to be adjudicated by the national court, unless one of the tribes waived its jurisdiction over its own tribal member in such a case. As one commentator wrote:

> It appears to me that a general court is appointed over the tribe so that if conflicts should develop within the gates of the cities, between one city and another, with regard to either the criminal or the civil law, where the citizen of one city causes damages to the resident of another from a single tribe, either to his person or his property; and similarly with regard to those matters

which are the general concern of municipalities such as its boundaries, fields, hamlets, and suburbs; these matters should be adjudicated by the general court of the concerned tribe . . . And if such matters should arise between tribes, they would come for judgment before the high court in Jerusalem.[641]

However, one may ask how and by whom inter-tribal disagreements or overlapping tribal jurisdiction would be dealt with, given the absence of any mention of a national court in the text before us? The rabbis suggested, however, that that such a court was implied in the wording of the text, *judges and officers shalt thou make thee.* "Whence do we learn that one of them should be appointed over all of them? From the verse *shalt thou make thee.*"[642] The inference from the biblical text is based on the text's use of the singular *thee,* which is taken as implying that all of Israel is to be treated as a corporate unit, thus indicating the need to establish *judges and officers* at the national level.

In this regard, it may be recalled that Moses earlier established a tiered corps of magistrates to render justice to the people as they traversed the wilderness, *and they judged the people at all seasons: the hard causes they brought unto Moses, but every small matter they judged themselves* (Ex. 18:26). In effect, Moses served as a superior court, an arrangement that would require another institutional form once Moses departed the scene, and since Moses is here instructing how the judicial establishment is to be organized when they enter and settle the land, it seems reasonable to assume that it was also his intention to establish a national court to deal with those legal issues that he dealt with personally up to this point, even though he does not specify such in his discourse.

By conflating the implications of the earlier biblical text with that under consideration here, it has been argued that Moses is establishing a judicial hierarchy that also encompasses an appeals system for matters over which the lower courts may be assigned original jurisdiction, and culminates in a final central judicial authority. Thus, based on the subdivision of the magistracy into *rulers of thousands, rulers of hundreds, rulers of fifties, and rulers of tens* (Ex. 18:21), one commentator argued that

Moses arranged that "there should be these four levels [of magistrates], each one higher than the next; the lowest will judge first and he who would protest against the judgment rendered will appeal to the next highest court, and so from the second to the third and from the third to the fourth."[643] Although this structure would now be superseded by a system of courts at the municipal, tribal, and national levels, the basic concept remains intact. The central national judicial authority would retain original jurisdiction in matters of vital national interest and scope in addition to serving as a court of final appeal. Initially, Moses was this national judicial authority, and it subsequently would have to reside in a collective successor—a supreme court, as suggested by the text, discussed below, which calls for irresolvable issues to be referred to a higher authority for decision (Deut. 17:8-11).

Recapitulating, the general rabbinic understanding of the text considers the judiciary to be constitutionally decentralized in a three level hierarchy, each level having a distinct area of original jurisdiction, corresponding to the national, provincial or tribal, and municipal subdivisions of the political entity. Moreover, it is also clear that the structure of the judiciary is contingent on the existence of a territorial state, a condition that should alleviate any concern that the three-level structure suggested by our present text is incompatible with the five-level hierarchy described in the book of Exodus, which was designed for the period before the nation became a territorial state.

The structure, as already indicated, also is understood by some as providing for an appellate process, culminating in the national high court, although some dispute this supposition. Thus, it has been argued, "the high court is not an appeals court; its role is to instruct the municipal courts."[644] That is, the high court may be considered as a court of appeal only in the sense that the lower courts may appeal to it when they experience difficulty in arriving at a judgment, but it is not envisioned as sitting in review of the decisions of lower courts on the basis of an appeal by a party to an already adjudicated dispute. In this view, the high court would thus serve as the final arbiter of the meaning and proper adjudication of the law, to ensure uniformity of justice throughout the country by limiting inconsistencies in judicial interpretations.

The role of the *officers* also requires some clarification. The linking of them with the judiciary would seem to suggest that they essentially are officers of the court whose mission it is to enforce the decisions of the judges. Alternatively, they may be viewed as a separate body of police whose primary purpose is to maintain social order in accordance with established law, which might include among other things, enforcing the decisions of the court when such is required. This issue had been addressed at some length in the rabbinic literature, which reflects diverse opinions on the matter.

Commenting generally on the present biblical text and those that follow, it has been pointed out: "After the commandments were given to the people as a whole [in earlier sections of Deuteronomy], he commanded with regard to the matter of their leaders. And these are the kings, the judges, the priests and the prophets through whose efforts the public interest would be well served and through whose corruption it too would become corrupted."[645] Conspicuous by its absence in the enumeration of the types of communal leaders given in this statement is any mention of "officers." This would suggest that the commentator does not consider officers to represent an element of political importance comparable to those he does mention, notwithstanding their being specifically mentioned in the biblical text. The commentator thus implicitly reflects the view that reads the text as imputing inherent executive power to the judiciary, and that the officers spoken of in the text are intended to serve as instruments of the coercive powers of the judiciary. As such the officers are not considered as a distinct co-equal element of government with the judiciary. Instead, they are viewed as a component of the judiciary that is clearly subordinate to the authority of the judges, and their primary function is to carry out and enforce the judgments rendered by the judicial authorities.

The basic source and ground for this interpretation is the cryptic note in the Talmud that, "an officer has a superior appointed over him."[646] Commenting on the latter statement, the preeminent medieval commentator on the Talmud affirms that it is understood to assert, in effect: "The judge is appointed over the officer, since the officer is appointed in order to apply pressure on whomever the judge shall order to be compelled."[647] In another place the same commentator describes the officers as *galearii* (Latin: "common soldiers") "who, on the word of the judges, strike with rods all who will not pay heed."[648] And, in specific reference to the biblical text, he defines *officers* as "those who subjugate the people in accordance with their [the judges'] commands; those who strike and compel with rod and lash until they accept the legal decision of the judge."[649] Numerous other commentators concur with this interpretation,[650] one going so far as to assert that "the officers are those appointed according to the instructions of the judges," which clearly makes them subordinate to the judiciary.[651]

Upon reflection, it seems evident that this interpretation of the text implicitly construes the executive powers of the judiciary as being limited to the enforcement of decisions rendered by the judges in the specific cases brought before them for adjudication. The judiciary, acting through its enforcement arm, the *officers*, thus exercises police powers only after a matter has been brought to its attention, and a ruling has been issued. This leaves open the question of who, if anyone, has the authority to initiate actions in the public interest that will be brought to the court for consideration.

To deal with this problem, there is a school of thought that would significantly enhance the executive powers of the judiciary, defining *officers* as "those who wield the rod and the lash. They stand before the judges; they make their rounds to the markets, squares, and shops, fixing prices, regulating weights, and correcting abuses. Their work is directed by the judges. Any person they find guilty of a misdemeanor is taken by them to court, and punishment corresponding to his offense is inflicted upon him."[652] Some take the role of the *officers* in policing the marketplace a step farther and associate them with the commissioners that are appointed to oversee the marketplaces.[653] This interpretation, in effect, would extend significantly the judiciary's executive power into the economic sector.

Some commentators extend greater implied powers to the *officers* while leaving their relationship to the judges unclear. Thus, one defines the *officers* as "those who have in their hand the power and the authority to bring to realization the law of the judges."[654] Although the *officers* are still linked to the judges to some extent in this interpretation, it clearly suggests that the authority of the judiciary is not the exclusive source of their own authority. Another goes farther and maintains that the *officers*, in addition to serving as coercive instruments of the courts, are rather the general enforcers of public order, subject to the direction of a number of political authorities.[655] Yet another considers the *officers* as also serving as military commanders.[656] It is noteworthy, however, that notwithstanding the extension of the powers of the *officers*, none of these commentators accord any independent statutory authority to them; they always remain a subordinate element of governance.

There is also a school of thought that maintains that the judiciary itself has no executive powers and therefore must rely on the *officers*, who are part of the executive branch of government, for their enforcement assistance. Thus, according to one early commentary on the biblical text, "Judges—these are the adjudicators; and officers—these are the managers that lead the community. R. Eleazar said: If there is no officer, there is no judge. How is that? When a person has been declared in court obligated to compensate his neighbor, unless there is an executor to collect from him . . . the judge has no power over him." The prooftext offered for this conclusion is the one that points out that David as king and chief magistrate *executed justice and righteousness unto all his people. And Joab the son of Zeruiah was over the host* (1 Chron. 18:14). The juxtaposition of these two verses suggests that although David rendered just decisions, their implementation was heavily dependent upon the mighty hand of Joab, commander of the army, standing behind him.[657] Commenting on this midrashic passage, it has been argued: "The text demonstrates that if there are no officers there is no obligation to appoint judges; that is, insofar as it is known that the people will not listen to the judges and that the judges cannot compel them, there is no obligation to appoint judges. However, where the people generally pay heed to the judges even without officers, they are obligated to appoint judges."[658] In this view, the only executive authority wielded by the judiciary is strictly moral in character.

Moreover, advocates of this position also maintain that the judiciary is not considered as possessing the authority to establish its own enforcement agencies.[659] One of the more emphatic proponents of this view asserts, "there is no doubt that the officers are not agents of the court," and bases his conclusion on the use of the term *officers* in other biblical texts where it is clear that the context is political and military leadership. Thus, Moses earlier declares, *So I took the heads of your tribes . . . and made them heads over you, captains of thousands . . . and captains of ten, and officers, tribe by tribe* (Deut. 1:15). The term is also used in this context in the later historical note, *And all Israel, and their elders and officers, and their judges, stood on this side of the ark and on that side before the priests* (Josh. 8:33). Similarly, it states: *And behold, Amariah the chief priest is over you in all matters of YHVH; and Zebediah the son of Ishamael, the ruler of the house of Judah, in all the king's matters; also the officers of the Levites before you* (2 Chron. 19:11). All of this indicates that the *officers* were considered a separate political entity from the judiciary. Accordingly, with regard to the use of the term in the present passage, he concludes, "the judges dealt with the matters between man and man, or with witnesses that testified to a transgression, and the officers would oversee the well-being of the state and would enact regulations and customs for the people."[660] The same commentator also assumed that the text implied that the judges would be permanently positioned in the various municipalities, whereas the *officers* would be sent from the central government to oversee the public as well as the judges.[661]

Focusing on the role of the judges, Moses demands, *they shall judge the people with mishpat tzedek,* translated as *righteous judgment.* The meaning of *righteous judgment,* however, is rather unclear, some rabbis defining it as judgment tinged with mercy,[662] and others as judgment weighted toward acquittal of the accused.[663] Thus, the New JPS translation renders the text as *they shall govern the people with due justice,* which is probably a more apt translation if the term *govern* is understood in the sense of adjudicate rather than in its usual political signification. Even closer to the mark is the translation that renders the statement as, *and they shall judge the people: judgment with justice.* As the translator and commentator notes, "regrettably it needs to be said: judgment and justice are not the same thing. Judges and lawyers can be part of one of the noblest endeavors of humankind: the law. When they fail to pursue justice in the performance of judgment, they pervert and degrade the law, and thus they demean humankind—nothing less."[664] In this regard, an earlier commentator defined *mishpat tzedek* as "receiving the arguments put forth by the litigants in a manner that will assure that that the case be justly concluded, that is that it should not be made easy for one and difficult for the other."[665] One is tempted to consider this understanding of the text as an early formulation of the much-discussed modern concept of justice as fairness.

The question that the text does not provide clear answer to is who assures that the judges render *mishpat tzedek*. The text seems to suggest that the responsibility of judicial oversight rests on the community that appoints them, but this is not very practicable. Accordingly, it may be inferred that the responsibility must fall on the shoulders of the person who holds executive power in the jurisdiction, its mayor or governor.[666]

Moses now directs his remarks to those who would undertake the responsibilities that attend judgeship.

> [16.19] *Thou shalt not wrest judgment; thou shalt not respect persons; neither shalt thou take a gift; for a gift doth blind the eyes of the wise, and pervert the words of the righteous.*

The phrase *lo tateh mishpat*, translated here as *thou shalt not wrest judgment*, more literally means that one should not lean toward one side in rendering judgment. In other words, it may be considered a caution against being one-sided and thereby perverting rather than rendering a just judgment; it may be understood as a call for unqualified neutrality on the part of a judge. The question this raises is how this squares with the assertion, mentioned above, that *righteous judgment* may be understood as judgment tinged with mercy. It has been suggested that these verses represent two different aspects of the judicial process. The first is that the judge must approach his task in a state of absolute neutrality, thus the admonition *thou shalt not wrest [pervert] judgment*. However, before judgment is pronounced, the concept of *righteous judgment* must be brought into play, demanding that the judge should lean toward mercy.[667] Another opinion suggests that the admonition *thou shalt not wrest [pervert] judgment* refers to the likely outcome if unqualified people are appointed to serve as judges.[668]

The demand that *thou shalt not respect persons* affirms the biblical rejection of the idea of social stratification with respect to the law. Although men may be characterized as unequal with regard to their physical nature, abilities, and aptitudes, "a person must never be regarded as an object or a commodity, but must be respected as a human being," a biblical concept that was alien to much if not all of the rest of the ancient world.[669] Accordingly each individual must be treated as having equal worth with all others before a court of law. Moses earlier had already elaborated further on the meaning of this demand, *Ye shall not respect persons in judgment; ye shall hear the small and the great alike* (Deut. 1:17), and *thou shalt not respect the person of the poor, nor favor the person of the mighty* (Lev. 19:15).

As a safeguard of the judge's integrity and disinterested objectivity, the text admonishes, *neither shalt thou take a gift; for a gift doth blind the eyes of the wise, and pervert the words of the righteous*, the latter expression suggesting that the temptations of bribery might cause otherwise righteous people to say dishonest things.[670] The rabbis point out that although "it goes without saying that this applies to acquitting the guilty and condemning the innocent, it applies also even to acquitting the innocent and condemning the guilty."[671]

Upon reflection, it would appear that the text we have just considered at some length is in essence a repetition of what Moses stated at the beginning of these discourses and does not add much to the earlier presentation: *Hear the causes between your brethren, and judge righteously between a man and his brother, and the stranger that is with him. Ye shall not respect persons in judgment; ye shall hear the small and the great alike; ye shall not be afraid of the face of any man; for the judgment is Elohim's* (Deut 1:16-17). Of course, the issues addressed are of such importance that they merit repetition, but it has also been suggested that in this instance, by contrast with the earlier iteration, they are not only directed to the judges but also to those who are instrumental in bringing about the appointment of the judges. That is, it is an admonition to appoint judges who are known to be able as well as ready and willing to abide by the stated stipulations. Moreover, in the course of choosing candidates, *thou shalt not wrest judgment* by practicing nepotism or favoritism in choosing candidates that you happen to like regardless of the prospective appointee's qualifications.[672] In this same regard, you should not *respect persons*, that is, choosing someone to be a judge because of his wealth or position in the community, or, alternatively, choosing a person because of a desire to provide an income to someone who is poor.[673] This emphasizes the point that excellent knowledge of the law and intellectual integrity in those given the responsibility of judging are critical to the proper functioning of the justice system.

Moses next offers an adjuration, seemingly directed not to the judges but to those who are likely to appear before them in a civil action.

> [16.20] *Justice, justice shalt thou follow, that thou mayest live, and inherit the land which YHVH thy Elohim giveth thee.*

The wording of this adjuration is less than clear and has been interpreted in a variety of ways. From the perspective of the rabbis it is directed primarily to those who have need for adjudication of disputes, urging them to seek out courts that are reputed to render proper judgments and dispense true justice.[674] The implicit presumption in this notion is that, notwithstanding the hierarchical structure of the court system, the people are to have the freedom of choice as to which court they turn to for justice. In other words, contrary to the system with which we in modern times are familiar, in which a bureaucrat assigns a case to a particular court, this interpretation of the text effectively institutes a competitive system of courts in which those with the best reputations for fairness and competence will attract very heavy workloads while inferior courts will have a lot of spare time, an embarrassment that should serve as a spur to the latter to do what is necessary to enhance their reputations. With a competent and righteous judiciary in place, *thou mayest live, and inherit the land which YHVH thy Elohim giveth thee.* That is, with justice as its keynote, the land will offer the stability and viability that will assure the future of the children of Israel there. "Israel's occupation of the land depends entirely on her obedience to God's law, which includes ensuring that no one is hampered from securing his proper rights. It is only through the maintenance of justice that the community will be able to guarantee right relations between man and God and man and his neighbor."[675]

In this regard, it also has been suggested that the adjuration is directed primarily to those who select the judges; that they should choose judges who primary attribute is a passion for justice, even if they are somewhat deficient in some of the other criteria for selection. It is noteworthy that the commentator chose for a prooftext the following passage describing the prophet Samuel's attempt to discover which of the sons of Jesse was to be anointed as God's choice for Israel's king. Samuel observed one son and said: *'Surely YHVH's anointed is before Him.' But YHVH said unto Samuel: 'Look not on his countenance, or on the height of his stature; because I have rejected him; for it is not as man seeth: for man looketh on the outward appearance, but YHVH looketh on the heart'* (1 Sam. 16:6-7).[676] Thus it has also been suggested that the meaning of the adjuration is that in appointing judges you should not be satisfied with any of the potential candidates that meet your stipulated criteria, but should seek out only those that excel among them.[677]

An alternate reading of the text *Justice, justice shalt thou follow* takes note that it does not state "Justice, justice shalt thou render through thy judgment," but rather that you should "follow" or "pursue" justice. The presumed implication of this is that if reason tells you that a person found guilty of some violation is actually innocent or if the judgment rendered is unjust, there is a moral obligation not to simply consider the matter closed because the court rendered a decision, but rather to continue to search for justice in the matter—judicial decisions are reversible,[678] but not necessarily in every case. In this regard, the rabbis stated as a matter of law, "In non-capital cases they may reverse a verdict either to acquittal or to conviction; but in capital cases they may reverse a verdict to acquittal but not to conviction,"[679] a rule that reflects the implicit disdain for capital punishment discussed below. In this same vein it has been proposed that the text is referring to two aspects of justice, thus accounting for the repetition of the word. The first is justice from the standpoint of proper adjudication according to the law, and the second is justice from the standpoint of the litigants, that is, through exhaustive investigation to determine that there is no deception involved in the claims of the litigants.[680]

Moses interrupts the flow of his discourse with a brief digression once again excoriating any pagan practices among the people.

> [16.21] *Thou shalt not plant thee an Asherah of any kind of tree beside the altar of YHVH thy Elohim, which thou shalt make thee.* [16.22] *Neither shalt thou set thee up a pillar, which YHVH thy Elohim hateth.*

It has been suggested that the reason for interposing this and the following passage here, in the midst of a discussion of the role of the judiciary, is to make the point that "whoever appoints an unworthy judge is as though he plants an *Asherah* in Israel."[681] The implication of this being that the prohibition against planting an *Asherah* applies equally to installing an unfit judge, both representing a corrupting influence that needs to be prevented from taking root. Moreover, it has been proposed that the insertion of this text here serves to emphasize that one of the primary initial responsibilities of the judge is to help root out idolatry from Israelite society.[682] In this regard, it seems reasonable that these texts were introduced here in order to give the people and the judges appointed by them some immediate insight into what awaits them. Thus, Moses provides some examples of transgressions meriting serious punishment by the courts.[683]

Alternatively, it has been argued that the placement of these texts here is intended to make a somewhat broader point. The previous texts described the structure of the judiciary, with the high court located at the national sanctuary, from which the tentacles of the law stretched out throughout the land. And, although there was to be but one sanctuary for the nation, every place where there was a court was to be considered an extension of the divine presence from the national center. And just as the sanctuary had to be guarded against those practices abhorrent to God, so too did this apply throughout the land.[684]

With regard to the text of this passage, it was pointed out that Moses had earlier commanded the people *And ye shall . . . burn their*

Asherim with fire (Deut 12:3), "from which it follows by reasoning from the minor to the major that one certainly should not plant them," thus making the present text seemingly superfluous. It should be borne in mind that an *Asherah* is a tree that was supposed to be under the special protection of a god or goddess, whose presence and influence could be assured by tending the tree and making it thrive.[685] Thus it has been suggested that Moses is prohibiting the planting of any kind of tree, which may be used as an *Asherah*, anywhere in the vicinity of the altar of the sanctuary, as a precautionary measure against recidivism with regard to popular pagan practices.[686] Indeed, the placement of an *Asherah* near an altar used for worship of God was considered so intolerable that the rabbis later extended the symbolic significance of the *Asherah* by forbidding the placement of any wooden structure near the altar.[687]

With regard to the prohibition against setting up a *matzevah* or *pillar*, the rabbis understood this term to refer to a pedestal made of a single stone on which the representation of a god might be placed.[688] Moses thus prohibits the setting up of a pillar made of a single stone even if it is for the worship of God, *which YHVH thy Elohim hateth* because it was commonly used by the Canaanites in their pagan rites of worship. Moses ordains this notwithstanding that the erection of votive pillars was considered acceptable during the period when the Israelites were in the wilderness, as it states: *And Moses wrote all the words of YHVH, and rose up early in the morning, and builded an altar under the mount, and twelve pillars, according to the twelve tribes of Israel* (Ex. 24:4).

However, even at that time, it was already becoming clear that what was acceptable in the wilderness would no longer be so once the children of Israel settled the land promised to them. In this regard, God had already commanded, *An altar of earth thou shalt make unto Me . . . And if thou make Me an altar of stone, thou shalt not build it of hewn stones; for if thou lift up thy tool upon it, thou hast profaned it* (Ex. 20:21-22). By definition, this would preclude the shaping of a stone into a pillar for purposes of worship. Accordingly, while a *matzevah* is prohibited, a *mizbeah*, or an altar made up of stones (plural), is perfectly acceptable. It has also been suggested that any of the appurtenances

298

related to idolatrous worship should be rejected as abhorrent, but an exception must be made with regard to altars, which are essential to the sacrificial rite.[689]

As a corollary to the prohibition of using a pillar as a sacrificial altar, Moses raises another concern regarding the quality of the animals to be brought for sacrifice.

> *17.1 Thou shalt not sacrifice unto YHVH thy Elohim an ox, or a sheep, wherein is a blemish, even any evil thing; for that is an abomination unto YHVH thy Elohim.*

Moses admonishes the people not to stint with regard to the quality of the animals brought to the sanctuary for sacrifice to God. Only flawless creatures are to be offered, ones without *blemish, even any evil thing.* The offering of a flawed animal would be *an abomination unto YHVH thy Elohim.* Because the sacrificial animal is intended to express the surrender of our own being to God, it must be void of any quality that might mar the pure expression of our total commitment to this act of worship.[690] It would have the same effect as appearing at the sanctuary dressed immodestly or ritually impure.

Although the meaning of *blemish* as referring to some visible flaw seems quite clear, that of *kol davar ra* or *any evil thing* begs for explication. Some rabbis argued that both descriptions refer to the same visible flaw, the distinction being that a *blemish* is considered as referring to an animal "born without a blemish which later became blemished," whereas *any evil thing* refers "to an animal congenitally blemished from its mother's womb." An alternate opinion considers *any evil thing* to apply not to a physical defect in the animal but rather to some improper act with regard to the animal, such as the purchase of an animal that had originally been set aside for pagan sacrifice or one purchased with a "harlot's hire,"[691] which would be considered as detracting from the suitability of the animal in question as a sacrifice to God.

The spirit of Moses' admonitions is perhaps best captured in the words of the prophet Malachi concerning the person who has a perverted sense of his obligations to God. Referring to the sacrifice of blemished and maimed animals in violation of the divine command *that ye may be accepted, ye shall offer a male without blemish . . . But whatsoever hath a blemish, that shall ye not bring* (Lev. 22:19-20), the prophet declaimed, *Ye offer polluted bread upon Mine altar. And ye say: "Wherein have we polluted Thee?" . . . And when ye offer the blind for sacrifice, it is no evil! And when ye offer the lame and sick, it is no evil! Present it now unto thy governor; will he be pleased with thee? Or will he accept thy person? Saith YHVH of hosts* (Mal. 1:7-8).

Continuing with the theme of his concern about the attractions of paganism and the need to root it out of the community of Israel, Moses turns to the matter of dealing with the problem judicially.

> *17.2 If there be found in the midst of thee, within any of thy gates which YHVH thy Elohim giveth thee, man or woman, that doeth that which is evil in the sight of YHVH thy Elohim, in transgressing His covenant, 17.3 and hath gone and served other gods, and worshipped them, or the sun, or the moon, or any of the host of heaven, which I have commanded not; 17.4 and it be told thee, and thou hear it, then shalt thou inquire diligently, and, behold, if it be true, and the thing certain, that such abomination is wrought in Israel; 17.5 then thou shalt bring forth that man or that woman, who have done this evil thing, unto thy gates, even the man or the woman; and thou shalt stone them with stones, that they die. 17.6 At the mouth of two witnesses, or three witnesses, shall he that is to die be put to death; at the mouth of one witness he shall not be put to death. 17.7 The hand of the witnesses shall be first upon him to put him to death, and afterward the hand of all the people. So thou shalt put away the evil from the midst of thee.*

In this passage, Moses directs his attention to an Israelite *that doeth that which is evil in the sight of YHVH thy Elohim, in transgressing His covenant.* Moses is not speaking here of someone who violates one of the numerous provisions deriving from the authority of the covenant, but rather someone whose transgression effectively and unilaterally undermines the covenant itself. The definition of such a covenant-breaking transgressor is one who *hath gone and served other gods, and worshipped them, or the sun, or the moon, or any of the host of heaven, which I have commanded not.* It has been suggested that the phrase, *which I have commanded not,* is a euphemism the intention of which is to assert that the kinds of service and worship mentioned are not merely things that God did not command to do but actually forbade.[692] Such a person, in Moses' view, has no place in Israelite society, and if the suspected transgressor is proven guilty of this seditious act, which is to be considered a capital offense, he or she is to be dealt with accordingly.

It has also been suggested that the text regarding one who *hath gone and served other gods, and worshipped them, or the sun, or the moon, or any of the host of heaven,* clearly implies something more than may appear at first glance. That is, if mention of *the sun, or the moon, or any of the host of heaven* is intended to refer to the worship of celestial bodies as deities typical of religions of the time, it surely was already encompassed by the phrase *and served other gods,* seemingly making it redundant. One explanation suggests that the reason for reiterating the admonition was for the sake of the worshippers of the heavenly bodies that, accepting the idea that those celestial bodies were nothing more than servants of God, may have believed erroneously that they were honoring Him by adoring His closest servants; the specific admonition was to inform them that they would be committing a grave error by so doing.[693] In this regard, it has been argued that mention of *the sun, or the moon, or any of the host of heaven* is intended to convey the idea that they are all physical bodies,[694] and, because God created all the heavenly bodies, their unauthorized worship, *which I have commanded not,* is an affront to Him.[695] The prohibition announced here by Moses is, by logical extension, applicable to the worship of any created thing, a concept that significantly broadens the potential scope of the prohibition of idolatry.

Injunctions against idolatry or idolatrous forms of worship are repeated numerous times in the biblical texts, and for good reason. The evidence of the biblical texts is that the struggle with idolatry was a problem that plagued Israel from its very beginning as a nation, primarily because of the penchant for if not obsession with the visual, something that pagan religions afforded in abundance and something that the biblical conception of God emphatically rejected. In this regard, worship of the ancient Canaanite gods Baal and Astarte (Ashtaroth) and their associated fertility rites became widespread in ancient Israel. Thus, following the death of Joshua, who like Moses was able to maintain a fairly strong grip on the people, the biblical texts record repeated and widespread religious anarchy. *And the children of Israel did that which was evil in the sight of YHVH, and served the Baalim. And they forsook YHVH, the Elohim of their fathers, who brought them out of the land of Egypt, and followed other gods, of the gods of the peoples that ere round about them, and worshipped them; and they provoked YHVH. And they forsook YHVH, and served Baal and the Ashtaroth* (Judg. 2:11-13). It was precisely this that Moses hoped to avert by affirming that apostasy was a grievous act of sedition that undermined the very basis for the nation's existence, and therefore had to be dealt with forcefully.

Because of the severity and irreversibility of the penalty, the charge of perpetrating such a transgression had to be verified by at least two corroborating witnesses, and a determination through a thorough cross-examination of the witnesses that their testimony *be true, and the thing certain* before the court might pronounce a sentence of capital punishment by stoning in the public square. A thorough investigation of the testimony had to be undertaken because such deviant behavior was not likely to have been done openly in places frequented by the public, but is far more likely to have been done in seclusion, making disclosure problematic.[696] It is noteworthy that the stipulation, *At the mouth of two witnesses, or three witnesses, shall he that is to die be put to death; at the mouth of one witness he shall not be put to death,* has been understood by the rabbis to apply not only in the case discussed here but in all cases involving capital offenses.[697] It may be pointed out that there can be no unimpeachable assurance that witnesses are telling the truth, no matter how many corroborate their assertions. What we have here, in effect, is a concession to practical necessity, recognizing that while it is possible that two or more witnesses might collude to offer false testimony against someone for unspecified reasons, as a general proposition the identical testimony of two or more vetted witnesses should be deemed reliable and trustworthy.

The assertion, *At the mouth of two witnesses, or three witnesses, shall he that is to die be put to death*, has also been understood as predicated on the assumption that the perpetrator of the capital offense had been cautioned prior to the act regarding its prohibition and the penal consequences that would follow from it. Thus, by committing the act, to which the witnesses will attest, the perpetrator is already considered as condemned to death when he appears before the court, "and the task of the court is rather to try and find some possible ground for remitting the death penalty."[698] In this regard, it has been suggested that the intention of the statement, *At the mouth of two witnesses, or three witnesses*, is that it is desirable to obtain as many witnesses as possible to assure that the truth of the matter be established beyond any doubt. This is the essential meaning of the adjuration, *then shalt thou inquire diligently*. That is, one should attempt to discover as many corroborating witnesses as possible, but that there must be at least two for imposition of capital punishment.[699] Another suggests that the implication of *at the mouth of two witnesses, or three witnesses* is that once one finds two witnesses the search for more should not immediately cease.[700] Still another possibility is that what the text is suggesting that in a case where two witnesses disagree a third witness that corroborates one of the two testimonies will be necessary before a judgment can be rendered.[701]

It also is noteworthy that there is no reference here to an effort to elicit a confession from the alleged perpetrator, voluntary or coerced, a reflection of a leading principle of Jewish law that no person can be convicted of a capital offense on the basis of his own testimony.[702] In this vein, the rabbis pointed out that the text speaks of capital punishment being inflicted on *that man or that woman* who was convicted on the basis of two trustworthy witnesses of his or her conscious and knowing guilt; "not one who was coerced, nor one who did it inadvertently, nor one who is (innocently) misled."[703]

Presumably as added insurance for the veracity of the testimony of the witnesses, Moses ordained that they must be the first to cast stones at the convicted perpetrator, to be followed in this act of public execution by the public at large. The rabbis pointed out, however, that this provision made sense only if the condemned survived the initial stoning by the witnesses.[704] In other words, this provision should not be understood as authorizing public desecration of a corpse, something considered abhorrent in Judaic thought. Public participation in the punishment, where appropriate, would presumably reinforce its consciousness of the enormity of such a transgression, and in this way, Moses assured the people, *thou shalt put away the evil from the midst of thee.* That is, the public will learn thereby to take responsibility for the well being of the society of which they are a part. Moreover, this requirement would forces the community that imposes capital punishment to accept responsibility as a community for the lives it takes. Obligating the public to play the role of executioner changes capital punishment from a spectacle performed by others into an intimate personal experience that few will relish. In this regard, it has been suggested that this requirement was one of the factors that ultimately led to virtual de facto elimination of capital punishment in addition to the stringent evidentiary requirements for imposition of such a penalty under rabbinic law.[705]

Moses next turns to the judges that are appointed to preside over the tribal and municipal courts and advises them how to deal with cases that arise for which the established law does not provide sufficiently clear guidance to enable them to reach a sound judgment.

> [17.8] *If there arise a matter too hard for thee in judgment, between blood and blood, between plea and plea, and between stroke and stroke, even matters of controversy within thy gates; then shalt thou arise, and get thee unto the place which YHVH thy Elohim shall choose.* [17.9] *And thou shalt come unto the priests the Levites, and unto the judge that shall be in those days; and thou shalt inquire; and they shall declare unto thee the sentence of judgment.* [17.10] *And thou shalt do according to the tenor of the sentence, which they shall declare unto thee from that place which YHVH shall choose; and thou shalt observe to do according*

to all that they shall teach thee. ¹⁷·¹¹ According to the law which they shall teach thee, and according to the judgment which they shall tell thee, thou shalt do; thou shalt not turn aside from the sentence which they shall declare unto thee, to the right hand or to the left. ¹⁷·¹² And the man that doeth presumptuously, in not hearkening unto the priest that standeth to minister there before YHVH thy Elohim, or unto the judge, even that man shall die; and thou shalt exterminate the evil from Israel. ¹⁷·¹³ And all the people shall hear, and fear, and do no more presumptuously.

As indicated above, the passage has been read as implying that Moses is ordaining the establishment of a national high court that would exercise ultimate judicial authority in the state. The court is to be located at *the place which YHVH thy Elohim shall choose*, that is, at the site of the central sanctuary, thus exemplifying the connection of the law as given and guarded by the priests with the law as applied in practice in accordance with the judgment of the high court. Moses emphasizes that the decisions of the court, *which they shall declare unto thee from that place which YHVH shall choose*, are final and must be followed. In this regard the rabbis taught, with particular reference to cases involving capital offenses, "when the priesthood is functioning, the judge functions; but when the priesthood is not functioning, the judge may not function."⁷⁰⁶ That is, the rabbis concluded that because of the wording of this text capital punishment could only be imposed by the high court at a time when the priests were officiating at the central sanctuary. According to this reading of the text, following the destruction of the Temple in Jerusalem in the first century, imposition of capital punishment ceased to be an authorized sentence from the standpoint of rabbinic law.

It should be noted that the text speaks only of referrals for judgment from a lower court; there is no indication here that the high court also was to serve as a court of appeal, which as discussed earlier is a matter of controversy among commentators. The basis for such referral is the statement, *ki yipale mimkha davar lamishpat*, translated above as *if there arise a matter too hard for thee in judgment*. It has been noted in this regard that the term *yipale* derives from a root employed to refer to something that has no discernible connection with the existing order of things. Accordingly, what the text is saying is that if a case arises that is so baffling that you cannot find a basis for rendering a verdict one way or the other, it should be referred to the high court for adjudication.[707] That is, where the stated law is insufficiently clear with regard to how a particular question should be resolved, it is essential that it be resolved definitively by the high court because, as one commentator put it, "general agreement on anything is rare, disagreements will multiply and the Torah will be transformed into a multiplicity of Torahs. Scripture therefore determined that we should pay heed to the high court . . . with regard to all that it may dictate to us concerning the interpretation of the Torah."[708] This suggests that the high court not only constitutes the highest national judicial entity, but also serves as the ultimate repository of the authoritative interpretation of the Torah. This view is predicated on the assumption that it was Moses' intention to make the high court "the ultimate authority on whose shoulders rests the responsibility for the authentic tradition and interpretation of the Torah, as well as making all arrangements for its being kept correctly." The high court is endowed with the power to make final decisions in this regard, and the people generally, as well as those appointed to teach them the Torah, are obligated to accept and act upon them without challenging the legitimacy of the court's judgments.[709]

With regard to the subject matter of the issues regarding which the lower court may be stymied in rendering judgment, *between blood and blood, between plea and plea, and between stroke and stroke, even matters of controversy within thy gates*, there are only varying degrees of agreement among commentators. Thus, according to the rabbis, *between blood and blood* "implies between clean blood and unclean blood,"[710] and refers to the question of the ritual purity or impurity with regard to "the blood of a menstruant, childbirth, and gonorrhoea."[711] By contrast, the phrase has also been understood as referring to the difficulty in determining whether a homicide was intentional or accidental.[712] In either case, clear guidelines for making the required determination are needed and can only originate from the central national authority. Thus it was with regard to the religious issue of ritual impurity that the prophet spoke of the responsibility of the priesthood: *And they shall teach My people the difference between the holy and the common, and cause them to discern between the clean and the unclean* (Ezek. 44:23).

With regard to *between plea and plea*, it is assumed by some that it refers to the inability to assess the relative merits of divergent claims in a suit before the court.[713] The rabbis, however, gave it a broader frame of reference, associating it with issues relating to "capital or civil cases, or cases involving flagellation. In capital cases, the issue is whether the biblical stipulation, *then shalt thou give life for life* (Ex. 21:23), should be understood literally or figuratively as referring to monetary compensation. In corporal punishment cases, the issue is over the size of the court that is permitted to render such sentence, three judges or twenty-three.

With regard to *bein nega lanega*, translated as *between stroke and stroke*, the term *nega* is also used in the sense of disease, and the rabbis read this text as saying, *between [leprous] plague spots and plague spots*, "including leprosy in man, houses and garments."[714] Others, however, relate it to issues involving mayhem.[715] As for *matters of controversy within thy gates*, the rabbis related the statement to a variety of complex religious issues;[716] whereas a straightforward reading suggests that it refers to any other matters of inconclusive controversy besides those mentioned that might arise.

The passage also indicates that the high court should be composed of *the priests the Levites*, and *the judge that shall be in those days*. The reference to the *priests the Levites*, a designation often found in the Torah, reflects the reality of the Mosaic era in which the role of minister and priest was transferred from the eldest sons of the tribes exclusively to the tribe of Levi, the ministry becoming the responsibility of the Levites and the priestly functions delegated to Aaron and his male descendents. Presumably, this changeover did not take place in practice overnight, and may even have been resisted in some quarters.[717] Thus, the text's repeated mention of *the priests the Levites* is intended to make it clear that only levitical priests were authorized to function in such capacity.

It is noteworthy that the designation *priests the Levites* has also been understood as depicting priests functioning in the common role of the Levites, the authorized priests also being members of the tribe of Levi, as teachers of the public, and that they are referred to as levitical priests "when this aspect of their calling is discussed."[718] It is not clear, however, that this explanation of the expression fits well with its repeated use in the text. An alternative argument is that "originally all the Levites were priests," but the descendents of Aaron subsequently made the priesthood the special preserve of their family, relegating the other Levites to a secondary role.[719]

On an initial reading, the text seems to be saying that the high court should be comprised of levitical priests, presumably because it was they to whom maintaining the integrity of the revealed law was entrusted, and presided over by *the judge that shall be in those days.* The wording, however, is ambiguous and lends itself to a variety of interpretations. Thus, the rabbis interpreted the text as indicating: "It is a positive commandment to have priests and Levites in the court; but lest that one should think that, since this is a commandment, if a court does not have them, it is disqualified, the verse goes on to say, *And unto the judge*—even if the court has no priests and Levites, it is legal."[720] In this interpretation, a court composed of priests and Levites is preferred but not absolutely necessary. Alternatively, the text could be understood as indicating that a properly constituted court should consist of priests and at least one judge, the former serving as authorities on the received law and on matters that fall in the category of those things that are between man and God, the latter serving as expert authority on matters between man and man. This of course would provide for a rather lopsided court, but given Moses' major and immediate concern with the issue of strengthening the faith of the people in God, a court well versed in divine law and its application may have been his priority at the time. In this regard, it has been suggested that there is a balance between the priests, who because of their service in the sanctuary are attuned to an intuitive grasp of the truth, and the judge who, in the sense of this passage refers to one capable of probing to the essence of the matter through investigation and an appreciation of what is required for the benefit of the state and society.[721]

In any case, the reference to *the judge that shall be in those days* raises questions as to its meaning and intent. Thus, one rabbi asked rhetorically: "Would it occur to you to go before a judge who is not living in your own days? Rather this means a judge who is qualified and approved in those days. If he had been a relative [of one of the parties through marriage, which would have disqualified him] and subsequently ceased being so, he is qualified."[722] Although this opinion reflects that of the majority of the rabbis, a minority view maintains that "if a man's daughter died and left children, her husband still counts as a kinsman," and therefore would be disqualified from hearing a case that involved the family of his deceased wife.[723] Some rabbis also drew another inference of import from the text, namely "that you must be content to go to the judge who is in your days."[724] That is, that the appointed judges at any particular point in time have absolute authority even though they may be of a lesser stature than those who preceded them. "As long as they perform their functions faithfully their judgments have the force of law and no one may call their competence into question."[725]

The high court is intended to be the ultimate judicial authority in the Israelite state, from whose decisions there can be no appeal to any human authority. Thus Moses declares: *According to the law which they shall teach thee, and according to the judgment which they shall tell thee, thou shalt do; thou shalt not turn aside from the sentence which they shall declare unto thee, to the right hand or to the left.* Although there is general agreement about the meaning and intent of this passage, there is some argument regarding the meaning of its final clause, *thou shalt not turn aside from the sentence which they shall declare unto thee, to the right hand or to the left.* Some took the position that this meant that, "even if they point out to you that right is left and left is right, obey them."[726] In other words, this opinion demands a total suspension of personal knowledge and judgment in favor of that of the court. In support of this view, it has been argued that its acceptance is essential, because the Torah has been given in writing, but it is self-evident that issues for which the Torah does not provide a clear answer will arise and it will be difficult to gain a consensus. Accordingly, it is vital to establish the unimpeachable authority of the high court to render definitive judgment on such matters.[727] Nonetheless, some rabbis found the arbitrariness of this position quite unacceptable, and insisted that one must accept the court's judgments as valid only if they affirm that what is right is right and what is left is left.[728] That is, the obligation to obey the court without challenge applies as long as the court does not render a judgment that defies common sense.

Applying speculative etymology to the text, it has been suggested that the text under consideration seems to imply that these decisions by the high court essentially take one of two forms: *according to the law which they shall teach thee,* and *according to the judgment which they shall tell thee,* corresponding to the use of the phrases *they shall teach* and *they shall tell* in these formulations. The first is understood as implying that the teaching will consist of a determination that the court arrives at either "by means of the hermeneutical rules sanctioned by the Lawgiver for the interpretation of and research into His Torah, or a decree, an institution designed for the practical maintenance of the Torah." By contrast, the second is understood as implying that what *they shall tell thee* is based on "pure tradition."[729] Alternatively, what *they shall tell thee* has been understood as referring to a decision based on their "wisdom."[730] In other words, acknowledging that what baffled the lower court was the lack of clarity as how to deal with the problem before it because the law failed to address it specifically, and its correlation to existing law was not self-evident, the high court would determine the relevant law either by the application of the accepted rules of deduction and inference from established law, a safeguard to protect the established law from inadvertent trespass, or by relying upon an existing tradition that is itself not necessarily based on established law, or their best intuitive judgment.

As for *the man that doeth presumptuously,* that is, who consciously and deliberately rejects the judgment of the court, refusing to *hearken unto the priest that standeth to minister there before YHVH thy Elohim, or unto the judge,* such a person must be deemed a danger to the society and punished appropriately. There is a presumption that when the text speaks of *the priest* or *the judge* it is referring to the high priest or the chief of the high court, which often would be the same person. This would not have been considered awkward in antiquity, where the priests, by virtue of their vocation, which excluded them from the normal economy and related occupations, made them the intellectual elite of the society, the most educated and the most familiar with the laws of the covenant that were entrusted to them for safekeeping. Accordingly it would have been expected that the high priest would also serve as chief justice. However, the text speaks of *the judge*, presumably referring to the lay chief justice in the event that the high priest, for some reason, was unavailable or unable to fill that role.[731]

In considering this text, the rabbis assumed that it was not referring to an ordinary citizen who might simply dislike the ruling of the court on a particular matter. Such a person would more than likely be considered incompetent and the decision of the court simply would be carried out with or without his cooperation; he would not be considered a threat to the stability of the society. Accordingly, they reasoned that the text must have been intended to apply to one of the elders of the society, possibly even a member of the high court who disagreed with the majority, whose opinions carried significant weight among the people. In the rabbinic literature, such a person is characterized "a rebellious elder." Because the text makes clear that it is concerned with *the man that doeth presumptuously*, it is assumed to be referring to a person of stature, and not to the mere disciple of such a person,[732] who actually *does* that which the court ruled should not be done. It is not considered as applicable to one who simply teaches that the law should be or actually is contrary to what the court has decided; "he is liable only for deed, not for teaching."[733] However, other rabbis expanded on this opinion and taught: "He is not liable unless he acts upon his ruling, or states his ruling to others, who act thereon."[734] In other words, teaching as such carries no liability. However, if teaching influences someone to violate the law, it too becomes a deed that carries liability.

Because such a rebellious elder undermines the authority of the court and with it the entire constitutional structure, he is deemed a danger to the society. Therefore, he must meet the same fate as those determined to be guilty of sedition, as discussed earlier; *that man shall die; and thou shalt exterminate the evil from Israel.* The rabbis wisely noted with regard to the last statement that suggesting such measures will *exterminate the evil from Israel* is probably somewhat of an overstatement and recommended that the assertion be understood in a more limited but also more realistic fashion as "exterminate the evildoers from Israel," which seemed more practicable than the elimination of evil, as such.[735]

The next topic on Moses' agenda concerned the establishment of an executive arm of government. It may seem strange that in setting forth the forms of governmental leadership that are to apply in the state-in-the-making the discussion of the king takes second position to that of the judges. "The reason is that whereas sound judicial administration by impartial judges is at the very heart of Israel's covenant theocracy, monarchy as a particular form of political authority is not."[736] That is, there is general agreement that there must be a form of executive leadership for the nation, but the nature of that leadership, as will be seen below, is a matter of contention.

> [17.14] *When thou art come unto the land which YHVH thy Elohim giveth thee, and shalt possess it, and shalt dwell therein; and shalt say: 'I will set a king over me, like all the nations that are round about me';*

The text repeatedly has given expression to Moses' concern about transforming the nation from a tribal confederacy to a federation with a strong national government, a change he considered essential to the viability of the nation in the land divinely allotted to them. Moses now turned to the question of the nature of the central political leadership of the nation, a subject he raised with God earlier in anticipation of his death. Thus we are told, Moses *spoke unto YHVH, saying: 'Let YHVH . . . set a man over the congregation, who may go out before them, and may come in before them, who may lead them out, and who may bring them in; that the congregation of YHVH be not as sheep without a shepherd'* (Num. 27:15-17). It should be noted that the emphasis in this passage appears to be on military leadership, although it surely implies political leadership as well. As one commentator remarked, what Moses is asking for is a successor "who combines the capacity of leadership in warfare with the vigorous prosecution of the general duties that devolve upon the head of a nation."[737] It is noteworthy that there is no specification in the text cited as to the form the requested leadership is to take.

By contrast, in the present text, the form of leadership appears to be stipulated as that of kingship. As one medieval writer put it, "Because the natures of men differ from one another, and the will of one is opposed to that of another, except for a single ruling authority over them there would be no agreement concluded between them and conflict would be rife. Therefore we have the precepts regarding judges and officers, and the establishment of a king over the people to rule them and guide them in the straight path."[738] Similarly it has been argued, "It is impossible for mankind to constitute a civilization without making one among them a chief over the rest . . . for the opinions of men differ from one to the other and they will never agree to a single understanding in order to accomplish a single thing."[739] The author then continues: "We are commanded to appoint a king over us from among the people of Israel who will gather us all and lead us according to his will . . . [because] of the benefit that accrues to the people by having over them a single person as chief and commander, because otherwise civilization could not be maintained in peace."[740]

With regard to the present text, I have ventured to say only that it "appears" to reflect this perspective, because the meaning and implications of the text are matters of profound disagreement among commentators from antiquity to the present. Before pursuing this point further, it should be noted that there are at lest two important differences between the two biblical texts. In the earlier passage the matter of national leadership is raised in the context of the nation wandering in the wilderness; the present text is predicated on the establishment of a national territory, as it states, *When thou art come unto the land.* That is, the appointment of a king is directly related to the effective occupation and possession of what is to be the national homeland. The implication that may be drawn from this is that the nature of the institution that is to embody the executive functions of government may differ in accordance with whether or not the nation is constituted as a territorially based political entity. In the absence of an established state, a politico-military chieftain may suffice for the needs of the people, as was the case with Joshua and the Judges that served as his successors for some two centuries after Moses' death. For the governance of a settled country, the text appears to suggest that something more is required. A second distinction of some importance is that in the earlier text, the primary military leadership role of the national leader is specified, whereas the functions of the king, in the present text, are unspecified, leaving open a number of possibilities ranging from figurehead to generalissimo.

But what, we may ask, is the essential difference between a king and a national leader not so designated, such as Moses and after him Joshua? Did they not have the same effective powers as any monarch? Moreover, it has been observed that in the previous discussion of the judges, the text treated the subject as quite natural to the people, whereas here it seems to emphasize that monarchy is essentially alien to the spirit of the children of Israel, something done not naturally but in emulation of other nations.[741] As a practical matter, the only discernible difference is that each national leader must be chosen individually, whereas a king implies a dynastic succession, as acknowledged below in the text that speaks of the proper king, *that he may prolong his days in his kingdom, he and his children, in the midst of Israel.*

Among a fractious people such as the children of Israel, choosing a national leader by consensus would prove to be an unrealizable ideal. God chose Moses, and Moses chose Joshua. But despite his exceptional competence, Joshua did not have the stature to choose his own successor, and therein lay the problem that Moses was alluding to in this text. Following Joshua there was little expectation that a new leader would emerge that would be able to bind the nation together, and indeed, no such leader arose throughout the entire period of the Judges, which endured for some two centuries. Thus Moses anticipated that the time would come when the leaders of the tribes would conclude that their own self-interest demanded that they establish a national leadership that would have centralized authority that could be passed automatically to a dynastic successor, and thus eliminate the contentiousness of an internal struggle for power that served to debilitate the country in the face of the challenges it faced from unrelenting enemies around and within it.

The controversy among commentators over the meaning and intent of the text results from its ambiguous wording: *and shalt say: 'I will set a king over me, like all the nations that are round about me.'* One school of thought read this text as clearly mandating the appointment of a king, whereas opponents of this reading argued that Moses made the statement "only in anticipation of their future murmurings."[742] The issue, as explained by one modern commentator is as follows: "According to R. Judah it is a commandment; I command you that you shall say to the prophet and the Sanhedrin: I will set a king over me; for the phrase *and shalt say* is not to be interpreted as meaning, 'if you should say,' for it is written *thou shalt in any wise set him [king over thee].* They are thus commanded to establish a king . . . R. Nehorai's understanding is that where it is written, *I will set a king over me*, it is not a commandment to do so. It is rather in reference to the shame of Israel that the text speaks, as if to say, that you will in the future murmur and speak in such a manner." Indeed, the sage went farther and asserted, "They demanded a king only so that he might lead them into idolatry," and that this is the import of they meant by expressing the desire to be *like all the nations that are round about me.*[743]

In support of those who argue that the establishment of a monarchy is optional rather than mandatory, the text may be read as suggesting Moses anticipated that a time of crisis would arise sometime in the future when the people would become convinced that they would be better off if their country were organized around a more powerful central leadership in the manner of the nations that surrounded them, in place of the more power diffuse federal system promoted by Moses because of his interest in preserving the tribal structure. The text therefore may be understood as saying that the centralization of power in a monarchy was not part of Moses' original scheme, and indeed contradicted the fundamental biblical teaching that attributed sovereignty to God alone. As the rabbis put it, "When kings arose over Israel and began to enslave them, God exclaimed: 'Did you not forsake Me and seek kings for yourselves?' Hence the import of the statement, *I will set a king over me.*"[744] Understood from this perspective, appointment of a king is necessarily optional rather than mandatory. Nonetheless, the controversy over this point has never been resolved satisfactorily or definitively, and both sides of the argument have received support from prominent thinkers throughout the centuries.

One advocate of the view that the establishment of a king is a biblical requirement essential to the proper ordering of society elevates it to become one of the six hundred and thirteen basic precepts of the Torah,[745] rationalizing this position in terms reminiscent of Greek political thought. "It being the will of God that our race should exist and be permanently established, He in His wisdom gave it such properties that men can acquire the capacity of ruling others. Some persons are therefore inspired with theories of legislation, such as prophets and lawgivers; others possess the power of enforcing the dictates of the former, and compelling the people to obey them, and to act accordingly. Such are kings, who accept the code of the lawgivers."[746] The idea that a monarchy is the necessary and most beneficial form of societal governance has been advocated by many in the literature of Judaism from the eleventh to the turn of the twentieth century. Thus in an early poem we find the line, "There is no good for the people in the absence of kings,"[747] and in the late medieval period, "Man, by nature, has need of political existence, and to gather with his kind to form a political society, and to be perfected through the strength of a just king."[748] Similarly in modern times, we find the assertion, "It should be understood that in the order of perfection [of the nation] the appointment of a king is antecedent to everything else, for without a king there is no people, and therefore a king is fundamental."[749]

An alternate and less absolute approach to the question stresses the importance of a strong leader but does not make the case that a king is the necessary or preferred form that central authority should take. Thus, it has been argued that "Conventional law cannot exist unless there is a ruler, or a judge, or a king, placed at the head of the group or city, who compels the people to repress wrong and observe the law so as to secure the welfare of the group. It follows that the establishment of a king or ruler or a judge is almost imperative for the continuation of the human species, seeing that man is political by nature."[750] Accordingly, a king may be necessary in conventional societies but whether such is necessary in a society governed in accordance with the Torah remains an open question.

Others go a step farther and argue that the entire question of whether kingship is mandatory or optional is only relevant under a set of particular socio-historic conditions. In the case of Israel, it becomes relevant only if its leaders truly wish to pattern it after the other nations, as the text puts it, if they truly want it to be *like all the nations that are round about me.* In the absence of this sentiment, which amounts to a rejection of much of the covenant, the need for a king is dubious, although the need for strong central leadership remains a necessity.[751] In this regard, in an apparent attempt to bridge the opposing positions on this issue, it has been argued that God "did not command unconditionally and absolutely that Israel should appoint a king over themselves, except when the people feel that they have the need for such . . . In the event that the people should feel weak . . . [then] it is not only permissible but mandatory to appoint a king over them."[752]

At the further end of the spectrum of opinion on the issue, there are those who insist that there is no historical evidence to support the notion that a king is necessary to produce cohesion in a political society, or that justice is better served when there is a king. Indeed, it is argued that collective leadership is far superior to that of a monarch in that it is likely to be less corruptible, less arbitrary, and more socially responsible. The conclusion, therefore, is that a king is not necessary for a people, neither for the improvement of the polity nor for the purpose of bringing about harmony, continuity, or exercising ultimate political authority. Accordingly, appointing a king is entirely optional.[753]

Another proponent of this position goes so far as to argue that although the appointment of a king is optional, it is nonetheless undesirable. He argues, "the permission to appoint a king is the same as the permission to marry a *woman of goodly form* [Deut. 21:11] which suggests that the end will be to hate her and give birth through her to a rebellious son, such as happened to David in the matter of Absalom."[754] The allusion to a *woman of goodly form* is to the biblical text that discusses the question of marrying an attractive female who is taken as a prisoner of war. This is what happened to David, who married a captive that gave birth to Absalom, who turned out to be a rebel that attempted to overthrow his father. By drawing this analogy, the commentator is suggesting that, even though it is permissible to establish a monarchy, it is not desirable because, once in power, the king may and most likely will tend to use his authority and power for purposes other than originally intended by those who put him in office. Thus the king is compared to a beautiful captive who appears most desirable at first glance, but whose allure may obscure other features that promise eventual incompatibility and regret.

It has also been argued that it is inconceivable that there should be a biblical requirement for the establishment of a monarchy, since such an unequivocal commandment might prove incompatible with the nature of the people who are to be governed. Thus, one finds "there are states that cannot tolerate the idea of monarchy, and there are states that, in the absence of a king, are like a ship without a captain . . . Therefore, it is not possible to command absolutely the appointment of a king so long as the people have not agreed to accept the yoke of kingship on the basis of the observation that surrounding states are conducted in a more proper order thereby."[755]

Putting aside the unresolved issue of whether the appointment of a king is mandatory or optional, Moses seems to make it clear that even if it is optional, the people do not have the option of choosing the person who is to be so elevated. Instead,

> [17.15] *thou shalt in any wise set him king over thee, whom YHVH thy Elohim shall choose; one from among thy brethren shalt thou set king over thee; thou mayest not put a foreigner over thee, who is not thy brother.* [17.16] *Only he shall not multiply horses to himself, nor cause the people to return to Egypt, to the end that he should multiply horses; forasmuch as YHVH hath said unto you: 'Ye shall henceforth return no more that way.'* [17.17] *Neither shall he multiply wives to himself, that his heart turn not away; neither shall he greatly multiply to himself silver and gold.*

This text is widely understood as saying that the choice of a king will be made by God, and presumably transmitted to the people through a prophet,[756] which effectively gives the prophet control over the appointment, a notion discounted by some who argue that the primary role in this aspect of the political process is played by the national high court.[757] However, some rabbis took issue with both of these suppositions as not being supported by the actual wording of the biblical text, which states, *Thou shalt in any wise set him king over thee.* It does not say, "I will set," but rather that *Thou shalt . . . set,* "which indicates that it is dependent upon you."[758] In addition to being understood as an argument against the mandatory appointment of a king,[759] this opinion seems to imply that, since the actual appointment of the king is to be by those who requested it, that is, the elders of the people, rather than the prophet, what is sought from the prophet is sanction for appointing a king, and not the nomination of one. Presumably, once approved in principle, the people's choice will be found acceptable to God.[760]

Alternatively, it has been suggested that, "hidden in the text of this verse is the concept that Hashem [God] is the absolute Master of whomever claims leadership among men and even over everything in nature."[761] For this reason it states *thou shalt in any wise set him king over thee* only after the people say *I will set a king over me, like all the nations.* That is, as the prophet Samuel later told the people when they insisted *a king shall reign over us; when YHVH your Elohim was your king* (1 Sam. 12:12). Accordingly, the appointment of a king that meets the criteria set forth by Moses becomes obligatory only after the people make the demand.[762] As it states in a later text, even a king will eventually come to realize that *God Most High ruleth in the kingdom of men, and that He setteth up over it whomsoever He will* (Dan. 5:21). In this regard, some rabbis asserted, "Even a superintendent of a well is appointed in heaven."[763] That is, all political authority is assumed to derive from a divine mandate.

The only critical prerequisite for the selection of a king for Israel is that *one from among thy brethren shalt thou set king over thee; thou mayest not put a foreigner over thee, who is not thy brother.* The reason for this restriction, according to one opinion, is that "no individual has ever been the chief of a religious community to whose race he did not belong, without doing it great or small injury." It suggested further that the biblical text itself provides evidence of this, noting that prior to the appointment of Israel's first king, the genealogy and origin of the kings of Edom (Gen. 36:31-40) reveals that none of them was Edomite in origin, and "they tyrannized over the *children of Esau* and humiliated them."[764] Alternatively, it has been suggested that the restriction on a candidate *who is not thy brother* was intended to preclude a descendent of Esau, that is, an Edomite, from becoming king, even though Esau was in fact the brother of Jacob. The implication being that *thy brother* refers exclusively to the descendents of Jacob.[765] It is noteworthy in regard to the latter opinion that Herod, the post-biblical king of Judea, who ruled as a tyrant, was of Edomite (Idumean) descent.

However, there is an implicit problem with this text, given the idea that God's selection will be made known through a prophet. If the latter is the case, is it conceivable that God would choose a non-Israelite to be the king of His people? Accordingly, it is suggested that this text needs to be read as containing an implicit stipulation that you are to set over yourself the king that God will choose if God makes His choice known to you, but if for some unknown reason He does not provide you with the appropriate guidance and you choose to act anyway, *thou mayest not put a foreigner over thee, who is not thy brother.*[766]

It has been pointed out that, by contrast with judges, priests, and prophets, with regard to whom the text alludes to both their authority and rights and the duty of obedience to them, the law about the king says nothing about the extent of his authority and power or any executive functions or responsibilities. Instead, it focuses on "limiting the power and prestige of human authorities," and deemphasizes that of the role of the king most of all.[767] In place of a discussion of his powers, the text speaks of the personal disabilities to which the king is subjected, restrictions that are designed to impede any tendency on his part to confuse his public responsibilities with his private ambitions and interests. These are reflected in the three injunctions: *he shall not multiply horses to himself . . . neither shall he multiply wives to himself . . . neither shall he greatly multiply to himself silver and gold.* "This means to say, even though you may have a king like the kings of other nations, he shall display the minimum of the characteristics of the other kings, as there are kings that strive for the multiplication of horses and chariots. But a king of Israel may multiply to himself neither horses, nor wives, nor silver and gold. There are kings who make a principle of attaining these things. However, a king of Israel will be deficient in this and will instead make a principle of the Torah and the fear of Heaven."[768] In this same vein another commentator remarks that the text imposes on the king the duty of self-regulation with regard "to just those factors which, according to the experience of all ages have been the rocks on which the virtue of rulers has come to grief and the happiness of their people shattered. These are: the passion for military glory and renown, women and possessions."[769] In short, the need to abide by these restrictions would tend to make wearing the crown a far less enticing prospect for the politically ambitious. It may reasonably be assumed that the aim of the restrictions is to deter the king from adopting "a culture alien to the spirit of Israel and the diversion of his heart from the Mosaic law."[770]

With regard to the first of these injunctions, the rabbis taught: "He shall not multiply horses to *himself*. I might think not even such as are required for his horsemen and chariots. Scripture therefore states: 'to himself': for himself he may not multiply, but he may multiply as many as are required for his chariots and horsemen."[771] The implication of this interpretation is that, while it is appropriate that the king build a mobile army as large as he deems necessary to meet the nation's needs, he may not exploit his authority to build up armed forces that only serve his personal vanity. Moreover, maintaining many horse-mounted troops, as has occurred repeatedly throughout ancient and medieval history, generally involves the emergence of a small upper class that needs to be serviced by a large class of serfs or servants, a development that the Torah seeks to forestall through this and other restrictive stipulations.[772] Another interpretive approach views the injunction as relating to the king personally. Thus, it has been asserted that "Scripture only prohibits him from having horses which stand idle in his stables and which are ready for him to ride upon on any day he pleases or to paraded before him as is done by the kings of other nations. Indeed, he is only permitted to have a single horse upon which to ride, like any other person."[773] In effect, this injunction demands that the king personally portray a degree of modesty not formally demanded of wealthy private citizens.

In principle, the biblical injunction relates not only to horses. The dictum is phrased in terms of horses because, in the context of biblical times, horses represented both wealth and military power. In the present day, the same injunction would apply to vehicles and aircraft. The implication of the text is that the king is constrained to remain constantly aware of the purpose for which he is enthroned and empowered, and that purpose decidedly is not self-aggrandizement, but rather to attend to the needs of the nation—to the exclusion of personal desires and ambitions. Alternatively, it has been argued that the intent of the injunction is to prevent the king from becoming over-reliant on sheer military power in place of maintaining his trust in God.[774] Toward this end, the injunctions applied to the king far exceeded those that apply to the people at large—who are not enjoined to possess but one horse, nor are they cautioned about counting any such possessions among their wealth.

In addition, the injunction also includes the rule that the king is not to *cause the people to return to Egypt, to the end that he should multiply horses; forasmuch as YHVH hath said unto you: 'Ye shall henceforth return no more that way,'* a text that lends itself to a number of possible interpretations. The Israelites were liberated from Egypt by God only four decades earlier, and Moses here informs them implicitly that for them to return to Egypt, even if only for the purpose of business transactions such as trade in horses, would be an affront to God. Indeed, by the time of Solomon, Egypt was noted as an exporter of horses and chariots, with Israelites serving as agents for the international transactions, as it states: *And a chariot came up and went out of Egypt for six hundred shekels of silver, and a horse for a hundred and fifty; and so for all the kings of the Hittites, and for the kings of Aram, did they bring them out by their means* (1 Kings 10:29).

Alternatively, the text has been understood as permitting one to go to Egypt on business or for the purpose of conquering it. The injunction applies only to settling there.[775] It is noteworthy that the latter opinion, which does not fit well with the straightforward reading of the text, may well have been considered an interpretation necessitated by the fact of a very large and in some cases long-established Israelite or Jewish population in Alexandria at the beginning of the first century.

Indeed, to deal with the latter being in apparent contradiction to the biblical demand, it had been argued that the biblical injunction under consideration was only intended to apply to a return to living in Egypt from the land of Israel but not from other places in the Diaspora.[776]

It has been observed that the divine injunction, *Ye shall henceforth return no more that way*, implies that they previously had gone to Egypt repeatedly, and were to do so no more, which would suggest that the text is not referring to their most recent departure from that country. Indeed, according to the biblical narratives, Egypt had long been seen as a place of refuge from the vicissitudes of drought and famine in the land promised to the Patriarchs. Thus, Abraham went there because of famine (Gen. 12:10), Isaac was about to go there for the same reason before he was dissuaded from doing so by God (Gen. 26:2), and Jacob and his sons also went there for the same reason. The injunction against doing so again in the future seems intended to cause the children of Israel to stop viewing Egypt as a naturally superior land because of its lack of dependence on rain as its source of water and fertility. It insists "you shall not go from Palestine to Egypt as in the past to obtain from there any national necessities which your own land does not supply. You are not to make yourselves dependent on Egypt."[777] Instead, they are to conduct themselves according to the covenant, and by so doing they will ensure their continued wellbeing in the land to which they are about to enter, and will have no further need of an external refuge in times of crisis.

The personal disabilities imposed on the king are perhaps best exemplified by the injunction *neither shall he multiply wives to himself, that his heart turn not away*. Here again the injunction applies exclusively to the king, and not to the people at-large. It is the king above all others who must be wary of submitting to a life of licentiousness and profligacy. His personal morality must be exemplary. The injunction clearly reflects the realities of court life in the ancient Middle East from antiquity to modern times, where "the evils and intrigues of harem-rule" were commonplaces.[778]

It is noteworthy that the rabbis of the land of Israel, living under Roman rule, apparently did not view this text from the latter perspective, perhaps because polygamy was not an acceptable Roman practice and Roman rulers did not maintain harems. Thus we find the curious assertion that the injunction *neither shall he multiply wives to himself* means that he may have no more than eighteen wives,[779] *that his heart turn not away.* As one commentator notes, the passage does not say that the king should not have many wives because "they will turn his heart away," but rather that *his heart turn not away.* The intent of this is that "even without any direct corrupting influence, his heart will become estranged from the spiritually high seriousness of the life of duty of a king."[780] This view finds expression, albeit somewhat cryptically, in the often repeated rabbinic fable concerning King Solomon's penchant for collecting spouses. "When Solomon married Pharaoh's daughter, Gabriel descended and stuck a reed in the sea, which gathered a sandbank around it, on which was built the great city of Rome."[781] By his act—which contributed to his violation of the biblical injunction against a king having many wives—Solomon is considered as having precipitated a series of events that ultimately led to the destruction of the Second Hebrew Commonwealth by the Romans. The significance of this fable in rabbinic thought has been summarized as follows: "By this, his moral weakness, he [Solomon] laid the foundations of a hostile world, symbolized by the Talmud as Rome, which overthrew Israel."[782]

With regard to the third of the biblical injunctions directed at the king, concerning the accumulation of wealth, *neither shall he greatly multiply to himself silver and gold*, the rabbis taught: "I might think [this applied] even for *aspanya* [supply and pay for the army]. Therefore Scripture writes *to himself*; only for himself he may not multiply silver and gold, but he may do so for *aspanya*."[783] Some view this restriction as a disincentive for the king to levy extortionate taxes on the public or to engage in remunerative but illegitimate financial practices.[784]

> [17.18] *And it shall be, when he sitteth upon the throne of his kingdom, that he shall write him a copy of this Torah in a book, out of that which is before the priests the Levites.* [17.19] *And it shall be with him, and he shall read therein all the days of his life; that he may learn to fear YHVH his Elohim, to keep all the words of this Torah and these*

statutes, to do them; [17.20] *that his heart be not lifted up above his brethren, and that he turn not aside from the commandment, to the right hand, or to the left; to the end that he may prolong his days in his kingdom, he and his children, in the midst of Israel.*

Moses insists that the future king, once ascending to the throne, is to reinforce his understanding of his obligations and constraints by obtaining a personal *copy of this Torah*, without specifying precisely what he meant by *this Torah*. Thus the translators that produced the Septuagint assumed that it referred to the entirety of the book containing the discourses of Moses, and therefore named it the Second Law or Deuteronomy. The rabbis considered it as containing all five books of the Pentateuch because it states that the king is *to keep all the words of this Torah and these statutes,* and this encompasses more than what is mentioned in Deuteronomy.[785] In this regard, some have argued that the phrase *mishne haTorah*, translated as *a copy of this Torah*, literally means "a doubling of the Torah," indicating that the king was to write two copies of the Torah, one to be retained in his treasury and the other to accompany him at all times.[786] However, it has been suggested that the copy that the king carried with him at all times was not the entire Torah, which would have been impractical, but rather just the Decalogue.[787] Alternatively, the text could be considered as referring particularly to the section of the Torah discussed in this chapter, that is, the section dealing with the organization of government and its institutions, which would be of paramount concern to a person entrusted with the fate of the nation.

In any case, the king's *copy of this Torah* is to be written *in a book, out of that which is before the priests the Levites.* That is, since the levitical priests were the designated guardians of the biblical revelations, the king's copy was to be made from the actual codex in their possession, and not from another copy of it, to assure that it contained no scribal errors that might mislead him with regard to the true meaning and intent of the inscribed law. However, this requirement was not intended to be purely symbolic; Moses not only demands that *it shall be with him,* but also that *he shall read therein all the days of his life; that he may learn to fear*

YHVH his Elohim, to keep all the words of this Torah and these statutes, to do them. The book of the law is to be his constant guide as he proceeds to deal with the innumerable problems and issues that will confront him as ruler of a nation and a state. Studying it continually will not only imprint its wisdom on his mind, but will inspire him to profound reverence for God and to observance of all that God expects of him as His viceroy. It has also been suggested that the underlying rationale for this demand is because once he ascends the throne, as a rule, no one will dare to rebuke him for any of his actions. Accordingly, constant study of the Torah will serve as a constant reminder of his position relative to God and thus serve as a safeguard against the arbitrary and improper use of his power.[788]

In this regard, one of the avowed purposes of the king's continuous engagement with the text of the Torah, as Moses puts it, is *that his heart be not lifted up above his brethren.* Study of the Torah will impress upon him that before God he is no different or better than any other Israelite who is faithful to the covenant. He must never allow the trappings of his office, and the privileges that pertain thereto, to mislead him into thinking of himself as more than just an ordinary human entrusted with great responsibilities for the welfare of the people of whom he is a member. A second goal is *that he turn not aside from the commandment, to the right hand, or to the left; to the end that he may prolong his days in his kingdom, he and his children, in the midst of Israel.* It is a reminder to every future king that his tenure and that of his dynasty is wholly dependent upon God's favor, and that may be expected to continue for as long as the king is a trustworthy adherent to the covenant, which he must follow faithfully and without deviation for the sake of expediency. In this regard, it has been suggested that the demand *that he turn not aside from the commandment* means that "the king too is forbidden to put himself at a distance from the Torah of Moses even by so much as a hairbreadth . . . and there is no difference between the king and the people except with regard to financial matters as well as those matters that touch upon the life of the nation. These are acquiesced in because of the general welfare realized through the improvement of the state. However, in the absence of this circumstance, the law of the Torah reassumes its position of primacy."[789]

Addressing the role of the priesthood and the Levites in the constitutional framework he is setting forth, Moses emphasizes, presumably based on his own experience growing up as a member of Egyptian royalty, that the abuses typical of a priestly class empowered by material wealth must be precluded as a matter of urgency. The priesthood must be prevented from attaining material power in addition to that which they exercise almost by definition over the spiritual and emotional lives of the people by virtue of their vocation. Accordingly, their income may not come from landed wealth but from the contributions of worshippers.

> *18.1 The priests the Levites, even all the tribe of Levi, shall have no portion nor inheritance with Israel; they shall eat the offerings of YHVH made by fire, and His inheritance. 18.2 And they shall have no inheritance among their brethren; YHVH is their inheritance, as He hath spoken unto them.*

Moses affirms that the levitical priests, as well as the entire tribe of Levi, are to lose their tribal status, because they are not to have a share in the land. Instead, they are to become a fundamental component of the central government, with special status in regard to all matters of a religious nature, including both worship and education. As such, they are to have no political allegiance to any tribe or clan among which they may work and reside. Freed from direct time consuming participation in the agricultural economy, they can devote their energies entirely to the spiritual needs of the nation, a task essential to its future viability. As indicated earlier, the functions of the priests and the Levites are differentiated by priestly and ministerial functions, the priests' primary concern being the complex sacrificial rites, that of the Levites with the maintenance and upkeep of the sanctuary and the highly significant role of teacher to the masses, a role also performed by the priests between tours of duty at the sanctuary, as indicated by the text referring primarily to the Levites but also to some priests and laymen, *And they taught in Judah, having the book of the Torah of YHVH with them; and they went about throughout all the cities of Judah, and taught among the people* (2 Chron. 17:9).[790] Because of the vast disparity in numbers between the levitical priests and the Levites, their sources of income must reflect their relative numbers, and are addressed separately in the following passages.

With regard to the priests and the Levites, their income, in part, shall derive from *the offerings of YHVH made by fire, and His inheritance.* The *offerings* are understood to refer to the burnt offering; the meal offering; the thanksgiving offering, and the trespass offering, certain parts of which belong to the priests. By *His inheritance*, the text is referring to what is appropriated to God and from Him to the tribe of Levi, which includes such as the heave-offerings, the tithes, and the first fruits.[791] The phrase, *as He hath spoken unto them*, appears to be a reference to the earlier text: *And YHVH said unto Aaron: 'Thou shalt have no inheritance in their land, neither shalt thou have any portion among them; I am thy portion and thine inheritance among the children of Israel* (Num. 18:20).

> [18.3] *And this shall be the priests' due from the people, from them that offer a sacrifice, whether it be ox or sheep, that they shall give unto the priest the shoulder, and the two cheeks, and the maw.* [18.4] *The first fruits of thy corn, of thy wine, and of thy oil, and the first of the fleece of thy sheep, shalt thou give him.* [18.5] *For YHVH thy Elohim hath chosen him out of all thy tribes, to stand to minister in the name of YHVH, him and his sons forever.*

The opening of this passage, *And this shall be the priests' due from the people*, clearly indicates that what follows represents the in-kind payment owed to the priests. However, there is also a subtlety in the Hebrew text that is largely obscured by the translation. Thus the Hebrew phrase, *mishpat hakohanim*, translated as *the priests' due*, more literally speaks of the "judgment of the priests," which led some rabbis to argue that this meant "these dues may be claimed through the judges."[792] That is, according to this reading, the priests would have an enforceable legal claim to such dues, which seems reasonable given that they were to be a primary source of income for the priests, who were effectively shut out from direct participation in the economy, for, as the text states, *YHVH thy Elohim hath chosen him out of all thy tribes, to stand to minister in the name of YHVH, him and his sons forever.* Since the priesthood is established by divine fiat, and there is no element of voluntarism on their part involved, their support and maintenance becomes a legally enforceable public obligation. In effect, the dues referred to in this passage, which augment those previously mentioned elsewhere, "those which accrued from the animals slaughtered for ordinary consumption, as distinguished from those brought as sacrifices,"[793] are a mandated in-kind tax to support the staff of one of the major institutions of Israelite government. However, some dispute this interpretation of the text on the basis that "the notion of sending parts of every animal slaughtered for food, in every part of the country, to the priests at the central sanctuary is unrealistic."[794] Nonetheless, it appears that this was the way the text was read and understood in antiquity, as may be inferred from the early commentary, "but from the victims which are sacrificed away from the altar, in order to be eaten, it is commanded that three portions should be given to the priest, an arm, and a jaw-bone, and that which is called the paunch."[795] However, neither the text nor the latter commentary, which dates from the period when the sacrificial rites were still performed, actually specifies that the priests to whom these dues are owed must be present at the central sanctuary; they might as well be located in the communities around the country where they performed the same role as the Levites, as teachers.

It is noteworthy that some later rabbis challenged the notion that an individual priest might make such a legal claim for the dues on the basis that "it is property which has no definite claimant."[796] That is, it is illogical to argue that any individual priest could make a legal claim to these dues, since every priest could make the identical claim prior to its actually having been given to someone. And since this is the case, the *mishpat hakohen* must be understood as implying that the dues "are to be distributed by the [advice of the] court."[797] In other words, since the priests, as a class, have legal claim to these dues, but cannot make a valid claim as individual priests, the court must determine the manner of equitable distribution among the priesthood.

In this regard, it should be borne in mind that over time the descendents of Aaron, who were marked for the priesthood from birth, would far exceed the number present at the time of Moses' delivery of this discourse. Indeed, within a few generations the number of priests would far exceed the number required for service in the sanctuary, and a system of shifts or watches would have to be instituted to provide opportunities for them to participate in the sacred rites. This would mean that serving as a priest in the sanctuary, perhaps with the exception of the high priest and his retinue of assistants, would become in effect a part-time job, making the matter of the sustenance of the priests a matter of national concern, an issue addressed in the biblical texts only to a very limited extent.

As already intimated above, the phrase, *zovehei hazevah*, translated as *them that offer a sacrifice*, has traditionally been understood as meaning *those who perform the slaughter*, as in the ArtScroll translation, referring to the slaughter of non-consecrated animals,[798] the consecrated gifts having been discussed in detail earlier (Num. 18). Accordingly, of the oxen or sheep brought for slaughter for personal consumption, *they shall give unto the priest the shoulder, and the two cheeks, and the maw*, or stomach. The reason for dedicating precisely these parts of the animals for the priests is not given, and the rabbis, who evidently were unable to come up with any plausible rationale for it, tended to refer to some allegorical and metaphorical explanations for the choices of body parts that seem rather strained and will not be discussed here.[799] Others, in search of a more reasonable explanation, have connected the choices of animal parts with the second order of dues listed in the text, *the first fruits of thy corn, of thy wine, and of thy oil, and the first of the fleece of thy sheep*. It has been asserted, "all first produces have been assigned to God so that the moral quality of generosity be strengthened and the appetite for eating and for acquisition be weakened. The *Priest's* receiving *the shoulder, the two jaws, and the stomach* has the same meaning; for *jaws* are a primary part of the body of the animal, and *the shoulder* is the right shoulder and is also the first part that has branched off from the body, and the *stomach* is the first of all the intestines."[800] In this regard, it has been observed that the *jaws* as such are merely bones and of no particular value, and hardly worthy of being given as a gift to the priests. Accordingly, the sages rendered the term *lehayayim*, translated as *jaws*, as "cheeks," the modern meaning of the term, and defined it as including everything "from the bend of the jaw to the knob of the windpipe," which includes the tongue.[801] Alternatively, it has been suggested that the body of the animal was divided into three parts, the head, the trunk, and the extremities, and part of each was to be given to the priests.[802] Another opinion suggests a symbolic significance to the several parts; the *shoulder* being an allusion to the power of motion, the *jaws* to the power of speech, "for the stream of speech could not flow out without the motion of these jaws,"[803] and the *stomach* to the power of nourishment. By giving these gifts to the priest, the donor symbolically dedicates all of his power to the service of God.[804] With regard to *the first of the fleece of thy sheep*, the people are admonished: "It is up to them to see that their priests get the wherewithal to dress respectably so that their outward appearance should not be prejudicial or detrimental in any way to the influence they are to exert among the people."[805]

Finally, the expression, *to stand to minister in the name of YHVH*, was understood as stipulating that the priests service had to be performed while standing; "only standing, in the position of awaiting the orders of a superior and carrying them out, does he bear the character of having been chosen for service."[806] The rabbis thus ruled that any sacrifice performed while sitting was invalid.[807]

Having dealt with the dues owed to the levitical priesthood, Moses turns to the much larger body of levitical ministers before God, the non-priestly members of the now economically disenfranchised tribe of Levi.

> [18.6] *And if a Levite come from any of thy gates out of all Israel, where he sojourneth, and come with all the desire of his soul unto the place which YHVH shall choose;* [18.7] *then he shall minister in the name of YHVH his Elohim, as all his brethren the Levites do, who stand there before YHVH.* [18.8] *They shall have like portions to eat, beside that which is his due according to the fathers' houses.*

In this passage, Moses implicitly acknowledges that the economic disenfranchisement of the Levites creates some potentially problematic issues relating to their economic welfare, similar to but far exceeding is scope that discussed above with regard to the priests. For one thing, the text acknowledges that only a relatively small number of the Levites will actually be able to live in the capital, and that at the same time, being landless, generally will have no permanent homes. In effect they will be sojourners among the tribes of Israel, earning their keep from being teachers and recipients of the numerous provisions mentioned elsewhere for their material sustenance. Moreover, as with the priests, a system of shifts or watches would be required to allow a rotation of levitical personnel to serve the needs of the sanctuary, which is their primary divinely mandated mission. According to one tradition recorded by the rabbis, Moses instituted eight *mishmarot* or watches, which were sufficient to accommodate the numbers of clergy in the early years. However, by the time of David, some three centuries later, they were increased to twenty-four watches to meet the need.[808] On the other hand, it has been suggested that a plain reading of the text indicates that Moses issued this instruction as a temporary measure prior to the finalization of the system of watches.[809] Given the tenuous nature of their subsistence as sojourners, the periodic tour of duty at the sanctuary assured a level of economic security otherwise unavailable to most other Levites at the same time, and was therefore highly prized.

What Moses appears to be addressing in this passage is the concern that among the Levites there will be some, possibly many, who will feel a spiritual need to *come with all the desire of his soul unto the place which YHVH shall choose*, at a time other than when his assigned period of rotation is to commence. Moses is concerned that the appearance of such unscheduled Levites at the sanctuary may be resisted by those Levites serving there in their normal rotation. The presence of additional Levites, without a commensurate increase in the number of worshippers, would mean an automatic redistribution of income to them. Nonetheless, from Moses' perspective, it would be unconscionable to refuse to allow a Levite, who came to the sanctuary out of devotion to God, to carry out the functions for which he was economically disenfranchised so that he might perform them without extraneous concerns. Accordingly, Moses ordained, *he shall minister in the name of YHVH his Elohim, as all his brethren the Levites do, who stand there before YHVH.*

It is noteworthy that the text also asserts *They shall have like portions to eat, beside that which is his due according to the fathers' houses.* The phrase, *levad mimkarav al ha'avot,* translated as *beside that which is his due according to the fathers' houses,* literally states, "besides his sales according to the fathers." This presumably refers to the proceeds of the sale of personal possessions inherited from his ancestors, or of private income accruing to him for services rendered such as giving lessons.[810] It has also been suggested that the phrase refers to income derived, during periods of heavy attendance at the sanctuary, when the volume of sacrifices and tithes far exceeded the ability of the officiating priests and Levites to consume the portions of the gifts allocated to them, and the surplus was sold to off-duty persons eligible to eat of them.[811] The point Moses is making is that the availability of such extra income in no way invalidates his right to share emoluments given to the sanctuary along with the others. Put in modern terms, no personal means test is to be applied to an itinerant priest or Levite before they may share in the dues allotted to those officiating in the sanctuary.

Of course, this should not be a serious problem, and one that the Levites on duty at the sanctuary could accommodate easily, if it concerned only a random levitical pilgrim. However, it would become a more serious problem if large numbers of such unscheduled levitical pilgrims appeared in the capital at any one time. Once again, the text does not deal with the practical implications of Moses' ruling, and it is not clear how the problem was dealt with historically, if it ever arose in practice. However, it does exemplify the consideration that many of the edicts given by Moses are actually precepts rather than detailed rules or even guidelines, the responsibility for working out the latter falling upon later authorities.

It should be noted, however, that the rabbis interpreted the entire passage as relating exclusively to the priests and not at all to the Levites as such. The presumed rationale for this is the statement, *then he shall minister in the name of YHVH his Elohim,* which "refers to those who are fit for ministering, thus excluding Levites who are not fit for ministering."[812] This argument, of course, is necessarily predicated on a very restricted view of what constitutes ministering, essentially ignoring the variety of activities performed by the Levites that were part of the sanctuary ritual, such as providing music and song, and assisting the priests. Indeed, there is a minority opinion among the rabbis that clearly supports the notion that our text does refer to the Levites and not the priests, on the basis that the text *then he shall minister in the name of YHVH his Elohim* refers to providing song, and it is the Levites and not the priests that sang in the sanctuary.[813] Although many or perhaps even most traditional commentators have adopted the majority view of the rabbis,[814] it nonetheless may be inconsistent with the plain meaning of the text, which can be read as referring to the ministry of the Levites,[815] and has been so understood by some.[816] Moreover, by excluding the Levites from the scope of the text, it leaves a substantial gap in accounting for the situation of the Levites at the sanctuary.

Moses now returns once again to the theme that seems to haunt him throughout the discourses, his concern about the future viability of the nation and state in the land they are about to enter, which in his view is wholly dependent upon compliance with the covenant. And the greatest threat to such compliance is the seeming inability of the people to comprehend in their inner being that the covenant is predicated on unconditional acceptance of monotheism, and that any deviation from this constitutes a breach of the covenant that portends the potential consequences of extreme divine displeasure. His immediate concern, given his assessment of the state of the people in this regard, is with the challenges presented by the variety of polytheistic practices of the peoples they will encounter in the land they are about to enter, practices abhorrent to God but undertaken with alacrity by those peoples.

> [18.9] *When thou art come into the land which YHVH thy Elohim giveth thee, thou shalt not learn to do after the abominations of those nations.* [18.10] *There shall not be found among you any one that maketh his son or his daughter to pass through the fire, one that useth divination, a soothsayer, or an enchanter, or a sorcerer,* [18.11] *or a charmer, or one that consulteth a ghost or a familiar*

spirit, or a necromancer. ^{18.12} *For whosoever doeth these things is an abomination unto YHVH; and because of these abominations YHVH thy Elohim is driving them out from before thee.* ^{18.13} *Thou shalt be wholehearted with YHVH thy Elohim.*

Moses opens with a general warning, *thou shalt not learn to do after the abominations of those nations*, and then proceeds to a comprehensive outline of what those *abominations* consist. First and foremost, he categorically forbids the common pagan practice of child sacrifice, making *his son or his daughter to pass through the fire*, which was an essential component of the worship of Moloch.[817] Next in order of priority is the prohibition of *divination*, which takes a number of forms, such as soothsaying, auguring, or sorcery. Next he forbids dealing in spells such as snake charming, holding séances to communicate with ghosts or familiar spirits, or necromancy or attempting to communicate with the dead. Anyone who participates in such practices is an abomination to God.

Moses emphasizes that it is precisely because of these abominable practices by the peoples of the land that God is facilitating their expulsion by the Israelites about to enter the land and displace them. And, he warns further, it is inconceivable that God would tolerate in Israel the same abominable practices carried on by those He was expelling from the land in their favor. Accordingly, Moses declares, viability as a nation in the land demands that *thou shalt be wholehearted with YHVH thy Elohim.* But what constitutes wholeheartedness? Given the context of the passage, in one opinion, it means you should expect to find through God alone that which others seek through these various abominable practices.[818] Or, as another put it, you should not attempt to find a place in your belief system for demoniacal powers or evil superstitions.[819] As indicated below, God will assign prophets to convey to the people that which He wishes them to know. As the pagan seer Balaam put it: *For there is no enchantment with Jacob, neither is there any divination with Israel* (Num. 23:23). It also has been suggested that the thrust of the latter adjuration is that one should not be overly concerned about the unforeseeable future and should desist from attempting to divine it through devious methods. Instead, one should place complete trust in God and wholeheartedly accept what God has in store for him.[820]

It is noteworthy that when Abraham was about to enter into the covenant through the act of circumcision, God announced, *I am El Shaddai; walk before Me and be thou wholehearted* (Gen. 17:1). Although this may be interpreted as saying put all pagan beliefs and practices behind and by so doing you will be wholehearted, it seems a rather stretched explanation, given that Abraham had surely put such things behind long before. In this instance, it has been suggested that the adjuration *be thou wholehearted* means not asking why God is demanding circumcision.[821] According to this interpretation, being wholehearted means suspension of intellect in favor of total unquestioning acceptance, a stance that others reject completely, arguing that being wholehearted with God does not mean naïve and simplistic acceptance, but rather attainment of profound philosophical insight that will convince one of the follies of belief in things like sorcery.[822]

However, it has also been pointed out that the text is speaking of wholehearted acceptance of what comes with respect to God, but not necessarily with respect to man. Man has been given free will, which includes the ability to perpetrate evil, and what he may choose to do should not be construed as though it were divinely ordained. Accordingly, "if one man treats another harshly, the victim need not accept this as the will of God, but has the right to take action to protect himself."[823]

It has been observed that the injunction in this passage is *thou shalt not learn to do after the abominations of those nations*, which raises the question of whether you should learn and teach your children how to act against them to curtail if not eliminate their influence entirely. As the rabbis put it: "You might think that you are not permitted to learn and instruct about them, or to understand them; therefore the verse says, *to do*—you may not learn (their ways) in order to do them, but you may learn them in order to instruct and to understand.[824] With this in mind, it has been proposed that, at least for those who might have to sit in judgment with regard to a violation of this injunction, they be "somewhat acquainted with astrology, the arts of diviners, soothsayers, sorcerers, the superstitious practices of idolaters, and similar matters, so that they be competent to deal with cases requiring such knowledge."[825]

> [18.14] *For these nations, that thou art to dispossess, hearken unto soothsayers, and unto diviners; but as for thee, YHVH thy Elohim hath not suffered thee so to do.* [18.15] *A prophet will YHVH thy Elohim raise up unto thee, from the midst of thee, of thy brethren, like unto me; unto him shall ye hearken;* [18.16] *according to all that thou didst desire of YHVH thy Elohim in Horeb in the day of the assembly, saying: 'Let me not hear again the voice of YHVH my Elohim, neither let me see this great fire any more, that I die not.'* [18.17] *And YHVH said unto me: 'They have well said that which they have spoken.* [18.18] *I will raise them up a prophet from among their brethren, like unto thee; and I will put My words in his mouth, and he shall speak unto them all that I shall command him.* [18.19] *And it shall come to pass, that whosoever will not hearken unto My words which he shall speak in My name, I will require it of him.'* [18.20] *But the prophet, that shall speak a word presumptuously in My name, which I have not commanded him to speak, or that shall speak in the name of other gods, that same prophet shall die.'*

Moses acknowledges that it is part of human nature to want to know the secrets of the universe, of life and death, and what lies beyond the grave, secrets that are beyond man's grasp, and that in pursuit of such knowledge and insight men have erroneously turned to charlatans such as diviners and soothsayers. Such as these, however, are mere pretenders to secret knowledge, which they do not and cannot possess, but to which the heathen nations turn nonetheless. *But as for thee, YHVH thy Elohim hath not suffered thee so to do.* Accordingly, Moses asserts, instead of turning to such charlatans, *A prophet will YHVH thy Elohim raise up unto thee, from the midst of thee, of thy brethren, like unto me; unto him shall ye hearken.* The divinely appointed prophet is not intended to be a surrogate for these charlatans, for which Israel has no need.[826] Instead, he will tell you truthfully what you can or cannot know, and more to the point, how you should act in the absence of the certain knowledge of that which you may desire to obtain, but will never achieve while you yet live.

In this text, Moses announces the institutionalization of prophecy as a constitutionally mandated component of political society, but does not specify what the function of the prophet is and how it relates to the other institutions of government. Nonetheless, upon close examination, the statement *A prophet will YHVH thy Elohim raise up unto thee, from the midst of thee, of thy brethren, like unto me; unto him shall ye hearken* may be seen as containing five elements from which a fuller picture of the prophetic institution may be inferred.

The first element is reflected in the statement *A prophet will YHVH thy Elohim raise up unto thee*, which makes it quite clear that the true prophet and prophecy originates from God's wish to communicate to the people. In this regard, one view sees the prophet serving as a complement to the priest with regard to the divine communications to Israel. As one commentator put it: "The role of the priest is to preserve the Torah [the divine revelations granted to Moses at Horeb] . . . The role of the prophet is to relate to the people the word of God that was revealed anew."[827] Another takes the position that the primary function of the prophet is to elaborate on the practical application of the biblical precepts, in accordance with some ill-defined legislative authority that presumably has been granted to him. It is argued that this is imperative in order to ensure that there be an authoritative standard accepted by the people as bearing the divine imprimatur, "for if we were to defer in these matters to our own opinions, our views would differ and we would not agree on anything."[828] Similarly, it has been argued that prophecy is necessary so that "men may be guided toward eternal happiness, that they may know through what is agreeable to God and what is not, and that they may attain to the destiny intended for mankind by doing those things which are agreeable to God."[829] This approach is "predicated on the assumption that man is both in need of, and entitled to, divine guidance. For God to reveal His word through the prophet to His people is an act of justice. The purpose of prophecy is to maintain the covenant, to establish the right relationship between God and man."[830]

These views of the prophet and prophecy obviously are rather different than the notion of a prophet as a seer relating visions of the future, or as a human transcription machine repeating messages received from on high. This is not to suggest that, through divine inspiration, prophets may not prove extraordinarily capable of profound insight into the probable course of events. However, such a capability is never conceived of in the biblical literature as an end in itself, but is always employed didactically by the prophet in pursuit of the higher moral purpose of redirecting men to the proper moral and political path. As one writer phrased it: "The function of the prophet is to admonish the people in order that they should follow the path of the Torah, and . . . not to depart from the Torah to follow an unpaved way; also to give abundant warning that their end will be bad and bitter if they abandon the Torah of Moses."[831] In sum, these opinions all agree that the principal purpose of the prophetic institution "is not to foretell the future or to regulate particular matters that interest individuals, such as are communicated by diviners and star-gazers, but to enable a whole nation or the entire human race to attain human perfection."[832]

These opinions are also all predicated on the proposition that the course that will lead to human perfection is fully charted in the Torah, and it is through adherence to and observance of the precepts of the Torah that man will find his way along the road. It becomes the mission of the prophet to assist the wayward by reorienting them to the appropriate path. Accordingly, the prophet who is true to his responsibility can only be one whose predilections and prescriptions are in conformity with the fundamental aims and precepts of the Torah.

The implication of this description is that, in essence, the prophetic institution called for in the Torah is intended to be reformist in character rather than revolutionary, by contrast with a typically modern notion of what makes one a prophet. The biblical prophet does not seek to overturn the government and assume direct political leadership. On the contrary, he seeks to bring about the realization of the good society within the framework of existing legitimate institutions. He is a reformer, not a revolutionary. However, where such institutions are plagued by corruption, he does not hesitate to raise his voice publicly in an effort to bring about the necessary reforms. The true prophet does not create an organization around his central leadership. His position and function are unique and personal, and therefore are not transferable to others. *A prophet will YHVH thy Elohim raise up unto thee*; it is God alone that makes one a prophet. "In a sense, the calling of the prophet may be described as that of an advocate or champion, speaking for those who are to weak to plead their own cause. Indeed, the major activity of the biblical prophets was interference, remonstrating about wrongs inflicted on other people, meddling in affairs which were seemingly neither their concern nor their responsibility."[833]

The second element in the statement, *A prophet will YHVH thy Elohim raise up unto thee, from the midst of thee*, has been understood by the rabbis as meaning "from the midst of thee and not outside the land."[834] In other words, the institution of prophecy, after Moses, is conceived as functionally related to the maintenance of an organized political society in the territorial context of the land of Israel. Although the literature provides a number of possible explanations of the fact that the biblical writings provide examples of prophecies that took place outside the confines of the land, the central point is that the prophetic institution was a critical component of the Israelite state, created *from the midst of thee*, making it both unnecessary and inappropriate to seek guidance from abroad, that is, from the wise men of the surrounding nations.

If the text had concluded at this point, it could be interpreted as suggesting that there would always be prophets in the land of Israel, irrespective of the character of the population inhabiting the country. Accordingly, a third element is added to the text, *A prophet will YHVH thy Elohim raise up unto thee, from the midst of thee, of thy brethren*. The last clause, *of thy brethren* has been interpreted as suggesting that the prophet that emerges will be someone known to you, "no mysterious secret obscurity will hover over them . . . they will be human beings and claim to be nothing but human beings."[835] Moreover, the text thus indicates that the prophetic institution must exist within a distinctively Israelite national context. The stipulation, *of thy brethren*, is considered as excluding from prophecy anyone not *of thy brethren*, that is, of anyone not considered an Israelite.[836] The prophetic institution is thus considered uniquely related to the people of Israel on account of their special covenantal relationship to the Torah. In this manner, institutional prophecy will become a truly national phenomenon, but only when the nation is constituted within its prescribed national territory.

The fourth element in the biblical text, *A prophet will YHVH thy Elohim raise up unto thee, from the midst of thee, of thy brethren, like unto me*, is somewhat more problematical. An early Aramaic translation renders the phrase *like unto me* as meaning, "as I am with respect to divine inspiration."[837] The implication of this is that the prophet must in some way be comparable to Moses. However, any such comparison is fraught with obstacles in view of the explicit biblical assertion *there hath not arisen a prophet since in Israel like unto Moses, whom YHVH knew face to face* (Deut. 34:10). The nature of the relationship between Moses and his prophetic successors becomes critical to the determination of the character and scope of their authority, as well as the criteria for acceptance as a prophet. In this regard, it is noteworthy that nowhere in the Torah including the text just cited is Moses actually referred to as a prophet; he is called *My servant* (Num. 12:7-8) or *man of Elohim* (Deut. 33:1). This should not be misconstrued as asserting that Moses was not a prophet, which he was, but rather that he was also much more. "Apparently, despite the status of the prophet as God's messenger, the title 'prophet' was felt to be too narrow and too restricted, at least in the popular mind, to oracular, divinatory, and magical functions to be applied to a figure as exalted and comprehensive as Moses."[838]

It should be borne in mind that the prophetic role is an individual one, even though it has institutional characteristics. It involves the authority and mission of the single prophet. There is no subordinate organization to which he can delegate functions or powers. Moreover, there are no procedures for succession. Accession to the position of prophet is by divine selection alone. Nonetheless, since it is an individual that is selected for the office, there must be some basic means by which the public readily can determine his probable legitimacy. This, presumably, is provided for by Moses' declaration that the successor to the office of prophet shall be *like unto me*.

After examining the character of the various adjectives used to describe Moses in the biblical writings, the rabbis derived certain fundamental criteria by which to determine if one in their midst is in fact comparable to Moses. Thus, one opinion held, "The Holy One does not permit His Presence to rest except upon one who is strong, wealthy, wise, and humble, and all [these criteria] are derived from Moses."[839] Another view asserts, "The Holy presence does not rest except upon one who is wise, strong, wealthy and tall."[840] Despite the obvious difference between "humble" and "tall" as qualifying criteria, the essential point of these listings of criteria make the same point, which is that the prophet must be capable of exuding charisma, if he is to be successful in his mission. That is, his status and obvious qualities must be such as to command attention and respect.

There are, however, two distinct schools among commentators on the matter of these criteria, one interpreting the stipulated criteria metaphorically, the other school taking them literally. The metaphorical school bases its interpretation of the criteria on the manner in which one noted rabbinic sage taught: "Who is wise? He who learns from all men . . . Who is strong? He who subdues his passions . . . Who is wealthy? He who rejoices in his portion."[841] An influential medieval advocate of this approach wrote: "The spirit of prophecy does not rest on any other than a wise man, great in wisdom, strong in his attributes, such that his desires do not overpower him in regard to anything in the world, but that he always overcomes his desire by force of his intellect, and maintains comprehensive and highly proper opinions."[842]

The metaphorical interpretation is rejected by the literalists, who insist that "where the Talmud speaks of strong, it means the word literally—that he should be a man of physical strength, and the same with wealthy—that he should literally have a large amount of money."[843] This is not to suggest that the literalists reject the values promoted by the metaphorical interpretation, but rather that they insist that the prophet must literally possess these characteristics in order to gain sufficient credibility with the masses of the people, so that he also gain acceptance of the message that he brings to them. The literalist position is predicated on the judgment that the large majority of the people will show greater deference to intellect, wealth, and physical power in their ordinary meanings, qualities that are widely admired, than to less demonstrable spiritual attributes. It is therefore to be expected that the public will pay greater attention to a prophet who reflects these popular aspirations.[844] In this regard, it has been argued that all of these attributes were present in Moses, and that his prophetic successors should possess them as well, "because these attributes of the strong, the wise and the wealthy are the greatest virtues in the eyes of man . . . it is proper that a prophet, the messenger of the Lord, should not be deficient in them, and they [the rabbis] added [humility to the list of criteria] in order that he should not show pride in these attributes, that he should be as humble with respect to all these as was Moses."[845] Another commentator take the literalist position even farther by arguing that the literal interpretation of the criteria applies, not because of the likelihood of greater public acceptance of the prophet, but rather because without these attributes the prophet would be unable to carry out his mission properly. "God does not pick out weaklings, simpletons, or those who are socially dependent on others to be messengers of His Word."[846] Indeed, in that writer's view, "only an independent person, who requires nothing for himself and asks nothing for himself, can look on and understand men and things in that complete objectivity, without any, even subconscious, reference to himself, which is so necessary for a messenger of God."[847]

As suggested earlier, one of the basic stumbling blocks in making comparability to Moses a criterion for prophetic selection is the incompatibility of the text, *like unto me*, with *there has not arisen a prophet since in Israel like unto Moses* (Deut. 34:10). Since every prophet is necessarily considered comparable to Moses with regard to his attributes—irrespective of the different interpretations of the metaphorists and the literalists—the differences between Moses and his successors cannot be personal ones, and therefore must relate to the very nature of their missions as prophets. The distinguishing factor of paramount importance between Moses and the other prophets is generally considered to be the unique legislative role of Moses. With the issuance of the precepts and laws of the Torah, the superstructure of divine law is considered to be complete. As the text states: *These are the commandments which YHVH commanded Moses for the children of Israel on Mount Sinai* (Lev. 27:34). As read by the rabbis, this text affirms: "*These* are the commandments; no prophet is authorized to legislate anew from this time on."[848] Accordingly, the rabbis asserted, "You should not argue that another Moses has arisen that brings us a new Torah from heaven; there remains no other such Torah in heaven."[849]

It would thus appear that the role of the prophet lies primarily in preaching and moralizing to the public in a sustained effort to raise its ethical and religious awareness. However, the constitutional provision, *unto him ye shall hearken*, which announces an unequivocal obligation on the part of society to pay heed to the prophet, which would also apply to members of the other institutions that in the aggregate comprise the government of the Israelite state, seems to indicate a responsibility beyond that of exhorting reform of man and society. In effect, this text makes the prophet the highest authority in the land; even the king is obligated to heed him.

The rabbis understood this provision to mean that "even if he says to you: Transgress one of the precepts of the Torah . . . in accordance with the needs of the hour, you shall listen to him."[850] Thus, while the prophet is denied legislative authority, the rabbis inferred from the biblical text that this restriction only applied to permanent amendments to the Torah. However, there is a presumption that the prophet has been granted full ad hoc legislative authority to abrogate the law temporarily, in accordance with the needs of society at any particular point in its social and political life. The exception to this blanket ad hoc legislative authority concerns matters that could lead to the undermining of the foundations of the society. For example, the prophet's authority would not extend to even temporary abrogation of the laws forbidding idolatry, murder, or incest, crimes that traditionally have called for martyrdom rather than complicity in face of external compulsion. In other words, the prophet's ad hoc legislation must be geared toward meeting a particular social or political need that, in the long run, would derogate from the observance and fulfillment of the covenant in greater degree than would take place through a temporary abrogation of the law.

The nature of the prophetic mission and the scope of the prophet's authority and its place within the governmental framework set forth by

Moses present a highly complex prospect that is not dealt with in the biblical text, but is treated at length in the interpretive literature. Suffice it note at this point that the prophet appears to have been intended to play a unique constitutional role. He or she was to be possessed of the moral authority that would enable the prophet to offset the abuse of authority and power by any of the other constituent elements of government. It was partly through the creative tension fostered by the presence of the prophet that the promise of the properly ordered political society was to be realized.

Moses reminds the people that at Horeb, when they were privileged to hear the voice of God directly, they demurred, *'Let me not hear again the voice of YHVH my Elohim, neither let me see this great fire any more, that I die not.'* They preferred to hear the voice of God through His prophet Moses. *And YHVH said unto me: 'They have well said that which they have spoken. I will raise them up a prophet from among their brethren, like unto thee; and I will put My words in his mouth, and he shall speak unto them all that I shall command him. And it shall come to pass, that whosoever will not hearken unto My words which he shall speak in My name, I will require it of him.'* The people had made a choice and would have to stick with it. They would have to accept that whatever Moses and the prophets that followed him told them reflected the divine wish and had to be obeyed. Any who refused to do so would have to render account before God. The dilemma this created was that if the prophet that claimed to be the mouthpiece of God said things that came from his own mind and not from God, the people could be led to violate the covenant without concern that they were committing a transgression. It has been suggested in this regard that the people were obligated to obey the prophet, but only if he had previously established his prophetic bona fides, presumably by showing a sign as did Moses at the outset of his prophetic career.[851]

But, God warns, *the prophet, that shall speak a word presumptuously in My name, which I have not commanded him to speak, or that shall speak in the name of other gods, that same prophet shall die.* It has been pointed out that the statement, *which I have not commanded him to speak*, contains a nuance that merits explication. If the whole intent of the text is to refer to a prophet who says things that God did not, the text could have simply stated, "which I have not commanded to speak." By including the word *him* the text, according to the rabbis, seems to be suggesting that the prophet is not to say anything that was not communicated to him directly, that is, he is not to repeat something that might have been revealed to another prophet.[852]

As for the prophet that improperly purported to be speaking in God' name things that were of his own invention, or who had the temerity to *speak in the name of other gods,* which would be considered a capital offense, *that same prophet shall die.* A straightforward reading of the text would suggest that this meant that God would take his life at a time of His choosing and manner. Nonetheless, the rabbis reached the conclusion that any unspecified imposition of a sentence of death in the Torah signifies strangulation.[853] The presumed rationale for this is that of all the modes of execution by man, strangulation, in the manner specified by the rabbis, is either the most lenient, or in one view the one that leaves no visible mark on the body, just as a normal death by God leaves the body intact, a condition which, among the authorized forms of execution, only strangling fulfills.[854]

Having completed the verbatim citation of God's words, Moses turned to the obvious dilemma that needed to be resolved if the punishment of the deviant prophet was to be a death imposed by a court of law.

> *18.21 And if thou say in thy heart: 'How shall we know the word which YHVH hath not spoken?' 18.22 When a prophet speaketh in the name of YHVH, if the thing follow not, nor come to pass, that is the thing which YHVH hath not spoken; the prophet hath spoken it presumptuously, thou shalt not be afraid of him.*

The text clearly seems to be speaking of a prophet whose bona fides have already been established, since the question raised does not concern whether or not he or she is a prophet but rather whether the prophecy truly reflects the divine word. But why would this issue even arise unless, as has been suggested, another acknowledged prophet contradicted the announced prophecy? Accordingly, the issue raised in the text concerns how to determine which voice truly is conveying the divine word.[855]   In this regard, Moses already made it clear that if a prophet that has established his bona fides should say: *'Let us go after other gods, which thou hast not known, and let us serve them'; thou shalt not hearken unto the words of that prophet* (Deut. 13:2-4). Here, however, Moses is assumed to be referring to two prophecies that are consistent with the covenant, but only one of which can be true. The question that needs to be answered is *how shall we know the word which YHVH hath not spoken?*

The simple answer is that there is no way to establish the truth of the prophecy on an a priori basis. The best guidance that Moses can offer in such a case is to submit the prophecy to an empirical test. *When a prophet speaketh in the name of YHVH, if the thing follow not, nor come to pass, that is the thing which YHVH hath not spoken.* In other words, the empirical test of whether God had transmitted the word to the prophet that he pronounced is whether what he predicted actually occurs. An example of this found in a later text concerning the prophet Samuel: *And Samuel grew, and YHVH was with him, and did let none of his words fall to the ground. And all Israel from Dan even to Beer-sheba knew that Samuel was established to be a prophet of YHVH* (1 Sam. 3:19-20). Nothing he said in a prophetic sense failed to materialize, and on this basis he was acknowledged from one end of the country to the other as a true prophet.

The stipulated criteria for determining validity of the prophecy are *velo yiheyeh hadavar velo yavo* or *if the thing follow not, nor come to pass*, which seem redundant. However, it has been argued, although both phrases refer to something that does not occur, they refer to two different classes of events. The verb root *haya* employed with regard to prophecy in the first phrase, *velo yiheyeh hadavar* or *if the thing follow not*, is used typically in the biblical text to describe "the occurrence of a miracle in the sphere of nature which has been previously prophesied," such as those extraordinary events that Moses brought on before Pharaoh in Egypt, which are described with the use of this verb. By contrast, the verb root *bo* employed with regard to prophecy in the second phrase, *velo yavo* or *nor come to pass*, is typically used with regard to "the occurrence of events in the sphere of human conditions."[856] A failure in either category is sufficient to discredit a prophet and his prophecy.

This empirical approach to verification of the true prophet seems reasonable in the case where a prophet says it is necessary to do something to avert a particular imminent crisis or critical situation. However, if his word relates to a longer-term issue, it is difficult to see how the guidance is particularly helpful in reaching a conclusion before the covenant may be subverted to a significant extent. In any case, the text affirms, if the predicted situation did not arise, *the prophet hath spoken it presumptuously.* That is, the prophet is to be held liable for his presumptuousness in predicting in God's name something he was not told. In such a case, Moses instructs the people, *thou shalt not be afraid of him*; you may set aside the previous warning that *whosoever will not hearken unto My words which he shall speak in My name, I will require it of him* as inapplicable in this situation, and you should not desist "from arguing for his condemnation."[857]

Having concluded his description of the constitutional arrangement he has set forth, Moses turned his attention to the problem of phasing out the ancient custom of the blood avenger, to be discussed below, by absorbing this time-honored function within the framework of the national legal system to be established in the land. The first step in this direction involves the creation of cities of refuge.

> [19.1] *When YHVH thy Elohim shall cut off the nations, whose land YHVH thy Elohim giveth thee, and thou dost succeed them, and dwell in their cities, and in their houses;* [19.2] *thou shalt separate three cities for thee in the midst of thy land, which YHVH thy Elohim giveth thee to possess it.* [19.3] *Thou shalt prepare thee the way, and divide the borders of thy land, which YHVH thy Elohim causeth thee to inherit, into three parts, that every manslayer may flee thither.*

The text already noted that Moses had set aside three cities in Transjordan to serve as sites *that the manslayer might flee thither, that slayeth his neighbor unawares, and hated him not in time past* (Deut.

4:42). He now instructs the people to do likewise in the land they are about to enter, after they conquer and settle it. It has been observed that Moses stipulates *thou shalt separate three cities for thee*, the phrase *for thee* indicating that these cities of refuge were intended solely for the children of Israel and not for aliens found among them.[858] The rationale for this qualification appears to be that the covenant requires that in order for a wrongful death caused by one of its adherents to be considered the capital crime of murder, punishable by the imposition of a death penalty, the perpetrator must be forewarned against its commission. In the absence of such forewarning, which serves to determine whether the act was deliberate and not accidental, the presumption of innocence must assure that no harm comes to the manslayer before a thorough investigation of the incident is concluded. Aliens, who are not parties to the covenant, are not afforded such protection, and their flight to a city of refuge will be of no avail.[859]

Moses specifies further that the cities of refuge be located *in the midst of thy land*, presumably for ease of access, and not on its periphery. Moreover, *Thou shalt prepare thee the way*. That is, you are to make sure that access to these cities is not hampered by poor roads or obstructions; an implicit reminder that such ready access to a city of refuge may literally be a matter of life or death. Finally, you are to *divide the borders of thy land, which YHVH thy Elohim causeth thee to inherit, into three parts, that every manslayer may flee thither*. For purposes of selecting sites to serve as cities of refuge, the country should be subdivided into three parts and a city located in the heart of each subdivision to facilitate equal access to it for someone seeking refuge from any section of the designated region.

Moses then turns to a discussion of manslaughter as opposed to murder to clarify why such a measure as the provision of cities of refuge is considered essential.

> [19.4] *And this is the case of the manslayer, that shall flee thither and live: whoso killeth his neighbor unawares, and hated him not in times past;* [19.5] *as when a man goeth into the forest with his neighbor to hew wood, and his hand fetcheth a stroke with the axe to cut down the tree, and*

the head slippeth from the helve, and lighteth upon his neighbor, that he die; he shall flee unto one of these cities and live; [19.6] lest the avenger of blood pursue the manslayer, while his heart is hot, and overtake him, because the way is long, and smite him mortally; whereas he was not deserving, inasmuch as he hated him not in time past. [19.7] Wherefore I command thee, saying: 'Thou shalt separate three cities for thee.' [19.8] And if YHVH thy Elohim enlarge thy border, as He hath sworn unto thy fathers, and give thee all the land which He promised to give unto thy fathers [19.9] (if thou shalt keep all this commandment to do it, which I command thee this day, to love YHVH thy Elohim, and to walk ever in His ways) then shalt thou add three cities more for thee, beside these three; [19.10] that innocent blood be not shed in the midst of thy land, which YHVH thy Elohim giveth thee for an inheritance, and so blood be upon thee.

By definition, manslaughter is characterized as a category of wrongful death caused by someone who *killeth his neighbor unawares, and hated him not in times past.* That is, the death was not caused deliberately and there is no basis for suspicion that the manslayer had any motive for causing harm to the victim. For an example of a case of manslaughter, Moses posits a situation in which *a man goeth into the forest with his neighbor to hew wood, and his hand fetcheth a stroke with the axe to cut down the tree, and the head slippeth from the helve, and lighteth upon his neighbor, that he die.* In modern parlance, such an instance of causing a death would be termed "homicide by misadventure."[860] The rabbis read this text as purposive and attributed legal significance to the locale where the misadventure took place. "What is the nature of this forest? It is a domain affording [free] access to the injured as well as to the injurer. In like manner every place [of injury] must be a domain of free access to the injured as to the injurer [to involve liability for injury]."[861] That is, attribution of "homicide by misadventure" would not apply if the same event took place while one was chopping wood in his backyard and a neighbor intruded without first announcing his presence and obtaining permission to enter and was struck by a flying axe head. In other words, the example chosen by the text makes the critically important point that the injured party had the same right to be in the place as the injurer. The evident purpose of the example is to begin to set parameters for the application of the law of homicide.

In such a case, the manslayer *shall flee unto one of these cities and live; lest the avenger of blood pursue the manslayer, while his heart is hot, and overtake him, because the way is long, and smite him mortally.* The concern expressed here is that one who kills another unintentionally and by accident should not be subject to the wrath of the *avenger of blood* and unjustifiably be put to death for something for which *he was not deserving, inasmuch as he hated him not in time past.* However, this is not to suggest that the manslayer was to be adjudged innocent of murder and allowed to return to his home. By contrast with other inadvertent transgressions that may be atoned for by a sin-offering or a guilt-offering, that of bloodshed must be atoned for in a more direct manner. The fact that one did cause another's death, even if by accident, still demands expiation, and the law Moses sets down here is that his bloodguilt shall be expiated by his extended residence in the city of refuge, presumably as the only reasonable alternative to death at the hands of the awaiting *avenger of blood.*

It is generally assumed that the biblical *go'el hadam*, translated as *avenger of blood*, is a relic of ancient vendetta law. This form of homicide law is not concerned with matters such as motives or circumstances. It dictates that if a member of one clan kills a member of another clan, the latter must retaliate in kind, for if it fails to do so the injured clan would become the target for assault by others. In other words, retaliation in kind, life for life, helps maintain the existing power balance among competing clans or other such groups. It seems self-evident that a system of justice that takes into account motive, intention, and circumstances in determining whether a homicide merits a death penalty cannot coexist with vendetta law, which is not at all concerned with such matters. "Vendetta law is, in effect, a perpetual civil war between constituent elements of a state, and that its unbridled practice can have no other result than the destruction of the state."[862] Under vendetta law, the warrant to slay the perpetrator of homicide was assigned by custom to the clan or family *go'el,* whose purpose and mission was to restore the inter-clan or inter-tribal power balance.

It should be noted, however, that a serious misconception of the meaning of these terms seems to be in play here. The term *go'el* does not actually mean *avenger,* which is rendered by the Hebrew *nokem.* Quite to the contrary, *go'el* refers to one who is a *redeemer,* and the term *go'el hadam,* means not *avenger of blood,* but *redeemer of bloodguilt,* the translation that I will use henceforth, as may be reasonably inferred from the following text concerning the new laws of homicide introduced by Moses. *So ye shall not pollute the land wherein ye are; for blood, it polluteth the land; and no expiation can be made for the land for the blood that is shed therein, but by the blood of him that shed it. And thou shalt not defile the land which ye inhabit, in the midst of which I dwell; for I YHVH dwell in the midst of the children of Israel* (Num. 35:33-34). This same point is made more concisely in the passage under discussion, *that innocent blood be not shed in the midst of thy land, which YHVH thy Elohim giveth thee for an inheritance, and so blood* [better *bloodguilt*] *be upon thee.* Why does the shedding of innocent blood cause bloodguilt to be assigned to the nation? Although the text offers no explanation, it would seem that the reason is that for such a crime to take place in the *land which YHVH thy Elohim giveth thee for an inheritance* is itself evidence that the society has not done enough to prevent such from happening, and must be held liable to some extent for failing to institute sufficient safeguards.

The idea that human bloodshed has a polluting effect on the earth itself was already given clear expression in the story of Cain and Abel. After Cain kills his brother, God tells him, *the voice of thy brother's blood crieth unto Me from the ground. And now cursed art thou from the ground, which hath opened her mouth to receive thy brother's blood from thy hand* (Gen. 4:10-11). In the case of Cain, the punishment was removal and exile from the ground he polluted with his act of homicide. In the passages cited above, which anticipate entry into the promised land, *no expiation can be made for the land for the blood that is shed therein, but by the blood of him that shed it.* Exile from the land, as in the case of Cain, is no longer an option. Moses thus proclaims that bloodguilt contaminates the sanctity of the place where the divine presence dwells, and that sanctity must be redeemed by the transformation of the family or clan *go'el* into the *go'el hadam* of the state.

> The *go'el* was the member of the family who, when it lost its head, was the next friend; a kind of sublimated executor and guardian, who looked after the interests of his kinsmen in trouble. And now it was the state whose new measures and principles avowed that it had incurred blood-guilt (*dam, damim*); that an evil fate threatened the country, unless this blood-guilt was redeemed or removed. A *go'el* or redeemer was needed, and thus the *go'el ha-dam*, a being never heard of before, was created. He was the state's redeemer from blood-guilt, not the avenger of the victim's blood. Had he been the latter, he would have been *nokem ha-dam*.[863]

This view is seconded by another commentator who wrote, "While the term *go'el* is frequently used of a family's accredited agent charged with recovering property, the fact that in the one case of murder the phrase has been expanded would in any event seem to indicate that a different person from the family *go'el* was being described."[864] Since the primary use of the expanded term *go'el ha-dam* is in connection with the cities of refuge, it seems clear that the bearer of that title fulfills a specific function with regard to those cities and their purpose.

As suggested at the outset of this discussion of the cities of refuge, Moses evidently set out to eliminate the ancient vendetta law, which well served a tribal society but was not suitable for the centralized state he knew would become necessary following the conquest and settlement of the land they were about to enter. Such a state could not allow such rough justice to be carried out by the many clans and extended families that made up the tribes of the children of Israel. A uniform system of justice was required, and the first modest but at the same time dramatic step in this direction was to transform the ancient family *go'el* into a sheriff and public executioner in each of the three subdivisions of the country with a city of refuge at its center, the *go'el hadam*, the *redeemer of blood guilt* on behalf of the nation. By the end of the rather anarchic period of the Judges, for the most part, the *go'el hadam* would also be dispensed with as the judicial and executive functions of the national constitutional structure set forth by Moses began to go into effect.

The three cities of refuge called for in this passage, in addition to the three already established for the tribes living in Transjordan, presumably were sufficient in number for the purpose at the time. However, Moses was also concerned about their adequacy in the future, *if YHVH thy Elohim enlarge thy border, as He hath sworn unto thy fathers, and give thee all the land which He promised to give unto thy fathers.* Although the text repeatedly makes reference to the territories of the seven nations found in the promised land, the initial divine promise to Abraham also specifically included some territories beyond the borders of those seven nations, as it states: *Unto thy seed have I given this land, from the river of Egypt unto the great river, the river Euphrates; the Kenite, and the Kenizzite, and the Kadmonite, and the Hittite, and the Perizzite, and the Rephaim, and the Amorite, and the Canaanite, and the Girgashite, and the Jebusite* (Gen. 15:18-21). It is presumed that the anticipated extension of Israelite control beyond the bounds of the seven nations refers to the incorporation of the territories of *the Kenite, and the Kenizzite, and the Kadmonite.*[865] When such an expansion takes place, *then shalt thou add three cities more for thee, beside these three.* To accommodate such extension of territory, an additional three cities of refuge are to be established, placing the total of such refuges at nine.[866]

Having dealt with the matter of "homicide by misadventure," Moses then turned to the question of whether the intentional murderer may also seek sanctuary in the cities of refuge.

> [19.11] *But if any man hate his neighbor, and lie in wait for him, and rise up against him, and smite him mortally that he die; and he flee into one of these cities;* [19.12] *then the elders of his city shall send and fetch him thence, and deliver him into the hand of the redeemer of bloodguilt, that he may die.* [19.13] *Thine eye shall not pity him, but thou shalt put away the bloodguilt of the innocent from Israel, that it may go well with thee.*

In the case of intentional and deliberate homicide, Moses makes it clear that the murderer cannot seek or receive sanctuary in a city of refuge. As the rabbis understood these texts, anyone who slays a human being, whether by error or by design, proceeds first to a city of refuge. The court then sends messengers to bring him to trial, and he who is found guilty is condemned to death and is executed, as it is said, *Then the elders of his city shall send and fetch him thence, and deliver him into the hand of the redeemer of bloodguilt, that he may die.* He who is found not guilty of murder is acquitted of the charge, *and the congregation shall deliver the manslayer out of the hand of the redeemer of bloodguilt.* However, if he is found guilty of manslaughter, *the congregation shall restore him to his city of refuge, whither he was fled; and he shall dwell therein until the death of the high priest* (Num. 35:25).[867] Apparently, the death of the high priest was deemed an appropriate occasion for the declaration of amnesty for those held guilty of manslaughter. However, to ensure that the manslayer, who is thus placed in internal exile in the country but is not incarcerated, does not violate the sanctuary he has been granted, the law stipulates that *if the manslayer shall at any time go beyond the border of his city of refuge, whither he fleeth; and the redeemer of bloodguilt find him without the border of his city of refuge, and the redeemer of bloodguilt slay the manslayer; there shall be no bloodguiltiness for him; because he must remain in his city of refuge until the death of the high priest; but after the death of the high priest the manslayer may return unto the land of his possession* (Num. 35:26-28).

With regard to the convicted murderer, Moses admonishes, *Thine eye shall not pity him*; that is, there should be no argument that "since the victim has already been slain, why should we become responsible for the blood of the slayer?" Instead, Moses insists, *thou shalt put away the bloodguilt of the innocent from Israel*, that is, you shall remove those who do evil from the body of Israel, their very presence polluting it. The passage ends with *that it may go well with thee*, the meaning of which in this context is not self-evident. In this regard, it has been suggested that what Moses is saying here is that the earth itself rejects innocent blood, and so it remains a stain on the surface visible to all, as though crying out for vengeance, a point made in an earlier text and already referred to above, that *no expiation can be made for the land for the blood that is shed therein, but by the blood of him that shed it* (Num. 35:33). Accordingly, the presumption here is that once the killer is punished the earth will accept the victim's blood and so the bloodguilt for his murder is expiated, allowing Israel to continue on the land without un-expiated bloodguilt.[868]

Moses next turns to an issue with serious consequences for the social harmony that is to be reflected in the covenantal society. It has been suggested that the connection of what follows with the preceding is that together they exemplify the idea that "life and property are the two principle valuables which are to be placed under the protection of the Laws of God administered by the State, and their inviolable sanctity in the Land of God's Torah proclaimed immediately that land is taken into possession."[869]

> *19.14 Thou shalt not remove thy neighbor's landmark, which they of old time have set, in thine inheritance which thou shalt inherit, in the land that YHVH thy Elohim giveth thee to possess it.*

Moses is keenly aware that the children of Israel, wandering in the wilderness for four decades, are impatient to enter the promised land and establish roots there. The land, once conquered will have to be distributed among the tribes, and then among the individual family units. Because the allocated plots of land will not be consistent in quality due to terrain, access to water, and other natural factors, disgruntlement among those who receive less desirable land parcels than their neighbors was to be expected. What was of concern to Moses was the potential for such disgruntlement to lead to encroachment on a neighbor's property, which was delimited by landmarks that in many instances may easily be moved. To do so, would in effect be stealing another's property, and this is intolerable *in the land that YHVH thy Elohim giveth thee to possess it.* Moreover, just as the spilling of innocent blood pollutes the earth of the place where the presence of the divine dwells, so too does the stealing of property.[870]

Moses is also aware that in the initial subdivision of the land, not all land parcels would be equal in dimensions because of topographic features as well as the difficulty of obtaining accurate surveys. To avoid later arguments, to the extent possible, about land distribution equity, Moses establishes the rule that initial landmarks must be accepted as proper and legitimate for the purpose of establishing ownership of the land. Accordingly, he forbids moving a landmark, *which they of old time have set.*

Reflecting his abiding concern with laying the groundwork for a just society, Moses once again returns to the theme of assuring a rational system of justice predicated on the principles outlined in the Torah. In the following passage he addresses the perennial problem of the reliability of eyewitnesses.

> *19.15 One witness shall not rise up against a man for any iniquity, or for any sin, in any sin that he sinneth; at the mouth of two witnesses, or at the mouth of three witnesses, shall a matter be established. 19.16 If an unrighteous witness rise up against any man to bear perverted witness against him; 19.17 then both the men, between whom the controversy is, shall stand before YHVH, before the priests and the judges that shall be in those days. 19.18 And the judges shall inquire diligently; and, behold, if the witness be a false witness, and hath testified falsely against his brother; 19.19 then ye shall do unto him, as he had purposed to do unto his brother; so shalt thou put away the evil from the midst of thee. 19.20 And those that remain shall hear, and fear, and shall henceforth commit no more any such evil in the midst of thee. 19.21 And thine eye shall not pity: life for life, eye for eye, tooth for tooth, hand for hand, foot for foot.*

To begin with, Moses declares the eyewitness testimony of a single witness unacceptable as sufficient evidence for conviction of an alleged perpetrator of *any iniquity, or for any sin, in any sin that he sinneth.* As the rabbis understood this rule, it applied to both criminal and civil offenses.[871] To establish the reliability of eyewitness testimony, a minimum of two corroborating witnesses are required. Additional witnesses will further assure trustworthiness of the testimony, providing of course that all witnesses corroborate each other's testimony. However, if two witnesses fail to corroborate their accounts, the witnesses must themselves be subjected to investigation and discovery. If it is found that one of them *be a false witness, and hath testified falsely against his brother; then ye shall do unto him, as he had purposed to do unto his brother.* In this manner *shalt thou put away the evil from the midst of thee.* The punishment of the false witness with the same penalty that his testimony, if accepted, would have been imposed on the person charged with the deed would serve as a clear warning to others to desist from bearing false testimony. *And those that remain shall hear, and fear, and shall henceforth commit no more any such evil in the midst of thee.* It has been observed that wording of this verse is rather unusual in that the usual formula with regard to violations of the covenant is *and all the people,* or *and all Israel,* whereas here it states *and those that remain.* The difference, it is pointed out, is that the present text is referring specifically to witnesses and, as a matter of law, not all of the people or all Israel are eligible to serve as witnesses.[872]

It should be noted that the text seems to draw a distinction between *eid hamas,* translated as *an unrighteous witness,* and *eid sheker,* translated as *a false witness,* both designations referring to the same person. The distinction is held to be that a *false witness* is one who testifies to something that he did not or could not have witnessed, without regard for the consequences of his testimony. By contrast, *an unrighteous witness* is one testifies falsely for the purpose of causing harm to the person against whom he testifies. In the situation postulated by Moses, the *unrighteous witness* intended that his testimony lead to a conviction that would cause harm to the person against whom he testified. However, once his design was thwarted by the challenge to the veracity of his testimony, he reverts to the status of a *false witness,* and is adjudged accordingly.[873]

Bearing this distinction in mind, it is noteworthy that the interpretation of this text was the subject of a major controversy between the Pharisees and Sadducees, the latter insisting that the death sentence was imposed on the false witness only if it was actually carried out on the accused, that is, if the false witness was actually *an unrighteous witness*. The Pharisees, on the other hand, maintained that the sentence would be carried out on the false witness only if it had not been carried out on the accused. The ostensible basis for the two approaches is considered as resting in the wording of the text. Thus the Sadducees argued that the text demands *life for life*, which implies that a life had to be taken before the *unrighteous witness* suffered the same fate. The Pharisees, however, argued that the indictment in the text states, *ye shall do unto him, as he had purposed to do unto his brother*, the phrase *purposed to do* clearly indicates that that it had not yet been done, and that the accused was still alive.[874]

Commentators have argued, however, that the underlying rationale for the Pharisee position is predicated on the assumption that if the accused had been executed, notwithstanding that it was on the basis of false testimony, he must have been guilty of some transgression that merited the punishment he received because God would not allow an innocent life to be taken away by a court functioning in accordance with divine law. Accordingly, in such a case, the accused must have already effectively been under a sentence of death, the implementation of which was caused by the false testimony. In this case, then, there is no justification for taking the life of the false witness, who indeed deserves punishment, but not at the hands of the court.[875] In this regard, it has been argued that God has a way of bringing justice to the guilty that have not been convicted by a court of law.[876] Alternatively, it has been argued that the political rationale for the Pharisee position on the question is simply that it was necessary to safeguard public confidence in the courts, which would be seriously impaired if it became known that the court put someone to death on the basis of a false witness. As a practical matter it would better serve the public interest to put the false witness to death before such sentence was imposed on the accused rather than after the fact.[877] Another commentator suggests that, notwithstanding that putting the false witness to death only if the accused has not been executed seems illogical, "in a particular respect, 'conspiring' is worse than 'doing.' For causing the court to issue a verdict which they cannot carry out creates a tension which is not present when the court carries out its verdict, even wrongfully."[878] In this regard, it has been suggested that the text, *ye shall do unto him, as he had purposed to do unto his brother*, requires that the court put the false witness to death because, "from the point of view of the law, it is the aggrieved party, since the witness has threatened to subvert its ability to judge correctly."[879]

Once again Moses demands, *thine eye shall not pity* the false witness, presumably arguing that because the person charged with the crime was not punished for it; in the instance of a death penalty case it might seem unreasonable to put the false witness to death for his unsuccessful attempt to support the conviction of his fellow. Moses, however, insists that the appropriate punishment of the false witness should be *life for life, eye for eye, tooth for tooth, hand for hand, foot for foot*, the terminology being that common to the ancient law of retaliation, but with the understanding that with the exception of *life for life*, the remaining reciprocities must be understood as metaphors for monetary compensation, because bodily mutilation is rejected by biblical law as an appropriate punishment.[880]

Moses next turns to several questions concerning warfare, something the people are about to begin engaging in for an indeterminate period once they cross the river into Cisjordan. It is suggested that this topic is introduced here because it is directly related to matters of life and death, as discussed above.[881]

> [20.1] *When thou goest forth to battle against thine enemies, and seest horses, and chariots, and a people more than thou, thou shalt not be afraid of them; for YHVH thy Elohim is with thee, who brought thee up out of the land of Egypt.* [20.2] *And it shall be, when ye draw nigh unto the battle, that the priest shall approach and speak unto the people,* [20.3] *and shall say unto them: 'Hear, O Israel, ye draw nigh this day unto battle against your enemies; let not your heart faint; fear not, nor be alarmed, neither be ye affrighted at them;* [20.4] *for YHVH your Elohim is He that goeth with you, to fight for you against your enemies, to save you.'*

The passage opens with the curious statement, *to battle against thine enemies*, leading one to ask who else one would go to battle against? Since it is so obvious, why trouble to mention it; the text could simply have said *When thou goest forth to battle*? It has been suggested that Moses is reminding the people that the nations they are about to confront are enemies in a very personal sense, namely that no mercy can be expected of them for either those wounded in battle or captured,[882] and that no mercy should be shown to them.[883]

The primary issue of concern to Moses in this passage with regard to warfare is the morale of the people. The Israelite army under the leadership of Joshua, at this stage of its development, is comprised entirely, for all practical purposes, of infantry. However, Moses is evidently well aware that the enemies they will face, particularly in the lowlands, will have relatively large and highly mobile cavalry and chariot forces, giving them a distinct tactical advantage over the Israelites. Moreover, he also knows that, in the aggregate, the armies defending their territory are larger than his own forces. Moses therefore takes the occasion to assure the people that they have one countervailing force that will shift the military balance decisively in their favor—God is on their side. With the certain knowledge that *YHVH thy Elohim is with thee, who brought thee up out of the land of Egypt*, they may rest assured that He did not nurture them for forty years in the wilderness in order to abandon them when they are engaged in realizing the promise God made to their ancestors, and reaffirmed in the covenant with them, that He would bring the children of Israel to the land where He revealed himself to Abraham, Isaac, and Jacob. Therefore, he adjures the people, *thou shalt not be afraid of them*, regardless of how powerful they may appear to be; God is immeasurably more powerful, and with Him on our side, we will prevail.

Moses is aware, however, that mere exhortation to trust in God is insufficient for a people, significant segments of which have proven repeatedly to be less than stalwart in their faith in God and commitment to the covenant. Accordingly, as a morale-building procedure, Moses ordains that before every battle a ceremony take place that will leave a visual impression on the minds of the people. A specially designated priest serving with the army[884], a chaplain, known to the troops, such as Phinehas the son of Eleazar, and grandson of Aaron, who Moses sent *to the war, with the holy vessels and the trumpets for the alarm in his hand* (Num. 31:6), will convene them in an assembly and deliver an inspirational message to them that will remain in their consciousness during the ensuing struggle: *Hear, O Israel, ye draw nigh this day unto battle against your enemies; let not your heart faint; fear not, nor be alarmed, neither be ye affrighted at them; for YHVH your Elohim is He that goeth with you, to fight for you against your enemies, to save you.* The priest begins his oration with *Hear, O Israel,* the opening words of the declaration of faith in God, perhaps implicitly alluding to it as a battle cry. He then admonishes them against succumbing to the four methods of psychological warfare commonly practiced by armies to demoralize their adversaries before engaging in battle. He thus urges, "*let not your heart faint* at the neighing of their horses, *fear not* the crashing of their shields and the tramp of their nail-studded shoes, *nor be alarmed* at the sound of the trumpets, *neither be ye affrighted* at the sound of their shouting."[885] He then assures them that not only is God on their side in the abstract, He is actually accompanying them on the battlefield as a comrade in arms, and with such a champion fighting for your cause, there should be no fear whatever of the enemy you will confront.

Because Moses emphasizes that they should have no fear of enemies with superior numbers and military capabilities since the divine presence will be with them in the battle, it becomes essential that those engaging in combat not be distracted from this critical idea by extraneous personal concerns. Since the absolute number of men on the battlefield is a less significant factor for success than high morale, Moses proceeds to set forth a number of personal circumstances that justify deferment from participation in combat. Indeed, the very idea that Moses would grant such deferments reflects his absolute confidence that as long as those engaging in battle do so with single-minded awareness of the divine role in what is about to take place, victory will be theirs, regardless of their absolute numbers. Moreover, to avoid causing embarrassment to those who might qualify for deferment but be reluctant to request one, the army commanders are directed to identify those that should be granted deferments, whether they request such or not.

> *20.5 And the officers shall speak unto the people, saying: 'What man is there that hath built a new house, and hath not dedicated it? let him go and return to his house, lest he die in battle, and another man dedicate it. 20.6 And what man is there that hath planted a vineyard, and hath not used the fruit thereof? Let him go and return to his house, lest he die in battle, and another man use the fruit thereof. 20.7 And what man is there that hath betrothed a wife, and hath not taken her? Let him go and return unto his house, lest he die in battle, and another man take her.' 20.8 And the officers shall speak further unto the people, and they shall say: 'What man is there that is fearful and faint-hearted? Let him go and return to his house, lest his brethren's heart melt as his heart.' 20.9 And it shall be, when the officers have made an end of speaking unto the people, that captains of hosts shall be appointed at the head of the people.*

The first basis for deferment would be the case of a soldier who built a house for his family but had not yet lived in it; *let him go and return to his house, lest he die in battle, and another man dedicate it.* Moses suggests that it would be inadvisable for someone in this situation to go into battle wondering and worrying what will happen to his new home if he were not to survive the battle. It appears to be Moses' judgment that a person in such a frame of mind will be more of a hindrance than an asset in battle; primarily because of the deleterious effects his expression of such concerns may have on the morale of his fellow combatants.

The second basis for deferment is the case of one *that hath planted a vineyard,* but had not yet tasted the fruit thereof. The text literally states, *And what man is there that hath planted a vineyard, and hath not made it profane?* Although, as a practical matter, the translation of the final clause as *and hath not used the fruit thereof* is accurate, it is also somewhat misleading. It should be noted that an earlier text earlier states: *And when ye shall come into the land, and shall have planted all manner of trees for food, then ye shall count the fruit thereof as forbidden; three years shall it be as forbidden unto you; it shall not be eaten. And in the fourth year all the fruit thereof shall be holy, for giving praise unto YHVH. But in the fifth year may ye eat of the fruit thereof* (Lev. 19:23-25). Accordingly, in the case of one who plants a vineyard but has not yet tasted of its fruit, depending upon when the planting took place, the deferment from combat may extend as much as five years. Nonetheless, Moses ordains: *Let him go and return to his house, lest he die in battle, and another man use the fruit thereof.* The person who received a plot of land of his own and went to the trouble of planting a vineyard that had not yet produced any yield might be distracted by thoughts of it to the extent that he might affect the morale of his unit. It would therefore be best if he remained at home for this battle and be recalled for a subsequent one, after eating from the fruit for the first time.

The third basis for deferment is the case of a man who *hath betrothed a wife, and hath not taken her;* that is, the betrothal took place but the marriage had not yet been consummated. Moses did not think sending someone into battle under such circumstances was a very good idea. In battle one needed to focus entirely on the danger before him and not daydream about the bliss of married life. *Let him go and return unto his house, lest he die in battle, and another man take her.*

It has been suggested that these three situations have been highlighted because they reflect the three happiest moments in a man's life, building his own home, establishing his economic base, and starting a family through marriage. It is at those precious moments, when his mind is preoccupied with them, a person is most vulnerable in a battlefield situation, and is therefore granted deferment.[886] It is noteworthy that in a later prophecy, completely unrelated to a battlefield situation, Jeremiah echoes the passage under consideration with his declaration in the name of God, *Build ye houses, and dwell in them, and plant gardens, and eat the fruit of them; take ye wives, and beget sons and daughters* (Jer. 29:5-6). The question that this raises once again is why these three aspects of life are singled out as deserving of special consideration. It has been suggested that, "each of these facets is interwoven with the concept of *kiddushin* - sanctification. The sanctification of place, time, and people . . . The Torah's primary concern is that of realization and completion. Acts of holiness and sanctification are to be completed. The Torah encourages us (before risking our lives on behalf of others) that if we have begun any of these acts of *kiddushin*, we must endeavor to complete them. We must choose life but we must choose a life that is endowed with a recognition of holiness and wholeness."[887]

Finally, the *officers*, which in this context refers to the army commanders, are to speak frankly to their troops and caution them that any among their ranks who is still afraid of facing the enemy should declare himself and be excused from participation in the battle. *Let him go and return to his house, lest his brethren's heart melt as his heart.* A person able to admit such fear and faintheartedness can demoralize those with whom he has to serve, fear being infectious, and will therefore be a liability rather than an asset. Of course, it may well be in some instances that a person's fear of confessing fear might be translated into bravery, and asking someone openly to confess fear and faintheartedness may actually be a psychological device for causing him to overcome that fear.

One of the large questions that this text raises, and there are numerous others that I have discussed at some length elsewhere,[888] is how one can reconcile such deferments at a time of national crisis, when families are being torn apart by war and the losses of loved ones in battle. Struggling with this question, the rabbis concluded on the basis of a majority opinion on a highly controversial issue that these exemptions from national military service applied only "to discretionary wars," that is, wars of choice. However, in the case of biblically mandated wars, of which there are a number, "all go forth, even a bridegroom from his chamber and a bride from her canopy."[889] In other words, in the case of a mandatory war there are no exemptions from mobilization of persons otherwise capable of national service. As the rabbis put it, "in a battle waged in a religious cause all go forth, even the bridegroom out of his chamber and the bride out of her bedchamber."[890] And, according to a modern rabbinic authority, this precludes any deferments for reasons of religion. "In such a war, there are no rabbis or Torah scholars. Everyone is obligated to go out to the battlefield to destroy the enemy."[891] Moreover, even in the case of a discretionary war, those exempted from combatant service "return home and provide water and food and repair the roads."[892] In other words, even those deferred from active military duty may be mobilized to provide support services behind the lines.

Once the commanders complete their inquiries, and those whose service is being deferred are removed from the ranks, *captains of hosts shall be appointed at the head of the people.* That is, the various units will be reorganized to make up for those who left and unit commanders will be appointed. It is noteworthy that the rabbis understood this text rather differently. They asserted that the appointment of *captains of hosts . . . at the head of the people* was complemented by others at the rear of the people; "they stationed warriors in front of them and others behind them with axes of iron in their hands, and if any sought to turn back the warrior was empowered to break his legs, for with a beginning in flight comes defeat."[893]

Moses continues with mention of some basic rules of warfare that the children of Israel are to observe as they fight to conquer the land divinely allocated to them.

> *20.10 When thou drawest nigh unto a city to fight against it, then proclaim peace unto it. 20.11 And it shall be, if it make thee answer of peace, and open unto thee, then it shall be, that all the people that are found therein shall become tributary unto thee, and shall serve thee. 20.12 And if it will make no peace with thee, but will make war against thee, then thou shalt besiege it. 20.13 And when YHVH thy Elohim delivereth it into thy hand, thou shalt smite every male thereof with the edge of the sword; 20.14 but the women, and the little ones, and the cattle, and all that is in the city, even all the spoil thereof, shalt thou take for a prey unto thyself; and thou shalt eat the spoil of thine enemies, which YHVH thy Elohim hath given thee. 20.15 Thus shalt thou do unto all the cities which are very far off from thee, which are not of the cities of these nations.*

> *20.16 Howbeit of the cities of these peoples, that YHVH thy Elohim giveth thee for an inheritance, thou shalt save alive nothing that breatheth, 20.17 but thou shalt utterly destroy them: the Hittite, and the Amorite, the Canaanite, and the Perizzite, the Hivite, and the Jebusite; as YHVH thy Elohim hath commanded thee; 20.18 that they teach you not to do after all their abominations, which they have done unto their gods, and so ye sin against YHVH your Elohim.*

First and foremost, as a general proposition, it is preferable to resolve territorial and other interstate disputes by peaceful means, war being a solution of last resort. Accordingly, Moses instructs the army commanders, *When thou drawest nigh unto a city to fight against it, then proclaim peace unto it.* Negotiations from a distance are unlikely to resolve an issue worth fighting over. However, when it is clear to the rulers or elites of a city that you are preparing to attack and destroy it, and your forces sufficient for the task are being maneuvered into position for an assault, that is the time to offer terms for peaceful surrender, a moment when the credibility of your intentions is patent for all to see. If the leaders of the city respond favorably to your offer, *and open unto thee, then it shall be, that all the people that are found therein shall become tributary unto thee, and shall serve thee.* It is noteworthy that thus far the text is not speaking of dispossessing the people of the city or even of the children of Israel moving into it. It speaks only of become tributary to the children of Israel, that is, paying an annual ransom for the safety of the city. Moreover, it is presumed that by *all the people that are found therein* Moses includes even numbers of people from the seven nations that they are to destroy as such.[894]

If the proffer of peaceful surrender is rejected, indicating a preference for war, *then thou shalt besiege it.* Having shown a preference for war rather than pay tribute and retain their freedom, the city is to be made to feel the brunt of the consequences of their rejection of peace, and *thou shalt smite every male thereof with the edge of the sword.* That is, every male capable of wielding a weapon is to be killed, thereby destroying any potential for reconstituting the independence of the city as a political entity. However, *the women, and the little ones, and the cattle, and all that is in the city, even all the spoil thereof, shalt thou take for a prey unto thyself.* Everything else of value in the city, human, animal, or goods, may be taken as booty, *and thou shalt eat the spoil of thine enemies, which YHVH thy Elohim hath given thee.* It should be noted, however, that this does not constitute a license for the killing or abuse of the women and children taken prisoner, who presumably will be taken as slaves in accordance with the accepted practice of the age.

At the same time, Moses makes clear, *Thus shalt thou do unto all the cities which are very far off from thee, which are not of the cities of these nations,* the latter phrase clearly referring to the cities of the Amorites, Canaanites, and the other nations that God had promised to deliver into their hands, to conquer and dispossess. Thus, the rules just announced apply only to wars that take place outside the confines of the territories assigned to the children of Israel under the covenant. But within the territories of the nations that the children of Israel are to dispossess, the rules are quite different. *Howbeit of the cities of these peoples, that YHVH thy Elohim giveth thee for an inheritance, thou shalt save alive nothing that breatheth, but thou shalt utterly destroy them: the Hittite, and the Amorite, the Canaanite, and the Perizzite, the Hivite, and the Jebusite; as YHVH thy Elohim hath commanded thee.* As pointed out earlier, this statement should not be misconstrued as a justification for genocide, which would make it quite incompatible with the repeated warnings against fraternization with or assimilation to those same nations. The policy announced by Moses pertains to these peoples as nations; as such their national presence is to be destroyed. It does not relate to the people of these nations as individuals living under Israelite rule. Moses also provides an explanation of this policy, which essentially repeats what he told the people on an earlier occasion, namely that this harsh approach must be taken to ensure *that they teach you not to do after all their abominations, which they have done unto their gods, and so ye sin against YHVH your Elohim,* a comment that attests to the susceptibility of some among the children of Israel to assimilation to alien cultures. The implication of *that they teach you not to do after all their abominations* is that if they abandon these practices, they may continue to live among you.[895]

Moses concludes this brief reprise of some laws and policies relating to the existential struggles for survival in the land that will soon begin with an interesting environmental note regarding the conduct of hostilities.

> ^{20.19} *When thou shalt besiege a city a long time, in making war against it to take it, thou shalt not destroy the trees thereof by wielding an axe against them; for thou mayest eat of them, but thou shalt not cut them down; for is the tree of the field man, that it should be besieged of thee?* ^{20.20} *Only the trees of which thou knowest that they are not trees for food, them thou mayest destroy and cut down, that thou mayest build bulwarks against the city that maketh war with thee, until it fall.*

Moses cautions his forces not to let the heat of battle affect the norms of proper behavior, and in the case of a lengthy siege of a city not to wantonly destroy the natural environment of the area. He thus declares: *thou shalt not destroy the trees thereof by wielding an axe against them.* That is, you are not to deliberately cut down a fruit-bearing tree. *Thou mayest eat of them, but thou shalt not cut them down.* It would seem commonsensical not to destroy something that provides benefit to man, in this case fruit trees that the children of Israel did not plant. They may destroy those trees that they know are not fruit-bearing, and even then only for purposes of making use of the lumber for a legitimate military purpose, for example, *that thou mayest build bulwarks against the city that maketh war with thee, until it fall.*

Nonetheless, the rationale for the restrictive rule provided by Moses makes a rather different and decidedly emphatic point, reflected in the rhetorical question, *for is the tree of the field man, that it should be besieged of thee?* That is, the tree is not an enemy like the man you would besiege and kill. The tree only offers benefit and takes nothing from you. Indeed, the creation narrative makes clear that it was for the benefit of man that God planted a garden in Eden in which to place him, where God made *to grow every tree that is pleasant to the sight, and good for food . . . And YHVH Elohim commanded the man, saying:*

"of every tree of the garden thou mayest freely eat [with one exception] (Gen. 2:9, 16). Accordingly, Moses instructs that the tree may not be destroyed arbitrarily and the fruit bearing tree not at all. The implicit lesson in this is that man needs to condition himself never to forget that which has benefited him, even in the fog of war and heat of battle.[896]

Moses now returns to an earlier theme, the polluting effect of the shedding of innocent blood and the bloodguilt that demands expiation. Whereas he earlier addressed how to deal with the perpetrator of homicide, he now turns to the problem of expiating bloodguilt for a victim in a case where the perpetrator is unknown. It will be observed that the following passage is wedged in the midst of paragraphs dealing with issues relating to war, a fact that begs for some explanation. It has been suggested, in this regard, that the placement of the section here is appropriate because during the course of a military conflict it is common to find dead bodies in the field.[897] Moreover, the placement of the passage here may serve to dissuade anyone from thinking that he might kill a personal enemy during battle, and have it concealed among the other battle casualties.[898]

> [21.1] *If one be found slain in the land which YHVH thy Elohim giveth thee to possess it, lying in the field, and it be not known who hath smitten him;* [21.2] *then thy elders and thy judges shall come forth, and they shall measure unto the cities which are round about him that is slain.* [21.3] *And it shall be, that the city which is nearest unto the slain man, even the elders of that city shall take a heifer of the herd, which hath not been wrought with, and which hath not drawn in the yoke.* [21.4] *And the elders of that city shall bring down the heifer unto a rough valley, which may neither be plowed nor sown, and shall break the heifer's neck there in the valley.* [21.5] *And the priests the sons of Levi shall come near—for them YHVH thy Elohim hath chosen to minister unto Him, and to bless in the name of YHVH; and according to their word shall every controversy and every stroke be.* [21.6] *And all the elders of that city, who are nearest unto the slain man, shall wash their hands over the*

heifer whose neck was broken in the valley. ^{21.7} *And they shall speak and say: 'Our hands have not shed this blood, neither have our eyes seen it.* ^{21.8} *Forgive, O YHVH, Thy people Israel, whom Thou hast redeemed, and suffer not innocent bloodguilt to remain in the midst of Thy people Israel.' And the bloodguilt shall be forgiven them.* ^{21.9} *So shalt thou put away the innocent bloodguilt from the midst of thee, when thou shalt do that which is right in the eyes of YHVH.*

In the event that a body, visibly having been killed by unnatural means, is found in a field, *thy elders and thy judges shall come forth, and they shall measure unto the cities which are round about him that is slain.* The rabbis understood this as asserting that the *elders* referred to in this statement are members of the national high court.[899] This seems eminently reasonable because no city would be anxious to claim responsibility for the bloodguilt associated with the murder, and using members of the national court to measure the distance between the body and the nearby cities would eliminate concern about fraud in determining which city had to accept the responsibility for the murdered body. In the absence of a known perpetrator, the un-expiated bloodguilt is thus assigned to the city closest to where the corpse was discovered. The elders of that city[900] must *take a heifer of the herd, which hath not been wrought with, and which hath not drawn in the yoke.* It is noteworthy that the criteria that the heifer must satisfy are almost identical with that of the Red Heifer, *faultless, wherein is no blemish, and upon which never came yoke* (Num. 19:2), which was sacrificed and its ashes used in a ceremony as *a purification for sin* (Num. 19:9). The elders of the city *shall bring down the heifer unto a rough valley, which may neither be plowed nor sown, and shall break the heifer's neck there in the valley.* The elders *shall wash their hands over the heifer whose neck was broken in the valley,* symbolically disowning the community's guilt in the affair,[901] before the levitical priests who apparently serve as a judicial body overseeing the expiation rite, and declare the innocence of their city before the priests, *Our hands have not shed this blood, neither have our eyes seen it.* The meaning of this declaration, according to the rabbis, is that the dead person "did not come to us for help and we dismissed him without supplying him with food, we did not see him and let go without an escort."[902] The text also does not state why the heifer is to be killed in a barren valley. The rabbis, however, saw a profound symbolism in the requirement, suggesting that the rationale was because God said, "Let something which did not produce fruit have its neck broken in a place which is not fertile and atone for one who was not allowed to produce fruit,"[903] that is, for a person who died prematurely. Alternatively, it has been suggested that the purpose of killing the animal in a barren valley is so that "the blood of the heifer may sink into the uncultivated soil and remain undisturbed. For the primitive intention of the ritual is to transfer the guilt which rests on the local community, and which is thought of in materialistic terms, from the local town to this desert place."[904]

The elders were then to plead for forgiveness, presumably for not having taken the appropriate steps to prevent the crime from having been committed in the first place, and that their city not bear the burden of bloodguilt for the slain one. Some suggest that it is the priests who utter the prayer for forgiveness on behalf of the community. Following completion of this procedure, *the bloodguilt shall be forgiven them.* Moses concludes with the comment, *So shalt thou put away the innocent bloodguilt from the midst of thee, when thou shalt do that which is right in the eyes of YHVH.* In effect, by assuming responsibility for expiating the bloodguilt instigated by an unknown assailant, who may not have been a resident of their city, the elders acknowledged the absolute need to expiate the sin of innocent bloodshed that cast a pall on the sanctity of the land that God gave them. And this, Moses declares, is an example of doing *that which is right in the eyes of YHVH.* Alternatively, this final text has been understood as saying, if the murderer is discovered following the ceremony that had been completed, and the bloodguilt expiated, he must nonetheless be put to death, *which is right in the eyes of YHVH.*[905]

NOTES

1   Mittleman, *The Politics of Torah*, p. 63.

2   Davies, *The Territorial Dimension of Judaism*, pp. 8-9.

3   Levinas, *Outside the Subject*, p. 130.

4   Luzzatto, *Perush al Hamisha Humshei Torah* on Deut. 1:1.

5   Abraham Sofer, *Ktav Sofer*, pp. 232a-b.

6   Abravanel, *Perush haTorah* on Deut. 1:1.

7   Ramban, *Perushei haTorah* on Deut. 1:1.

8   *Babylonian Talmud* (henceforth *BT*) *Megillah* 31b.

9   Attar, *Or haHayyim* on Deut. 1:1.

10   Munk, *The Call of the Torah* on Deut. 1:1.

11   *Sifre*, Piska 1.

12   Ibid.

13   Ephraim Solomon of Luntshits, *Perush Kli Yakar haShalem* on Deut. 1:1.

14   *BT Arakhin* 15a.

15   Rashi, *Perushei Rashi* on Deut. 1.1.

16   Sforno, *Biur al haTorah* on Deut. 1:1-2.

17   Friedman, *Commentary on the Torah* on Deut. 1:3.

18   Abulafia, *Mafteah haTokhahot*, p. 5.

19   *Seder Olam Rabbah* 10.

20   Tigay, *The JPS Torah Commentary: Deuteronomy*, p. 418.

21   Wright, *Deuteronomy*, p. 21.

22   Weinfeld, *Deuteronomy 1-11*, p. 129.

23   Ehrlich, *Mikra kiFeshuto* on Deut. 1:5.

24 Sforno, *Biur al haTorah* on Deut. 1:5.

25 Gordon, *Hamishah Humshei Torah* on Deut. 1:6.

26 Jacob ben Asher, *Perush Baal haTurim* on Deut. 1:6.

27 *Sifre*, Piska 40; *Midrash Rabbah: Leviticus* 35:6.

28 Wright, *Deuteronomy*, p. 25.

29 Sforno, *Biur al haTorah* on Deut. 1:8.

30 Abravanel, *Perush haTorah* on Deut. 1:9.

31 Friedman, *Commentary on the Torah* on Deut. 1:9.

32 Caro, *Toledot Yitzhak* on Deut. 1:9.

33 Tigay, *The JPS Torah Commentary: Deuteronomy* on Deut. 1:11.

34 Peli, "Torah Today," *Jerusalem Post International*, July 23, 1988.

35 Sforno, *Biur al haTorah* on Deut. 1:12.

36 *Sifre*, Piska 12.

37 Ibn Ezra, *Perushei haTorah* on Deut. 1:12.

38 *Sifre*, Piska 12.

39 Firer, *Hegyonah shel Torah*, vol. 5, p. 18.

40 Hertz, *The Pentateuch and Haftorahs* on Num. 11:17.

41 Berlin, *HaAmek Davar* on Deut. 1:15.

42 Grossman, "The Differences between Devarim and Earlier Accounts."

43 *Targum of Jonathan ben Uziel* on Deut 1:16, p. 560.

44 Bazak, "How Shall I Bear Alone."

45 Jacob ben Asher, *Perush haTur haArokh* on Deut. 1:18.

46 Ramban, *Perushei haTorah* on Deut. 1:18.

47 Elijah ben Solomon Zalman of Vilna, *Aderet Eliyahu* on Deut. 1:15. See also Mecklenburg, *HaKtav vehaKabbalah* on Deut. 1:15.

48 *BT Hagigah* 14a.

49 Hoffmann, *Sefer Devarim* on Deut 1:15.

50 Malbim, *HaTorah vehaMitzvah* on Deut. 1:16.

51 Gordon, *Sefer Devarim* on Deut 1:16.

52 Hertz, *The Pentateuch and Haftorahs* on Deut. 1:16.

53 *BT Sanhedrin* 7b.

54 *Targum of Jonathan ben Uziel* on Deut 1:16, p. 560.

55 *Sifre,* Piska 16.

56 *BT Sanhedrin* 7b.

57 *Sifre*, Piska 16.

58 Hertz, *The Pentateuch and Haftorahs* on Deut. 1:16.

59 *BT Sanhedrin* 7b.

60 *Mishnah Avot* 1:8.

61 *Sifre*, Piska 17.

62 *BT Sanhedrin* 8a.

63 *Sifre*, Piska 17.

64 Ibid.

65 Porto, *Minhah Belulah*, p. 165a.

66 *BT Sanhedrin* 8a.

67 Gikatilla, *Gates of Light*, p. 200.

68 *BT Sanhedrin* 6b.

69 Tigay, *The JPS Torah Commentary: Deuteronomy* on Deut. 1:17.

70 Bahya ben Asher, *Biur al haTorah* on Deut. 1:17.

71 *Sifre*, Piska 17.

72 Tigay, *The JPS Torah Commentary: Deuteronomy* on Deut. 1:18.

73 Sforno, *Biur al haTorah* on Deut. 1:19.

74 Berlin, *HaAmek Davar* on Deut, 1:21.

75 Berlin, *HaAmek Davar* on Deut, 1:22.

76 Grossman, "The Differences between Devarim and Earlier Accounts."

77 Mecklenburg, *HaKtav vehaKabbalah* on Deut. 1:22.

78   Malbim, *HaTorah vehaMitzvah* on Num. 13:2 and Deut. 1:22.

79   Berlin, *HaAmek Davar* on Deut, 1:23.

80   Ibid.

81   *Yalkut Shimoni* #742 on Num. 13.

82   Attar, *Or haHayyim* on Num. 13:2.

83   Firer, *Hegyonah shel Torah*, vol. 5, pp. 18-19.

84   Caro, *Toldot Yitzhak* on Deut. 1:22-23.

85   Arama, *Akedat Yitzhak: Devarim*, sect. 87.

86   Hertz, *The Pentateuch and Haftorahs* on Deut. 1:2.

87   Hoffmann, *Sefer Devarim* on Deut 1:24-25.

88   Wahrhaftig, "The People's Responsibility for Their Leaders' Actions."

89   Munk, *The Call of the Torah* on Deut. 1:26.

90   Phillips, *Deuteronomy*, p. 19.

91   Berlin, *HaAmek Davar* on Deut, 1:27.

92   Although the Hebrew term *yam suf*, when used in connection with the exodus narrative, is properly rendered as *Sea of Reeds*, it is extremely unlikely that it has the same significance with regard to the period of wandering in the wilderness. It is most unlikely that they would have gone anywhere as close to Egypt as the site of the exodus and the destruction of the Egyptian army in its wake. Accordingly, the term in the present context probably refers to an extension of the Red Sea farther to the east, most likely to the Gulf of Eilat, the area where they crossed into Transjordan.

93   Abravanel, *Perush haTorah* on Deut. 1:22.

94   Keil and Delitzsch, *Commentary* on Deut. 1:34-36.

95   Tigay, *The JPS Torah Commentary: Deuteronomy* on Deut. 1:41.

96   Hirsch, *The Pentateuch* on Deut. 1:41.

97   Firer, *Hegyonah shel Torah*, vol. 5, pp. 20-22.

98   Thompson, *Deuteronomy*, p. 89.

99   Hertz, *The Pentateuch and Haftorahs* on Deut. 1:45.

100   *Seder Olam Rabbah* 8.

101   Thompson, *Deuteronomy*, p. 90.

102   Gersonides, *Perushei haTorah* on Deut. 2:2.

103   Hoffmann, *Sefer Devarim* on Deut 2:4-7.

104   Rashbam, *Perush haTorah* on Deut. 2:4; S.D. Luzzatto, *Perush al Hamisha Humshei Torah* on Deut. 2:4.

105   Munk, *The Call of the Torah* on Deut. 2:1.

106   Munk, *The Call of the Torah* on Deut. 2:9.

107   Gersonides, *Perushei haTorah* on Deut. 2:12.

108   Hirsch, *The Pentateuch* on Deut. 2:10.

109   *Tosafot* on *BT Baba Batra* 121a.

110   Aharoni and Avi-Yonah, *The Macmillan Bible Atlas,* map 52.

111   *BT Baba Batra* 121b; Rashi, *Perushei Rashi* on Deut. 2:16-17.

112   Hirsch, *The Pentateuch* on Deut. 2:16-17; Rashi, *Perushei Rashi* on Deut. 2:16-17.

113   Hoffmann, *Sefer Devarim* on Deut 2:16-19.

114   Cohen, *Joshua-Judges* on Josh. 13:3.

115   *BT Hullin* 60b.

116   For a concise summary of the contending positions on this question, see Ofir Cohen, *Divrei Shalom.*

117   Hirsch, *The Pentateuch* on Deut. 2:30.

118   Graetz, *History of the Jews,* vol. 1, p. 27.

119   Hertz, *The Pentateuch and Haftorahs* on Num. 21:34.

120   Tigay, *The JPS Torah Commentary: Deuteronomy* on Deut. 2:24 and 2:34-35.

121   Ramban, *Perushei haTorah* on Num. 32:33.

122   Firer, *Hegyonah shel Torah: Devarim,* p. 263.

123   Porto, *Minhah Belulah,* p. 166b.

124   *Sifre,* Piska 26.

125   *Sifre al Sefer Bamidbar* 134.

126 Rashi, *Perushei Rashi* on Deut. 3:24.

127 Maharal, *Gur Arye* on Deut. 3:24.

128 Berlin, *HaAmek Davar* on Deut. 3:24.

129 Hirsch, *The Pentateuch* on Deut. 3:24.

130 *Midrash Rabbah: Deuteronomy* 2:7.

131 *Sifre*, Piska 27.

132 Hertz, *The Pentateuch and Haftorahs* on Deut. 3:25.

133 Friedman, *Commentary on the Torah* on Deut. 3:26.

134 Berlin, *HaAmek Davar* on Deut. 3:26.

135 Thompson, *Deuteronomy*, p. 100.

136 Hertz, *The Pentateuch and Haftorahs* on Num. 20:11.

137 Rashi, *Perushei Rashi* on Deut. 3:28.

138 *The Zohar*, vol. 5, p. 344.

139 Gersonides, *Perushei haTorah* on Deut. 3:28.

140 Mecklenburg, *HaKtav vehaKabbalah* on Deut. 4:1.

141 Malbim, *HaTorah vehaMitzvah* on Deut. 4:1.

142 Ibn Ezra, *Perushei haTorah* on Deut 4:1.

143 *Mishnah Avot* 1:17.

144 Plaut, *The Torah* on Deut. 4:1.

145 Hertz, *The Pentateuch and Haftorahs* on Deut. 4:1.

146 Munk, *The Call of the Torah* on Deut. 4:1.

147 Hirsch, *The Pentateuch* on Deut. 4:1.

148 *Sifre*, Piska 58.

149 *BT Kiddushin* 37a.

150 *BT Keritot* 13b.

151 Berlin, *HaAmek Davar* on Deut. 4:1 and Lev. 18:5.

152 Porto, *Minhah Belulah*, p. 167b.

153 Friedman, *Commentary on the Torah* on Deut. 4:2.

154 Munk, *The Call of the Torah* on Deut. 4:2.

[155] Maimonides, *Mishne Torah: Hilkhot Mamrim* 2:9; *The Book of Judges: Rebels* 2:9.

[156] Ramban, *Perushei haTorah* on Deut. 4:2.

[157] *TJ: Megillah* 1:5.

[158] Malbim, *HaTorah vehaMitzvah* on Deut. 4:2.

[159] Hezekiah ben Manoah, *Hizzekuni* on Deut. 4:2.

[160] Gibschtein, *Daat Torah*, part 2, p. 50.

[161] Gersonides, *Perushei haTorah* on Deut. 4:2.

[162] Sforno, *Biur al haTorah* on Deut. 4:3.

[163] Hertz, *The Pentateuch and Haftorahs* on Num. 25:4.

[164] The disproportionate impact of the plague on the tribe of Simeon is made clear in the census that was taken shortly afterward.

[165] It is noteworthy that there is a tradition that this verse is recited aloud by the congregation immediately preceding the reading of the Torah during the synagogue service.

[166] Malbim, *HaTorah vehaMitzvah* on Deut. 4:3-4.

[167] Abraham Isaac Kook, quoted by Leibowitz, *Studies in Devarim*, p. 47.

[168] Hirsch, *The Pentateuch* on Deut. 4:3.

[169] Tigay, *The JPS Torah Commentary: Deuteronomy* on Deut. 4:5.

[170] Malbim, *HaTorah vehaMitzvah* on Deut. 4:6.

[171] Rashi, *Perushei Rashi* on Deut. 4:8.

[172] Sforno, *Biur al haTorah* on Deut. 4:8.

[173] Bahya ben Asher, *Biur al haTorah* on Deut. 4:6.

[174] Luzzatto, *Perush al Hamisha Humshei Torah* on Deut. 4:6.

[175] Goldberg, "The Torah's Many layers of Reason."

[176] Firer, *Hegyonah shel Torah*, vol. 5, pp. 45-46.

[177] Ramban, *Perushei haTorah* on Deut. 4:5.

[178] Hirsch, *The Pentateuch* on Deut. 4:5.

[179] Steinsaltz, *We Jews*, p. 179.

180   Ibn Ezra, *Perushei haTorah* on Deut. 4:9.

181   Munk, *The Call of the Torah* on Deut. 4:15.

182   Sforno, *Biur al haTorah* on Deut. 4:9.

183   Malbim, *HaTorah vehaMitzvah* on Deut. 4:9.

184   Heschel, *God in Search of Man*, p. 140.

185   *Mishnah Pesahim* 10:5.

186   Tigay, *The JPS Torah Commentary: Deuteronomy* on Deut. 4:9.

187   Munk, *The Call of the Torah* on Deut. 4:10.

188   Berlin, *HaAmek Davar* on Deut. 4:10.

189   Sicker, *The Ten Commandments*, pp. 2-9.

190   Maimonides, *The Guide of the Perplexed* 2:33.

191   Maimonides, *The Guide of the Perplexed* 3:9.

192   Hirsch, *The Pentateuch* on Deut. 4:11; S.D. Luzzatto, *Perush al Hamisha Humshei Torah* on Deut. 4: 11.

193   *Mekilta de-Rabbi Ishmael,* "Bahodesh" 8; *Midrash Rabbah: Exodus* 47:6..

194   *Talmud Yerushalmi: Shekalim* 6:1.

195   Phillips, *Deuteronomy*, p. 33.

196   Bahya ben Asher, *Biur al haTorah* on Deut. 4:5.

197   *BT Nedarim* 37a.

198   Rashi, *Perush al Mishlei.* 23:23.

199   *The Zohar*, vol. 5, p. 344.

200   Israel, "Idolatry."

201   *BT Avodah Zarah* 55a.

202   Maimonides, *The Guide of the Perplexed* 2:5.

203   *The Minor Tractates of the Talmud: Sefer Torah* 1:9; *BT Megillah* 9b.

204   Rashbam, *Perush haTorah* on Deut. 4:19.

205   Mecklenburg, *HaKtav vehaKabbalah* on Deut. 4:19.

206 Epstein, *Tosefet Berakhah* on Deut. 4:19.

207 Hoffmann, *Sefer Devarim* on Deut. 4:19.

208 Ramban, *Perushei haTorah* on Lev. 18:25.

209 *BT Shabbat* 156a-b. See also *BT Nedarim* 32a.

210 Ibn Ezra, *Perushei haTorah* on Ex. 20:1 (Introduction to the Decalogue).

211 Ibn Ezra, *Perushei haTorah* on Deut. 4:19.

212 Gibschtein, *Daat Torah*, part 2, p. 51.

213 Scherman, *The Chumash*, Deut. 4:21.

214 *Sifre al Sefer Bamidbar* 75.

215 Meir Simha HaCohen, *Meshekh Hokhmah*, p. 257.

216 *Mekilta deRabbi Ishmael*, "Amalek" 2; *Sifre al Sefer Bamidbar* 135.

217 Cited from *Midrash Tannaim* 178 and translated by Ginzberg, *The Legends of the Jews*, vol. 3, p. 422.

218 Munk, *The Call of the Torah* on Deut. 4:22.

219 Ramban, *Perushei haTorah* on Deut. 4:25.

220 *BT Gittin* 88a.

221 Rashi, *Perushei Rashi* on Deut. 32:1.

222 Phillips, *Deuteronomy*, p. 36.

223 Bahya ben Asher, *Biur al haTorah* on Deut. 4:28.

224 Maimonides, *The Guide of the Perplexed* 1:47.

225 *BT Ketuvot* 110b.

226 Munk, *The Call of the Torah* on Deut. 4:29.

227 Attar, *Or haHayyim* on Deut. 4:29.

228 Tigay, *The JPS Torah Commentary: Deuteronomy* on Deut. 4:34.

229 *BT Hagigah* 11b.

230 *The Wisdom of Ben Sira* 3:21-24. This text is cited with approval in *BT Hagigah* 13a.

231 Munk, *The Call of the Torah* on Deut. 4:35.

232 Sforno, *Biur al haTorah* on Deut. 4:36.

233 *Targum Yonatan ben Uziel* on Deut. 4:37; Ibn Ezra, *Perushei haTorah* on Deut. 4:37.

234 Hoffmann, *Sefer Devarim* on Deut. 4: 37-38.

235 Sforno, *Biur al haTorah* on Deut. 4:39.

236 Bahya ibn Pakuda, *The Duties of the Heart,* The First Gate: 2.

237 Bahya ben Asher, *Biur al haTorah* on Deut. 4:39.

238 A. Cohen, *Proverbs,* p. 166.

239 *Midrash Rabbah: Deuteronomy* 2:26-27.

240 Keil and Delitzsch, *Commentary* on Deut. 4:41-43.

241 Malbim, *HaTorah vehaMitzvah* on Deut. 4:41.

242 Hertz, *The Pentateuch and Haftorahs* on Deut. 4:45.

243 Kimhi, *Perush haRadak* on Psalm 119.

244 Tigay, *The JPS Torah Commentary: Deuteronomy* on Deut. 4:1.

245 Hoffmann, *Sefer Devarim* on Deut. 6:20.

246 *B.T. Yoma* 67b.

247 Bahya ben Asher, *Biur al haTorah* on Deut 5:1.

248 Hertz, *The Pentateuch and Haftorahs* on Deut. 5:1.

249 Hirsch, *The Pentateuch* on Deut. 5:1.

250 *BT Yevamot* 109b.

251 Rashi, *Perushei Rashi* on Deut. 5:3.

252 *Pesikta Rabbati* 21:6.

253 Attar, *Or haHayyim* on Deut. 5:19.

254 Luzzatto, *Perush al Hamisha Humshei Torah* on Deut. 5:21.

255 *BT Berakhot* 33b.

256 Malbim, *HaTorah vehaMitzvah* on Deut. 6:2.

257 Hirsch, *The Pentateuch* on Deut. 6:1-3.

258 *BT Bekhorot* 6b, 7b.

259 Hirsch, *The Pentateuch* on Deut. 6:4.

260 Eldad, *Hegyonot Mikra*, p. 240.

261 Jacobson, *Meditations on the Torah*, p. 270.

262 *Yalkut Shimoni* #833.

263 Rashi, *Perushei Rashi* on Deut. 6:4.

264 *Mishnah Berakhot* 2:2.

265 Greenberg, *Foundations of a Faith*, p.2. See also Silberman, "God and Man," in *Great Jewish Ideas*, p.151.

266 Rashbam, *Perush haTorah* on Deut. 6:4.

267 Meszler, *Witness to the One*, pp. 2-3.

268 Wyschogrod, "This One—and No Other," p. 97.

269 Berkovits, *Man and God*, p.29.

270 Ibn Ezra, *Perushei haTorah* on Deut. 6:4. A biblical example in support of Ibn Ezra's interpretation is I Chron. 29:1, where the word *ehad* (one) is clearly used in the sense of "alone."

271 Ibn Gabirol, *Keter Malkhut* 2, pp. 8-9. See also translation by Zangwill in *Selected Religious Poems of Solomon ibn Gabirol*, pp. 83-84.

272 Modena, *Magen vaHerev*, p. 22.

273 Bokser, *Judaism: Profile of a Faith*, p. 43.

274 Hertz, *The Pentateuch and Haftorahs* on Deut. 6:4.

275 Philo, *Allegorical Interpretation* 2:1:2-3.

276 Maimonides, *Mishneh Torah: Hilkhot Yesodei haTorah* 1:7. See also, *The Guide of the Perplexed* 1:57, 2:1.

277 Bleich, "One G-d, One People," in *Ehad: the Many Meanings of God is One*, p. 5.

278 Barth, *The Modern Jew Faces Eternal Problems*, p. 30.

279 Cohen, *Religion of Reason*, p. 41.

280 Montefiore, *Outlines of Liberal Judaism*, p. 54.

281 Munk, *The Call of the Torah* on Deut. 5:4.

282 *The Complete ArtScroll Siddur*, p. 485.

283   Wright, *Deuteronomy*, p. 97.

284   Hirsch, *The Pentateuch* on Deut. 6:5.

285   Maimonides, *The Book of Knowledge: Repentance* 10:3.

286   Tillich, *Love, Power, and Justice*, p. 26.

287   Ibid., p. 31.

288   Hermann Cohen, *Religion of Reason*, p. 159.

289   Rosenberg, *More Loves than One*, p. 35.

290   Hertz, *The Pentateuch and Haftorahs* on Deut. 6:5.

291   Schneur Zalman of Liadi, *Likutei Amarim*, Part 2, p. 283.

292   Bahya ibn Pakuda, *The Duties of the Heart*, p. 441.

293   Schneur Zalman of Liadi, *Likutei Amarim*, Part 2, pp. 283-285.

294   Maimonides, *Mishne Torah: Hilkhot Yesodei haTorah* 2:2; *The Book of Knowledge: The Foundation of the Torah* 2:2.

295   M.H. Luzzatto, *Mesillat Yesharim*, p. 16.

296   Steinsaltz, *Simple Words*, p. 200.

297   *Sifre*, Piska 32.

298   M.H. Luzzatto, *Mesillat Yesharim*, p. 16.

299   *Sifre*, Piska 32.

300   Meiri, *Bet haBehirah* on *Avot* 2:16.

301   Hirsch, *The Pentateuch* on Deut. 6:5.

302   Ibn Ezra, *Perushei haTorah* on Deut. 6:5.

303   Hoffmann, *Sefer Devarim* on Deut. 6:5.

304   Astruc, *Midreshei haTorah*, p. 189.

305   Luzzatto, *Perush al Hamisha Humshei Torah* on Deut. 6:4.

306   *Sifre*, Piska 32.

307   *BT Berakhot* 61b.

308   Mizrahi, supercommentary on Rashi on Deut. 6:5.

309   Hertz, *The Pentateuch and Haftorahs* on Deut. 6:5.

310   Astruc, *Midreshei haTorah*, p. 189.

311 *Sifre*, Piska 32.

312 Gersonides, *Perushei haTorah* on Deut. 6:7.

313 *The Zohar*, vol. 5, p. 364.

314 Hertz, *The Pentateuch and Haftorahs* on Deut. 6:7.

315 Hirsch, *The Pentateuch* on Deut. 6:8.

316 Tigay, *The JPS Torah Commentary: Deuteronomy* on Deut. 6:8.

317 *BT Menahot* 35b.

318 Friedman, *Commentary on the Torah* on Deut. 6:8.

319 *BT Menahot* 34a.

320 *BT Yoma* 11a.

321 Maimonides, *The Commandments*, Positive Commandment #7.

322 Ramban, *Perushei haTorah* on Deut. 6:13.

323 Moses of Coucy, *Sefer Mitzvot Gadol: Lo Taaseh* #4.

324 Ramban, *Perushei haTorah* on Deut. 6:16; Hirsch, *The Pentateuch* on Deut. 6:16.

325 Hirsch, *The Pentateuch* on Deut. 6:18.

326 Hertz, *The Pentateuch and Haftorahs* on Deut. 6:25.

327 Hoffmann, *Sefer Devarim* on Deut. 6:24-25.

328 Hirsch, *The Pentateuch* on Deut. 6:24.

329 Mecklenburg, *HaKtav vehaKabbalah* on Deut. 6:25.

330 Munk, *The Call of the Torah* on Deut. 6:20.

331 Israel, "Idolatry."

332 Wright, *Deuteronomy*, p. 110.

333 Phillips, *Deuteronomy*, pp. 60-61.

334 Albo, *Sefer Ha-Ikkarim* 3:37, pp. 347-348.

335 The phrase *thousand generations* may be understood as a poetic way of saying "forever," considering that if a generation is reckoned as thirty years, there are only approximately one hundred generations between Moses and ourselves, making a thousand generations the equivalent of thirty thousand years.

336 Rashi, *Perushei Rashi* on Deut. 7:9.

337 Onkelos, *Targum* on Deut. 7:10; Rashi, *Perushei Rashi* on Deut. 7:10.

338 *Sifre*, Piska 37.

339 *Midrash HaGadol* on Deut. 7:12, p. 154-155.

340 Malbim, *HaTorah vehaMitzvah* on Deut. 7:12.

341 Ibid.

342 Ephraim of Luntshits, *Perush Kli Yakar haShalem* on Deut. 7:12.

343 Onkelos, *Targum Onkelos* on Deut. 7:12.

344 Scherman, *The Chumash*, Deut. 7:12.

345 Sforno, *Biur al haTorah* on Deut. 7:12.

346 Hirsch, *The Pentateuch* on Deut. 7:12.

347 Berlin, *HaAmek Davar* on Deut. 7:14.

348 Tigay, *The JPS Torah Commentary: Deuteronomy* on Deut. 7:13.

349 Sorotzkin, *Insights in the Torah* on Deut. 7:15.

350 Ibid.

351 Gersonides, *Perushei haTorah* on Deut. 7:15.

352 Sforno, *Biur al haTorah* on Deut. 7:15.

353 *Talmud Yerushalmi: Shabbat* 14:3.

354 Likutei Peshatim, Parashas Ekev, Internet Edition Vol. 18 No. 41, August 5, 2004.

355 Sorotzkin, *Insights in the Torah* on Deut. 7:16.

356 Malbim, *HaTorah vehaMitzvah* on Deut. 7:16.

357 Hirsch, *The Pentateuch* on Deut. 7:16.

358 Ramban, *Perushei haTorah* on Deut. 7:16.

359 Malbim, *HaTorah vehaMitzvah* on Deut. 7:17.

360 Abravanel, *Perush haTorah* on Deut. 7:17.

361 Hertz, *The Pentateuch and Haftorahs* on Deut. 7:22.

362 Tigay, *The JPS Torah Commentary: Deuteronomy* on Deut. 7:22.

363 Gersonides, *Perushei haTorah* on Deut. 7:22.

364 Berlin, *HaAmek Davar* on Deut 7:23.

365 Sforno, *Biur al haTorah* on Deut. 7:24.

366 Berlin, *HaAmek Davar* on Deut 7:24.

367 Bekhor Shor, *Perush al haTorah* on Deut. 7:25.

368 Maimonides, *The Guide of the Perplexed* 3:37.

369 Malbim, *HaTorah vehaMitzvah* on Deut. 8:1.

370 Hertz, *The Pentateuch and Haftorahs* on Deut. 8:1.

371 Ibn Ezra, *Perushei haTorah* on Deut. 8:1.

372 Berlin, *HaAmek Davar* on Deut. 8:1.

373 Malbim, *HaTorah vehaMitzvah* on Deut. 8:2.

374 *B.T. Berakhot* 32a.

375 Wright, *Deuteronomy*, p. 122.

376 Ibid., p. 123.

377 Munk, *The Call of the Torah* on Deut. 8:16.

378 *The Midrash on Psalms* 23:4; *Midrash Rabbah: Song of Songs* 4:11:2.

379 Cited but not specifically endorsed by Ibn Ezra, *Perushei haTorah* on Deut 8:4.

380 Hoffmann, *Sefer Devarim* on Deut. 8:4.

381 Ibn Ezra, *Perushei haTorah* on Deut. 8:4.

382 Ramban, *Perushei haTorah* on Deut. 8:4.

383 Berlin, *HaAmek Davar* on Deut. 8:5.

384 Attar, *Or haHayyim* on Deut. 8:5.

385 *Midrash Tanhuma*, "Ki Tetze," 3, on Deut. 22:6.

386 Malbim, *HaTorah vehaMitzvah* on Deut. 8:7.

387 Munk, *The Call of the Torah* on Deut. 8:7.

388 Ramban, *Perushei haTorah* on Deut. 8:9.

389 *The Targum of Jonathan ben Uziel* on Deut. 8:9.

390 *Jerusalem Targum* on Deut. 8:9, imbedded in text of *The Targum of Jonathan ben Uziel.*

391 Ramban, *Perushei ha Torah* on Deut. 8:9.

392 Recanati, *Perush ha Torah* on Deut. 8:10.

393 Horowitz, *Shnei Luhot haBrit*, "Shaar haGadol."

394 Berlin, *HaAmek Davar* on Deut. 8:11.

395 Hirsch, *The Pentateuch* on Deut. 8:11.

396 Ibn Ezra, *Perushei ha Torah* on Deut. 8:14.

397 Hirsch, *The Pentateuch* on Deut. 8:18.

398 Bahya ben Asher, *Biur al ha Torah* on Deut. 8:18.

399 Attar, *Or haHayyim* on Deut. 9:2.

400 Sforno, *Biur al ha Torah* on Deut. 9:6.

401 Tigay, *The JPS Torah Commentary: Deuteronomy* on Deut. 9:9.

402 Muffs, *Biblical Theology*, p. 31.

403 *BT Berakhot* 32a.

404 The following analysis of the biblical text is derived from my earlier work, *The Convocation at Sinai*, pp. 127-130.

405 Epstein, *Tosefet Berakhah* on Ex. 32:11.

406 *Midrash haGadol* on Ex. 32:11.

407 *Midrash Rabbah: Exodus* 43:3.

408 Gersonides, *Perushei ha Torah* on Ex. 32:11.

409 Abravanel, *Perush ha Torah* on Ex. 32:7.

410 The reference to the Patriarchs as Abraham, Isaac, and Israel appears only one other time in the biblical writings, and then also only at a time of national crisis (1 Kings 18:36).

411 *BT Berakhot* 32a.

412 Attar, *Or haHayyim* on Ex. 32:14.

413 *BT Shabbat* 87a.

414 Gersonides, *Perushei ha Torah* on Ex. 32:19.

415 Hirsch, *The Pentateuch* on Deut. 9:17.

416 Gersonides: *Perushei haTorah* on Deut. 9:17; Firer, *Hegyonah shel Torah*, vol. 2, pp. 201-203.

417 Hoffmann, *Sefer Devarim* on Deut. 9:18-19.

418 Rashi, *Perushei Rashi* on Ex. 32:21.

419 Ramban, *Perushei haTorah* on Ex. 32:21.

420 Cassutto, *Perush al Sefer Shemot* on Ex. 32:22.

421 *BT Megillah* 25b.

422 See, for example, the discussion of this text by Munk, *The Call of the Torah* on Ex. 32:24.

423 Ramban, *Perushei haTorah* on Ex. 32:22.

424 Gersonides: *Perushei haTorah* on Deut. 9:20.

425 Sofer, *Torat Moshe: Sefer Devarim*, p. 25b.

426 Hoffmann, *Sefer Devarim* on Deut. 10:1-2.

427 Ehrlich, *Mikra kiFeshuto* on Deut. 10:1.

428 Hirsch, *The Pentateuch* on Deut. 10:2.

429 Jacob, *The Second Book of the Bible* on Ex. 34:1.

430 Ehrlich, *Mikra kiFeshuto* on Deut. 10:6.

431 Hertz, *The Pentateuch and Haftorahs* on Ex. 32:29 and Deut. 10:8.

432 Malbim, *HaTorah vehaMitzvah* on Deut. 10:8-9.

433 Hertz, *The Pentateuch and Haftorahs* on Deut. 10:12.

434 Moses Hayyim Luzzatto, *Mesillat Yesharim*, ch. 19, p. 312.

435 Albo, *Sefer Ha-Ikkarim* 3:31.

436 Attar, *Or haHayyim* on Deut. 10:12.

437 *BT Shabbat* 31a-b.

438 Gerondi, *Shnaim Assar Derushim*, #5, p. 39.

439 Tillich, *Dynamics of Faith*, p. 3.

440 Scherman, *The Chumash* on Deut. 10:12.

441 *BT Berakhot* 33b.

442 Lazarus, *The Ethics of Judaism*, Part 1, pp. 113-14.

443 Buber, *Israel and the World*, p. 71.

444 *Midrash Tanhuma*, "Bereshit," 6, on Gen. 3:22.

445 *Sifre*, Piska 49.

446 *B.T. Sotah* 14a. See also *B.T. Megillah* 31a; *Midrash Tanhuma*, Buber edition, "Vayera" p.42a-43b; *Midrash Rabbah: Genesis* 8:13; *Midrash Rabbah: Ecclesiastes* 7:2, #2-#3.

447 See Maimonides, *The Commandments*, Positive Commandment #8; Moses of Coucy, *Sefer Mitzvot Gadol*, "Aseh," #7; *Sefer haHinukh* #608.

448 Bokser, *Judaism: Profile of a Faith*, p. 162.

449 Schechter, *Some Aspects of Rabbinic Theology*, pp. 203-204.

450 Ibid.

451 *Mekilta de-Rabbi Ishmael*, "BaHodesh," 6.

452 Malbim, *HaTorah vehaMitzvah* on Ex. 20:5.

453 Berkovits, *Man and God*, pp. 251-252.

454 Gersonides, *Perushei haTorah* on Deut. 10:12.

455 Spero, "After All, The Lord Does Not Ask For Much!" p. 155.

456 Ibid., p. 156.

457 Hertz, *The Pentateuch and Haftorahs* on Deut. 10:16.

458 Ibn Ezra, *Perushei haTorah* on Gen. 1:1.

459 Malbim, *HaTorah vehaMitzvah* on Deut. 10:17.

460 Munk, *The Call of the Torah* on Deut. 10:19.

461 Hermann Cohen, *Religion of Reason*, p. 145.

462 Hertz, *The Pentateuch and Haftorahs* on Deut. 10:21.

463 Hertz, *The Pentateuch and Haftorahs* on Deut. 11:6.

464 *Midrash HaGadol* on Deut. 11:12, p. 203.

465 Attar, *Or haHayyim* on Deut. 11:13.

466 Hertz, *The Pentateuch and Haftorahs* on Deut. 11:16.

467 *Sifre*, Piska 48.

468 *Sifre*, Piska 49.

469 *Sifre*, Piska 51.

470 *Sifre*, Piska 52.

471 Leff, *Kol Yaacov*, "If Dogs Could Talk."

472 For an in depth consideration of this issue, see my *Between Man and God*, pp. 21-40.

473 Gersonides, *Perushei haTorah* on Deut. 11:26.

474 Hirsch, *The Pentateuch* on Deut. 11:26.

475 Sforno, *Biur al haTorah* on Deut. 11:26-28.

476 Attar, *Or haHayyim* on Deut. 11:26.

477 Astruc, *Midreshei haTorah*, p. 192.

478 Elijah of Vilna, *Aderet Eliyahu* on Deut. 11:26.

479 Hirsch, *The Pentateuch* on Deut. 11:27.

480 *The Torah: The Five Books of Moses*, Deut. 11:28, and translator's note, p. 347.

481 Ephraim of Luntshits, *Perush Kli Yakar haShalem* on Deut. 11:27.

482 Porto, *Minhah Belulah*, p. 176b.

483 Onkelos, *Targum Onkelos* on Deut. 11:29.

484 Ramban, *Perushei haTorah* on Deut. 11:29.

485 *Sifre*, Piska 55.

486 *Mishnah Sotah* 7:5.

487 S.D. Luzzatto, *Perush al Hamisha Humshei Torah* on Deut. 11:29.

488 Gersonides, *Perushei haTorah* on Deut. 11:32.

489 *Sifre*, Piska 58.

490 Friedman, *Commentary on the Torah* on Deut. 11:30.

491 For a concise discussion of the problem and some proposed solutions, see Tigay, *The JPS Torah Commentary: Deuteronomy* on Deut. 11:30.

492 Steinberg, *Millon haTanakh*, p. 146.

493 Hurlbut, *A Bible Atlas*, p. 40.

494 Hoffmann, *Sefer Devarim* on Deut. 11:30.

495 *Sifre*, Piska 59; *BT Kiddushin* 37a.

496 Sforno, *Biur al haTorah* on Deut. 12:1-5.

497 Rashi, *Perushei Rashi* on Deut. 12:3.

498 Mecklenburg, *HaKtav vehaKabbalah* on Deut. 12:3.

499 *BT Avodah Zarah* 45a-b.

500 Hoffmann, *Sefer Devarim* on Deut. 12:2-3.

501 Gersonides, *Perushei haTorah* on Deut. 12:3.

502 *Sifre*, Piska 61.

503 *BT Hullin* 13b.

504 *Sifre*, Piska 61; *BT Shevuot* 35a-b.

505 *Sifre*, Piska 62.

506 Friedman, *Commentary on the Torah* on Deut. 12:5.

507 Ibid.

508 Keil and Delitzsch, *Commentary* on Deut. 12:2, 3.

509 Ephraim of Luntshits, *Perush Kli Yakar haShalem* on Deut. 12:4.

510 Hertz, *The Pentateuch and Haftorahs* on Deut. 12:5.

511 *Sifre*, Piska 63.

512 Sforno, *Biur al haTorah* on Deut. 12:7.

513 Ibn Ezra, *Perushei haTorah* on Deut. 12:8.

514 Hertz, *The Pentateuch and Haftorahs* on Lev. 17:7.

515 Ramban, *Perushei haTorah* on Deut. 12:8.

516 Ehrlich, *Mikra kiFeshuto* on Deut. 12:8.

517 *Sifre*, Piska 71.

518 Ibid.

519 Hirsch, *The Pentateuch* on Deut. 12:19.

520 Hoffmann, *Sefer Devarim* on Deut. 12:20.

521 Ramban, *Perushei haTorah* on Deut. 12:21.

522   *BT Hullin* 28a.

523   Gersonides, *Perushei haTorah* on Deut. 12:22.

524   Jacob ben Asher, *Perush haTur haArokh* on Deut. 12:23.

525   Luzzatto, *Perush al Hamisha Humshei Torah* on Deut. 12:23.

526   Hertz, *The Pentateuch and Haftorahs* on Gen. 9:4.

527   Hirsch, *The Pentateuch* on Deut. 12:23.

528   Sforno, *Biur al haTorah* on Deut. 12:23.

529   Cited by Hertz, *The Pentateuch and Haftorahs* on Lev. 1:5.

530   *Sifre*, Piska 79.

531   Malbim, *HaTorah vehaMitzvah* on Deut. 12:28.

532   Hezekiah ben Manoah, *Hizzekuni* on Deut. 13:1; Jacob ben Asher, *Perush haTur haArokh* on Deut. 12:31.

533   Hirsch, *The Pentateuch* on Deut. 12:29.

534   Ibn Ezra, *Perushei haTorah* on Deut. 13:2.

535   Maimonides, *The Book of Knowledge: The Foundations of the Torah* 8:2.

536   Ramban, *Perushei haTorah* on Deut. 13:2.

537   *BT Sanhedrin* 90a.

538   Hertz, *The Pentateuch and Haftorahs* on Deut. 13:4.

539   Sforno, *Biur al haTorah* on Deut. 13:3.

540   Hoffmann, *Sefer Devarim* on Deut. 13:2-6.

541   *BT Sanhedrin* 90a.

542   Munk, *The Call of the Torah* on Deut. 13:5.

543   Malbim, *HaTorah vehaMitzvah* on Deut. 13:2.

544   Hoffmann, *Sefer Devarim* on Deut. 13:7-12.

545   *Sifre*, Piska 87.

546   Sorotzkin, *Insights in the Torah* on Deut. 13:7.

547   *The Septuagint Version*, Deut. 13:6.

548   *Sifre*, Piska 87.

549 Hertz, *The Pentateuch and Haftorahs* on Deut. 13:7.

550 Malbim, *HaTorah vehaMitzvah* on Deut. 13:9.

551 Philo, *The Special Laws 1*, 58 (315).

552 *Mishnah Sanhedrin* 7:10.

553 *Sifre*, Piska 87.

554 Hoffmann, *Sefer Devarim* on Deut. 13:7-12.

555 Ibid.

556 *Sifre*, Piska 93.

557 *Mishnah Sanhedrin* 10:4.

558 Hirsch, *The Pentateuch* on Deut. 13:14.

559 *Sifre*, Piska 92.

560 Hoffmann, *Sefer Devarim* on Deut. 13:13.

561 Friedman, *Commentary on the Torah* on Deut. 13:16.

562 The following discussion regarding the Deluge and Sodom and Gomorrah is drawn directly from my *The Trials of Abraham*, pp. 117-128.

563 In an otherwise engaging examination of the discussion between Abraham and God, Alan M. Dershowitz, writing from a juridical perspective, tends to use the terms law and justice as well as righteousness and innocence interchangeably, thus confusing the issue and, in my view, missing some of the essential points of the interchange (*The Genesis of Justice*, pp. 69-93).

564 For an in-depth discussion of the biblical concept of communal responsibility, see Daube, *Studies in Biblical Law*, chapter 4. It is noteworthy that, in his discussion, Daube, writing from the perspective of a jurist, seems to have entirely missed the critical distinction being made here between righteousness and innocence, and their political as opposed to jurisprudential implications.

565 *Etz Hayim: Torah and Commentary*, note on 18:24, p. 103.

566 *Tosefta Sanhedrin* 14:1.

567 Ehrlich, *Mikra kiFeshuto* on Deut. 14:1.

568 *Sifre*, Piska 96; *BT Kiddushin* 36a.

569 Malbim, *Hatorah vehaMitzvah* on Deut. 14:1.

570 Munk, *The Call of the Torah* on Deut. 14:1.

571 Hertz, *The Pentateuch and Haftorahs* on Lev. 19:28.

572 *Sifre*, Piska 96.

573 *BT Yevamot* 13b-14a.

574 Tigay, *The JPS Torah Commentary: Deuteronomy*, p. 137.

575 Luzzatto, *Perush al Hamisha Humshei Torah*, p. 407, note citing Luzzatto's article originally published in the journal *Hamishtadel*.

576 Hoffmann, *Sefer Devarim*, pp. 204-205.

577 Hertz, *The Pentateuch and Haftorahs* on Lev. 11:8.

578 Hertz, *The Pentateuch and Haftorahs* on Lev. 11:12.

579 *Sifre*, Piska 103.

580 Malbim, *HaTorah vehaMitzvah* on Ex. 34:26. Maimonides also suspected that this had something to do with idolatry, although he was unaware of any evidence to support such a conclusion (*The Guide of the Perplexed* 3:48). The evidence for this, as reported by Cassutto, has indeed been discovered at Ugarit in contemporary times (*Perush al Sefer Shemot* on Ex. 23:19). He also notes that a similar practice persists to this day among the Bedouin.

581 Phillips, *Deuteronomy*, p. 100.

582 Sforno, *Biur al haTorah* on Ex. 34:18.

583 *Mishna Rosh Hashanah* 1:1.

584 Bekhor Shor, *Perush al haTorah* on Ex. 34:26. This interpretation also is cited by Hezekiah ben Manoah, *Hizzekuni* on Ex. 34:26.

585 *Sifre*, Piska 107.

586 Ibn Ezra, *Perushei haTorah* on Deut. 14:28.

587 *Sifre*, Piska 109.

588 Luzzatto, *Perush al Hamisha Humshei Torah* on Deut. 14:28.

589 The following discussion of this passage is drawn primarily from my *The Political Culture of Judaism*, pp. 99-100.

590 Ibn Ezra, *Perushei haTorah* on Deut. 15:2.

591 *Mishnah Sheviyit* 10:4; *BT Gittin* 36a.

592 Luzzatto, *Perush al Hamisha Humshei Torah* on Deut. 15:4.

593 Levinthal, *Judaism Speaks to the Modern World*, p. 108.

594 *Mishnah Avot* 3:21.

595 Richard G. Hirsch, "There Shall Be No Poor," p. 237.

596 *BT Eruvin* 41b.

597 *Exodus Rabbah* 31:14.

598 *BT Berakhot* 6b.

599 R.G. Hirsch, "There Shall Be No Poor," p. 238.

600 Herberg, *Judaism and Modern Man*, pp. 151-52.

601 The present discussion of the distinction between the "poor" and the "needy" is drawn from my *The Idea of Justice in Judaism*, pp. 111-112.

602 Rashi's commentary on *BT Baba Metzia* 111b; Shlomo Goren, *Torat haMedinah*, pp. 368-70.

603 Rashi, *Perushei Rashi* on Deut. 14:7.

604 *Sifre*, Piska 116.

605 Rashi, *Perushei Rashi* on Deut. 15:8.

606 *Sifre*, Piska 116; *BT Ketuvot* 67b.

607 *Mekilta de-Rabbi Ishmael*, "Kaspa," 1.

608 Maimonides, *The Commandments*, Positive Commandment 197, p. 211.

609 Maimonides, *The Book of Civil Laws*, "Creditor and Debtor," 1:1, p. 78; *Mishnah Torah: Hilkhot Malveh veLoveh* 1:1.

610 Joseph Caro, *Shulhan Arukh: Hoshen Mishpat* 97:1.

611 Jakobovits, *Journal of a Rabbi*, p. 114.

612 *Mekilta de-Rabbi Ishmael.* Nezikin 1.

613 *BT Kiddushin* 14b.

614 Ibid.

615 Harlap, "The Hebrew Slave in the Light of Peshat."

616 Wright, *Deuteronomy*, p. 193.

617 *BT Kiddushin* 20a.

618 Lauterbach, *Rabbinic Essays*, p. 278.

619 *Sifre*, Piska 122.

620 Hertz, *The Pentateuch and Haftorahs* on Deut. 15:17.

621 *BT Sotah* 23b.

622 Luzzatto, *Perush al Hamisha Humshei Torah* on Deut. 15:12.

623 *Sifre*, Piska 122.

624 *Sifre*, Piska 118. See *BT Kiddushin* 18a-b for additional distinctions and qualifications.

625 Hertz, *The Pentateuch and Haftorahs* on Deut. 16:2.

626 Margalit, "*Matzot Mitzrayim uMatzot Dorot*," p. 330.

627 Sarna, *Exploring Exodus*, p. 90.

628 Hertz, *The Pentateuch and Haftorahs* on Lev. 23:42.

629 Bekhor Shor, *Perushei haTorah* on Deut. 16:11.

630 Munk, *The Call of the Torah* on Deut 17:20.

631 Ibn Ezra, *Perushei haTorah* on Deut. 16:18.

632 Firer, *Hegyonah shel Torah*, vol. 5, pp. 134-37.

633 *BT Sanhedrin* 3b.

634 Gersonides, *Perushei haTorah* on Deut. 16:18.

635 Ephraim of Luntshits, *Perush Kli Yakar* on Deut. 16:18.

636 *Sifre*, Piska 144; S.D. Luzzatto, *Perush Shadal al Hamishah Humshei Torah* on Deut. 16:18.

637 *Sifre*, Piska 144; *BT Sanhedrin* 16b.

638 Epstein, *Torah Temimah* on Deut. 16:18.

639 Ramban, *Perushei haTorah* on Deut. 16:18.

640 *Tosafot* on *BT Sanhedrin 16b*.

641 Emden, *Hiddushim veHagahot* on *BT Sanhedrin* 16b.

642 *Sifre*, Piska 144; *BT Sanhedrin* 16b.

643 Sforno, *Biur al haTorah* on Ex. 18:21.

644 Hoffmann, *Sefer Devarim*, p. 305.

645 Sforno, *Biur al haTorah* on Deut. 16:18.

646 *BT Sotah* 42a.

647 Rashi, commentary on *BT Sotah* 42a.

648 Rashi, commentary on *BT Sanhedrin* 16b.

649 Rashi, *Perushei Rashi* on Deut. 16:18.

650 Rashbam, *Perush haTorah* on Deut. 16:18; Jacob ben Asher, *Arba Turim: Tur Hoshen Mishpat* 1:2a; Abravanel, *Perush haTorah* on Deut. 16:18.

651 Bertinoro, *Amar Neke* on Deut. 16:18.

652 Maimonides, *The Book of Judges: Sanhedrin* 1:1; *Mishmeh Torah: Hilkhot Sanhedrin* 1:1. See also Gersonides, *Perushei haTorah* on Deut. 16:18; Maharal, *Gur Aryeh* on Deut. 16:18; and Mecklenburg, *HaKtav vehaKabbalah* on Deut. 16:18.

653 Meyuhas ben Elijah, *Perush al Sefer Devarim* on Deut. 16:18.

654 Porto, *Minhah Belulah*, p. 181b.

655 Anatoli, *Malmad haTalmidim*, p. 167a.

656 Samuel ben Hophni, *Perush haTorah*, p. 520.

657 *Midrash Tanhuma* (Rosen edition), "Shofetim" 2.

658 Attar, *Or haHayyim* on Deut. 16:18.

659 Ibn Ezra, *Perushei haTorah* on Deut. 16:18; Kimhi, *Sefer haShorashim*, p. 383.

660 Luzzatto, *Perush Shadal al Hamishah Humshei Torah* on Deut. 16:18.

661 Ibid.

662 *Midrash Tanhuma*, "Shofetim" 4.

663 *Midrash haGadol* on Deut. 16:18.

664 Friedman, *Commentary on the Torah* on Deut. 16:18.

665 Sforno, *Biur al haTorah* on Deut. 16:18.

666 Berlin, *HaAmek Davar* on Deut. 16:18.

667 Munk, *The Call of the Torah* on Deut. 16:19.

668 Gersonides, *Perushei haTorah* on Deut. 16:19.

669 Munk, *The Call of the Torah* on Deut. 16:19.

670 Luzzatto, *Perush Shadal al Hamishah Humshei Torah* on Deut. 16:19.

671 *Sifre*, Piska 144.

672 Gersonides, *Perushei haTorah* on Deut. 16:19.

673 Elijah of Vilna, *Aderet Eliyahu* on Deut. 16:19; Malbim, *HaTorah vehaMitzvah* on Deut. 16:19.

674 *Sifre*, Piska 144; *BT Sanhedrin* 32b.

675 Phillips, *Deuteronomy*, on Deut. 16:20.

676 Sforno, *Biur al haTorah* on Deut. 16:20.

677 Attar, *Or HaHayyim* on Deut. 16:20.

678 Malbim, *HaTorah vehaMitzvah* on Deut. 16:20.

679 *Mishnah Sanhedrin* 4:1.

680 Mecklenburg, *HaKtav vehaKabbalah* on Deut. 16:20.

681 *BT Avodah Zarah* 52a.

682 Ibn Ezra, *Perushei haTorah* on Deut. 16:20.

683 Kiel, *Commentary* on Deut. 16:18-17:7, vol. 1, p. 924.

684 Hoffmann, *Sefer Devarim*, pp. 296-97.

685 Hirsch, *The Pentateuch* on Deut. 16:21.

686 *Sifre*, Piska 145.

687 *BT Tamid* 28b.

688 *Mishnah: Avodah Zarah* 3:7.

689 Ramban, *Perushei haTorah* on Deut. 16:22.

690 Hirsch, *The Pentateuch* on Deut. 17:1.

691 *Sifre*, Piska 147.

692 Luzzatto, *Perush Shadal al Hamishah Humshei Torah* on Deut. 17:3.

693 Bahya ben Asher, *Biur al haTorah* on Deut. 17:3.

694 Sforno, *Biur al haTorah* on Deut. 17:3.

695 Ibn Ezra, *Perushei haTorah* on Deut. 17:3.

696 Bahya ben Asher, *Biur al haTorah* on Deut. 17:2.

697 *Sifre*, Piska 150.

698 Hirsch, *The Pentateuch* on Deut. 17:6.

699 Ramban, *Perushei haTorah* on Deut. 17:6.

700 Luzzatto, *Perush Shadal al Hamishah Humshei Torah* on Deut. 17:6.

701 Ibn Ezra, *Perushei haTorah* on Deut. 17:6.

702 Hertz, *The Pentateuch and Haftorahs* on Deut. 17:6.

703 *Sifre*, Piska 149.

704 *Sifre*, Piska 151.

705 Friedman, *Commentary on the Torah* on Deut. 17:7.

706 *BT Sanhedrin* 52b.

707 Hirsch, *The Pentateuch* on Deut. 17:8.

708 Ramban, *Perushei haTorah* on Deut. 17:11.

709 Hirsch, *The Pentateuch* on Deut. 17:8-13.

710 *BT Niddah* 19a.

711 *BT Sanhedrin* 87b.

712 Luzzatto, *Perush Shadal al Hamishah Humshei Torah* on Deut. 17:8.

713 Ibid.

714 *BT Sanhedrin* 87b.

715 Ibn Ezra, *Perushei haTorah* on Deut. 17:8.

716 *BT Sanhedrin* 88a.

717 Ibn Ezra, *Perushei haTorah* on Num. 16:1 and Deut. 17:9.

718   Hirsch, *The Pentateuch* on Deut. 18:1.

719   Ibn Ezra, *Perushei haTorah* on Num. 16:1; Friedman, *Commentary on the Torah* on Deut. 17:9.

720   *Sifre*, Piska 153.

721   Berlin, *HaAmek Davar* on Deut. 17:12.

722   *Sifre*, Piska 153.

723   *Mishnah Sanhedrin* 3:4.

724   *BT Rosh Hashanah* 25b.

725   Munk, *The Call of the Torah* on Deut. 17:9.

726   *Sifre*, Piska 154.

727   Ramban, *Perushei haTorah* on Deut. 17:11.

728   *JT Horayot* 1:1.

729   Hirsch, *The Pentateuch* on Deut. 17:10.

730   Elijah of Vilna, *Aderet Eliyahu* on Deut. 17:10.

731   Hoffmann, *Sefer Devarim* on Deut. 17:8-11, pp. 311-14.

732   Elijah of Vilna, *Aderet Eliyahu* on Deut. 17:12.

733   *Sifre*, Piska 155.

734   *BT Sanhedrin* 88b.

735   *Sifre*, Piska 155.

736   Wright, *Deuteronomy*, p. 207.

737   Hertz, *The Pentateuch and Haftorahs* on Num. 27:17.

738   Anatoli, *Malmad haTalmidim*, p. 167a.

739   *Sefer haHinukh* #97.

740   *Sefer haHinukh* #493.

741   Luzzatto, *Perush Shadal al Hamishah Humshei Torah* on Deut. 17:14.

742   *BT Sanhedrin* 20b; *Sifre*, Piska 156.

743   Malbim, *HaTorah vehaMitzvah* on Deut. 27:14 and *Sifre*, Piska 156.

744 *Midrash Rabbah: Deuteronomy* 5:8.

745 Maimonides, *The Commandments*, Positive Commandment #173.

746 Maimonides, *The Guide for the Perplexed* 2:40. In this instance, the Friedlander translation is much clearer than the Pines translation used elsewhere in this study.

747 Samuel HaNagid, *Ben Mishlei*, #828, p. 238.

748 Shalom, *Nevei Shalom*, p. 108.

749 J.M. Epstein, *Arukh haShulhan heated: Sanhedrin*, "Hilhot Melakhim" 71:3.

750 Albo, *Sefer Ha'Ikkarim* 1:73.

751 Malbim, *Mikra'ei Kodesh* on 1 Sam. 8:6 and *HaTorah vehaMitzvah* on Deut. 17:14.

752 Hoffmann, *Sefer Devarim*, p. 333. Luzzatto, *Perush Shadal al Hamishah Humshei Torah* on Deut. 17:14, makes essentially the same argument.

753 Abravanel, *Perush haTorah* on Deut. 17:14.

754 Sforno, *Biur al haTorah* on Deut. 17:14.

755 Berlin, *HaAmek Davar* on Deut. 17:14.

756 Ibn Ezra, *Perushei haTorah* on Deut. 17:15.

757 Ramban, *Perushei haTorah* on Deut. 17:14.

758 *JT Sanhedrin* 2:6.

759 Margoliot, *Pneh Moshe* on *JT Sanhedrin* 2:6. See also Epstein, *Torah Temimah* on Deut. 17:14.

760 Commentary by an anonymous author on *JT Sanhedrin* 2:6, in the Cracow edition of 1609, reprinted in *Talmud Bavli veYerushalmi*.

761 Munk, *The Call of the Torah* on Deut. 17:15.

762 Attar, *Or haHayyim* on Deut. 17:14.

763 *BT Baba Batra* 91b.

764 Maimonides, *The Guide of the Perplexed* 3:50.

765 Ibn Ezra, *Perushei haTorah* on Deut. 17:15.

766 Ramban, *Perushei haTorah* on Deut. 17:15.

767 Tigay, *The JPS Torah Commentary: Deuteronomy*, p. 166.

768 Bahya ben Asher, *Biur al haTorah* on Deut. 17:16.

769 Hirsch, *The Pentateuch* on Deut. 17:16.

770 Firer, *Hegyonah shel Torah*, vol. 5, p. 147.

771 *BT Sanhedrin* 21b.

772 Friedman, *Commentary on the Torah* on Deut. 17:16.

773 Maimonides, *Commentary on the Mishnah: Tractate Sanhedrin* 2.

774 Ramban, *Perushei haTorah* on Deut. 17:16.

775 *JT Sanhedrin* 10:8; Maimonides, *The Book of Judges: Kings and Wars* 5:8.

776 Munk, *The Call of the Torah* on Deut. 17:16.

777 Hirsch, *The Pentateuch* on Deut. 17:16.

778 Hertz, *The Pentateuch and Haftorahs* on Deut. 17:17.

779 *Sifre*, Piska 159; *Mishnah Sanhedrin* 2:4.

780 Hirsch, *The Pentateuch* on Deut. 17:16.

781 *BT Sanhedrin* 21b.

782 Judah J. Slotki commentary in *Babylonian Talmud: Sanhedrin*, p. 117, n. 11.

783 *BT Sanhedrin* 21b; *Sifre*, Piska 159..

784 Ibn Ezra, *Perushei haTorah* on Deut. 17:17.; Gersonides, *Perushei haTorah* on Deut. 17:17.

785 *Sifre*, Piska 160.

786 *BT Sanhedrin* 21b.

787 Munk, *The Call of the Torah* on Deut. 17:18. Munk cites this in the name of the Tosafot but does not indicate where it is stated, and refers to a remark cited in Nathan ben Jehiel, *Sefer haArukh*, "Tefel," p. 588 to the effect that some medieval scholars, evidently working with a variant manuscript of the Torah, asserted that since the number of letters in the Decalogue was 613 (which is

not the count in the received Masoretic text), corresponding to the 613 commandments, the Decalogue could be considered as constituting the entire law of the Torah.

788 *Sefer haHinukh* #494.

789 Chajes, *Torat Neviyyim*, p. 48.

790 Ibn Ezra, *Perushei haTorah* on Deut. 18:1.

791 Hertz, *The Pentateuch and Haftorahs* on Deut. 18:1.

792 *Sifre*, Piska 165.

793 Hertz, *The Pentateuch and Haftorahs* on Deut. 18:3.

794 Tigay, *The JPS Torah Commentary: Deuteronomy* on Deut. 18:3.

795 Philo, *The Special Laws* 1:147.

796 *BT Hullin* 130b.

797 Ibid.

798 Ramban, *Perushei haTorah* on Deut. 18:3.

799 *Sifre*, Piska 165; *BT Hullin* 134b.

800 Maimonides, *The Guide of the Perplexed* 3:39.

801 *Mishnah Hullin* 10:4.

802 Luzzatto, *Perush Shadal al Hamishah Humshei Torah* on Deut. 18:3.

803 Philo, *The Special Laws* 1:147.

804 Hoffmann, *Sefer Devarim* on Deut. 18:3-5.

805 Hirsch, *The Pentateuch* on Deut. 18:1.

806 Hirsch, *The Pentateuch* on Deut. 18:5.

807 *Mishnah Zevahim* 2:1.

808 *BT Taanit* 27a.

809 Hoffmann, *Sefer Devarim* on Deut. 18:6-8.

810 Ibn Ezra, *Perushei haTorah* on Deut. 18:8.

811 Luzzatto, *Perush Shadal al Hamishah Humshei Torah* on Deut. 18:8.

812 *Sifre*, Piska 168.

813   *BT Arakhin* 11a; *Midrash haGadol* on Deut. 18:7.

814   Rashi, *Perushei Rashi* on Deut. 18:6-7, and numerous others.

815   Hoffmann, *Sefer Devarim* on Deut. 18:6-8.

816   Bekhor Shor, *Perush al haTorah* on Deut. 18:6; Hezekiah ben Manoah, *Hizzekuni* on Deut. 18:6; Elijah of Vilna, *Aderet Eliyahu* on Deut. 18:6-7.

817   *BT Sanhedrin* 64a-b.

818   Ramban, *Perushei haTorah* on Deut. 18:13.

819   Hertz, *The Pentateuch and Haftorahs* on Deut. 18:13.

820   Rashi, *Perushei Rashi* on Deut. 18:13.

821   Ibn Ezra, *Perushei haTorah* on Gen. 17:1.

822   Lichtenstein, "Temimut veShleimut." Comment on Maimonides, *The Book of Knowledge: Idolatry* 11:16.

823   Munk, *The Call of the Torah* on Deut. 18:13.

824   *Sifre*, Piska 170.

825   Maimonides, *The Book of Judges: Sanhedrin* 2:1.

826   Hirsch, *The Pentateuch* on Deut. 18:15.

827   Hoffmann, *Sefer Devarim*, pp. 342-343.

828   Saadiah, *The Book of Beliefs and Opinions*, pp. 145-147.

829   Albo, *Sefer Ha-Ikkarim*, vol 3, p. 109.

830   Heschel, *The Prophets*, p. 202.

831   Chajes, *Torat Neviyyim*, p. 13.

832   Albo, *Sefer Ha-Ikkarim*, vol. 3, p. 107.

833   Heschel, *The Prophets*, p. 205.

834   *Sifre*, Piska 175.

835   Hirsch, *The Pentateuch* on Deut. 18:15.

836   *Sifre*, Piska 175.

837   *Targum Yonatan ben Uziel* on Deut. 18:15.

838   Tigay, *The JPS Torah Commentary: Deuteronomy* on Deut. 18:15.

839 *BT Nedarim* 38a.

840 *BT Shabbat* 92a.

841 *Mishnah Avot* 4:1.

842 Maimonides, *Mishneh Torah: Hilkhot Yesodei haTorah* 7:1 (my translation); *The Book of Knowledge: The Foundation of the Torah* 7:1.

843 Joseph Caro, *Kesef Mishneh* on *Hilkhot Yesodei haTorah* 7:1.

844 Gerondi, *Shnaim Assar Derushim* #5, p. 34.

845 Edels, *Hiddushei Aggadot* on *BT Nedarim* 38a.

846 Hirsch, *The Pentateuch* on Ex. 2:11-12.

847 Hirsch, *The Pentateuch* on Ex. 6:14-27.

848 *Torat Kohanim (Sifra), Parshat beHukotai*, 13:7.

849 *Yalkut Shimoni: Netzavim* 30, p. 665.

850 *BT Yevamot* 90b; *Sifre*, Piska 175.

851 Ramban, *Perushei haTorah* on Deut. 18:21.

852 *Sifre*, Piska 177: *Mishnah Sanhedrin* 11:5.

853 *Sifre*, Piska 155 and 178.

854 *BT Sanhedrin* 52b.

855 *Sifre*, Piska 178.

856 Hirsch, *The Pentateuch* on Deut. 18:21-22.

857 *Sifre*, Piska 178.

858 *Sifre*, Piska 180.

859 Pardo, *Perush Sifre deVei Rav* on Piska 180.

860 Sulzberger, "The Ancient Hebrew Law of Homicide," part 2, p. 306.

861 *BT Makkot* 7b.

862 Sulzberger, "The Ancient Hebrew Law of Homicide," part 2, p. 304.

863 Ibid., p. 309.

864 Phillips, *Deuteronomy* on Deut. 19:6.

865 Rashi, *Perushei Rashi* on Deut. 19:8.

866 *Sifre*, Piska 185.

867 *Sifre*, Piska 186/87.

868 Mecklenburg, *HaKtav vehaKabbalah* on Deut. 19:13.

869 Hirsch, *The Pentateuch* on Deut. 19:14.

870 Hoffmann, *Sefer Devarim* on Deut. 19:14.

871 *Sifre*, Piska 188.

872 *BT Sanhedrin* 89a.

873 Hoffmann, *Sefer Devarim* on Deut. 19:16-21.

874 *Mishnah Makkot* 1:6.

875 *Sefer haHinukh* #501; Munk, *The Call of the Torah* on Deut. 19:19.

876 Recanati, *Perush haTorah* on Deut. 19:19.

877 Abravanel, *Perush haTorah* on Deut. 19:19.

878 Commentary on Rashi, *The Torah: With Rashi's Commentary Translated, Annotated, and Elucidated by Yisrael Isser Zvi Herczeg*, on Deut. 19:19, note 8, pp. 208-209.

879 Tigay, *The JPS Torah Commentary: Deuteronomy* on Deut. 19:19.

880 *Sifre*, Piska 190.

881 Hoffmann, *Sefer Devarim* on Deut. 20:1.

882 *Mishnah Sotah* 8:1.

883 Rashi, *Perushei Rashi* on Deut. 20:1.

884 *BT Sotah* 42a.

885 *Sifre*, Piska 192; *BT Sotah* 42b.

886 Recanati, *Perush haTorah* on Deut. 20:5.

887 Berkowitz, "Parashah Commentary: Shofetim."

888 Sicker, *The Political Culture of Judaism*, pp. 119-144.

889 *Mishnah Sotah* 8:7.

890 *Mishnah Sotah* 8:7.

891 Avraham Horowitz, "Tehukat haTzavah haIvri leOr haHalakhah," p. 108.

892 *Mishnah Sotah* 8:2.

893 *Sifre*, Piska 198; *Mishnah Sotah* 8:6.

894 *Sifre*, Piska 200.

895 *Sifre*, Piska 202.

896 Luzzatto, *Perush Shadal al Hamishah Humshei Torah* on Deut. 20:19.

897 Jacob ben Asher, *Perush Baal haTurim al haTorah* on Deut. 21:1.

898 Munk, *The Call of the Torah* on Deut. 21:1.

899 *Mishnah Sotah* 9:1; *Sifre*, Piska 205.

900 *Mishnah Sotah* 9:5.

901 Hertz, *The Pentateuch and Haftorahs* on Deut. 21:6.

902 *BT Sotah* 46b.

903 *BT Sotah* 46a.

904 Phillips, *Deuteronomy* on Deut. 21:4.

905 Hertz, *The Pentateuch and Haftorahs* on Deut. 21:9.